Cases
and
Exercises
in
Marketing

W. Wayne Talarzyk
The Ohio State University

The Dryden Press
Chicago   New York   Philadelphia   San Francisco
Montreal   Toronto   London   Sydney   Tokyo
Mexico City   Rio de Janeiro   Madrid

Acquisitions Editor: Rob Zwettler
Project Editor: Nancy Shanahan
Design Director: Alan Wendt
Production Supervisor: Diane Tenzi
Permissions Editor: Doris Milligan
Director of Editing, Design, and Production: Jane Perkins

Copy Editor: David Talley
Compositor: Pam Frye Typesetting
Text Type: 10/12 California

Library of Congress Cataloging-in-Publication Data

Talarzyk, W. Wayne.
    Cases and exercises in marketing.

    Includes index.
    1. Marketing—Case studies.   2. Marketing—Problems,
exercises, etc.   I. Title.
HF5415.T324   1987   658.8   86-11673
ISBN 0-03-007643-9

Printed in the United States of America
789-066-987654321

Address orders:
383 Madison Avenue
New York, NY 10017

Address editorial correspondence:
One Salt Creek Lane
Hinsdale, IL 60521

CBS COLLEGE PUBLISHING
The Dryden Press
Holt, Rinehart and Winston
Saunders College Publishing

The Dryden Press
Series in Marketing

Balsley and Birsner
Selling: Marketing Personified

Barry
Marketing: An Integrated Approach

Blackwell, Engel, and Talarzyk
Contemporary Cases in Consumer Behavior,
Revised Edition

Blackwell, Johnston, and Talarzyk
Cases in Marketing Management and Strategy

Block and Roering
Essentials of Consumer Behavior, *Second Edition*

Boone and Kurtz
Contemporary Marketing, *Fifth Edition*

Churchill
**Marketing Research: Methodological
Foundations,** *Fourth Edition*

Dunn and Barban
Advertising: Its Role in Modern Marketing,
Sixth Edition

Engel, Blackwell, and Miniard
Consumer Behavior, *Fifth Edition*

Futrell
Contemporary Cases in Sales Management

Futrell
Sales Management: Behavior, Practice, and Cases

Green
Analyzing Multivariate Data

Hutt and Speh
**Industrial Marketing Management: A Strategic
View of Business Markets,** *Second Edition*

Kurtz and Boone
Marketing, *Third Edition*

Marquardt, Makens, and Roe
**Retail Management: Satisfaction of Consumer
Needs,** *Third Edition*

Park and Zaltman
Marketing Management

Rachman
Marketing Today

Rosenbloom
Marketing Channels: A Management View,
Third Edition

Schary
Logistic Decisions: Text and Cases

Schellinck and Maddox
**Computer-Assisted Learning for Marketing
Research**

Schnaars
**MICROSIM
A marketing simulation available for IBM-PC®
and Apple®**

Sciglimpaglia
Applied Marketing Research

Sellars
**Role Playing the Principles of Selling:
College and University Edition**

Shimp and DeLozier
**Promotion Management and Marketing
Communications**

Talarzyk
Cases and Exercises in Marketing

Terpstra
International Marketing, *Fourth Edition*

Young and Mondy
Personal Selling: Function, Theory, and Practice,
Second Edition

Zikmund, Lundstrom, and Sciglimpaglia
Cases in Marketing Research

Zikmund
Exploring Marketing Research, *Second Edition*

About the Author

Dr. Wayne Talarzyk is Chairman and Professor of Marketing in the College of Administrative Science at The Ohio State University. His teaching and research interests lie primarily in the areas of managerial attitudes and emerging technologies in marketing.

He received his bachelor's degree in electrical engineering from Purdue University. For three years he was a flight test engineer for the Atlas missile systems at General Dynamics Astronautics in California. Dr. Talarzyk returned to Purdue and received his master's degree and Ph.D. in industrial administration.

His research projects, many of which have been concerned with the applications of consumer attitudes, lifestyle research, and Videotex, are regularly reported through authored or coauthored articles appearing in professional journals and conference proceedings. He is active in the business community serving as a professional consultant and is also a frequent participant in executive seminars, continuing education programs, and professional association conferences. He is also involved with the religious community and serves as faculty advisor to Campus Crusade for Christ at Ohio State.

Dr. Talarzyk is author or coauthor of 14 college textbooks, three research monographs, and three professional manuals. He has received Outstanding Teaching Awards from Purdue University as a graduate instructor and from the College of Administrative Science at Ohio State, including being named Marketing Professor of the Year.

Preface

This book is the culmination of almost 20 years of analyzing, writing, developing, teaching, and publishing cases in the discipline of marketing. It is not a new book per se, but builds on all of this experience with the end result of providing students and instructors with a very contemporary and progressive approach to the analysis of marketing cases.

The book is contemporary in the sense that it focuses on a variety of the types of issues presently confronting marketers. It builds on the base established by two of the author's previous books, *Contemporary Cases in Marketing* and *Cases for Analysis in Marketing*.

The approach in this book is progressive, through the types of cases presented and the levels of analysis expected. Part I provides a series of very short cases with directed discussion questions. Part II has medium-length cases with Case Analysis Forms to help structure the analyses. Part III presents a set of more comprehensive cases that allow students to develop their own problem statements, relevant questions, and recommendations.

This approach to organizing the book provides students with a progressive learning experience. They start with relatively straightforward questions focusing on the principles of marketing. Then they progress to longer cases dealing with some of the managerial issues in marketing. The Case Analysis Forms allow an intermediate step to studying cases by giving some structure to the relevant issues in each case. Students are then given the opportunity to utilize their cumulative analytical skills on comprehensive cases where no specific directions are given.

A variety of objectives guide the use of cases in a marketing course. This book is designed to facilitate the following objectives:[1]

☐ To give students experience in applying marketing principles and concepts in real-world situations.
☐ To help students to reason better through the use of questions and problems.
☐ To teach students to apply analytical skills and techniques.
☐ To show students how to organize and interpret facts and draw relevant conclusions.
☐ To give students the opportunity to evaluate and interpret quantitative data.
☐ To improve students' communications skills, both written and oral.
☐ To assist students in identifying key problems as compared to symptoms.

In order to accomplish these and other objectives, this book provides a variety of features to assist the student and the instructor. Some of these distinctive features include:

☐ Cases with familiar names and real-world data. Almost all of the cases involve well-known organizations. Even in those few instances where the name is fictitious, the information provided is real. This enables the student to view some of the products in local markets and, if appropriate, do library research on the industries and organizations involved.
☐ Many of the cases provide opportunities to assess the need for marketing research or analyze actual research data.

---

[1]These objectives have been adapted from Cynthia J. Frey and Raymond F. Keyes, "Marketing Case Instruction at the Undergraduate Level," *Journal of Marketing Education*, Summer 1985, pp. 51–59.

☐ Several international cases are included, along with other cases that have international dimensions and implications.

☐ Cases of a variety of lengths are included to facilitate the progressive approach to analysis discussed earlier.

☐ Also as mentioned earlier, discussion questions and Case Analysis Forms are included in Parts I and II to give direction and structure to analyses. Instructors may want to assign questions for the comprehensive cases in Part III based on information from the *Instructor's Manual.*

☐ Organizations included range from some of the largest in the world to two- and three-person operations. Some not-for-profit organizations are also included.

☐ A variety of products and services are represented, including quick-service restaurants, soft drinks, funeral service, agricultural services, new technologies in marketing, religion, and many others—even desserts for dogs.

☐ **Instructor's Manual** with case analyses and solutions available to adoptors free.

It has been very enjoyable to prepare this collection of cases. My hope is that it will satisfy the needs and expectations of students and instructors. Both groups are encouraged to provide any comments or suggestions for improvements to the author. Such input will be quite helpful in planning future editions. Thank you.

Acknowledgments

Many people and organizations were instrumental in the successful completion of this collection of contemporary marketing cases. With extreme gratitude, all of these individuals and organizations are acknowledged.

Special appreciation is extended to Professors Geoffrey Lantos and William Kaven for permission to include their original case manuscripts in this text. Thanks are also given to my coauthors on other casebooks: Roger D. Blackwell, James F. Engel, and Wesley J. Johnston. Their influence on previous books can be seen in this new casebook.

Appreciaton is also expressed to the following individuals for their willingness to cooperate in the development of cases based on their organizations and sources:

Jane Anderson	Diane Hopkins
Zelma Bishop	John Huston
Richard Blanchard	Joy Vander Laan
Mary Bonelli	Patricia Mastin
Judyth Box	Joseph C. Modaff
Richard T. Brigham	Paul R. Raab
Barbara Brooks	John A. Russell
Mary Kay Fenner	L. Thomas Williams, Jr.
Suzanne Glickman	Jay H. Wardell
Michael L. Hayes	Marvin E. Williams
Lisa Henry	Graydon D. Webb

The assistance of Marjorie King is gratefully recognized. She gave much of her time in all phases of the preparation of this casebook. It is also a pleasure to acknowledge the helpful cooperation of the people at The Dryden Press. Mary Fischer, Rob Zwettler, Nancy Shanahan, and Doris Milligan all were of major assistance in planning this project and bringing it to completion.

W. Wayne Talarzyk
Columbus, Ohio
September, 1986

Contents

Marketing Principles Cases

Part I

This first part of the book is divided into five sections: Overview of Marketing (Cases 1–3), Environment for Marketing (Cases 4–6), Marketing Research (Cases 7–9), Buyer Behavior (Cases 10–12), and Market Segmentation (Cases 13–15). These five sections relate to some of the basic issues that each organization has to think about in developing a marketing strategy.

The cases in Part I all relate to well-known companies, industries, or products. It should be fairly easy to do library research or field studies on these types of cases if appropriate for the course and expected by the instructor.

All of the cases are short and designed to introduce one or two basic principles of marketing. Three questions at the end of each case will guide preparation and discussion.

Coca-Cola Company: Classic Coke—New Coke—Cherry Coke

Case 1

Coca-Cola Company introduced its new, reformulated Coke in April 1984. The company shocked the nation by replacing the world's leading soft drink with what it termed a "new improved taste." Some six weeks later, in response to a massive public outcry, the company brought back the old flavor as Coca-Cola Classic. This response caused some comedians to quip, "Coke is them," playing on the company's long-standing commercial tag-line, "Coke is it." Company executives believed that demand for the original product would soon diminish and that the new Coke would emerge as the clearly favorite product and survivor.

U. S. Sales Mix

The basic objective behind the new Coke was to provide a sweeter-tasting product to appeal to Pepsi-Cola drinkers. In recent years, Pepsi had begun to outsell Coke in bottles and cans, specifically in situations where consumers were given a choice. Coca-Cola retained an overall gallonage lead due to its dominant position in restaurants, sporting arenas, and other areas where only Coke was available. Extensive taste-testing research indicated that, in blind tests, consumers preferred the reformulated Coke to the old Coke. Based on these research results and Pepsi's increasing market share, Coca-Cola Company decided to change its formula and come out with the new Coke.

In October 1985, Coca-Cola confirmed for the first time that Coke Classic was outselling the new Coke. Coca-Cola officials would not discuss the Classic/new Coke sales ratios nationally, but an informal survey conducted by *Advertising Age* in early 1986 indicated that Classic Coke was emerging as ". . . the all-American favorite hands down."

Based on sales through major food outlets for September and October 1985, *Advertising Age's* informal survey showed Classic outselling new Coke two to one. Market shares for that period were 11.6 percent for Classic Coke and 5.6 percent for new Coke. The total share of the sugar-cola market for Coke, including Cherry Coke which also was introduced in 1985, was 20.1 percent. This was up from 18.8 percent a year earlier when Coke's only sugar colas were regular Coke and caffeine-free Coke.

Source: Material presented here has been adapted from "Coke 'family' sales fly as new Coke stumbles," *Advertising Age*, January 27, 1986, pp. 1+; Scott Kilman, "Coke's earnings increased 12% in 3rd quarter," *The Wall Street Journal*, October 18, 1985, p. 9; and "New Coke is it in Canada?" *Advertising Age*, January 27, 1986, p. 36.

3

The Canadian Market

New Coke was introduced into the Canadian market at about the same time it made its debut in the United States. After receiving about 500,000 telephone calls on a special toll-free number, Classic Coke was launched in Canada in mid-September 1985. According to an audit by A.C. Nielsen during October and November 1985, new Coke had 12.8 percent of the total Canadian soft-drink market, compared with 9.4 percent for Classic Coke. Before the introduction of new Coke, regular Coke had 21.4 percent of the market.

According to a company spokesperson, of total sales for both brands from mid-September to year-end, new Coke accounted for 53 percent while Classic Coke represented 47 percent. The figures included fountain and restaurant sales where only new Coke was available.

Focal Topics

1. Do you think it was wise for Coca-Cola to change to new Coke in the first place?
2. Was it a good strategy to bring back the original as Classic Coke?
3. How do you suggest that Coca-Cola attempt to position new Coke and Classic Coke in the future?

Newman's Own, Inc.:
Paul Newman's Products   Case 2

Paul Newman's lines of spaghetti sauce, salad dressing, and gourmet popcorn have been major successes since his company, Newman's Own, Inc., was formed in 1982. It is estimated that as of 1985, Newman's spaghetti sauce had about 1.3 percent of the $770 million market, his salad dressing had a 3 percent share of the $600 million market, and his gourmet popcorn may have owned as much as 10 percent of that $30 million market. The company plans to introduce microwave popcorn soon, and possibly a line of men's toiletries in the future. Even a commercialized version of a granola-type cereal made by Newman's wife, actress Joanne Woodward, remains a possibility.

Company Background

Newman's Own, Inc. started as a lark when Newman and his friend, author A. E. Hotchner, decided to market the homemade salad dressing Newman gave his friends each Christmas. The product was marketed locally in Connecticut under the Newman's Own label. In a few months, requests for the product were being received from throughout the country. A chance meeting with a food broker led to national distribution. Newman's Own products are now sold in about 80 percent of the supermarket chains in the United States.

In 1983, the company introduced its Industrial Strength Venetian Spaghetti Sauce. Newman explained that he chose that name because he thought it signified that the sauce was "the real thing." Later the company brought out its gourmet popcorn.

At the outset, the two partners never expected to make any money. After a year of phenomenal success, they decided to give away the profits. So far the company has given away over $7 million to some 200 groups including the Sloan-Kettering Center for Cancer Research, Catholic Relief for Ethiopia, and Recording for the Blind. Overall, about 20 percent of the price of a jar of Newman's spaghetti sauce goes to charity.

Marketing Strategy

When they first started the company, the partners sought marketing advice. After receiving estimates of $500,000 for test marketing and a probable loss of $1 million in the first year, they decided to go it on their own. Each partner put up $20,000 to set up the company, and had his investment back in six weeks.

Source: Materials presented here have been adapted from "Paul Newman is packing 'em in at the supermarket," *Business Week*, November 4, 1985, p. 38 and a product review in *Consumer Reports*, October 1985, p. 630.

The company's sales philosophy can probably best be described by a small banner that reportedly hangs above a Ping-Pong table in the three-room corporate headquarters furnished with patio furniture: " 'If we ever have a plan, we're screwed'—Paul Newman to himself at the Stork Club urinal, 1983." The company does not advertise and only occasionally distributes coupons.

Newman's smiling face does appear on the label of each product. He has explained the products' success by saying that people first try the products because of his name, but because they are good food, customers buy again. The label on the spaghetti sauce states: "La stella della salse e la salsa delle stelle." "The star of the sauces, the sauce of the stars."

Focal Topics

1. From a marketing perspective, how would you explain the success of Newman's Own? His popularity is an asset

2. In what ways might marketing be of help to the company?

3. What sort of marketing strategy would you recommend for Newman's Own?

Detyzco, Inc.: Pet 79 Frozen Dog Dessert

"Pet 79 is a nutritionally balanced, frozen dessert for your dog—fortified with vitamins and minerals. Your dog will love it!" are the words used on the package to describe Detyzco's new product aimed at dog lovers. The firm has achieved selected distribution in the Midwest for its product and would like to attain national market coverage.

Product Description

Pet 79 Frozen Dog Dessert is packed in a six-serving carton. Each individual serving is in a four-ounce plastic cup. The product can be served to dogs in its frozen state or thawed in the refrigerator and served as a creamy pudding.

The product is currently retail priced at $1.39 per six-pack carton. At this price, retailers have a margin of about 25 to 30 percent. Food distributors receive a markup of 15 percent for handling the product from Detyzco to the retailer.

Following is information from a product brochure distributed to potential customers in supermarkets:

> Doesn't your dog deserve dessert? Won't you feel better giving "man's best friend"—and yours—a treat that is actually *good* for him?
>
> PET 79 FROZEN DOG DESSERT is a nutritionally complete, well-balanced food made with only the highest quality proteins and with vitamins and minerals added. And it contains *absolutely no sugar*.
>
> PET 79 FROZEN DOG DESSERT can be fed like ice cream or it can be thawed in the refrigerator and spooned over dry dog food. And it can be refrozen for your convenience.
>
> Can't you just imagine how pleased your pet will be to have a change of taste in its diet after eating the same thing meal after meal?
>
> Feed PET 79 FROZEN DOG DESSERT with the confidence that you're feeding the *best!* And have fun watching your pet truly enjoy *a real dessert treat!*

Following is a description of an introductory television advertisement for the product:

Source: This has been edited from the original case, which appeared in W. Wayne Talarzyk, *Cases for Analysis in Marketing.* Hinsdale, Ill.: Dryden Press, 1985.

Video	Audio
Full head shot of dog	Pet 79 is the newest in dog desserts. It's frozen!
Full screen of both packages	Now for the first time you can reward your dog with a tasty dessert that's good for him and absolutely unique. It's frozen!
Zoom in on one package with (6) six desserts	Pet 79 is a healthful, nutritious dessert that can be stored easily in your freezer.
Model spooning dessert—dog eating dessert	When your dog is ready for this tasty treat, just spoon it into his bowl or serve it over his favorite dry dog food.
Full screen of package	So ask your grocer or pet store for Pet 79—or call 279-3922.
Superimposed phone number	Because doesn't your dog deserve dessert today!

Focal Topics

1. What do you see as the "real business" of Detyzco? — *Pet owners*
2. How would you market Pet 79?
3. How would you handle any "service responsibility" issues that might come up regarding this product?

Black & Decker: Responding to Market Changes

Test

Case 4

Black & Decker is a global manufacturer and marketer of quality products for use by consumers in and around the home and for professional applications. With its products marketed in over 50 countries, the company enjoys worldwide recognition of its brand name and a strong reputation for quality, value, and innovation. A pioneer in cordless, rechargeable technology, Black & Decker provides a variety of electrical household products and small appliances. The company is the world's leading producer of power tools.

1985 Operating Results

On November 12, 1985, Laurence J. Farley, Chairman of Black & Decker, announced a major restructuring involving an after-tax write-off of $205 million. This charge resulted in a $153 million loss for the fiscal year compared to earnings of $95 million in 1984. Farley revealed that the company's plants were operating at about 50 percent of capacity, barely enough to cover fixed costs, according to one industry analyst.

Because anticipated consumer demand did not reach expected levels, high inventories of Black & Decker products resulted in backed up retail and wholesale distribution channels. Earnings were reduced by costs associated with aggressive advertising and dealer incentive programs designed to stimulate sales of power tool products. Promotion costs also rose as the company increased rebate programs on some of its consumer products.

Competitive Environment

Some industry analysts suggest that Black & Decker may have caused some of its own problems through superior products. The company can now make motor tools that are 25 percent smaller and more powerful than its old products and that last for many years.

Imports from Japan and West Germany have also impacted the company's market share. Black & Decker has concentrated much of its distribution in hardware stores and mass merchandisers, like K mart, while Japan's Makita has aimed its competitive products at the growing number of warehouse home centers.

Source: Materials presented here have been adapted from Black & Decker's 1985 Annual Report and Christopher S. Eklund, "Why Black & Decker is cutting itself down to size," *Business Week*, November 25, 1985, pp. 42 + .

9

Changes in Marketing

To seek lower manufacturing costs, Black & Decker plans to shift more production overseas. Labor costs at its Singapore factory are $2 to $2.50 per hour compared to about $16 in the United States. The company hopes to be able to raise prices on its products an average of 4 percent during 1986. Plans also call for a globalization strategy, which will reduce its eight worldwide design centers to two and reduce the number of different motor sizes it produces from over 250 to a "handful." Possible new products include security systems, outdoor items, painting systems, and other items typically found in hardware stores.

As stated in its annual report, objectives for 1986 include:

☐ Achieving a substantial earnings turnaround
☐ Increasing emphasis on effective marketing, brand position and customer satisfaction
☐ Continuing new product introductions and globalization
☐ Successfully managing the restructurings

Focal Topics

1. In what ways has the consumer social/cultural environment impacted Black & Decker? *— Not many people wanted to buy*

2. In what ways has the competitive environment impacted Black & Decker?

3. What marketing strategies would you recommend to Black & Decker to deal with its changing environment?

I really feel that advertising on T.V., radio, news etc is an excellent way to get the product sold.

New Products
New uses

Surveys ask what consumers would like in a black & decker product

Japan

California Beef Council:
Light Cooking with Beef

Case 5

Individual beef producers throughout California have for many years recognized their shared need for a single research, education, and promotion channel for beef. In 1957, legislation was passed establishing the California Beef Council (CBC). The law set four objectives for the council: research, consumer education, public information, and promotion.

In recent years, the CBC has seen the need to increase the awareness and usage of beef as a light, fashionable, contemporary, nutritious food consistent with today's active, healthy lifestyles. Toward that end, the CBC developed the "Light Cooking with Beef" campaign.

Program Background

The CBC recognized the need to begin working with the food-service industry to assist operators in keeping beef on their menus and in presenting it in new and exciting ways. No data existed that could assist the CBC in program development. Therefore, a series of focus group interviews were conducted to explore the "Beef Usage and Attitudes among the White Table Cloth and College/University Foodservice Market Segments."

The findings implied that, despite its universally acknowledged food appeal, beef was not perceived as linked with the emerging image of lightness and fitness sought by today's trend-sensitive consumer. The study also implied that beef was not perceived as something new to offer the discriminating diner or the selective restauranteur seeking new offerings for demanding clientele. With this background, the "Light Cooking with Beef" campaign was designed to communicate beef's fashionability and nutrition to California food-service employees, food editors, health-care providers, retailers, and active, health-conscious consumers.

Scope of Program

The program distributed 10,000 recipe cards to the food-service industry; it also distributed 50,000 copies of "Light Cooking with Beef" and 100,000 copies of "More Light Cooking with Beef." The food-service recipe cards, featuring beef round recipes under 400 calories per serving, were distributed at the National Restaurant Association and the California Western Association shows. The recipes were also offered through restaurant trade publications. A Light Beef Recipe contest is also held yearly to encourage the industry to develop innovative ways to serve beef.

Source: The material presented here has been adapted from information provided by the California Beef Council.

11

The food-service recipes were converted to consumer portions for inclusion in the booklet "Light Cooking with Beef." This booklet was developed for use by health-care professionals in counseling settings or by health-conscious consumers, to learn about the role of beef in a balanced diet consistent with recommendations to limit total fat, calories, and cholesterol.

"Light Cooking with Beef" was distributed through health fairs, conventions of health-care professionals, and reader action cards in a national nutrition newsletter. In addition, the booklet was offered directly to consumers through food editor releases and through advertisements in the health and fitness sections of leading newspapers such as *The Wall Street Journal.*

At the retail level, the booklet was made available at points of purchase. In cooperation with Ralph's Supermarket, the recipes in "Light Cooking with Beef" were produced as a label to be applied to packages of beef round in the meat department. This special promotion distributed 10,000 copies of the booklet in the first three days.

Focal Topics

1. What changes in the marketing environment have impacted the demand for beef?

2. What is your overall evaluation of the "Light Cooking with Beef" campaign?

3. What other things should the CBC do to help market beef?

Hyundai Excel:
Minipriced Import Cars

Hyundai (rhymes with Sunday) is the first South Korean company to export cars to the United States. In recent years, several Korean companies, including Samsung, Goldstar, and Daewoo, have successfully introduced television sets, videocassette recorders, and personal computers into the U.S. market. Since wages are generally lower in South Korea compared to many other countries, Korean products often sell for 25 percent less than competitors' brands.

Changing Automobile Competition

In 1985, U. S. car buyers purchased some 11 million cars costing in total $131 billion. Many foreign car manufacturers, including the Japanese producers Toyota, Honda, and Nissan, moved to bigger cars with more power and plushness to attract American buyers who could afford more luxury. It is estimated that in 1985, cars that were larger and more expensive than subcompacts accounted for half of Japan's U. S. car sales. Honda's Accord and Prelude, Nissan's Maxima, and Toyota's Celica GT-S were all priced from $12,000 to $20,000.

While South Korea is introducing the Hyundai to the U. S. market, an even lower priced entry is coming from Yugoslavia. The Yugo resembles a cross between the Chevrolet Chevette and the early Volkswagen Rabbit. It is two feet shorter than Chevette, but weighs some 350 pounds more. Fuel economy for the Yugo is limited to about 25 miles per gallon on the highway and 17 in the city.

The Yugo is priced at around $4,000, partially because of Yugoslavia's status as a favored trading partner with the United States. The main reason for the low price, however, lies in labor rates. The factory where the Yugo is manufactured pays labor rates of about $1 an hour, compared to $2 to $3 in Korea, $6 in Japan, and $12 in the United States.

Hyundai Excel

Hyundai, whose Pony subcompact is already the best-selling import in Canada, introduced its new Excel, a front-wheel-drive car, at various U. S. automobile shows in February 1986. With a base price of $4,995, the company announced plans to launch the Excel with a $25 million advertising campaign and hopes of selling 100,000 vehicles in its first year in the United States.

Source: Materials presented here have been adapted from "The Excel Has Landed," *Time*, February 10, 1986, p. 67, and "Minipriced Import Cars Lead New Invasion of U.S.," *U. S. News & World Report*, October 28, 1985, pp. 43 + .

The four-door Excel comes as a sedan or hatchback and includes an AM-FM cassette stereo, five steel-belted tires, and fabric interior. The car is powered by a four-cylinder, 1.3 liter engine producing 75 horsepower.

The Excel is expected to intensify competition among the makers of subcompact cars. Alternatives available to U. S. consumers include Ford's Escort (base price $6,052), Chrysler's Omni and Horizon ($6,209), the Toyota Tercel ($5,598), the Nissan Sentra ($5,649), and the Honda Civic ($5,649).

A Canadian automobile dealer commenting on the success of Hyundai said that consumers perceive it as a quality car because it comes from the Orient. This is a result of the reputation of many Japanese products. It is interesting to note that Japan's Mitsubishi owns 15 percent of Hyundai and supplies the technology for the Excel's engine and transmission.

Focal Topics

1. How has the marketing environment for automobiles changed in the United States in recent years?

2. What marketing strategies would you recommend for Hyundai's Excel?

3. As a subcompact competitor of the Excel, what marketing strategies would you use?

DuPont: Market for Control Garments

Panty hose began the assault. They eliminated one function of the girdle—holding up stockings. Then the attrition accelerated with the rapid changes in dress which accompanied new casual lifestyles until the girdle—once worn almost universally by women of all ages and backgrounds—seemed doomed to extinction. DuPont decided to do a series of focus group interviews to try and understand why the market had changed. Following are some selected results from the research.

Reasons for the Girdle Decline

☐ There always was resentment toward girdles. Women disliked girdles, but wore them anyway because there was no option.

☐ Many believe that girdles cause physical problems. Many women are convinced that girdle-wearing causes loss of muscle control and problems with circulation.

☐ Changing lifestyles and changing attitudes toward dress have made girdles optional. Today's emphasis is on "naturalness."

☐ Women do not want to admit that they are out of shape. To many women, wearing a girdle is a psychological blow.

☐ Wearing a girdle to correct faults simply exchanges one problem for another. In smoothing a fanny or a tummy, you create a bulge somewhere else.

☐ Girdles are viewed as dull. There is nothing exciting about buying or wearing a girdle; the word itself is unappealing.

☐ Women are not aware of the full range of lightweight controlling garments available today.

Motivations to Wear Control Garments

Following are the most important reasons given by interviewees as to why they wear control garments:

1. Under certain clothes, especially revealing ones, they create sleeker lines, eliminate bulges. A flat tummy was the most common objective. Even the most liberated women were conscious of their sexual role in marriage and wanted to look pretty for their husbands.

Source: This case is an edited version of "Control Garments: Do They Have a Future?" a report prepared by DuPont. It originally appeared in W. Wayne Talarzyk, *Contemporary Cases in Marketing.* Hinsdale, IL: Dryden Press, 1979.

2.   For many, they are "morale builders," giving self-confidence — a psychological as well as a physical sense of well-being. It was found that many women, both slim and heavy, thought a body garment "gets it together," eliminates "looseness" and "flabbiness." One woman commented, "I hate the need for a girdle, but I feel more comfortable with one, because without it I look sloppy."

3.   They give support and reduce fatigue.

4.   They improve posture.

5.   They satisfy good grooming requirements for dress-up occasions.

6.   They serve as a gentle reminder against over-eating.

7.   Some women gain weight in the winter and will wear some light control for their "winter figures."

8.   They provide extra warmth in the winter.

Focal Topics

1.   What are the relative advantages and disadvantages of using focus group interviews as opposed to other methods of gathering research data?

2.   Based upon the research reported here, what recommendations would you make to control garment marketers?

3.   What other types of research should be undertaken at this time?

Burger King: Measuring Marketing Effectiveness

Case 8

Burger King's "Battle of the Burgers" campaign started in October 1982. In the original advertising, Burger King boasted that the Whopper had beaten McDonald's Big Mac in a national taste test. Both McDonald's and Wendy's sued to stop the advertisements claiming they made false claims. Burger King dropped those advertisements, but brought out new ones of a similar nature that pushed its broiled hamburgers over the competitors' fried ones.

In the fall of 1985, Burger King management announced a basic change in marketing strategy. The firm decided to stop direct attacks on products of competitors and focus more on topics such as fast service, a varied menu, and improved restaurant decor. The feeling was that the comparative advertising had lost its glamour.

Marketing Focus

Burger King, a subsidiary of Pillsbury, decided to change its marketing strategy after a $30 million advertising campaign designed to promote its meatier Whopper hamburgers failed to attract many new customers. Executives felt that the comparative approach was losing its zing.

As part of the change, the company announced plans to invest around $100 million to remodel most of its 4,300 restaurants by 1987. The interiors will move away from the plastic currently common in the restaurants and focus more on natural materials, such as wood and plants. As part of a continuing effort to expand the menu, Burger King is experimenting with new hamburger toppings such as taco sauce and mushrooms. Soft-drink machines that dispense free refills will also be installed. The company also announced plans for a $20 million advertising campaign to emphasize the quality of the food at Burger King.

The Herb Campaign

On November 24, 1985, television commercials announced the search for Herb, a hapless fellow who had never tried Burger King's Whopper. In a planned $40 million plus promotion, the company hoped to create excitement for its restaurants and products by getting people talking about this unknown Herb and why he was not coming to Burger King.

Source: Materials presented here have been adapted from "Burger King takes the bite out of its ad," *Business Week*, October 28, 1985, pp. 38 + and "Burger King spices up Herb search with bucks," *Advertising Age*, January 20, 1986, pp. 1 + .

During the 1986 Super Bowl, two Burger King commercials reported that Herb had been found. The prematurely balding, bubble-faced nerd with horn-rimmed glasses had finally wised up and tried Burger King's hamburgers. The character Herb wore clashing plaid jackets and trousers, white socks with untied shoes, and wide ties emblazoned with a big *H*. The company continued the promotion by sending its "new customer" on a cross-country tour of its restaurants.

The plan involved Herb showing up unannounced at various Burger King restaurants throughout North America and moping around until someone spotted him. That person received $5,000 and every customer in the restaurant at that time received a free Whopper, french fries, and Pepsi. Herb also helped each customer register for the million dollar drawing that took place when the campaign wound up in March.

Focal Topics

1. What type of marketing research would you do to measure the effectiveness of the Herb campaign?

2. What other types of research would be helpful to Burger King as future marketing strategies are planned?

3. How would you conduct those types of research?

USA Today: The Nation's Newspaper

"*USA Today* is coming of age with our millions of curious, intelligent, affluent readers from New York to California who depend on *USA Today* for factual, comprehensive reports of top news across the USA and around the world everyday." This statement was on the cover of a special insert in *Advertising Age* promoting *USA Today* to potential advertisers. The insert also stated that *USA Today* was coming of age with advertisers in terms of number of pages of advertising.

Product Characteristics

USA Today, published by the Gannett Company, was introduced in September 1982. Positioned as "The Nation's Newspaper," the publication was rolled out in different geographic markets over the next two years. As of eary 1986, the newspaper was available in about 90 percent of the United States. Sales are made through newsstands, corner vending machines, and in some markets via home or office delivery.

At the end of the first year of publication, daily paid circulation reached around 800,000. A year later it had reached about 1.2 million. In early 1986, *USA Today* announced that its circulation rate base (number of copies sold) would move to 1.45 million on March 1. By way of comparison, the circulation of the *New York Daily News* at the start of 1986 was around 1.35 million and that of *The Wall Street Journal* at a little over 1.91 million. The introductory price of *USA Today* was a quarter. During 1985, the price was raised to 50 cents.

In the advertising insert, the newspaper was described as follows: "*USA Today* is different: filled with color and graphics, serious where it should be serious, fun when it's appropriate, and always introducing something new for our readers." The newspaper used many forms of direct reader response in 1985, including reader lotteries and special reader polls.

Selected Marketing Activities

During 1986, *USA Today* planned to spend around $4 million to advertise itself to potential readers and advertisers. A variety of media, including television, print, radio, and outdoor were used to advertise the newspaper. In a tie-in program, Neiman-Marcus, the Dallas-based department store chain, carried a *USA Today*

Source: Material presented here has been adapted from Janet Myers, "Gannett pushes *USA Today* as tomorrow's paper," *Advertising Age*, January 23, 1986, pp. 32 + and from an advertising insert for *USA Today* in *Advertising Age*.

subscription card in its winter catalog. A special promotion in the summer of 1985 with General Mills cereals offered consumers a free six-month subscription. That promotion yielded 450,000 new, but unpaid, subscribers.

A print advertisement to potential advertisers said in its heading, "A lot of media people are saying *USA Today* is neither fish nor fowl." Along side a sketch of a part fish, part chicken creature were the words "They're right!" The advertisement went on to say that readers viewed the publication as a newspaper, "bold, exciting, colorful and unique," while many advertisers saw it as a newsmagazine, "bold, exciting, colorful and unique." Concluding copy said, "The truth is, we don't much care what you call us. Just as long as you call us." The theme line, "The advertising might of *USA Today*," appeared at the bottom of the advertisement over the newspaper logo.

Focal Topics

1. What types of research should *USA Today* undertake to market itself to potential readers?

2. What types of research would be helpful to market *USA Today* to potential advertisers?

3. How might an advertiser in *USA Today* measure the effectiveness of its advertising?

) fun ad where reader to invited to comment on product.

Kenncorp Sports, Inc.: Hacky Sack Official Footbag

R. John Stalberger, Jr., injured his knee in 1970 before trying out for The University of Texas football team. To rehabilitate his knee after the injury, he invented what is today known as the Hacky Sack. Created as an exercise aid, the product has spawned a company, various footbag games, and a players' association. The ultimate goal of the association is to see footbagging become an internationally recognized sport and therefore an Olympic event.

Background Information

Mr. Stalberger developed a kicking game using a small object made of hand-stitched leather, called a Hacky Sack footbag. Because of his background in baseball, football, and other sports, he saw the games as a good off-season training and warm-up exercise. It enhanced bilateral control and versatility. Mr. Stalberger, also having a background in physical therapy, knew that such a workout for the heart and lungs was important for fitness. He wanted to develop the game as a conditioning exercise.

Mr. Stalberger poured all of his energies into developing the American Footbag Game. He was determined to make it a nationally accepted exercise game and sport. The American Footbag Games are the modern American versions of ancient kicking games, and they differ from all similar games in two main areas. First, using the body above the waist as a striking surface is prohibited (except in Freestyle). Second, the method of play utilizes five basic kicks that dictate the equal use of both feet.

Marketing Activities

Hacky Sacks have been promoted directly to consumers through advertisements in publications such as *National Lampoon*, *Sports Illustrated*, and *Boys' Life Magazine*.

Source: Hacky Sack is a registered trademark of and is patented by Kenncorp Sports, Inc. This has been edited from the original case which appeared in W. Wayne Talarzyk, *Cases for Analysis in Marketing*. Hinsdale, IL: Dryden Press, 1985.

Kenncorp has also marketed its products to the sporting goods industry by participating in various trade shows and by advertising in specialized publications such as *Sporting Goods Business, The Sporting Goods Dealer, Sports Retailer,* and *Sports Merchandiser.*

To support individual retailers in promoting the product, Kenncorp has developed a series of advertising slicks. Retailers can add their names and addresses to the copy and then run the advertisements in local newspapers. In addition to general themes for Hacky Sacks, the company has developed segmented advertising slicks tying the product to conditioning for other sports such as soccer, running, football, and skiing. On occasions, Kenncorp also provides Hacky Sack demonstrators to retail stores for promotional programs. A Hacky Sack with a book on how to play with it costs around $9 at retail.

Additional Dimensions

Hacky Sack sales seem to be taking off for Kenncorp. The company, however, would like to obtain additional capitalization on the product's success. To date it has lined up corporate sponsors for shoes, socks, and shorts. It is also negotiating deals with beer and soft-drink companies to sponsor Hacky Sack events. The company is also marketing additional tie-in products such as T-shirts and key chains.

Focal Topics

1.   What dimensions could the company use to segment the market for Hacky Sack? ~Kenncorp should segment~

2.   Which market segments do you think would be best for Kenncorp to pursue? Why? *Age, living area, athletics (soccer)*

3.   What marketing strategies would you recommend to reach those segments?

[handwritten marginal note: Youth students under 25(08)]

[handwritten]

1) If Kenncorp wanted to segment the market for Hacky Sack they could aim their product or rather use it as a competitive out-door product. The competitor being the frisbee. There are however many out door games like the frisbee. such as track-ball and jarts. They should aim the product at all young - high-school college individuals who an athletes as well - As was the game intention to warm-up, off season exersise,

2) I believe they should focus on the young male or female about age 10-25.

M & M Products, Inc.:
Black Hair-Care Products Case 11

In 1973, two young black pharmacists named Cornell McBride and Therman McKenzie each invested $250 and went into business marketing a hair spray for black men that would keep their hair soft. The two men developed the spray while studying pharmacy in Atlanta. After graduation, they worked during the day for a large drugstore chain and spent their evenings taking business courses and preparing to run their own company. In 1983, the company they started and still own had become the 11th largest black business in the United States, according to *Black Enterprise* magazine. Sales in 1983 reached $47.3 million.

Black Hair-Care Market

From all dimensions, the statistics for blacks in the United States are impressive. Blacks represent about 12 percent of the total population, with aggregate income estimated between $140 and $160 billion. With allowances for the generally recognized income differentials, on a per-capita basis it is a fair assumption that blacks represent at least 8 percent of all the dollars spent on consumer goods and services. In addition, all indications point to a disproportion in the way black consumers spend their dollars. In many categories, their expenditures significantly exceed the proportion of income devoted by consumers in general.

It is estimated that blacks use about 36 percent of the hair-care products sold in the United States. The general hair-care market has been growing at a rate of less than 5 percent annually while the rate of growth for ethnic hair-care products is rising at an annual increase of 15 to 20 percent, according to the American Health and Beauty Aids Institute, a 15-member association representing minority-owned hair-care and cosmetics companies.

During 1982, the health and beauty aids market in the United States was estimated at $10 billion. Blacks accounted for some $2 billion in that market, with more than $800 million being spent on ethnic products. It is estimated that blacks spend three-and-a-half to five times as much as whites on health and beauty aids, making the black market the fastest growing segment of the industry.

There are six basic product categories in the black hair-care market: conditioners and hair dress products, comb-easy conditioner lotions, blow-out and creme relaxers, hair sprays for sheen and aerosol products, perm products and permanent curl kits, and curl activators. Of these, the current hottest category is the permanent curl (or cold wave) treatment introduced by Jhirmack to the professional market in 1978. It was brought to the retail market in 1980.

Source: Adapted from Mill Roseman, "The Black Consumer Market: Problem or Opportunity," *Madison Avenue*, May 1983, pp. 66–70; Sarah Lum, "Ethnic Hair Care—A Growing Market," *Madison Avenue*, May 1983, p. 72; and Ezra K. Davidson, "Success of Hair Care Company Illustrates Progress of Black-Owned Businesses in the U.S.," *The Wall Street Journal*, September 15, 1983, p. 29ff. The original case appeared in David J. Rachman, *Marketing Today*, with cases by W. Wayne Talarzyk. Hinsdale, Ill.: Dryden Press, 1985.

M & M Products

Working in the basement of his three-room home, Mr. McBride and his partner, Mr. McKenzie, mixed the first batch of their hair spray in a 55-gallon drum and stirred it with a pool cue. Their families helped them mix and bottle the spray marketed under the brand name Sta-Sof-Fro. In the summer of 1974, a year after founding their company, both quit their jobs to devote full time to the business.

In the beginning, the two marketed the product themselves. Larger retailers were skeptical, so they focused on small stores, making deliveries in their own cars. The product caught on, and the big retailers became interested in carrying the product. In 1977, four years after its founding, M & M Products reached annual sales of more than one million dollars.

Around 1978, the "curl" style for blacks became popular, the first major change in hair styles for blacks since the Afro began in the late 1960s. M & M Products again recognized the need for specialized products and began to add to their growing array of consumer offerings. By 1983, the company was marketing 65 hair-care products with sales in Canada, Europe, Africa, and the Caribbean as well as in the United States. The company employs 400 people, most of them black, and spends nearly $4 million a year on advertising.

Focal Topics

1. What consumer behavior concepts do you feel are appropriate to consider in the marketing of hair-care products to all market segments?

2. How might these concepts apply differently to M & M Products' consumers compared with other consumer groups?

3. What types of marketing research would be helpful for M & M Products to better understand its consumers?

Royal Canadian Mint: 1988 Olympic Winter Games Coins

Case 12

The Royal Canadian Mint sent the customers on its mailing list information about the United States Mint's 1984 Olympic coins. In 1985, the United States Mint returned the favor by sending its customers ordering information for the Calgary 1988 Olympic Winter Games Sterling Silver Proof Coin Sets issued by the Royal Canadian Mint. A portion of the U.S. sales of those coins will go directly to the U. S. Olympic Committee.

The Product Offering

The complete Olympic Set will contain ten proof coins, issued two at a time every six months. The Royal Canadian Mint has limited the mintage to 5 million coins, of which 3.5 million coins (or 350,000 ten-coin sets) will be reserved for subscribers. Each coin will commemorate one of the rigorous athletic events of the Winter Games: Downhill Skiing and Speed Skating (Issue 1); Hockey and Biathlon (Issue 2); Cross-Country Skiing and Freestyle Skiing (Issue 3); Figure Skating and Curling (Issue 4); and Ski Jumping and Bobsled (Issue 5).

Specific features of the coins include:

□ Each coin is sealed in its own transparent capsule to preserve its radiant finish.

□ Each coin is incused with rate edge-lettering in English and in French, reading: "XV OLYMPIC WINTER GAMES" and "XVes JEUX OLYMPIQUES D'HIVER."

□ These coins are legal tender in Canada, carrying a face value of $20.

□ Each coin is struck more than once, using special dies, on polished blanks to give the coin its remarkable brilliant field and frosted relief.

□ Each coin is a superbly crafted work of art. Canada's finest artists competed for the honor of commemorating this historic event.

□ Each coin measures 40 millimeters in diameter and weighs 34.107 grams, of which 31.102 grams are pure silver (one Troy ounce).

Payment Options

The following information describes the two payment options as presented in the cover letter for the coins:

Source: The material here has been adapted from direct mailing pieces sent out by the United States Mint in cooperation with the Royal Canadian Mint.

Subscription 1:   Pay in Advance. You may pay the full price of $280 for the ten-coin set in advance, receiving two coins every six months. With this payment option, purchasers will receive free a 1985 brilliant uncirculated commemorative silver dollar, a first day of issue stamp, a ten-coin presentation case, and a Certificate of Authenticity.

Subscription 2:   Pay As You Go. Every six months you order a new issue of two coins. The price for the two coins is US$56, guaranteed for all subsequent issues. Purchasers will also receive free a first day of issue stamp, a ten-coin presentation case, and a Certificate of Authenticity. Purchasers who are not completely satisfied with the coins, may discontinue their subscriptions at any time.

Focal Topics

1. What consumer needs are being satisfied by the Royal Canadian Mint's product offering?

2. What consumer behavior concepts are relevant in the marketing of these types of products?

3. From a consumer behavior perspective, what is your evaluation of the two payment options?

Tandy Corporation:
Radio Shack Stores

Case 13

Charles D. Tandy, the late founder of the Tandy Corporation, acquired the nine store, Boston area Radio Shack chain in 1963, and built it into the largest chain of electronics specialty outlets in the world. With annual retail sales in excess of $3 billion, Tandy has over 9,500 stores and dealers worldwide. For over 20 years, the company has achieved annual double-digit sales and earnings increases and gross margins in the range of 60 percent, nearly double those of average specialty retailers.

Regional Discount Chains

Electronics "superstores," operated by companies like the Federated Group, Highland Appliance, and Circuit City, have offered lower prices in many areas. The superstores, which average about an acre of retail space, have twice the selling area of the biggest Radio Shack and have average markups of around 30 percent. Their size allows the superstores to offer a broad selection of name-brand stereos, televisions, video recorders, and even appliances. The superstores, which had about ten percent of the market in 1980 and around 16 percent in 1985, are expected to reach about 25 percent in 1990, according to industry analysts.

In 1985, Tandy purchased 207 Video Concepts stores from a division of Jack Eckerd Corporation and 21 stores from Scott/McDuff, a privately held company. These acquisitions marked an effort by Tandy to gain a foothold in the fast-growing name-brand audio, video, and appliance discount retailing market.

Future Activities

Some industry analysts believe that the new businesses will draw attention away from Tandy's main lines. John V. Roach, Chairman and CEO of Tandy, states that the new stores will not affect Radio Shack outlets because their product lines differ and management will be separate. The new operations will "enable us to compete in a broad section of the consumer electronics business where we aren't competing," he said. Mr. Roach also said that Tandy, compared to its competitors, will have smaller stores, but with more locations that will be more convenient to the customers.

(leather goods) - crafts - creative products
- Hobbies

Source: Materials presented here have been adapted from "Burned by Superstores, Tandy is fighting fire with fire," *Business Week*, October 28, 1985, pp. 62 + ; "Tandy sees end to its 1½ year slump amid increase in sales of its computers," *The Wall Street Journal*, August 5, 1985, p. 8; and company materials.

Tandy plans to invest some $80 million over the next five years to give its nearly 5,000 Radio Shacks a face lift. The objective is to use bright color schemes and sleeker displays to provide more of a high-tech patina. Tandy's stores in the past have been criticized by some people as "cluttered and dowdy."

Focal Topics

1.   How would you segment the market for consumer electronics and appliances?

2.   What is your evaluation of Tandy's decision to enter the electronics and appliance discount retailing market?

3.   How would you market Radio Shack stores to meet the competition of the electronic superstores?

American Express:
The Platinum Card
Case 14

Your long association with American Express and annual volume of travel and entertainment charges places you in a unique group — a group which requires and would appreciate a Card so personalized it's reserved for a select group of American Express Card members. By invitation only. Only for our best customers.

These words were part of a letter inviting certain holders of American Express cards to apply for The Platinum Card. With an annual fee of $250, The Platinum Card provided a number of special features and benefits over and above those of the American Express basic green card ($45 annual fee) and its gold card ($65 annual fee). Other selected information from the invitation letter included the following.

> As you would expect, The Platinum Card will continue to secure Card member services to which you are already accustomed. Worldwide charge privileges. Assured Reservations. No pre-set spending limit. Duplicate receipts. Emergency Card replacement. Emergency check cashing at hotels, motels, airline counters. Travel Accident Insurance. And Express Cash.
>
> What distinguishes The Platinum Card and sets it possessor on a new plateau of recognition, service and convenience are the customized services it provides.
>
> First and foremost, it commands immediate recognition and respect at the finest hotels, restaurants and selected stores worldwide.
>
> Secondly, you can enjoy complimentary nonresident membership privileges at 25 fine private clubs in New York, London, Hong Kong and other cities throughout North America, Europe and the Far East. Whether entertaining clients or friends, enjoying a fine meal or conducting a business meeting, the services of these clubs will be available to you through your membership in the Centurion Club, an exclusive benefit of The Platinum Card.
>
> What's more, the Platinum Card Personalized Travel Service will also assure customized attention to all your travel needs and arrangements 24 hours a day. We'll keep a record of your travel preferences — what hotels, airlines and ground transportation (limousines and car rentals) you prefer to use — so many of the bothersome travel details are easily taken care of in advance. And we'll be pleased to make en route changes to the original itinerary we booked for you should you have a change in plans.
>
> In addition, in keeping with The Platinum Card level of service, you will have increased Travel Accident Insurance protection — to a full $500,000 — every time you charge your common carrier travel

Source: American Express and Platinum Card are registered trademarks of American Express. Information presented here has been adapted from direct mail materials from American Express, sent to the author as a card holder and from Carole Gould, "American Express card holders going for the gold," New York Times News Service, February 11, 1986.

tickets to The Platinum Card. And should the need arise, you will now be able to cash your personalized check for up to $10,000 at participating American Express Travel Service Offices worldwide.

You will also be able to obtain up to $10,000 in Travelers Checques from our network of automated dispensers and up to $1,000 in cash from automated teller machines at participating U.S. financial institutions.

Arrangements for billings are similarly customized:

☐   You may choose the billing time most convenient for you — the beginning, middle, or end of the month.

☐   And at year end, you may receive a customized summary of all charges itemized by category of expense: retail, hotel, restaurants and the like.

As of early 1986, of the 22.2 million cards issued by American Express, gold cards accounted for 4 million (twice as many as 1981), while less than one half of 1 percent (about 120,000) were platinum.

Focal Topics

1.   Why do you think American Express brought out The Platinum Card?

2.   How would you describe the market segment toward which The Platinum Card is positioned? *Nuova Riche class.*

3.   What recommendations would you make to American Express in the marketing of its Platinum Card?

* Prestidge — upper-level type
Many priviledges

- Giving yourself an "ausa" of wealth with this card.

* Direct mail to the upper-echlon people.
* mailing lists. zip codes

Pepsi-Cola Company: Soft Drink Products and Advertising

Case 15

In response to a question about what kind of consumer Pepsi-Cola will appeal to in the foreseeable future, John Costello, senior vice president of sales and marketing for Pepsi-Cola U.S.A. said:

> Virtually everybody is a potential soft drink user, so we tend to get our advertising message across to the widest range of people. However, while we will continue to go against a broad target audience, you may see more segmented efforts from us. For example, we discovered with Slice that there are many consumers who are interested in combining the benefits of real juice and soft drinks. That's why we created a whole new product to go against that segment.

Product Offerings

At the present time, Pepsi-Cola U.S.A. has around 28 percent of the soft-drink market counting all of its brands (Pepsi, Diet Pepsi, Pepsi Light, Caffeine Free Pepsi and Diet Pepsi, Slice, and Mountain Dew.) Coca-Cola brands have a combined market share of 39 percent. Seven-Up accounts for about 7 percent of the market. Pepsi-Cola's recent changes in product offerings include:

- In early 1986, Pepsi-Cola announced plans to purchase Seven-Up Company brands from Philip Morris for $380 million. Despite the obvious fit between the two companies' bottling networks, industry analysts disagree on whether 7up and Pepsi's Slice brands will complement or cannibalize one another. Analysts did expect Seven-Up to scrap its planned introduction of juice-based Citrus 7, a direct competitor to Slice.
- Slice, with 10 percent juice and an estimated market share of 2.5 percent, added a mandarin orange flavor to go with the original lemon-lime flavor. Future plans call for additional flavors of Slice, including apple and cherry cola.
- Cherry Pepsi entered Canada in November 1985, just two days before test marketing began for Cherry Coke. Both Cherry Pepsi and Cherry Coke were launched in the United Kingdom in January 1986, with no test marketing. As of February 1986, Cherry Pepsi had not been introduced in the United States.

Source: Material presented here has been adapted from "Pepsi-Cola's John Costello," *Sales and Marketing Management,* October 7, 1985, pp. 36 + , Brian Lowry, "Stars to shine in Pepsi's ad push," *Advertising Age,* February 3, 1986, pp. 2 + ; and other articles.

Advertising Strategies

In commenting on Pepsi-Cola's advertising, Costello said:

> We are implementing a big-event marketing strategy. We are looking for things that are big, bold, new, and unexpected—events that can excite all of our consumers. At the time we signed Michael Jackson and Lionel Richie to do TV commercials, it had never been done before. Both of them symbolize the new generation and thus have enabled us to create large marketing events around them.

Pepsi-Cola is expected to invest over $150 million in measured media during 1986 for all its soft-drink brands. The flagship brand, Pepsi, will receive about $50 million in advertising. Among the planned television commercials for Pepsi are a two-minute ad featuring *Miami Vice* star Don Johnson and Grammy-nominated singer Glenn Frey, a 90-second high-tech image ad titled "Earth," two spots firing barbs at rival Coke, and "Copier," which shows Michael Fox drinking a Pepsi from a picture made from a copying machine.

Focal Topics

1. How would you segment the market for soft drinks?
2. What product strategies would you recommend to Pepsi-Cola to reach the various segments?
3. What advertising strategies do you think would be appropriate for Pepsi-Cola to use in reaching those segments?

Marketing Management Cases

Part II

This part of the book is divided into six sections: Marketing Research (Cases 16–18), Buyer Behavior (Cases 19–21), Product Strategies (Cases 22–24), Pricing Strategies (Cases 25–27), Advertising Strategies (Cases 28–30), and Distribution Strategies (Cases 31–33).

The first two sections relating to marketing research and buyer behavior tie in with some of the cases in the first part of the book. Here the objective is to study these key concepts in a little more detail with somewhat longer cases. The last four sections cover what is known as the four *P*s of marketing (product, price, promotion, and place). These are the elements of an organization's marketing mix.

Cases in this part can be taught using the traditional approach to the case method involving identification of the problem, development of alternatives, analysis of the alternatives, and specifying recommendations. Many instructors, however, may prefer to provide somewhat greater structure and direction in terms of specific topics for analysis. To meet the needs of this group of instructors, a special series of self-contained Case Analysis Forms has been developed for each case. These Case Analysis Forms provide space for students to respond to specific questions about each case.

Whirlpool Corporation: Researching Consumer Perceptions

Whirlpool Corporation is a leading manufacturer of major home appliances with corporate roots that go back to 1911. During the more than 70 years that the firm has been making appliances, the variety of consumer products and services has grown astronomically. At the same time, competition for the consumer's dollar has become fierce. Whirlpool has always placed quality first and foremost in the products it builds and in the after-purchase services it provides.

In an attempt to help understand more about consumers today, Whirlpool commissioned Research & Forecasts to conceive and execute a study that would uncover new information about the desires, expectations, and judgments of the consuming public, with emphasis on—but not limited to—an exploration of quality-related issues. The following material relates to that study.

Introduction

America's Search for Quality: The Whirlpool Report on Consumers in the 80s, brings together two issues of contemporary concern, one with a high level of public consciousness and one with a much lesser level.

The first is the concern about quality in our society's goods and services. As America's international economic role has been challenged and redefined in recent years, the issue of product quality and value has surged to the forefront of public scrutiny. The postwar concern for abundance has been superseded by a desire for quality in our production, in our environment, and in our lives.

The second issue is consumption. The words "to consume" or "consumer" may never have been completely attractive, but today after decades of attacks on "conspicuous consumption," "consumer society," and "consumption of natural resources," it is difficult to use them in a neutral way. The increased concern for preserving worldwide natural resources creates a negative context in most developed economies over the prospect of being called "consumers."

Yet consumers we are. Adam Smith stated the concept succinctly: "Consumption is the sole end and purpose of all production." Our current concern with

Source: This case has been adapted from "America's Search for Quality: The Whirlpool Report on Consumers in the 80s."

quality products has to include an equal and unbiased concern with consumption — with quality consumption.

The Whirlpool Report on Consumers in the 80s draws some conclusions about what it means today to be a quality consumer and poses some focused questions about products and services. What is quality consumption? Which Americans are most concerned with quality?

As more than a generation of marketing research has demonstrated, different perspectives on the American consumer are much like the proverbial blind men touching different parts of one elephant and coming to radically different conclusins about the animal. *The Whirlpool Report*, however, deals with the broad topic of quality and the American consumer. Rather than detailing specific profiles of markets for particular products or services, it outlines for our new "postconsumerist" era what it means today to be a quality consumer.

The Whirlpool Report was initiated in the spring of 1982 by surveying a representative sample of reporters, editors, researchers, producers, and program directors from print and broadcast media. These media representatives were specialists in either business, consumer, or home/lifestyle reporting. We assumed that these people would have a clear idea about what were the most important issues related to quality.

The results of this media survey were clear. The specialists nearly unanimously believed Americans are discontented with manufactured goods and believed Americans are even more dissatisfied — even angry and cynical — about services and service providers. The media said consumers do not feel they are getting their money's worth. They said consumers are becoming more active and demanding shoppers because of this discontent.

The Whirlpool Report's subsequent national public opinion survey tested these and many other related issues. Some of the results of the national opinion study confirm basic notions about the search for quality in everyday goods and services. Frequently, however, this study forces us to revise many stereotypes about the American consumer.

Some of the key questions explored in this report are:

☐ Do Americans feel surrounded by junk and poor quality goods and services available to them or are they satisfied?

☐ Do Americans think quality is becoming more scarce, or do they think the quality of goods and services has improved in recent years?

☐ Do consumers feel they have an adversary relationship with manufacturers and service providers?

☐ Does the public believe it is the pawn of advertising, or does it take advantage of the information available in advertising while maintaining a balanced perspective?

☐ Do they place more value on secondary considerations such as style and packaging over basic materials, workmanship, and safety?

☐ Are Americans insistent that goods and services be accompanied by the human touch — by evidence of workmanship in the products they purchase and of courtesy and integrity in consumer-provider interactions?

☐ Does the public feel there has been recent improvement or deterioration in available goods and services?

☐ Are they more or less demanding about quality than they have been in the past?

☐ Are consumers most likely to trust the information provided by the manufacturer, government, or consumer interest groups?

Methodology

A multistage research design was used in conducting this study of American attitudes to quality in goods and services.

Phase One.   The first phase consisted of qualitative and background research undertaken to generate hypotheses and develop topic areas for the general public survey stage of the project.

Phase Two.   The second phase consisted of a series of interviews with 50 representatives of the print and broadcast media from throughout the nation between May 24 and June 18, 1982. These media representatives were specialists in the areas of consumer interest, business and finance, and home/lifestyle reporting. In these interviews, topic areas for the general public survey were discussed at length in an open-ended interview format and suggestions as to issues of consumer concern were solicited.

Advisory Panel.   During Phase One and Phase Two of the project, the advice of experts in the consumer relations and consumer research fields was actively solicited through numerous telephone and face-to-face interviews. As a result of these conversations and on the results of the background research and media interviews, the research staff invited a number of experts to act as an advisory panel for the general public survey stage of the project. The advisory panel was particularly helpful in the questionnaire construction, in the phrasing of questions, and in ensuring that the questionnaire and the final report were both comprehensive and nonbiased.

Phase Three.   The third phase of the project was a general public survey. Twenty trained interviewers conducted phone interviews for a period of five weeks. Group A interviews took place from December 16, 1982 to December 23, 1982. Group B interviews were conducted from December 27, 1982 to January 23, 1983. Groups A and B were compared to determine if there were any differences in responses before and after the Christmas shopping season. No differences were found. The interviews were conducted on weeknights, between the hours of 6 p.m. and 10 p.m.; and on weekends, between the hours of 10:00 a.m. and 11:30 p.m. The interviews took an average of 34 minutes to complete.

Briefings were held before each daily interviewing session to discuss the data collection process. Interviewers were urged to ask questions at any time during the briefing period. Supervisors audited each interviewer periodically in order to ensure accuracy and to prevent bias.

In order to ensure that the respondents interviewed represented a random sample of the total U.S. population, at least four callbacks were made to each telephone number that had neither yielded a complete interview nor been disqualified. A final response rate of 63 percent was obtained. The components of the response rate are listed below.

Phase Four, Weighting.   In order to make valid projections to the entire population of the United States, the sample should match the total U.S. population on key demographic variables. Due to sampling fluctuations, it was necessary to weight the data to match Census figures on four characteristics: age, race, gender, and education. The final weighted sample matches Census figures very closely. The weighting produced a total weighted sample size of 1,002.

Statistical Analysis.   The bulk of analyses reported in the text are illustrated with cross-tabulation data. Relationships among variables were confirmed by reference to the Chi Square and Pearson's R Statistics, where applicable.

General Public Response Rate

Completed Interviews	1,002	(63%)
Nonresponse	591	(37%)
Refusals	339	
Terminated interviews	17	
Callbacks	165	
Deaf/Language problem	70	
Total Potential Respondents	1,593	(100%)
Excluded from Sample	2,020	
Disconnected	684	
Never answered	614	
Always busy	84	
Business/Government	533	
Not qualified	105	
Total Number of Calls	3,613	

Several three-way crosstabs were computed to test further for relationships among variables. An examination of the tables revealed no additional insights, but confirmed the analysis derived from an examination of the cross-tabulations.

Scale Construction. Seven scales or indexes were constructed for the analysis. The first is an Active Consumer Index. Respondents were asked whether they had purchased any of the following items new in the past year:

- Auto
- Major household appliance
- Home furniture
- Home electronics equipment
- Child raising equipment
- Small household appliances

Respondents were then placed in one of four categories, depending on the number of "yes" responses given to the question. The most active consumer scored three or more affirmative responses, while the least active consumer purchased none of the items listed. Those making one or two purchases from the list fell into the two middle categories.

The Personal Financial Sophistication Index. This is the second constructed index. Questions were asked about the respondents' financial investments in the following:

- Bank checking account
- Money market fund
- Property insurance
- Local department store credit card
- IRA or Keough plan
- Real estate other than permanent residence
- Bank savings account
- Life insurance
- Major national credit card
- Corporate stocks or bonds
- Will
- Municipal bonds or bond funds

The "very sophisticated" investor is one who has invested in or is in possession of six or more of the items in the list. The "somewhat sophisticated" investor has three to five of the items, while the least sophisticated have two or fewer of the items.

The Family Type/Family Responsibility Index.   This is the final construction. For this index, respondents were placed in one of seven categories according to their age, their marital and employment status, their spouse's employment status (where applicable), and whether or not they are parents. Those on the low end of the responsibility scale, without any appreciable family responsibilities, are single people, without children or spouse to care for and people aged 65 and older, many with diminished work and family responsibilities.

Those is the middle of the responsibility scale include married respondents who have no children and married people whose children are all over 18. In most cases the respondents in these categories have greater responsibilities than singles and older Americans, but fewer than those in the remaining three categories.

The first category of those with high levels of family responsibility is the traditional family type, consisting of people aged 18 to 64 who are married and have children 18 or younger. Only the husband in these families is employed. Another, the dual-career family type, resembles the traditional family, except that both spouses are employed. The final category consists of single parents who are not currently married, but have children 18 or younger with whom they live.

The fourth through seventh scales were constructed to identify the sources of information that are primarily relied upon by various people. A factor analysis was conducted based on all the variables from the questionnaire in which respondents indicated the level of importance to them of a source of information about goods and services. The factor analysis showed four distinct types of people: those who rely on advertising, those who rely on television and radio shows, those who rely on personal recommendations, and those who rely on consumer-interest media.

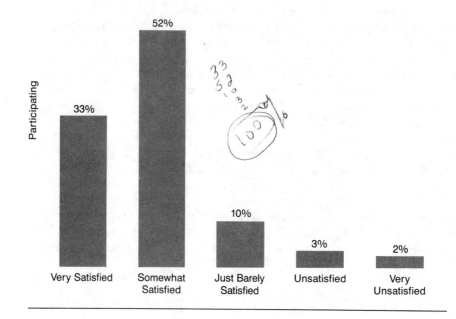

How satisfied are you with the manufactured goods you can purchase in your area? (992 respondents)

In general do you think the quality of goods in America has improved or deteriorated over the last few years? (988 respondents)

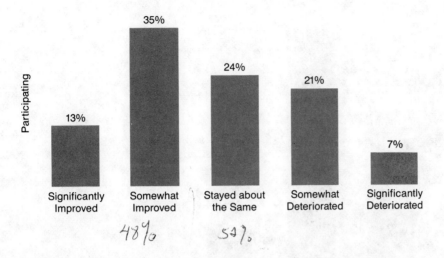

48% 52%

Overall would you say you are more or less demanding about the quality of goods in America than you were a few years ago? (999 respondents)

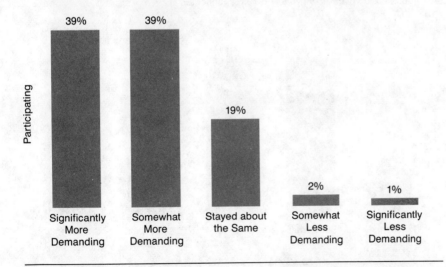

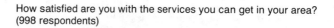

How satisfied are you with the services you can get in your area?
(998 respondents)

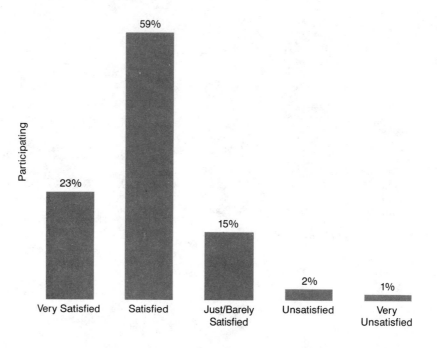

Do you think the quality of the services in your area has improved or
deteriorated over recent years? (979 respondents)

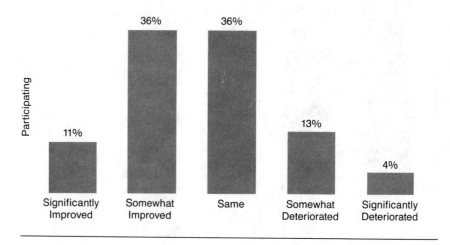

Changes in Service Quality

	Improved	Stayed the Same	Deteriorated
Supermarket Services (checkout, bagging, check-cashing, etc.)	46	42	12
Your Local Fire Department	45	53	2
Your Local Law Enforcement Agency	33	48	18
Residential Telephone Service	29	52	19
Your Local Garbage Collection and Sanitation	28	59	13
The U.S. Postal Service	24	54	22
Clothes Cleaning and Tailoring	26	58	16
Home Electronics Equipment Service (TV, stereo, radio, etc.)	35	47	18
Major Household Appliance Service (refrigerator, washer, dryer, etc.)	22	54	24
Home Repair and Services (plumbing, electrician services, painting, carpentry, etc.)	20	61	19
Automobile Service	17	33	50

All figures percentages

Do you do more do-it-yourself activities than you used to?
(987 respondents)

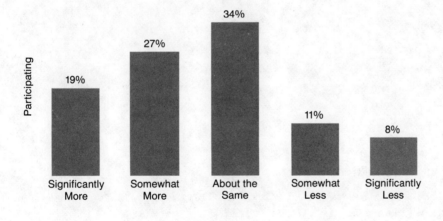

Frequency of Do-It-Yourself Activities

	More Than Once per Month	About Once per Month	A Few Times per Year	Once a Year or Less	Never
Home Repair	11	15	31	15	28
Auto Repair	9	15	24	8	44
Home Electronics Repair	1	5	12	17	65
Household Appliance Repair	1	4	10	19	65
Gourmet Cooking	8	11	22	8	52

All figures percentages

Important Characteristics of the Salesperson

	Always Important	Sometimes Important	Only a Little Important	Not At All Important
Knowledgeable about Specific Products—Sizes, Materials, Specifications, Etc.?	72	21	5	2
Knowledgeable about the Competing Brands?	45	38	9	9
Knowledgeable about Other Departments and Products in the Store?	39	42	12	8
Available to Help You As Soon As You Enter the Store?	37	41	12	10
Courteous?	91	8	1	0
Easily Identifiable by a Name Tag or the Clothes They Wear?	58	25	7	10
The Same Sex as You?	6	13	8	73
About the Same Age as You?	2	11	7	80
About the Same Ethnic Background as You?	3	9	5	83

All figures percentages

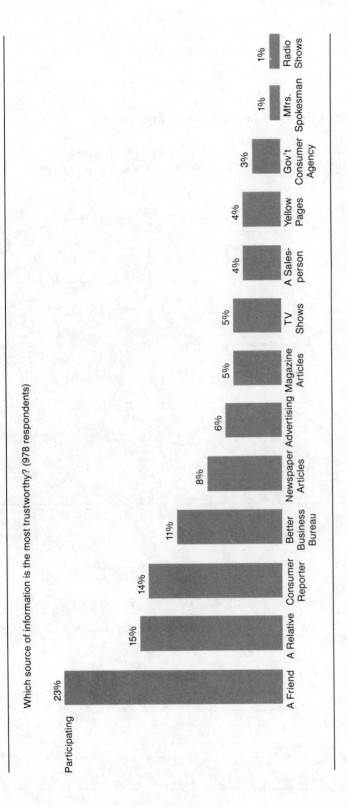

Which source of information is the most trustworthy? (978 respondents)

Participating

A Friend — 23%

A Relative — 15%

Consumer Reporter — 14%

Better Business Bureau — 11%

Newspaper Articles — 8%

Advertising — 6%

Magazine Articles — 5%

TV Shows — 5%

A Sales-person — 4%

Yellow Pages — 4%

Gov't Consumer Agency — 3%

Mfrs. Spokesman — 1%

Radio Shows — 1%

Case 16 Analysis Form

Whirlpool Corporation: Researching Consumer Perceptions

1. From the perspective of Whirlpool and recipients of the research (other businesses, academia, and the American public), why is this type of research valuable?

Whirlpool: _____

_____

_____

_____

_____

Other Businesses: _____

_____

_____

_____

_____

Academia: _____

_____

_____

_____

American Public: _____

_____

_____

_____

_____

2.   What is your evaluation of the research methodology used in the study?

_____

_____

_____

_____

_____

_____

_____

_____

_____

3.   What other types of data analyses would be helpful?

_____

_____

_____

_____

_____

_____

_____

_____

_____

4. *Test Ques.*

Discuss the relative advantages and disadvantges of using the following methods of gathering consumer research in a study like Whirlpool's.

Mail Survey: _____

_____

_____

_____

_____

_____

Telephone Survey: _____

_____

_____

_____

_____

_____

Product Survey: _____

_____

_____

_____

_____

_____

Focus Group Interviews: _____

_____

_____

_____

_____

_____

5. Based on the limited research results presented in the case, what conclusions do you draw in terms of the following?

Satisfaction with Good Services: _____

_____

_____

_____

_____

_____

Characteristics of Sales Personnel: _____

_____

_____

_____

_____

_____

Do-It-Yourself Behavior: _____

_____

_____

_____

_____

_____

Sources of Consumer Information: _____

_____

_____

_____

_____

_____

Tomorrow's Customers in Canada: Researching Consumer Trends

Each year, Clarkson Gordon/Woods Gordon, a Canadian management consulting organization, prepares an updated version of a publication titled *Tomorrow's Customers in Canada*. The publication is designed to serve their clients and friends in business, industry, and government by providing a clear, concise summary of social, economic, and business trends as they emerge. The following sections provide some of the consumer highlights from a recent edition of the publication.[1]

The Business Environment

The recovery from the disastrous recession of the early 80s is by no means complete; some industry sectors and regions of the country have not yet regained their former buoyancy. Even so, over the past 2½ years the Canadian economy has profited from the strongest economic expansion in North America in more than a decade. A leaner, tougher, and more aggressive Canadian business has now begun to emerge. These survivors are well-placed to accept the challenges of an increasingly competitive environment.

Renewed growth, much reduced inflation, and declining interest rates have increased business and consumer optimism. Some reduction in the degree of uncertainty associated with the economic environment has made the business climate more accommodating. As a result, the potential for further growth in our production, income, and standard of living is more significant than has been the case since 1979. The rapid dissemination of technology and know-how is dramatically increasing the intensity of competition. New products are needed for established markets, new markets for established products. In the successful pursuit of this, Canadian business must stress efficiency throughout all segments of its business; planning, research, finance, production, administration, marketing, distribution, and sales.

Population Trends

The past decade has seen some important shifts of emphasis in Canadian society which present an intriguing mix of problems and opportunities to marketers. Canadian consumers will look for an even broader range of products and services

---

[1]Marketing and Economics Group of Woods Gordon, P.O. Box 251, Toronto-Dominion Centre, Toronto, Canada M5K IJ7.

than before, demanding luxury quality on some items and cut prices on others. Marketers will be focusing their efforts on segments of the population with distinctive needs: on the affluent, many of whom have lifestyles based on the search for novelty and individuality, and on the rapidly growing number of singles.

Population growth continues to be slow, and Woods Gordon projections suggest a further decline in the years ahead due to:

☐   Low birth rates (currently averaging 1.7 per woman compared with 3.8 in 1961)
☐   Low net migration (currently about 40,000 a year compared with 120,000 ten years ago)
☐   A larger portion of "over 65s" in the population and hence more deaths

During the past decade, the pattern of migration between provinces has changed. Two major trends have emerged: Quebec's net outflow is slowing down while Alberta, which had a net inflow in the 1970s, now has a net outflow. Population growth for 1974–1984 averaged 1.1 percent a year; between 1984 and 1989 it is expected to drop to 0.8 percent, between 1989 and 1994 to less than 0.7 percent. Estimates place the population at 27 million (up from 25.1 million in 1984).

As the baby-boom generation matures, the balance of the age groups will change. Looking ahead to 1994, we see an important increase in the 35–49 and 65 + age groups and a substantial reduction in the number of young adults.

Middle Aged.   By 1994, there will be 1.6 million more people aged 35–49 and they will constitute 23.2 percent of the population, up from 18.6 percent today. A one-third increase in the number of people in the high-spending 35–49 age bracket will provide a stimulus for consumer durables and other household-related furnishings.

Seniors.   Ten years ago, 8.4 percent of all Canadians were 65 or over. Today the percentage has risen to 10.2 percent, or just over 2.5 million people. By 1994, with 518,000 more, they will constitute 11.4 percent of the total population. With 20 percent increase in the number of seniors, sensitivity will be required in marketing; studies show that seniors feel they are 10 to 15 years younger than they really are. Increased quality-of-life expectations will increase demands for hobby/ recreational equipment and travel packages developed specifically for seniors. Health-care and beauty products, prepared foods, health-promoting foods and food substitutes, and fashionable "easy-care, easy-wear" clothing will be in demand. In the longer term, the Affluent Senior will emerge, with distinctive needs and expectations.

Children.   It is estimated that by 1994, there will be 230,000 (6 percent) more young children aged up to nine years old than today. By 1994, there will be an estimated 234,000 (11 percent) fewer young people aged 15 to 19 than today. More young children in the population points to a greater need for day care, pre-school facilities, nannies, and child-care products and services. Child-raising is becoming a "managed" process and, with fewer children per family, parents are more willing to invest in educational toys and services.

Fewer teenagers in the population mix has implications for those industries that rely on this group for their source of labor or as customers. Obvious examples are fast foods and movies; others include the textbook and school-supply industries, clothing and accessories, as well as sports equipment.

Social Patterns

Housing

Annual housing starts continue to be lower than they were in the 1970s. Between 1985 and 1989, housing starts are expected to average 155,000 annually, representing two-thirds of the average annual starts of a decade ago. During the coming decade we will see an increase in the proportion of single-detached dwellings within the overall total. For the most part, these dwellings will be sought by families in the 35–49 year age group who tend to be more affluent than younger families and to have greater numbers of children.

As more elderly singles choose to live independently in their own homes rather than in institutions, there will be a greater need for housekeeping assistance, prepared meals, organized social activities, and house maintenance and repair services. In response to this trend, the Ontario Ministry of Municipal Affairs and Housing has undertaken a pilot project for 1985 to assess the potential of "granny flats"—detached and portable units designed to be placed on the grounds of a single-family home. Self-contained, these units would provide privacy, yet with access to a main house. If successful, this new type of dwelling should be a boon to the prefabricated housing industry.

Households

Trends in the number of households are important because sales of some products, such as major appliances, are more closely correlated with the number of households than with the size of the population. Over the last decade, the number of households has increased dramatically—up 37 percent since 1971. During that same time, the population increased by only 12.9 percent! Although household formation rates will continue to exceed population growth rates over the next ten years, the overall rate of household formation is declining. Almost 25 percent of total households in 1981 were nonfamily households, with the most dramatic growth occurring in single-person households. In 1961, they accounted for 9.3 percent of the total; by 1981 the percentage had risen to 20.3 percent.

Families

Over the last decade, the number of husband-wife families without children at home has grown over two-and-a-half times as quickly as those with children. The higher incidence of these husband-wife families reflects, in part, the decision among younger couples to postpone starting a family. However, the most extraordinary growth occurred in the number of single-parent families, stimulating demand for day-care centres, after hours shopping, and time- and labour-saving devices. In 1981, there were approximately 714,000 such families in Canada, representing more than a 50 percent increase over 1971.

Income

The Affluent Family

In 1983, 39.8 percent of all family income, or $91 billion, was acquired by the affluent top quintile (20 percent) of families—those with over $48,900 in total income. In 1983, of families in the affluent top quintile, only 11 percent had one income earner; 52 percent had two income earners, and 35 percent had three or more income earners. These families tend to live in large urban centres—46 percent have a professional or manager as the head of the family; 87 percent include two or more income earners. Over one-half of these families have no children under the age of 16.

The concentration of income among affluent Canadians will support a continued market for luxury goods and services. These include such things as high-end automobiles; sail boats; personal computers, software, and games; such time-saving devices as microwave ovens and frozen/take-out foods; foreign travel; health and recreational facilities and products, including tanning centres, spas, and home fitness equipment; the right restaurants for dining out and gourmet foods for dining in. Additionally, one-stop shopping, shop-at-home, and mail order services; in-home computer banking; and home maintenance, renovation, and catering services all answer a wide-spread need of the affluent to save time whenever and however possible.

The Affluent Single

In 1983, 47 percent of the aggregate income of singles, or $19 billion, was acquired by the top 20 percent of this group—those with over $23,000 in total income. Affluent singles are even more concentrated in urban centres than affluent families. Male singles constitute 60 percent of the group, 48 percent are managers or professionals. As the single lifestyle becomes more and more acceptable—not just an interim arrangement—there will be a substantial increase in the group's overall income. Affluent singles are actively seeking and acquiring their own homes, furniture, and appliances—traditionally the domain of families.

A Market for "High-Touch"

In the final analysis, beyond luxury goods and services, beyond time-saving devices and resources, affluent Canadians are manifesting the desire for new and different experiences. Satiated and often supersaturated with material possessions, the search is on for different pursuits. White-water rafting, African safaris, survival games, "Whodunit" weekends, chocolate-making classes, and bicycle tours of the French wine country are just a few examples. The operative words seem to be escape, challenge, and fantasy-fulfillment.

Saving and Spending

Saving: A New Importance for Old Reality

Over the last decade, saving once again assumed an important role. Government tax incentives encouraged investment in RRSPs and RHOSPs,[2] and concerns about a volatile economy, possible unemployment, and high interest rates provided further impetus. In the first quarter of 1982, savings peaked at 16.1 percent of personal disposable income. By 1984, the average level was down to 12.8 percent — still substantially higher than the 9.9 percent average of 1974. Homeowners in unprecedented numbers were paying off their mortgages to avoid fluctuating interest rates, while those without debt and able to do so took advantage of these same rates by saving. Proposed increases in RRSP contribution limits would further stimulate savings by the affluent. The upsurge in savings reduces the short-term demand for durables and increases demand for innovative investment vehicles. In particular, proposed changes to the Capital Gains Tax would stimulate new interest in equity-linked investment plans.

Spending: New Attitudes, New Approaches

The High Spenders.   Families where the husband is 45–54 years old have, in the past, been the heaviest spenders. In 1985, these families will each spend an average of $31,600 on goods and services. Families where the husband is 35–44 will spend about $30,900. Projections for the next decade indicate that these younger families, typically with children aged 5–15, will be the most numerous and will account for the greatest total spending, stimulating demand for large, family-oriented vehicles, recreation and sports equipment, and household furnishings.

Singles' Spending.   In 1985, there are twice as many single-person households as "conventional" households of two adults, two children. In 1985, singles living on their own will spend, in aggregate, almost $1 billion on products and services for their homes — only 30 percent less than the $1.4 billion collectively spent by families of four. The average single will spend about $13,400 on goods and services — almost half as much as that conventional family of four. Compared with families, proportionately more of singles' spending goes on shelter, public transportation, reading material, tobacco products, and alcoholic beverages. Singles living alone constitute a major market segment; as the trend to living alone increases, so will the group's market potential.

The "Scrimp and Splurge" Phenomenon.   Over the last decade the consumer has enjoyed an overall increase in personal disposable income. This, together with the changes in working patterns and lifestyles, has stimulated demand for luxuries and items that used to be considered luxuries, but are modern-day essentials, such as prepared foods, home maintenance help, and child-care facilities. These influences run counter to the experience of the recent recession, which has encouraged consumers to seek value and reexamine their real needs.

Today's more educated and demanding consumers are more confident in their own priorities. They are determining the product with the level of perfor-

---

[2]Types of personal retirement savings plans.

mance and quality necessary to meet their personal needs, and then obtaining it at the lowest cost by using coupons and looking for "deals" and off-price outlets. This has led to apparent contradictions in buyer behavior and to the birth of a hybrid: the "scrimp and splurge" consumer. This person holds back in some areas and lets go extravagantly in others. We save a few cents buying a generic laundry bleach, then blow the savings—and much more—on custom-blended coffee from a gourmet shop. We buy discount house T-shirts, but our health equipment is of health-club quality. Thus, while the need for discount stores, junior department stores, off-price outlets, and private label products will continue to escalate, so will the need for "gourmet-to-go" and other luxury specialty shops.

Case 17 Analysis Form

Tomorrow's Customers in Canada:
Researching Consumer Trends

Due three questions for case 17

1. From a general marketing perspective, what are some of the ways in which an understanding of social, economic, and business trends can be helpful?

From a marketing perspective, having an understanding of social, economic, and business trends can be helpful in that they show how the environment is. The environment, being as turbulent as it is, has an effect on all business behaviors. And it is up to the marketing people to decifer it and understand it, so that they can provide for, and tend to, the needs and wants of consumers

2. What are the potential benefits to a firm like Woods Gordon in doing and disseminating research of this type?

Doing a research of this type helps the firm understand the outside environment. This is important because the environment will determine the firms behavior. All organizations must modify their functions in order to coexsist with the ever changing environment. If a firm doesn't it will not survive

3.   Please indicate what suggestions you would make to the following groups based on the information in the case:

Retailing Organizations: _____

_____

_____

_____

_____

Advertising Agencies: _____

_____

_____

_____

_____

Consumer Appliance Manufacturers: _____

_____

_____

_____

_____

Publishing Firms: _____

_____

_____

_____

_____

4. What other types of research could Woods Gordon undertake that would be helpful to the organizations and groups it serves?

_____

_____

_____

_____

_____

_____

5. Compare the advantages and disadvantages of research like this using secondary data sources and a primary data study.

Secondary Study: _Dis. Information is done already_
- used someone else has done it!
Adv. much less expensive, you can
see trends perhaps.
Plus, you can pick out something
that isn't relevant anymore and
avoid repitition

_____

Primary Study: _Dis Very expensive, and long_
lead time especially in the scope
of their reports.
It becomes yours
Anything new you've discared.

_____

_____

6. Discuss some of the ways that a firm could keep aware of the changing values and emerging lifestyles of its consumers.

   Keep abreast of trends
   Constantly monitor the
   environment, and watch
   for changes.

7. How do the changing consumer characteristics in Canada compare to the changes occurring in the United States?

   - characteristics in Canada
   Compared

Impact Resources: Measuring Market and Media Audiences

Case 18

Impact Resources is a professional consulting firm specializing in media and retail marketing/management. More than 75 years of combined experience is held by Impact's principal professionals in the areas of media management, market research, acquisition analysis, retail marketing, strategic planning, communications, financial planning, target marketing, consumer profiling, and industry training and development. The firm is the sole provider of a unique media/retail market measuring system named MA-RT. MA-RT is a new pragmatic, total-system approach to the collection and analysis of usable consumer data.

Market Audience — Readership Traffic

Market Audience — Readership Traffic (MA-RT for short) was created by Dr. John Scott Davenport, a former professor of communications at Brigham Young University and a veteran of almost 40 years in media research and development. MA-RT is a total-system concept, not just another type of market survey. Most legitimate market surveys utilize probability sampling. MA-RT does not. Instead it uses what it calls "reality sampling."

MA-RT's survey seeks the greatest number of people or things practically possible to represent the item to be measured, sorts this larger sample by age and sex, and then uses census weights to keep disparities from biasing or distorting the total survey. MA-RT's sample would contain 3,000 to 5,000 interviews, depending on the size of the market. In some markets, the number of interviews could be even larger. The large sample does not improve the mathematical basis of the survey, but does enhance the degree and quality of the information gathered on the market and its competitive environment.

In sampling, MA-RT recognizes the fallacy of more being better, but requires the large number to identify the traffic patterns of less popular retail and media units and to enable the collection of demographic profiles on both units being measured. For example, consider a specialty store retailer with a target market of working women. A probability sample of 300 would provide the size of the market in total numbers and a broad age spectrum. A MA-RT sample of 3,000 to 5,000 would give market size plus a complete consumer profile such as an age range of 18 to 34 for the most frequent shoppers who listen to radio stations Z and X and read P, Q, and Y local newspapers and magazines, who tend to be clustered in zip codes, and who shop at the ABC Department store because of quality and selection.

Exhibit 18.1, prepared by the firm as part of its communications strategy, describes some of the features and benefits of MA-RT and what it can do for a client. Specifically a survey:

Exhibit 18.1   Features and Benefits of MA-RT

Now, for the first time, you can take the guess work out of understanding your *local* market.

MA-RT:

1. Pinpoints, targets, who and where your current and potential customers are.
2. Tells you specifically which *local* media best and most effectively reach your target consumer.
3. Gives you a return on the ad dollar you spend, "More bang for your buck." MA-RT allows you to concentrate your advertising dollars by placing ads only in media that truly reach your customers.
4. Matches and tags regular customers to the specific retailer they use, a competitive comparison.
5. Provides you with a clean consumer consumption report. MA-RT asks how many? how much? where? and why?
6. Gives you a catalog of consumer retail expenditures and tells you when consumers plan to purchase major items.
7. Is compatible with SRI (Stanford Research Institute) Val's Lifestyle Program: a nationally recognized program that helps you appeal to and attract customers.
8. Provides retail executives with practical decision-making information.
9. Gathers a *local* shopper profile that is directly usable by *local* merchants.
10. Gives you real marketplace information about your *local* market, with regional and national compatibility.

☐ Measures local consumer shopping patterns—who shops where, why they shop there, what they buy, and which media they use
☐ Simultaneously measures all media in a local market, including radio, television, newspapers, cable TV, magazines, etc.
☐ Obtains local consumer usage data on direct mail, Yellow Pages advertising, motion picture attendance, billboard ads, and telephone solicitations
☐ Collects in-depth and comprehensive demographic characteristics and consumer lifestyle behavior patterns

---

Data Gathering Approach

All data in a MA-RT survey is collected directly from consumers who personally fill out a questionnaire. Rather than walking up to consumers and asking them to participate in a survey, MA-RT surveyors are stationed at folding tables in shopping malls. Posted signs read "Give Us Your Opinion." Interested consumers are then asked to sit down with a questionnaire to complete. The respondents do not receive any incentive to participate.

The questionnaire was field-tested and fine-tuned over a seven-year period with more than 100,000 respondents. The questionnaire is highly sensitive, yet people friendly, as a literate 12-year old can easily respond to the questions. The questionnaire is totally compatible with MA-RT's computer systems, yet it was designed not to alienate respondents and bias answers by including a lot of technical jargon. MA-RT never sacrifices the humanity of personal data collection to expedite data processing.

MA-RT data is as clear a channel as it is possible to create. Data does not pass through an interviewer who is subject to bias. In being translated into computer language by editors and coders, questionnaires are subject to standard codes in 96 percent of the response areas. Areas of exception are the concern of specially trained editors who check the standard coding to minimize human error in translation. In the MA-RT system, there are few opportunities for biasing the data. There is an absolute minimum of data manipulation between the time the respondents fill in the questionnaire and the computer provides its reports.

A MA-RT measurement is taken rapidly. Generally, all questionnaires within a given market are completed within a 36-hour period. By taking large samples in a short period without forewarning to the local media or retailers, it is difficult for them to inflate, or hype, the size of the audience. The combination of a short period of measurement and a large number of interviews provides strong safeguards against and deterrents to manipulation of MA-RT results. In street parlance, it is a matter of getting in and getting out quickly; mathematically, it is a matter of the Law of Large Numbers.

Additional Information

MA-RT reports are available in a variety of formats. A company report provides specific information on a single organization's customers. An industry report provides data on all members of a given industry group. This might include, for example, all department stores in the market area, or all drug stores, or viewerships for all television stations. Total market reports include data on all media and all retailing organizations in the market area being studied.

In addition, Impact Resources can prepare special reports that define core customers, pinpoint special market needs, provide media profiles and analysis of media usage behavior, target the best media usage to maximize the return on a firm's advertising investment, and so forth. Price ranges for the alternative reports are presented in Exhibit 18.2

MA-RT has been used in a variety of ways. Exhibit 18.3 profiles some of these applications.

Exhibit 18.2   MA-RT Reports Pricing Schedule

	Market Size			
	Small: 250,000 to 500,000	Medium: 500,000 to 1 million	Metro: 1 million to 2 million	Super Metro: 2 million and Up
Company Report	$ 3,000	$ 4,000	$ 5,500	$ 7,500
Industry Report	5,000	7,500	9,000	13,500
Total Market Report	24,000	28,000	32,000	37,000
Special Reports	Customized Sorts and Prices			

Exhibit 18.3   How MA-RT Has Been Used

Shopping Center Gains Competitive Edge

From our association, ZCMI Center Mall has come from an information deficit to a leader in demographic data. By knowing who our customers are, where they consume their advertising messages and how much each spends per visit, we have a keen representation of where we are now and where we will be in the coming decade. MA-RT data has also helped us to relocate selected key mall tenants to smaller spaces. This action has reduced overhead cost for the retailers, increased their sales per square foot, and brought greater productivity and expansion opportunities to ZCMI Center.

ZCMI Center Mall, Salt Lake City, Utah

Hispanic Market Identified

A theater owner in New Mexico used MA-RT to find out the number of bilingual households in the area with an annual income of less than $15,000. When he had that information, he took out a $7.50 coupon ad in a small Hispanic newspaper. The first night after the ad appeared, the theater owner did $1,000 more business than usual.

Positive Selling Made Possible by MA-RT

I know of no other service available that is so comprehensive, yet so simple. KTRC believes in positive selling, and not by selling against another media. With the MA-RT reports it is now possible to sell our affirmative points without any notations of the negative points of our competitors. Keep up the excellent work, and don't hesitate to use KTRC as a recommendation.

KTRC, Santa Fe, N. M.

Market Share Increased

As you know, we are not the number one paper in circulation or advertising in Las Vegas. However, the MA-RT Study has been instrumental in helping us close the gap. We feel confident that with continuing research from MA-RT, there will be no gap.

Las Vegas Sun

Valued Data for Measuring Television

All television managers express their frustration concerning ARB and NSI and the variances of the data. Your data has application to television in the form of viewer preference for news talent, station perception, and local program/promotion awareness. You are on the right track.

Channel 3, Phoenix, Ariz.

Case 18 Analysis Form

Impact Resources: Measuring Market and Media Audiences

1. What is your overall evaluation of MA-RT?

Strengths: _____

_____

_____

_____

_____

_____

Weaknesses: _____

_____

_____

_____

_____

2. What other types of data should MA-RT consider gathering as part of the survey?

_____

_____

_____

_____

_____

_____

_____

_____

_____

3.   Why do you think consumers are willing to complete the surveys without compensation?

_____

_____

_____

_____

_____

_____

_____

_____

4.   What do you see as the specific value of MA-RT to the following?

Media: _____

_____

_____

_____

_____

Retailing: _____

_____

_____

_____

_____

Manufacturers: _____

_____

_____

_____

_____

5.   What do you see as the market potential for a service like MA-RT?

_____

_____

_____

_____

_____

_____

_____

_____

_____

_____

6.   What do you consider to be the basic problems facing Impact Resources in
      marketing MA-RT?

_____

_____

_____

_____

_____

_____

_____

_____

_____

_____

7.   Who do you see as the competitors for MA-RT?

_____

_____

_____

_____

_____

_____

_____

_____

8.   How would you suggest that Impact Resources market MA-RT to potential clients?

_____

_____

_____

_____

_____

_____

_____

_____

_____

_____

_____

_____

Cheryl's Cookies: Gourmet Cookies— and Brownies

Case 19

Cheryl's Cookies enters 1986 with plans to open 10 to 15 stores during the year and to position itself not just as a place to buy a cookie or brownie, but also as a gift shop. In a little over four years since the firm was founded, Cheryl's has grown from a single shop to a mininetwork of stores in Ohio, Indiana, New York, Missouri, and New Jersey. The company would like to have 100 stores open by 1990.

Company Background

People in Bellevue, Ohio, probably best remember Cheryl Krueger as the little farm girl who made cookies for various church groups. As the eldest of three children, Krueger was always baking. The aroma of cookies, cakes, brownies, and other baked goods always seemed to fill the family home.

A 1974 graduate of Bowling Green University, Krueger gained some of her early business experience as a buyer for Burdines, one of the Federated stores, and The Limited, based in Columbus. "Through my travels I saw David's Cookies and Mrs. Fields' Cookies, which operate on both coasts," she said. "We lived on a farm when I was a kid, and I was always baking things at home. I thought it would be great to bring something like David's or Mrs. Fields' to Columbus." At first, Krueger weighed the advantages and disadvantages of bringing one of those franchised operations to Columbus. "But, it would always be their store, and I didn't really want that," she said.

Krueger worked for The Limited for four years prior to opening her first store, and then lived in New York for three years as a vice president of Chaus, a manufacturer of women's apparel. During that time, she regularly flew back to Columbus on weekends to develop the cookie company with a school friend, Caryl Walker. The pair developed the product, originally a line of five cookies, and Krueger worked on the store design. In February 1984, Krueger returned to The Limited as a merchandise manager. It wasn't until May 1985 that she went to work full time as the president of her company, deciding, "If the cookie company was going to make it on its own, it needed full-time management."

The first Cheryl's Cookies was opened in September 1981. In January of the next year, the second store was opened. Sales for 1982 reached $250,000. By the end of 1985, the company had 14 stores with total sales of $2.5 million. Krueger estimated average monthly sales at about 280,000 cookies with around quadruple that to 1.2 million during the 1985 Christmas season. Overall, the company has some 130 to 150 full- and part-time employees. Krueger estimates sales from 25 to 30 units will top $5 million during 1986.

Product Description

The stores now feature about ten varieties of cookies, including chocolate chip and chocolate chunk, peanut butter, oatmeal, macadamian coconut, oatmeal raisin, white chocolate pecan, and others. Through product development, Krueger and Walker keep their assortment current with demands of the consumers. They are currently developing their line of brownies by adding more chips and switching varieties of pecans, finding that the brownies sell better than chocolate chunk cookies. When Cheryl's first started, the cookies were priced at $4 per pound. Today they sell for $4.95 per pound compared to competitors' prices that range up to $6.95 per pound. Exhibit 19.1 helps explain the product in more detail.

In addition to over-the-counter business, Cheryl's operates a good-sized mail order service, especially around Christmas. Orders can be placed at the store or by phone, charged to Visa or MasterCard, if preferred, and mailed anywhere in the continental United States. Cheryl's also has a corporate gift service that assists

Exhibit 19.1   Information about Cheryl's Cookies

A Culinary Note from Cheryl:

I've found that most people gain tremendous satisfaction from good, honest, "made from scratch" baked goods. All of us at Cheryl's Cookies share your respect for the finest of natural ingredients. That's why my cookies are freshly baked with generous amounts of fancy pecans, Hawaiian macadamia nuts, plump raisins, and rich, velvety imported chocolate.

You can enjoy the wonderful flavor of Cheryl's Cookies long after you've purchased them by following these suggestions:
Because there are no preservatives in Cheryl's Cookies, you should keep your cookies in an airtight container at room temperature. Placing a piece of bread inside the container will help keep the cookies soft. The cookies can be frozen; thaw or reheat them in your oven or microwave.

We hope you are pleased with our cookies. If you are—please tell your friends, if not— please tell us. We guarantee your satisfaction.

Sincerely,

Cheryl

organizations in arranging gifts for corporations, fund raisers, or any group purchase. Discounts for quantity purchases are available. In some of Cheryl's market areas, the firm's delivery service will deliver free of charge orders of $3 or more in designated downtown areas.

Cheryl's has recently introduced several new cookie packages, as well as packages that combine cookies with nonedible items like oven mittens and coffee mugs. As shown in Exhibit 19.2, Cheryl's offers three different sizes of cookie tins and two sizes of gift boxes. Four sizes of "gourmet dessert baskets" have been created and are priced from $39 to $75 each. In addition to brownies or cookies, the baskets contain such items as special sauces, gourmet coffee, imported chocolates, nuts, napkins, kitchen mittens, and coffee mugs.

Production and Store Format

All of Cheryl's cookie and brownie dough is prepared in Columbus and shipped frozen in 30-pound boxes via the company's own refrigerated trucks. "We're trying to have control of a highly perishable product," Krueger explains. Each location gets a four-week inventory per trip. The dough is thawed and baked as needed in each store. The centralized preparation enables the company to ensure consistent quality. There is no difference in taste between cookies baked from fresh or frozen raw dough.

This approach to product preparation also allows the company to operate in a very small retail space. "We can do 300 square feet," Krueger explains. "We don't have to have a kitchen in every store." Cheryl's Cookies has installed cookie units in leased space in department stores. A typical Cheryl's Cookies location is shown in Exhibit 19.3. The contemporary design is a black and white store with red accents and artfully accented with specially designed tins and boxes. The firm recently opened its largest Cheryl's Cookies in downtown Columbus. At 1,200 square feet it is about a third larger than any other unit. An even larger unit of 1,800 square feet is planned to open in the Roos Park Mall in Pittsburgh in August 1986.

To help use the additional retail space, the firm is introducing some gourmet innovations. For example, at the Columbus store, the firm is testing new ideas for the first time like muffins, croissants, and freshly squeezed orange juice in the morning, and different kinds of coffee. The store opens at 7 a.m. to capture the didn't-have-time-for-breakfast trade Monday through Friday. If there is a special evening event in the downtown area, the store will stay open for after-theater customers. For this group there will be espresso, cappuccino, and perhaps some gourmet desserts. Unlike the other Cheryl's Cookies, this store has tables at which to sit.

General Operating Philosophies

The following quotes from Cheryl Krueger represent some of the basic operating philosophies of the organization.

> We don't want to be over saturated in a market, like some of our competitors are. In the long run, we plan to stay east of the Mississippi. We have no plans for the South in 1986, although we probably will go south at some point in our growth.

Exhibit 19.2   Cheryl's Cookies Gift Offerings

Cheryl's Cookies

The Entertainment Gift Tin

The Snack Gift Tin

The Hostess Gift Tin

The One-Half Pound Gift Box

The Pound Gift Box

Cheryl's Gourmet Dessert Basket
The ultimate gift. Available in a variety of sizes and prices.

- **The Entertainment Gift Tin**
  16 Cookies—$12.00
  8 Brownies—$16.00

- **The Snack Gift Tin**
  5 Cookies—$4.95
  3 Brownies—$7.00

- **The Hostess Gift Tin**
  12 Cookies—$9.50
  7 Brownies—$13.50

- **The One-Half Pound Gift Box**
  5 Cookies—$2.95
  2 Brownies—$3.50

- **The Pound Gift Box**
  10 Cookies—$5.75
  4 Brownies—$7.00

  Add $3.95 per unit for shipping and handling of tins and boxes

- **Cheryl's Gourmet Dessert Basket**
  Prices range from $39.00 to $75.00

  Add $4.95 per unit for shipping and handling of Dessert Baskets

  Our gift items are available in 3 delicious varieties: Chocolate Chip · Cheryl's Gourmet Assortment · Fudge Brownies

  Quantity discounts available
  Prices good through 6/30/86

The key to success for Cheryl's Cookies is three-fold: the product, good service, and a unique store atmosphere.

I'm really involved in my work. I like to get out and see our customers a lot on weekends. I believe you have to be behind the counter to know what's going on.

Retailing fundamentals are the same, whether it's clothing or cookies.

We're not pigs. We don't work on the kind of mark-up some of the other people work on. We're not looking to get rich quick. We don't gouge the customer.

I love to come to work. It's exciting running a corporation. You test your planning skills, negotiating ability and see if you have people in the right positions.

Exhibit 19.3   Photograph of Typical Cheryl's Store

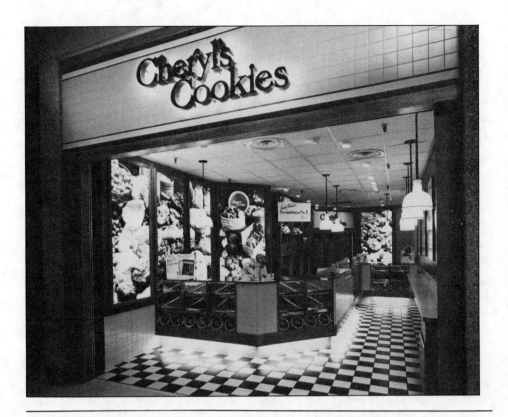

People say, "What happens as you get bigger if it all collapses?" My answer is, "So what." I never came from money. I'm not going to tell you that I don't enjoy the comfort levels that money can get you. I have a healthy respect for the downside, but I focus on the upside and the potential of the business. I work offensively, not defensively. If the business would fall apart, you would pay the bills and go on with your life.

Right now I don't have to go public; we're in a solid financial position. I can borrow at prime now, or a half-point above prime. If it gets back up, [going public] would be a factor to consider.

I guess I'm one of those gals that like to have it all. Until somebody proves me wrong, I'm going to go for it.

Case 19 Analysis Form

Cheryl's Cookies: Gourmet Cookies and Brownies

1. In terms of your analysis of the case and from a consumer behavior perspective, what do you see as:

The "real business" of Cheryl's Cookies? _____

_____

_____

_____

_____

_____

_____

The competition to Cheryl's? _____

_____

_____

_____

_____

_____

_____

_____

The marketing problems facing Cheryl's? _____

_____

_____

_____

_____

_____

2.   What are the benefits sought in a product like Cheryl's Cookies by each of the following market segments?

Consumer (Personal Use): _____

_____

_____

Consumer (Gift-Giving): _____

_____

_____

Organization (Fund Raising): _____

_____

_____

3.   What do you see as the relative advantages and disadvantages to Cheryl's in franchising its stores?

Advantages: _____

_____

_____

_____

_____

_____

_____

Disadvantages: _____

_____

_____

_____

_____

_____

_____

_____

4. Discuss possible marketing strategies that Cheryl's could use in a new market area for moving consumers through the stages of the adoption process.

Awareness: _____

_____

_____

_____

_____

Interest: _____

_____

_____

_____

_____

Evaluation: _____

_____

_____

_____

_____

Trial: _____

_____

_____

_____

_____

Adoption: _____

_____

_____

_____

_____

5. Based on your analysis, list your specific recommendations to Cheryl's (and supporting rationale) for each of the following decision areas:

Target Consumers to Reach: _____

_____

_____

    Rationale: _____

_____

_____

Promotional Appeals to Use: _____

_____

_____

    Rationale: _____

_____

_____

Media to Reach Consumers: _____

_____

_____

    Rationale: _____

_____

_____

Needed Marketing Research: _____

_____

_____

    Rationale: _____

_____

_____

Libb Pharmaceuticals:

Alive Toothpaste

Case 20

In terms of understanding consumer behavior and the subsequent formation of marketing strategy, the measurement of consumer attitudes is very important. Many firms have found that it is valuable and necessary to know how consumers perceive their brands along key product attributes.

During the late 1960s, management of Libb Pharmaceuticals became quite concerned when the market share of Alive toothpaste declined from about 15 percent to 10 percent. At a meeting of the product management team it was concluded that the firm should undertake some attitude research on the toothpaste market. Specifically the firm was interested in determining:

1. Can consumers' attitudes toward brands predict individual consumer brand preference?
2. What perceptions do people have of Alive toothpaste?
3. What are the preferences for and perceptions of the other major brands of toothpaste?
4. How can Alive toothpaste best be positioned in the marketplace?

Market share improved somewhat during the 1970s as management began a heavier emphasis on promotion. Alive's market position seemed to peak in 1980, however, with a 12 percent share. By 1983, the market share had declined to less than 9 percent. Management decided that it was time to replicate some of the attitude research it had conducted earlier on consumer attitudes toward Alive.

Background

The Company

Libb Pharmaceuticals traces its origin back to 1855 when the founder, Phillip L. Libb, developed an all-purpose skin ointment. The product achieved relatively large success within a regional trading area. From the outset, Libb devoted a significant proportion of the firm's profits to the development of new product lines and the improvement of existing ones.

By the early 1900s, the firm was manufacturing and distributing a wide line of pharmaceutical and personal care products. In addition, the firm was gradually expanding its marketing area and by 1920 had achieved national distribution for most of its products.

One of Libb's early product additions was in the area of toothpastes. At one point, the firm was marketing four separate brands of toothpaste. By the end of

World War II, all of the brands had been gradually phased out with the exception of Alive. The decision was made at that time that Alive would be the firm's only brand of toothpaste and that it would be modified and reformulated as appropriate to keep the brand competitive with changing market conditions and potentials.

The Product and Promotion

In the early 1970s, Alive toothpaste was positioned almost as an all-in-one mouth care product. Promotional claims for the product included such statements as, "Alive toothpaste polishes your teeth as bright as any other brand," "Alive contains special ingredients that freshen your breath like the leading mouthwashes," "Alive now contains a special fluoride to help reduce the threat of tooth decay," "Alive brightens and protects your teeth while it freshens your mouth."

Most of the brand's advertising budget was allocated to spot television commercials in both daytime and prime time. The basic themes of most commercials focused on boy meets girl and vice versa and "slice-of-life" types of situations. The second largest share of the brand's advertising budget goes to national magazines with some use being made of Sunday newspaper supplements.

As another form of promotion, couponing was utilized to some extent. Libb also tried several promotional efforts where Alive toothpaste was associated with some of the firm's other products. In essence, the firm only made limited attempts to concentrate on any specific market segments with its promotional efforts. Instead, the focus was on reaching as many consumers as possible with the amount of promotional dollars available.

Based on the initial attitude research results, the firm started placing more emphasis on the issue of decay prevention. While Alive was positioned more directly against Crest, the basic promotional themes still focused on all of the characteristics of the brand. The major change in marketing centered around an increase in the promotional support for the brand with specific concentrations on couponing and prime-time, spot television advertising.

Attitude Research

At a professional association conference in the late 1960s, Michael Leason, the director of marketing research for Libb, attended a special session on the use of attitude models to predict consumer brand preference. He learned that the elements that make up such predictive models could be utilized to assess the images and perceptions of individual brands.

A basic attitude model used in the prediction of individual brand preference was described as follows:

$$A_b = \sum_{i=1}^{n} W_i B_{ib}$$

where A_b = the attitude toward a particular brand b

W_i = the weight or importance of attribute i

B_{ib} = the evaluative aspect or belief toward attribute i for brand b

n = the number of attributes important in the selection of a given brand in the given product category.

A consumer attitude toward a particular brand was hypothesized to be a function of the relative importance of each product attribute and the beliefs about the brand on each attribute. The logical interpretation was that the more favorable the attitude score, the more preferred the brand.[1]

After reviewing his notes from the conference and discussing the ideas with members of the product management research team, Leason decided to conduct an attitude research project on the toothpaste market. The basic research methodology and the questionnaire used to gather the data are presented in the Appendix to this case.

Initial Consumer Research

Brand Preferences

As shown in Exhibit 20.1, Crest was ranked as the most preferred brand by 46.4 percent of the respondents. Alive was preferred by 10.5 percent of the respondents, while 22.7 percent and 22.3 percent ranked it as their second or third choices, respectively.

To gain a better understanding of brand preference across various levels of education, a cross-tabulation was developed (see Exhibit 20.2). It is significant to note that, in general, as education increases the preference for Alive decreases. The same phenomena holds true for Colgate while the opposite is true for Crest.

Attribute Importances

As part of the input to the attitude model, respondents were asked to rank the importance of five attributes of toothpaste. Exhibit 20.3 reports the ranking results for the total sample. Some 75 percent of the respondents ranked "Decay Prevention" as the most important attribute to them in selecting a brand of toothpaste. Price was ranked as least important.

With the model presented earlier, attitude scores were calculated for each respondent for each brand. Attribute important (W_1) came from Question 2 on the survey while the beliefs ($B_{1b}s$) toward each brand on each attribute came from Question 1. The attitude scores for each respondent were used to predict a rank order preference for that respondent for the five brands used in the research. These predicted rank order preferences were then compared with the actual preferences given by each respondent in Question 3 on the survey. Exhibit 20.4 shows the results of these comparisons.

As can be seen, the attitude model correctly predicted the actual most preferred brand for 74.9 percent of the respondents. The model also correctly predicted the second most preferred brand for 45.5 percent of the sample. The least preferred brand was successfully predicted 63.3 percent of the time. For 15.5

---

[1]For additional information on this particular model, see Frank M. Bass and W. Wayne Talarzyk, "An Attitude Model for the Study of Individual Brand Preference," *Journal of Marketing Research* (February 1972), pp. 93–96.

percent of the respondents, the model's predicted most preferred brand was actually their second preference.

Consumer Perceptions

Since the attitude model's predictions were relatively successful, the research team felt that the individual attribute ratings (Question 1) would probably fairly represent the images and perceptions that consumers held toward the alternative brands studied. It was decided that the average consumer ratings for each attribute should be calculated for each brand. It was also concluded that these average ratings on each brand should be first computed for those who ranked the brand as their most preferred, and then computed for those who stated first preference for any of the other brands. The results of these calculations are shown in Exhibit 20.5.

Alive was rated as a 1.27 (the lower the rating, the more satisfactory the brand is perceived on that attribute) on Taste/Flavor by those who prefer it and as a 2.23 by those who stated preference for some other brand. Respondents preferring Alive rated it as a 1.56 on Decay Prevention while those preferring Crest rated it as a 1.21 on that attribute.

1983 Consumer Research

After Alive's market share fell below 9 percent, Michael Leason decided it was time to replicate part of the earlier attitude research project. He went back to the consumer behavior literature to review some of the developments involving attitude formation and brand preference. He specifically studied some of the summary articles on attitude models in marketing.[2] Specialized models such as Fishbein's behavioral intentions model were also examined and evaluated.[3]

Due to budget constraints and a desire to have some comparability with the earlier study, the decision was made to stay with the same basic methodology. Selected results from the updated research project are presented in Exhibits 20.6 and 20.7.

Specific information is not provided on other brands since the brand preferences had shifted over the years between the two studies. In most cases, for those brands other than Alive that were still among the top five, there were few changes in the ways consumers perceived them. The major changes were observed for Alive as presented in Exhibits 20.6 and 20.7.

---

[2]W. L. Wilkie and E. A. Pessemier, "Issues in Marketing's Use of Multi-Attribute Attitude Models," *Journal of Marketing Research*, vol. 10 (November 1973), pp. 428–441; and M. B. Holbrook and J. M. Hulbert, "Multi-Attribute Attitude Models: A Comparative Analysis," in Mary Jane Schlinger (ed.), *Advances in Consumer Research*, vol. 2 (Chicago: Association for Consumer Research, 1975), pp. 375–388.

[3]Martin Fishbein and Ajzen Icek, *Belief, Attitude, Intention and Behavior: An Introduction to Theory and Research* (Reading, Mass.: Addison-Wesley, 1975); and P. W. Miniard, "Examining the Diagnostic Utility of the Fishbein Behavioral Intentions Model," WPS 80–71 (Columbus: College of Administrative Science, Ohio State University, 1980).

Research Methodology and Questionnaire

Four distinct steps were used in the development and execution of this toothpaste research. First, the relevant product attributes for toothpaste had to be determined. The second step involved designing the questions to be asked and testing consumers' ability and willingness to answer them. It was then necessary to test the overall questionnaire on a small sample under conditions similar to those that would prevail for the final survey. The last step was the nationwide administration of the final survey.

Product Attributes

The five product attributes used for toothpaste were ascertained from the results of 20 small focus group interviews. These interviews took the form of getting consumers involved in a general discussion about those things that consumers think about when selecting a brand of toothpaste. The five attributes used in this study were the ones mentioned most frequently in these interviews: (1) decay prevention; (2) taste/flavor; (3) freshens mouth; (4) whitens teeth; and (5) price.

Initial Questionnaire

Once the relevant product attributes were decided upon, a sample questionnaire was constructed and tested on a group of consumers to determine their ability and willingness to answer the questions. The results of this informal test indicated that the respondents were in general able and willing to answer these types of questions.

The Pretest

In order to insure that individuals would respond to this type of questionnaire under actual field conditions, it was decided to run a pretest of 100 panel households. A cover letter accompanied the questionnaire providing information about how to fill it out along with an incentive to participate in the form of a promised gift upon return of the completed questionnaire. Approximately 68 percent of this sample returned the questionnaire within two weeks. In general, the results were satisfactory, with no more than the anticipated number of omissions. With minor rewording of some of the questions, it was decided to go ahead with the complete sample.

Final Questionnaire

The final questionnaire was mailed to 2,000 households who were members of a national mail panel. The households were selected to provide a balanced sample which paralleled census data for the United States with respect to geographic divisions, and within each division by total household income, population density, degree of urbanization, and age of panel member. In each case, the questionnaire was to be completed by the female head-of-household. Each respondent was offered a small gift (retail value of about $2) for cooperating with the research. Within the predetermined six-week cut-off period, 78.5 percent of the 2,000 households had responded to the questionnaire. However, out of these 1,571 returned questionnaires, only 1,272 or 63.6 percent of the total sample were deemed usable for the entire analysis.

Basic Questions

In addition to the standard demographic characteristics, the following questions were asked of each respondent:

1. Now we would like for you to think about these attributes for the leading brands of toothpaste. Circle a "1" if you think the brand is very satisfactory in the attribute, "6" if you think it is very *unsatisfactory* in the attribute, or somewhere in between depending how well you are satisfied with the brand. *Please indicate your "feelings" about the brand even though you have not tried it or do not currently use it.*

Gleem	Satisfactory					Unsatisfactory
Decay prevention	1	2	3	4	5	6
Taste/Flavor	1	2	3	4	5	6
Freshens mouth	1	2	3	4	5	6
Whitens teeth	1	2	3	4	5	6
Price	1	2	3	4	5	6
Crest	**Satisfactory**					**Unsatisfactory**
Decay prevention	1	2	3	4	5	6
Taste/Flavor	1	2	3	4	5	6
Freshens mouth	1	2	3	4	5	6
Whitens teeth	1	2	3	4	5	6
Price	1	2	3	4	5	6
Alive	**Satisfactory**					**Unsatisfactory**
Decay prevention	1	2	3	4	5	6
Taste/Flavor	1	2	3	4	5	6
Freshens mouth	1	2	3	4	5	6
Whitens teeth	1	2	3	4	5	6
Price	1	2	3	4	5	6
Colgate	**Satisfactory**					**Unsatisfactory**
Decay prevention	1	2	3	4	5	6
Taste/Flavor	1	2	3	4	5	6
Freshens mouth	1	2	3	4	5	6
Whitens teeth	1	2	3	4	5	6
Price	1	2	3	4	5	6
Macleans	**Satisfactory**					**Unsatisfactory**
Decay prevention	1	2	3	4	5	6
Taste/Flavor	1	2	3	4	5	6
Freshens mouth	1	2	3	4	5	6
Whitens teeth	1	2	3	4	5	6
Price	1	2	3	4	5	6

2. Please rank the following attributes for toothpaste in their order of importance to you in selecting a brand. Write a "1" by the attribute which is most important to you, a "2" by the attribute which is next most important to you, and so on until you have ranked all five attributes.

   _____ Decay prevention
   _____ Taste/Flavor
   _____ Freshens mouth
   _____ Whitens teeth
   _____ Price

3. Now, we would like for you to rank these five brands of toothpaste by writing a "1" next to your favorite brand, a "2" next to your second favorite brand, and so on. If your favorite brand is not listed, please write it in the space provided. However, still rank the given brands in order of preference from 1 to 5, even if you are not currently using them.

   _____ Gleem
   _____ Crest
   _____ Alive
   _____ Colgate
   _____ Macleans
   _____ Preferred Brand

4. How many times a day is toothpaste used by all members of your family counted together?

   Don't use _____   1 to 2 _____   7 to 8 _____
                          3 to 4 _____   9 to 10 _____
                          5 to 6 _____   More than 10 _____

Exhibit 20.1   Frequency of Brand Preference Rankings (in Percent)

Brands	1st	2nd	Ranking 3rd	4th	5th
Gleem	9.0	28.1	25.0	29.9	8.0
Crest	46.4	19.6	19.8	9.8	4.4
Alive	10.5	22.7	22.3	30.1	14.5
Colgate	24.9	21.5	24.7	21.0	7.9
Macleans	9.2	8.2	8.2	9.2	65.2

Exhibit 20.2   Brand Preference Given Educational Level (in Percent)

Educational Level	Gleem	Crest	Alive	Colgate	Macleans	Others	
Some grammar school	5.5	18.4	16.6	44.8	2.7	12.0	100%
Completed grammar school	7.6	24.7	11.8	37.7	3.9	14.2	100%
Some high school	5.1	29.7	14.1	33.9	5.5	11.6	100%
Completed high school	5.1	33.4	10.9	31.5	5.9	13.2	100%
Some college	6.7	42.4	10.7	23.3	4.6	12.2	100%
Completed college	4.7	49.1	9.3	22.7	3.6	10.5	100%
Masters or doctorate degree	4.5	53.4	7.9	17.4	3.2	13.7	100%

Exhibit 20.3   Frequency of Attribute Importance Rankings (in Percent)

			Ranking		
Attribute	1st	2nd	3rd	4th	5th
Decay prevention	75.5	11.7	5.6	3.8	3.4
Taste/flavor	11.4	26.1	24.8	25.9	11.8
Freshens mouth	4.3	21.8	32.8	32.0	9.1
Whitens teeth	5.9	31.1	23.6	22.9	16.5
Price	2.9	9.3	13.2	15.4	59.3

Exhibit 20.4   Frequency of Actual Preference Rankings Given Predicted Ranking (in Percent)

Predicted Rank	Actual Rank					
	1st	2nd	3rd	4th	5th	
1st	74.9	15.5	5.4	3.0	1.2	100%
2nd	13.9	45.5	22.0	12.5	6.1	100%
3rd	6.5	22.7	39.4	21.3	10.0	100%
4th	3.2	11.7	24.5	41.1	19.4	100%
5th	1.4	4.5	8.6	22.2	63.3	100%

Exhibit 20.5   Average Consumer Ratings of Toothpaste Brands on Relevant Attributes

	Average Score on				
Brands	Decay Prevention	Taste/ Flavor	Freshens Mouth	Whitens Teeth	Price
Gleem					
A[a]	1.83	1.33	1.33	1.78	1.95
B[b]	2.64	2.26	2.06	2.34	2.27
Crest					
A	1.21	1.32	1.44	1.99	1.96
B	1.97	2.31	2.21	2.44	2.27
Alive					
A	1.56	1.27	1.28	1.80	2.11
B	2.40	2.23	2.13	2.45	2.24
Colgate					
A	1.40	1.26	1.25	1.80	1.96
B	2.39	2.04	1.98	2.50	2.24
Macleans					
A	1.89	1.64	1.28	1.35	2.14
B	3.03	3.39	2.66	2.38	2.50

[a]Row A = average ratings given the brand by respondents preferring *that brand*
[b]Row B = average ratings given the brand by respondents preferring *any of the other brands*

Exhibit 20.6   Frequency of Attribute Importance Rankings (in Percent) 1983 Study

Attribute	Ranking				
	1st	2nd	3rd	4th	5th
Decay prevention	70.2	13.1	7.3	4.8	4.6
Taste/flavor	14.8	25.5	26.5	21.1	12.1
Freshens mouth	4.9	20.2	32.0	34.0	8.9
Whitens teeth	6.9	34.2	25.2	19.4	14.3
Price	3.2	7.0	9.0	20.7	60.1

Exhibit 20.7   Average Consumer Ratings of Alive on Relevant Variables, 1983 Study

	Average Score on				
	Decay Prevention	Taste/ Flavor	Freshens Mouth	Whitens Teeth	Price
Alive[a]					
A[a]	1.40	1.39	1.47	1.95	2.40
B	2.63	2.45	2.51	2.67	2.55

[a]A = average ratings given the Alive by respondents preferring Alive
B = average ratings given Alive by respondents preferring brands other than Alive

Case 20 Analysis Form

Libb Pharmaceuticals: Alive Toothpaste

1. What do you see as the basic problem facing Libb Pharmaceuticals at this time?

_____

_____

_____

_____

_____

_____

2. In the following matrix, indicate how the four basic determinants of consumer behavior are involved in brand preference for toothpaste.

Needs	Motives
Perception	**Attitudes**

3. Indicate the impact that each of the following influences may have on the selection of a brand of toothpaste.

Social Influences:_____

_____

_____

Family Influences:_____

_____

_____

Cultural Influences:_____

_____

_____

4. Evaluate the research methodology used by Libb in studying the toothpaste market. In what ways could the research have been strengthened?

_____

_____

_____

_____

_____

_____

_____

_____

_____

_____

_____

_____

_____

_____

5.   What other types of analyses could have been done on the data?

_____

_____

_____

_____

_____

_____

_____

_____

_____

6.   What other types of research should Libb consider undertaking on the tooth-
     paste market?

_____

_____

_____

_____

_____

_____

_____

_____

_____

_____

_____

7. Based on your response to Question 1, indicate the specific recommendations you would make to Libb Pharmaceuticals at this time.

_____

_____

_____

_____

_____

_____

_____

_____

_____

_____

_____

_____

_____

_____

_____

_____

_____

_____

_____

DuPont Canada, Inc.: The Residential Carpet Market

Case 21

For each of the past 14 years, the Home Furnishings Division of DuPont Canada has prepared and distributed an informative report entitled "The Carpet Market As We See It." The information contained in the report is designed to help manufacturers, distributors, and retailers do a better job of preparing to serve the carpet market in Canada. The focus is on the coming five years, with specific emphasis on the next 12 months. Information is provided on both the residential and contract markets. This case concentrates on the information relating to the consumer market.

Economic Outlook

The medium-term outlook to 1990 will see a slower rate of underlying growth than during most of the post-war period. Between 1947 and 1973 economic growth averaged 5 percent per year. Since 1973, that underlying growth trend has been almost cut in half, and, although some improvement can be expected during the remainder of the 1980s, most forecasters do not expect to see a return to anything like the growth rates of the 1950s and 1960s. There are six principal reasons for this.

Slower Population Growth

A reduced rate of increase in Canada's population is expected during the coming decade. During the past 20 years, Canada's population rose by 1.5 to 2.0 percent per year. However, due to the declining birth rate and lower immigration, population growth today is slowing down. In fact, the increase in population last year was only 1.0 percent, about the same as it was in the late 1930s. By 1990, Canadians will number 26.7 million, reflecting an average growth since 1981 of only 1 percent annually.

Chronic High Unemployment

Despite the small number of younger people entering the labour market, labour force growth will outstrip population growth. More of the population will be working. In 1960, 30 percent of women between the ages of 25 and 35 were in the labour force. Today the ratio is over 70 percent and still rising. This, combined with technological change and continuing efforts by employers to minimize labour costs, will mean that unemployment is going to continue as a chronic social and economic problem. Canada's unemployment rate is expected to remain above 10 percent for several years to come. Even by the early 1990s, when a slowdown in labour force growth will become more pronounced, unemployment is not forecast to fall below 8 percent—still a very high level by historic standards.

Large Federal Deficit

The hard facts of life are, however, that given the size of the federal deficit, and the near-certainty that it will remain very large over the foreseeable future, Ottawa has no room to maneuver in terms of direct spending to create jobs. In fact, the size of the deficit is yet another reason why economic growth over the next few years will be below potential. If the deficit is not reduced, interest rates will remain high, and this will act as a severe brake on growth. At the same time, necessary action to reduce the deficit—i.e., higher taxes or reduced spending— also subtracts from growth possibilities, particularly over the short to medium term.

Inflation

Although there have been great strides in the battle against inflation, it has not yet been won. The expectation of a 5 percent inflation rate over the next few years is still a high rate of price escalation in comparison to the 1950s and 1960s. Thus, there will be an ongoing risk that inflationary pressures could break out at any time. Because of the deep-seated fear of this happening, interest rates will remain relatively high, and the monetary authorities will have a built-in bias toward restraint.

Poor Productivity Performance

Canada's productivity performance in recent years has been abysmal. Although the country should enjoy a cyclical improvement in productivity over the next couple of years, the Economic Council, The C. D. Howe Institute, the Conference Board, and others remain convinced that productivity performance will remain poor for the balance of the decade.

Exchange Rates

Both the Canadian and U. S. dollars are overvalued relative to most other currencies. In general, forecasters expect the value of the U. S. dollar to moderate over the next few years, and then stabilize at a new level for the balance of the decade. This forecast, if it comes to pass, would alleviate, but not remove the problem of overvaluation, as the U. S. dollar has risen by over 30 percent since 1979. However, there are significant risks that this realignment will not happen in an orderly or predictable fashion. High U. S. interest rates may continue to attract foreign capital, and political and economic problems worldwide may continue to cause capital to flow to the U. S. as a safe haven country.

Summary

What all this implies is that the country faces an environment replete with major uncertainties — the deficit, unemployment, inflation, foreign exchange rates, demographic shifts — and other possible troubles such as world and domestic energy conditions and international debt. On the positive side, however, there is a chance of moving onto a steadier, although moderate, growth path now that there is better control over inflation, and all sectors of the economy — business, labour, and government — have a better understanding of the consequences of unrealistic expectations. It is indeed possible, despite all the downside risks, that for the remainder of this decade the economic environment will be better than it has been since 1973. Growth should improve over that of recent years, but should not be taken for granted.

Consumer Factors and Housing

The key demographic factors shaping markets in the remainder of the century are first, that the rate of population growth is slowing to 1 percent per year, and second, that the population is aging. Ten years hence there will be fewer young people, and at the same time there will be a rapid increase in the 30–45 year olds (the baby-boom generation heading towards middle-age). This age group represents the traditional big spenders in society. The key for business is to make sure its products are geared to this group, and not to the younger people who dominated the marketplace during the 1960s and early 1970s.

For many products and services, such as housing, appliances, and furniture, the number of households is of primary importance. The age distribution of the population is one determinant here, but economic conditions are significant in dictating affordability. During the next ten years, growth in the total number of households, although diminishing, will be roughly double that of population, approximately 2 percent per year. Families will be smaller, and nonfamily households are projected to increase as a share of the total. The decline in household size that has already been observed will continue. From 3.5 persons per household in 1971 and 2.9 in 1981, average household size is expected to decline to 2.6 in 1991 and 2.5 in 2001. Past trends have followed, and the long-term trend in housing requirements will follow, these demographic patterns. As shown in Exhibit 21.1, however, the actual yearly pattern will also be determined by a combination of economic and financial factors.

Residential Carpet Market

As shown in Exhibit 21.2, the residential sector represents 60 percent of the unit volume sold in Canada in 1983, with the majority of this being replacement business. Although sales in 1983 started slowly, there was a marked improvement over 1982 in the residential carpet market. Consumer confidence improved with economic recovery as it spurred purchases. Governments introduced plans to

Exhibit 21.1   Canadian Housing Starts (000 Units)

Year	Units (000)
1970–74	233
1975–79	235
1980	159
1981	178
1982	131
1983	161
1984	164
1985	165
1986	169
1987	172
1988	172
1989	167
1990	161

stimulate the economy, such as home purchase grants, the opportunity to use tax-free RHOSP savings to purchase floor covering, as well as the suspension of sales tax on home furnishings in Ontario for a 90-day period.

Consumers are changing their buying habits, looking more carefully for value/quality, and are prepared to shop around in order to ensure better purchase decisions. Colour and texture continue to be the most important selection criteria, followed by price, appearance retention, and maintenance features. Increased advertising by companies at all levels of the industry has made the consumer more aware of the benefits of carpets of advanced-generation fibres.

The abundance of colour choices in 1983 will continue into 1984. Light, bright, clear, pastel colours are forecast. The colour cross-over from apparel to home furnishings is demonstrated by the importance of accent shades such as blue/white, true red, violet, quartz blue, and turquoise. Rich, dark, saturated colours represent 20 percent of the 1984/1985 palette. Tinted neutrals, greys, blues, greens, and roses enable design flexibility without having to rely as heavily on browns and earth tones as neutrals. Lustres in higher-end saxonies are being toned down for more wool-like aesthetics with higher lustres in the medium-priced carpets.

Consumer Studies

The following information was provided by focus groups of female heads-of-households in the age range of 35 to 60 with family incomes of $20,000 or more. Each consumer had either purchased carpet recently or intended to purchase carpet in the near future.

Most consumers appeared to have little detailed knowledge of carpet other than their personal preferences; in some cases, they had information gleaned from decorating courses. Their reason for contemplating a carpet purchase was a move to a new home, a desire to redecorate individual rooms, or an upgrading or replacement of existing carpets. Most consumers used fairly simple guidelines when looking for carpet. They expressed a preference for synthetic fibres for ease

Exhibit 21.2   Flow Chart for the Residential Carpet Market

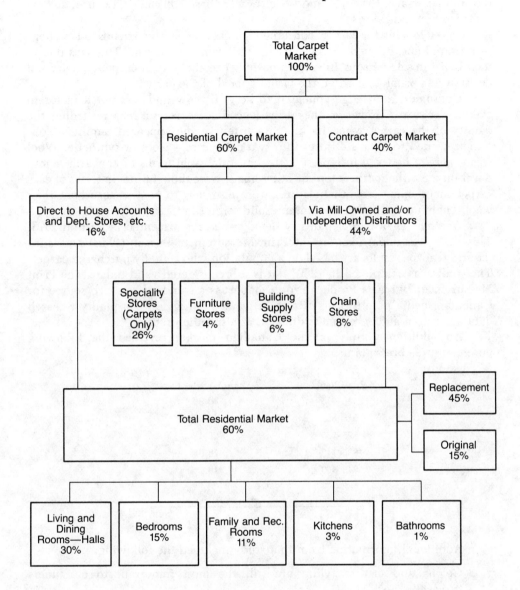

The chart illustrates the channels through which residential carpet flows after it leaves the mill. The chart was developed by surveying mills, distributors, and retailers, weighing their responses, and producing a compositive opinion.

of maintenance, and favored either plush or hardtwist to provide the durability they felt necessary. However, most choices were based on colour, texture, and expected performance.

When looking for carpet, consumers sought advice from friends. They shopped around and listened to salespersons with some skepticism. This was due to their belief in salespersons' interest in pushing certain types of carpets. Their final decision was usually based on the visual appeal of the carpet.

Consumer knowledge appeared to be fairly low and was not a factor in overall decisions. However, they experienced some reassurance regarding the quality of the carpet when the manufacturer's name appeared familiar. Consumers tended to separate fibres into two categories—wool or synthetic. Wool was generally believed to represent the best quality in terms of appearance and durability. Synthetic fibres, on the other hand, were thought best in terms of easy carpet maintenance. Synthetic fibres were also said to be less absorbent than wool, enabling easier liquid stain and solid soil cleanup.

Another set of carpet industry demographics is presented in Exhibit 21.3. This study was undertaken by the Print Measurement Bureau (PMB) and is interesting, as the results are based on a population who actually purchased carpet. The study was completed in 1980, but is still considered valid today. The Print Measurement Bureau's Product Profile Report is a standard research source for Canadian media practitioners. Its objective is to provide high-quality research data against an audience that is directed at a specific product.

An additional study of the Canadian market revealed the following purchase-price breakpoints:

Price Points	Share by Sales Level
$0–$15	6.9%
$15–$25	22.3%
$25–$35	26.4%
$35–$45	18.6%
$45–$60	19.1%
$60 +	6.7%

Additional information from that study included the following:

1. Colour and texture/styling are still the most important to consumers surveyed.
2. There has been a trend toward shorter, denser cut-pile constructions in the middle price ranges.
3. The average age of carpet in a home is perceived to be about one-half the actual average age.
4. At least three stores were visited when buying carpet.
5. The average price paid for carpet seems to indicate room-by-room renovations.
6. Nylon fibre was mentioned most often when asked about fibre type.

Exhibit 21.4 provides some results from a U.S. study on consumers' buying habits. The charts deal with consumer motivations, age of and reasons for replacement, and choices of styles and colours.

Exhibit 21.3   Carpet Purchaser Characteristics

The typical demographic group is determined as:

Target Group: Adults (Married) 25–49 years old
Household Income: $26,000–$45,000
Occupation: Skilled Service Labourers and Management
Education: Post-Secondary

1.   Adults 18 + Demographic Breakdown

   a.   Twenty-nine percent of the total adult 18 + population in Canada purchased wall-to-wall carpeting in 1979–1980.

   b.   Fifty-four percent of the total carpet purchasing population (4,862,000) are between the ages of 25 and 49 years old.

   c.   Thirty-three percent of the 25–49 year old population (7,946,000) purchased carpeting, 4 percent above the Canadian carpeting buying index.

2.   Male/Female Demographic Breakdown

   a.   No significant decision making differences between males and females.

3.   Marital Status

   a.   Seventy-six percent of the carpet purchasers are married.

4.   Education

   a.   As the level of education increased, more consumers purchased wall-to-wall carpeting.

   b.   Sixty percent of the carpet purchasers had either completed secondary school or a higher level of education.

5.   Occupation

   a.   Skilled service labourers purchased more carpeting in 1979–1980 than any other job demographic.

   b.   All levels of job demographics, except professional and primary industrial workers, were above the Canadian carpet buying index.

6.   Household Incomes

   a.   Household incomes of $26,000–$45,000 purchased more carpeting than any other demographic group.

   b.   Thirty-seven percent of the $26,000–$32,000 income group purchased carpeting, the highest percentage among all the demographic groups.

7.   Home Ownership

   a.   Seventy-six percent of all the home owners in Canada are between the ages of 25 and 64 years old.

   b.   Eighty percent of the adults 35–49 years old own a home.

Exhibit 21.4   Consumer Buying Patterns

Reasons for Replacement

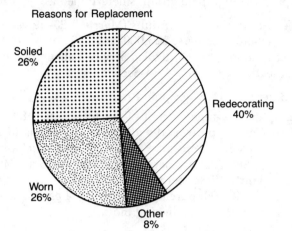

Style and Colour

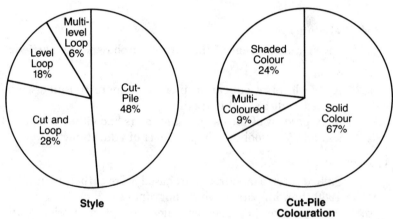

continued

Exhibit 21.4 *continued*

Age of Replaced Carpet

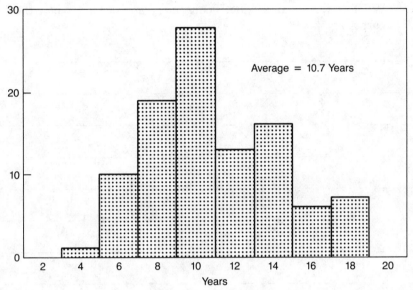

Motivations

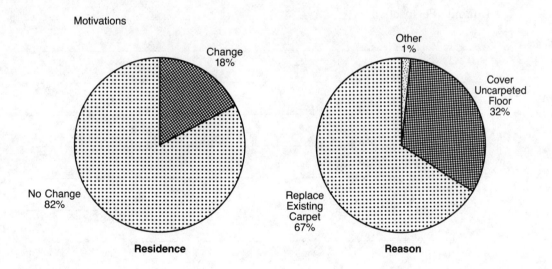

Although 82 percent of the population did not change their residence, 67 percent replaced existing carpet. This supports hypotheses of strong refurbishing trends. Only 32 percent bought carpet for previously uncarpeted floors.

continued

Case 21 Analysis Form

DuPont Canada, Inc.: The Residential Carpet Market

1. What is the "real product" consumers are seeking when they purchase carpeting?

_____

_____

_____

_____

_____

_____

2. From the perspective of DuPont and recipients of the report (manufacturers, distributors, and retailers), why is this type of research of value?

DuPont's Perspective:_____

_____

_____

_____

_____

Recipients' Perspective: _____

_____

_____

_____

_____

_____

3. Indicate the impact that each of the following influences may have on the decision to purchase carpeting.

Social Influences: _____

_____

_____

_____

Family Influences: _____

_____

_____

_____

Cultural Influences: _____

_____

_____

_____

4. Explain how the concept of cognitive dissonance may be relevant to a marketer of carpeting. What steps might be taken to deal with this issue?

Relevance of Cognitive Dissonance: _____

_____

_____

_____

_____

Ways to Deal with Cognitive Dissonance: _____

_____

_____

_____

_____

5. In the following matrix, indicate how the four basic determinants of consumer behavior are involved in the purchase of carpeting.

Needs	Motives
Perception	**Attitudes**

6. Based on your analysis of the case, what marketing recommendations would you make to a manufacturer of carpeting? Explain the logic behind your recommendations.

_____

_____

_____

_____

_____

_____

_____

7.   Based on your analysis, list your specific recommendations to a retailer of
carpeting (and supporting rationale) in each of the following decision areas:

Target Consumer to Reach: _____

_____

_____

_____

_____

    Rationale: _____

_____

_____

_____

_____

_____

Promotion Appeals to Use: _____

_____

_____

_____

_____

    Rationale: _____

_____

_____

_____

_____

_____

K mart Corporation: Jaclyn Smith's Maternity Collection

In October 1985, K mart Apparel, the clothing division of K mart Corporation, introduced the Jaclyn Smith signature line in 500 K mart stores across the country. The new line is part of an overall merchandising strategy of the retailer that began in 1980 when Bernard M. Fauber became company chairman. The collection was designed to fit into the new image K mart is attempting to develop through its five-year refurbishing and new merchandising plans. The objective is to continue to present a balance of quality merchandise at reasonable prices.

The K mart Story

In 1899, Sebastian Spering Kresge opened his first store in downtown Detroit with the slogan "Nothing over Ten Cents." The idea caught on, and by 1912 when it was incorporated, Kresge had 85 stores with annual sales of more than $10 million. Kresge's "five and ten" stores appealed to shoppers with low prices, open displays, and convenient locations. Kresge declared in 1912 that all executive management would come from within the company, promotions would be based strictly on merit and patronage would not be allowed.

Inflation in the World War I era forced Kresge to raise prices to 25 cents. In the mid-twenties, Kresge opened "green-front stores" to sell items at a dollar or less, often next to the red-front dime stores. Kresge went into the first suburban shopping center—Country Club Plaza in Kansas City, Missouri—in 1929. By 1930, variety-store chains had become commonplace because they provided a wide array of goods at low prices. Meanwhile, supermarket chains were introducing the public to self-service shopping.

The Kresge Company launched its newspaper advertising program in the early 1930s. Radio promotions followed 20 years later, and television was added in 1968. Today, print ads still dominate K mart's advertising program with 120 million circulars weekly for insertion in 1,700 newspapers nationwide.

Several discount houses emerged in the 1950s, leading Kresge President Harry B. Cunningham to study a similar strategy for his organization. The result was the opening of the first K mart discount department store in Garden City, Michigan in 1962. In K mart's first year of operation, corporate sales topped $483 million. By 1966, Kresge registered its first billion-dollar year with 162 K mart stores in operation. In 1984, sales reached a record $21.1 billion and K mart retained its berth as the nation's second largest general-merchandise retailer.

Today, there are more than 2,100 K mart stores in the continental United States, Puerto Rico, and Canada. The company still operates some Kresge variety units and Jupiter limited-line discount stores, but the name of the organization was changed to K mart Corporation in 1977 to reflect the fact that more than 95 percent of sales are generated by K mart stores.

Today's K mart differs greatly from its forerunner of the sixties and seventies. K mart emphasizes national-brand goods, but also has a strong program of private-label products for the value-conscious customer. Some new introductions to the merchandise lines include Jonathan Logan ladies' sportswear and designer jeans for men and women, name-brand athletic shoes, prestige cosmetics and fragrances, and many respected names in home improvement and health and beauty aids.

In addition to broad mechandise assortments, K mart stores also offer services. Many K marts have automotive service departments and pharmacies. Several other service possibilities are now under study including optical departments.

The company adheres to a "satisfaction always" policy, which means customers receive refunds and exchanges with ease. K mart discount department stores strive to sell at prices at least as low as those of their competitors.

Refurbished and new K marts now sport an updated interior design with innovations such as a fresh color scheme and contemporary hanging displays in the clothing departments. New departments feature expanded assortments of goods in areas of special interest, including Home Care Centers, Kitchen Korners, Domestic Centers, and Home Electronics Centers.

K mart and Apparel

K mart's overall merchandising strategy was modified in the early 1980s to seek out the more discriminating shopper by providing better-quality merchandise. The objective was to accomplish this while still building on the desire to have the reputation as the nation's lowest priced general-merchandise retailer.

Before the strategy was implemented, K mart stores devoted approximately 30 percent of their floor space to apparel sales, but netted only 20 to 22 percent of their overall business from that line. While size of store displays has not changed, traffic patterns and merchandise selection have been improved to reflect the varied tastes of shoppers. K mart began merchandising better quality apparel three years go when Names for Less was introduced.

Joseph Antonini, senior vice president of K mart Corporation and president of K mart Apparel, said, however, that merchandise is now placed in stores where it is most popular, not throughout the company's stores. Climate, income, and the personal tastes of shoppers affect the placement of merchandise.

Jaclyn Smith and K mart Apparel have joined forces to bring stylish, moderately priced clothing to American women with two major Jaclyn Smith collections, one in sportswear and the other in maternity. Exhibit 22.1 provides a biographical sketch of Ms. Smith. The sportswear line was introduced into 1,400 of the company's 2,100 stores in the summer of 1985. Skirts, trousers, and blouses made of natural and man-made fibers can be mixed for versatility and worn year-around. The merchandise is priced from $16.97 to $24.97.

"I like to have lots of different looks to suit my changing moods and demands of my active lifestyle," explained Ms. Smith. "The glamorous clothes that I wear on television are just not practical for my off-camera life. When I spend time with my son, Gaston, and my daughter, Spencer Margaret, I want to wear clothes that are comfortable yet stylish."

Exhibit 22.1   Jaclyn Smith Biography

Actress Jaclyn Smith is relishing the many roles she's playing these days. As wife, mother, and successful career woman, she is the epitome of the 1980s woman. Although she has gained international fame, Jaclyn's first priority is her family. Jaclyn's sense of self-esteem is deeply rooted in the loving and supportive home in which she was raised. Growing up as she did, it is not surprising that Jaclyn prefers spending her time with her family—husband Tony Richmond, three-year-old son Gaston Anthony, and daughter Spencer Margaret, born December 4, 1985.

Like those of many young girls, Jaclyn's early interests included fashion and ballet. She studied ballet in her native Houston, but gave up that dream and turned to acting instead. After a year of drama study at Trinity University, she joined various theatrical groups in New York. After playing a variety of roles in smaller productions, she moved onto Broadway where she performed in productions such as *West Side Story*, *Gentlemen Prefer Blondes*, and *Bye-Bye Birdie*.

While in New York, she came to the attention of an agent who felt that her classic beauty would make her a "natural" for television commercials. She signed as the Breck Girl, and her career as a commercial model took off in a new direction.

Success in commercials led to her first television acting role in *McCloud* and prompted her to move to Hollywood. Almost immediately, she landed guest starring roles in shows such as *The Rookies* and *Switch*. Her feature film debut followed with *The World of Disney*, *The Adventurers*, and *Bootleggers*.

When *Charlie's Angels* hit television in 1975, Jaclyn Smith had firmly established herself as a television star. The success of this series brought Jaclyn's unique sense of style to the small screen. As detective Kelly Garrett, Jaclyn led the phenomenally successful show through five seasons.

Jaclyn continued to expand her acting career by accepting roles markedly different from Kelly Garrett in films such as *Escape from Bogan County*, *The Users*, *Nightkill*, *Sentimental Journey*, and *The Night that Saved Christmas*.

Her most challenging roles have come in television miniseries. She played the title role in one of the highest-rated TV films, *Jacqueline Bouvier Kennedy*, an outstanding critical and ratings success. This was followed by *Rage of Angels*, the television adaption of Sidney Sheldon's best-selling novel. She also co-starred in the recently telecast *George Washington*, portraying Washington's long-time love interest, Sally Fairfax. Her success playing historic characters led to her most difficult role, that of *Florence Nightingale*, in a special for NBC.

Her latest movie is a feature film entitled *Deja Vu* that airs in May. This movie was directed by her husband, Tony Richmond, an Academy Award winning cinematographer.

Jaclyn recently authored a beauty book, *The American Look*, published by Simon and Schuster. Her latest venture is the realization of a life-long dream—a clothing line bearing her name. K mart and Jaclyn Smith, two famous names, have joined forces to bring affordable, quality fashion to working women.

K mart hopes the Jaclyn Smith line and K mart's reputation for reasonable prices will attract women who would not ordinarily consider K mart for clothes. The objective is to improve its apparel and attract the upscale, yet cost-conscious consumer. "Jaclyn Smith's name will help K mart get that message to our customers," says Antonini. "People realize that if Jaclyn Smith puts her name on something, the clothes will be of high quality."

"The Jaclyn Smith line reflects her style and good taste," Antonini said. "The line caters to the varied lifestyle of today's woman—working woman, mother, sports enthusiast, and homemaker." "I believe that we can design a wardrobe that is versatile and affordable," said Ms. Smith. "Because today's women have so little time to shop, they can appreciate clothes that are easily mixed and matched."

The Maternity Collection

"There is a tremendous need for fashionable, yet affordable maternity clothing," said Antonini. "K mart is taking a leading role by offering women maternity wardrobing that is comfortable, yet stylish at a reasonable price." Antonini added that this is the first time a celebrity has signed his or her name to a line of maternity clothing that has been designed especially for a mass-merchandise retailer.

As a busy actress and expectant mother, Ms. Smith is only too aware of the fashion problems pregnancy creates.

> The proverbial "tent dress" is, quite simply, too limiting for the woman who wants to feel fashionable and beautiful during her pregnancy. I realized just how frustrating these limitations can be while pregnant with my son, Gaston. When I was expecting my first child, I found it difficult to find well-made maternity outfits. My new signature line will help women dress stylishly during the most important time of their lives.

The maternity collection, as described in Exhibit 22.2, consists of 38 coordinated separates available in sizes 6 to 16 and priced reasonably from $15.97 to $20.97. Natural fibers and synthetics make up this collection, allowing transitional wear from season to season. "A woman's pregnancy usually spans two seasons. However, most women can't afford to buy maternity clothes for both warm and colder temperatures," says Smith. Jaclyn Smith's maternity fashions combine softly tailored separates with casual sportswear. Color coordinated wovens and knits offer an array of wardrobe options in solids, bold stripes, and stylish cabbage rose prints. The pieces include oversized shirts, blouse-knit tops, adjustable pants, and fashionable rib-knit tube skirts. Examples of the collection are shown in Exhibit 22.3.

The following statements reflect some of Ms. Smith's attitudes toward maternity fashions:

> My maternity signature collection will help women dress stylishly during the most important time of their lives.

> I like the flexibility of many pieces. This helps to create a maternity wardrobe that easily works together.

> There is no reason why maternity clothes can't be attractive, current, and affordable.

> The Jaclyn Smith maternity collection is adaptable and functional because we created it that way.

Exhibit 22.2   K mart/Jaclyn Smith Maternity Collection Fact Sheet

Debut	The Jaclyn Smith signature maternity collection will consist of coordinated separates designed for the varied lifestyles of today's expectant mother. The maternity collection will debut on October 11, 1985 in 500 K mart stores throughout the country.
Clothing	The 38 coordinated separates sizes in 6 to 16 will consist of the following: Oversized tops Boat-neck knit tops Chelsea-collared tops with contrasting bow ties Adjustable snap pants Softly ribbed knit skirts
Styling	The maternity line is fashionable and updated, featuring the quality workmanship women expect in a wardrobe. Designed to be mixed and matched, the collection features casual looks. Quality detailing such as band-bottom tops; solids, stripes, and floral prints; bow ties; mandarin collars; and button shoulder treatments complete the high-quality look of the collection.
Fabrics	The selected fabrics allow for comfort as well as fine styling: Polyester/cotton blending Soft, silky satinessa fabrics Woven stretch twill Cotton double knit
Colors	There is a selection of the soft tones of pastels — pink, powder blue, maize, and grey, as well as a wide assortment of bright tones — black, red, ivory, hot pink, turquoise, and yellow.
Price	The separates are reasonably priced from $15.97 to $20.97.
Jaclyn Smith Involvement	The wardrobe, designed under the creative eye of Jaclyn Smith, is consistent with her elegant, yet down-to-earth style. Jaclyn Smith's involvement spans all aspects of clothing design from the approval of sketches to fabric selection.
K mart's New Marketing Strategy	K mart is spending more than $2.2 billion over the next five years to refurbish its stores. K mart will carry more quality name brands and a wider selection of merchandise and establish a more convenient and pleasant atmosphere.
K mart Background	K mart is the world's second largest retailer with more than $21.1 billion in annual sales. The 2,100 K mart stores in the United Staes, Canada, and Puerto Rico sell merchandise ranging from apparel and personal goods to housewares.

Exhibit 22.3   Examples of Maternity Collection

A woman wants to look attractive and feel comfortable, especially when expecting a child.

When I was expecting my first child, I found it difficult to find well-made maternity outfits at reasonable prices.

Case 22 Analysis Form

K mart Corporation: Jaclyn Smith Maternity Collection

1. What do you see as the basic marketing problems facing K mart?

    - Some possible marketing problems that k-mart maybe facing is their reputation. K-mart has always been a store that had affordable items. Therefore, their target market are ordinary people perhaps the middle to low class. Therefore, in order for k-mart to attract a more discriminating shopper, they would have to provide higher-quality good. They will still attempt to provide these goods at an affordable prices, after all they want to be known as the lowest-priced general merchandiser. However, it may be more and more difficult to do this if in fact they want to sell better-quality merchandise.

2. How does the introduction of the Jaclyn Smith collection help deal with those problems?

3.   Discuss possible marketing strategies that could be used for moving potential customers through the stages of the adoption process as applied to the Jaclyn Smith maternity collection.

Stages	Marketing Strategies
Awareness	
Interest	
Evaluation	
Trial	
Adoption	

4.   What types of marketing research would be helpful to K mart in connection
       with this maternity collection?

_____

_____

_____

_____

_____

_____

_____

_____

5.   What kinds of product extension and expansion should K mart consider for
       the Jaclyn Smith collections?

Product Extension:_____

_____

_____

_____

_____

Product Expansion: _____

_____

_____

_____

_____

6.   What are the relative advantages and disadvantages for using celebrity product strategies?

Advantages: People recognize the celebrity and want to identify themselves with him or her. Therefore, the more popular the celebrity, chances are the more popular or higher demand you will have with the particular product.

Disadvantages: It becomes difficult at times, when using a celebrity for a particular item. Depending on the individual (celebrity) he/she may want all rights associated with that certain product. Span of control is limited. Residuals are almost always granted to the celebrity therefore, you may end up getting only a small portion of the pie.

7.   Do you think it was wise for K mart to develop and market the Jaclyn Smith maternity collection? Please support your conclusions.

Yes, it was wise for K-mart to develop and market the Jaclyn Smith maternity collection, because it gave K-mart recognition to a weider variety of consumers. It also tapped into a maternity market. More people will shop at K-mart knowing they can find Jaclyn Smith collection of maternity clothes there. Furthermore K-Mart wanted to attract a more prestigious shopper, and they have by enacting the Jaclyn Smith collection

The Executive Gallery: New Product Direct Marketing

Case 23

"How to Clean up Your Executive Act!"
"Kiss Executive Frustrations Goodbye!"
"The Perfect Executive Gift!"

These and other headlines appeared in newspaper and magazine advertisements to introduce and market a new management tool. Called the Executive ScanCard system, it acts as a portable control center for monitoring both business and personal projects on a daily basis. Information on each project is maintained on a ScanCard project card that stays in the system until the project is completed. The cards can be scanned daily in only a few minutes and notes can be added for the next review.

The Executive Gallery also markets an innovative product called SkyValet and a variety of audio cassettes of well-known speakers written under the label "The Executive Listening Library." The SkyValet wardrobe-on-wheels is a completely new kind of garment bag designed specifically for busy executives and other frequent travelers. Like conventional garment bags, it carries clothing flat without folding. Unlike other garment bags, however, travelers do not have to carry the SkyValet, they can wheel it.

Product Descriptions

Marvin E. Williams had worked at O. M. Scotts as marketing research director for more than 17 years. After that time, he purchased Scotts Lawn Care Service, which became known as Barefoot Grass Lawn Service. He later sold the company to Toro and stayed on as a vice president. After two years in that position, he decided to resign and go into the business of mail-order marketing.

Development of the ScanCard led to the formation of a company, Executive ScanCard Systems. The company later changed its name to The Executive Gallery. The firm ran its first advertisement in the Southwest edition of *The Wall Street Journal* on May 20, 1981. This first advertisement offered the Executive ScanCard System, including Pocket Idea File, 500 ScanCards, and free productivity guide for $39.95, plus $3.00 for handling and shipping.

The basic need for the system and the logic behind it was later described in one of the firm's promotional brochures, shown in Exhibit 23.1. The Executive ScanCard System is described in additional detail in Exhibit 23.2. The product mix grew to several major offerings of the basic system. They are shown in Exhibit 23.3, a brochure developed for use by retail stores in promoting the product.

Marvin Williams also developed the SkyValet, a garment bag on wheels. Tired of the inconveniences of carrying luggage, he planned the new product on the basis that business people and vacationers have more important things to do

---

Exhibit 23.1   The Basic Product Idea

An idea whose time has come...

In an era of sagging productivity comes this remarkable new management system

IT'S A PARADOX. A quirk of our times. American business productivity is sagging, at a time when space-age technology is making unparalleled strides in the field of computers and other business machines. Why?

The reason is fundamental. Individual management skills simply have not kept pace with the new technology. At a time when the economy and a faster-paced business environment are creating ever greater demands, many executives are still operating as they did decades ago. Some still rely on notes on scattered scraps of paper to remind them what needs to be done each day. Others write reminders on restaurant napkins or the backs of envelopes. Or even worse, they try to operate from memory.

As a result, deadlines are missed. Assignments are forgotten. And costly last-minute rushes become commonplace. The individual's productivity goes down...as job stress goes up. And the organization's productivity suffers accordingly.

You can double, even triple, your personal productivity.

Into such an environment comes the Executive ScanCard™ System, a simple yet effective way to improve personal and organizational productivity. Each project is written on a separate ScanCard™ project card that is merged into the system and stays there until the project is completed. Because of the system's unique design, the cards can be scanned daily, in only a few minutes, to jog your memory on what's due next on each activity...from whom...and when. *Nothing gets overlooked—ever!*

A proven success in many fields

Since its introduction approximately one year ago, more than 150,000 systems have been purchased by business and professional people around the world. At the corporate level, over 400 of the famed "Fortune 500" companies are currently using the systems to help their employees improve organizational productivity. Additionally, a wide assortment of business and professional people, such as doctors, teachers, lawyers, realtors, accountants, contractors, merchants and the clergy have found the system perfect for organizing all their activities and responsibilities.

And although each system is sold with a no-questions-asked guarantee of "satisfaction or your money back," less than 1% of purchasers have exercised that return privilege—for *any* reason.

In short, the Executive ScanCard System is an effective and proven way to improve personal and organizational productivity. It is an idea born of necessity, at a critical time in history. It is an idea whose time has come.

---

than concern themselves with headaches and backaches while traveling. Complete information on the SkyValet is shown in Exhibit 23.4, a retail store promotional brochure.

Advertising and Promotion

The initial advertising ran one a week for two months in the Southwest edition of *The Wall Street Journal.* The advertisement ran one-quarter page in size. Beginning in January 1981, the product was advertised nationally in *The Wall Street Journal* each week, again using quarter pages. Five different advertisements were used during the next six months.

Exhibit 23.2   Additional Details on the Executive ScanCard® System

Easy to use
Each project is recorded on a color coded ScanCard™ project card that stays in the system until the project is completed.

Fast follow up
Cards can be scanned daily, in only seconds, to jog your memory on what's to be done next. Puts an end to operating from memory or from scattered reminder notes.

A variety of extras
Everything from a built in multi-function calculator and additional ScanCard panels, to space for an 8½" × 11" tablet. See pages 3 through 15.

Management's New Productivity Tool!

No matter how effective and well organized you are today, the Executive ScanCard® System will help you become even better. Or your money back!

"It's amazingly simple, and it really works," That's a common comment among business and professional people who use the Executive ScanCard® System. It improves personal and organizational productivity dramatically—even among those who are already organized.

No more missed deadlines.
The system serves as a portable "control center", monitoring all of your projects, so you can stay on top of everything from start to finish. It helps eliminate missed deadlines, forgotten assignments and costly last minute rushes.

Each project is recorded on a separate ScanCard™ project card. The cards can be scanned daily, in only a few seconds to jog your memory on what's due next...from whom...and when. So everything stays on schedule. Nothing gets overlooked—ever!

Free personalization.
Each Executive ScanCard System is made of the finest materials in your choice of several convenient models. Each model so indicated on the following pages is personalized with the user's name or initials in handsome goldtone, at no extra charge.

Bonus gift ends note-filled pockets.
Most models of the Executive ScanCard System come complete with a handy Pocket Idea™ wallet. It lets you carry a small supply of ScanCards with you at all times. So you can jot down your new ideas or reminders "on the spot". Then you can merge the cards into the system later, so your notes will not be forgotten or overlooked. This puts an end to pockets filled with notes scribbled on restaurant napkins and the backs of envelopes.

Satisfaction guaranteed.
We are so sure you'll enjoy the Executive ScanCard System that we invite you to try it for 30 days. If, for any reason, you are not completely satisfied, you may return it for a prompt and courteous refund. You take no risk.

Many models available.
A wide variety of models of the Executive ScanCard System are available on the following pages. You may choose from several colors in handsome leather-like vinyl or in genuine leather. Plus an assortment of new exquisite "designer models" featured on pages 8-11.

Because the Executive ScanCard System is so compact, you can take it with you, to stay on top of all your projects...in the office...at home...or even when traveling.

At the same time, the firm began to run advertisements in airline flight magazines. These advertisements ranged in size from one-quarter to one-half to full page. In some cases the advertisements were in black and white, in others, in full color. After about nine months, responses from *The Wall Street Journal* advertisements began to fall off due to wearout. Responses from the airline magazines, however, remained steady.

In the fall of 1981, the Executive ScanCard System was also advertised in such publications as *Money, Venture, Fortune, U. S. News & World Report, Business Week, Forbes, Smithsonian, Christian Science Monitor*, and others. During 1982, the firm purchased selected mailing lists and began a direct-mail promotional program. Specialized folding brochures and catalogs in various formats were used in attempts to reach this market.

Exhibit 23.3   Retail Brochure for Executive ScanCard® System

Exhibit 23.4   Retail Brochure for SkyValet

The company has also participated in trade shows and conventions to reach specialized markets for the Executive ScanCard system. Specific groups reached include bankers, restaurant operators, home builders, electronics specialists, and others. Special inserts have also been included with the monthly statements sent by certain banks to their credit card holders. In addition, the company has attempted to work with certain associations in promoting the system to their members.

Other forms of promotion and distribution include working through office supply retailers. A national mailing to such retailers picked up only a few distributors. The company is also working with sales representatives to try to add more retailers to its distribution system. There has been some success recently in getting retail stores to carry Executive Gallery products.

Recent Developments

Initially, most of the orders came from upper and executive management levels. Later orders came from a variety of people, industries, and organizations. The company has directed limited efforts toward evaluating its consumers. The firm does know that most of its customers are male, 30–60 years of age, with annual incomes in excess of $25,000.

In 1983, the company began to expand its catalog activities by adding a variety of other products aimed at the same general market targets. One catalog in early 1985 contained, in addition to various versions of the Executive ScanCard System and SkyValet wardrobes-on-wheels, over 125 other executive-oriented items selected either to help the consumer perform his or her job or to enhance the executive lifestyle. Representative products included desk and office accessories, attaché cases, personal travel accessories, cameras and various electronic products, executive dress and casual shoes, and a limited selection of men's clothing. These expanded product offerings met with limited success, and in its 1985 Holiday Catalog the firm focused only on various versions of the Executive ScanCard System; SkyValet wardrobes-on-wheels; and selected educational, seminar, and self-help audio cassettes.

An additional development in 1985 involved the acquisition of The Executive Gallery by Hunt Manufacturing Company. From its origins as a pen-making company in 1889, Hunt has evolved into a leading producer of office and art/craft products through a strategic blending of acquisition and new product development. Among Hunt's major products are: pencil sharpeners, paper punches, paper trimmers, telephone indexes, desk accessories, metal office files, desk organizers, machine stands, furniture for computers, and pens, paints, inks, knives, blades, tools, and scissors for artists, hobbyists, and craft enthusiasts. The firm also offers miniature furniture kits through direct-response marketing.

Case 23 Analysis Form

The Executive Gallery: New Product Development Marketing

1. What is the "real product" being marketed by the Executive Gallery?

    - a certain "higher upper" executive
    - trying to make his life easier
    - portable secretary (scan cards)

2. What do you see as the basic marketing problems the organization is likely to
    face in the near future?

3.   What types of marketing research would be helpful to the organization at this time?

_____

_____

_____

_____

_____

_____

_____

_____

4.   What suggestions would you have for the company concerning product additions?

Extensions to Existing Products: _____

_____

_____

_____

_____

_____

Addition of Other Products: _____

_____

_____

_____

_____

_____

5.   Discuss the advantages and disadvantages of each of the following alternative retail channels for The Executive Gallery's products.

Department Stores

Advantages: _____

_____

_____

Disadvantages: _____

_____

_____

Discount Stores

Advantages: _____

_____

_____

Disadvantages: _____

_____

_____

Specialty Stores

Advantages: _____

_____

_____

Disadvantages: _____

_____

_____

Direct Mail

Advantages: _____

_____

_____

Disadvantages: _____

_____

_____

6.   In terms of your analysis of the case, what are your specific marketing rec-
      ommendations to The Executive Gallery? Please provide the rationale for
      your recommendations.

Recommendations: _____

_____

_____

_____

_____

_____

_____

_____

_____

_____

Rationale: _____

_____

_____

_____

_____

_____

_____

_____

_____

_____

_____

Cardinal Industries, Incorporated: Manufactured Modular Housing

Cardinal Industries has been supplying shelter products for 32 years. Since the introduction of modular products at its Columbus, Ohio plant in 1970, Cardinal has grown to become the nation's largest modular manufacturer and it is the fourth largest supplier of apartments. Cardinal provides employment for nearly 7,000 people. But today the name Cardinal Industries means more than leadership in housing. It means a complete shelter manufacturing, real estate development, and property management system that provides expertise across a broad spectrum of activities, both to Cardinal and to its customers.

Company Background

During the past 16 years, Cardinal's revenues have grown by an average of 20 percent yearly. In the past five years, annual revenues from all operations more than tripled to $527 million in 1985. Factors that contribute to this revenue are sales from Cardinal's various product lines, revenues from income-producing properties, management-fee income, and revenues from businesses the company operates. Some of these are a furniture leasing business, an insurance business, and a parts business. Exhibit 24.1 provides a variety of facts about the corporation.

Cardinal controls its destiny through vertical integration — in-house performance of every function vital to its success. As a result, fluctuations in the economy have little effect on the company. With five plants, thousands of employees, and five product lines, Cardinal Industries has expanded its corporate structure through support departments that strengthen the company's ability to manufacture, market, and manage its products. Five subsidiaries and 24 corporate support departments in areas as diverse as manufacturing, project planning, finance, and marketing lend their expertise. Exhibit 24.2 lists the various departments and subsidiaries of Cardinal that ensure the success of each product line.

Cardinal constantly monitors and fine-tunes the precision of its financial planning. Its mission statement reads: "It is Cardinal Industries' mission to be the largest and most efficient manufacturer and marketer of shelter products possible." To achieve this mission, the company develops a completely updated ten-year plan every year. This plan projects a conservative ten-year growth rate that will make Cardinal a $1 billion corporation by 1990.

All the various Cardinal divisions were developed from the company's determination to control those processes that influence its success, to gain immunity from fluctuations in the housing market, in the weather, and in the availability of money and labor.

Exhibit 24.1   Information about Cardinal Industries

Cardinal Industries Corporate Facts

Cardinal Industries Incorporated, a privately-held company with corporate headquarters in Columbus, Ohio, was founded in 1954 by Austin Guirlinger, who is president and chairman of the company's seven-member executive committee. During its first 16 years of operation, Cardinal Industries manufactured roof trusses and other housing components. Since 1970, Cardinal Industries has manufactured a standardized 12'-by-24' modular housing product for use in various configurations for the company's five product lines. The company employs, directly and/or indirectly, 6,911 people at its five plant locations and apartment, motel and retirement communities.

Scope of operations

As of January 1, 1986, Cardinal Industries had developed 917 properties with an additional four properties being constructed each week. The company manages more than 37,000 apartments in Ohio, Indiana, Michigan, Kentucky, Florida, Georgia, Maryland, Tennessee, and Illinois. Corporate-wide, the company maintains a 96 percent occupancy rate for its apartment communities.

Cardinal Industries also owns and operates the Knights Inn motel chain of 75 inns with a total of 8,250 rooms. The company has constructed and manages six Cardinal retirement communities.

Product lines

Apartments—Introduced in 1970. Represent 75 percent of current production.

Motels—Introduced in 1973. Represent 18 percent of current production.

Retail Housing—Introduced in 1979.

Commercial buildings—Introduced in 1981.

Retirement housing—Introduced in 1982.

These last three represent 7 percent of current production.

1985 financial information

Cardinal Industries had a dollar volume of approximately $527 million in 1985 from all operations, an increase of 15 percent over 1984 revenue. Projected income for all operations for 1986 is $656 million.

The company currently serves as general partner in more than 430 limited partnerships. Cardinal Industries has raised more than $295 million in equity through its investment sales operations.

Since 1970, Cardinal Industries has arranged $1.5 billion in mortgage financing from more than 500 banks and savings and loan institutions.

Industry rankings

A. **Nation's leading manufacturer of modular housing.** (Source: *Red Book of Manufactured Housing*, 1984 edition. Based on annual production figures.)

B. **Fourth largest developer of multi-family housing units.** (Source: *Building Design and Construction Magazine*, Dec. 1985. Based on dollar volume for apartment construction.)

C. **Sixth largest builder in U.S. in 1984.** (Source: *Builder Magazine*, July, 1985. Based on number of housing starts for 1984.)

Note: This information is for use from Jan. 1 to Mar. 31, 1986.

Production

In 1986, Cardinal's five plants will manufacture an estimated 23,800 modules, a 15 percent increase over 1985 production of 20,750 modules. As of January 1, 1986, Cardinal Industries has produced a total of 99,818 modules.

Cardinal Industries currently is positioned to serve a 17-state market area in the Midwest, East and Southeast, with a total population exceeding 100 million. The company delivers its modular product within a 350-mile radius of each plant location.

Plant information

Cardinal Industries
2040 S. Hamilton Road
Columbus, Ohio 43232
Year opened: 1960
Production space: 65,000 square feet
Current daily production: 25 modules (two shifts)
Annual production capacity: 8,000 modules
Current number of production employees: 258

Cardinal Industries
8400 E. Broad Street
Reynoldsburg, Ohio 43068
Year opened: 1982
Production space: 226,000 square feet
Current daily production: 24 modules (one shift)
Annual production capacity: 20,000 modules
Current number of production employees: 200

Cardinal Industries
4601 Welcome All Road
College Park, Georgia 30349
Year opened: 1982
Production space: 120,000 square feet
Current daily production: 16 modules (one shift)
Annual production capacity: 16,000 modules
Current number of production employees: 180

Cardinal Industries
3701 S. Sanford Avenue
Sanford, Florida 32771
Year opened: 1976
Production space: 125,000 square feet
Current daily production: 25 modules (two shifts)
Annual production capacity: 12,000 modules
Current number of production employees: 199

Cardinal Industries
333 South Hammonds Ferry Road
Glen Burnie, Maryland 21061
Year opened: 1985
Production space: 226,000 square feet
Current daily production: 4 modules
Current number of production employees: 80

CARDINAL
INDUSTRIES INCORPORATED

© Copyright 1985 Cardinal Industries, Inc.   85-2248

Exhibit 24.2   Activities and Businesses of Cardinal

Product Lines

Apartment Products
Commercial Products
Motel Products
Retail Products
Retirement Housing Products

Subsidiaries

Cardinal Securities Corporation
Cardinal Development Corporation
Cardinal Industries Mortgage Company
Cardinal Furniture Leasing, Inc.
Cardinal Parts Service

Departments

Land Acquisition
Apartment Management
Motel Management
Cardinal Village Management
Technical Services

Marketing Services
Transportation
Manufacturing
Investment Sales
Construction
Government Affairs
Corporate Communications
Public Relations
Accounting
Management Information Systems
Site Planning
Direct Sales
Purchasing
Personnel
Finance
Investment Administration
Project Planning
Research and Development
New Facilities Development
New Product Development

- ☐ The product is constantly being refined by in-house architects and engineers.
- ☐ Land representatives work more than a year in advance to seek out and purchase well-situated land for development.
- ☐ The Cardinal Mortgage Company provides or arranges suitable financing and services an increasing portfolio for the secondary market.
- ☐ Cardinal site planners plan every aspect of new developments.
- ☐ The Construction Division manages subcontractors in all phases of site development.
- ☐ Cardinal transportation crews transport the units to the site with a fleet of specially designed trucks and patented trailers.
- ☐ Cardinal's securities brokers syndicate investments in company developments.
- ☐ The company's Property Management Divisions step in before the job is finished and ensure properly operated developments.
- ☐ The marketing group staff conducts research and develops advertising, promotion and public relations programs.

Manufacturing of Product

Cardinal Industries captures the essence of form and function with its modular manufacturing method. The form allows the module to be assembled in a variety of configurations — apartments, motels, retail housing, retirement housing, commercial offices — while the functional design promotes standardization and volume production.

Cardinal Industries takes the benefits of factory-built housing one step further, however. By manufacturing a standardized product — a three-dimensional modular unit — the company's five plants can build thousands of nearly identical units every year. Volume production allows Cardinal to refine its product constantly through extensive research and development activities while employing the latest technologies to achieve even greater efficiencies. As annual volume approaches 45,200 modules by the end of the decade, Cardinal Industries will be positioned to invent its own technologies to further refine its manufacturing process.

Each patented 10,000-pound unit is sturdy enough to be lifted by its roof to be placed on its foundation. Every unit exceeds the most stringent of building codes, including the strict 125-mph wind-load requirement set by the state of Florida. Cardinal quality asserts itself at every step in its logical manufacturing process. Cardinal-engineered tooling shapes and aligns floors, walls, ceilings, and roofs. Every section is pneumatically nailed and glued to get the tightest fit possible. Exhibit 24.3 describes the assembly-line manufacturing process.

Through volume production, Cardinal Industries makes special purchase arrangements with name-brand suppliers—Georgia-Pacific, Weyerhauser, The Borden Company, Owens-Corning Fiberglass, and General Electric, among others. Besides quality, Cardinal builds energy efficiency into every unit. The

---

Exhibit 24.3   The Assembly Process

The basic building block of any Cardinal apartment community, Knights Inn® motel, condominium, home, congregate, or commercial product is the 12-by-24 foot module that's built inside a Cardinal factory.

The present factory assembly lines have a total of 121 modules in production at any one time and flow in a systematic fashion. The modules are assembled on dollies that ride along rails down one side of the factory. All subassemblies are fed onto the production line from the factory interior. Materials are unloaded from docks located along the assembly line close to the points of use.

Each module moves through the production process in exactly the same way and is subjected to strict quality controls at each stage of completion. The subassembly lines produce floors, walls, ceilings, and roofs built to precise tolerances using custom-designed equipment. These components are both glued and nailed for extra rigidity. They meet at the production line where they are assembled into modules strong enough to be carried to the building site by a fleet of modular transporters, lifted by their own framing members with a special patented lifting frame, and set on their foundations by crane. When the modules leave the factory, they contain complete plumbing and electrical systems, carpeting, vinyl-coated fabric wallcovering, heating and cooling units, built-in cabinets, and appliances—even lightbulbs.

The manufacturing process results in a standardized product. This standardized product and the manufacturing process itself can be controlled and refined. Constant refinements since 1970 have made the production system extremely efficient, and as volume increases, the opportunities for cost reduction become more obtainable.

Factory construction also eliminates delays due to bad weather, keeps labor productivity high, and protects valuable inventory. In short, the manufacturing process results in higher-quality housing at a guaranteed cost—an outstanding value to the end user and a higher profit potential to the investor.

company's Energy Envelope® design keeps units cool in summer and warm in winter, while keeping utility bills low.

The company's commitment to landscaping is unique in the housing industry. In 1986, Cardinal plans to spend over $19 million in landscaping new and existing properties, while planting 3.3 million flowers.

Quality materials, quality manufacturing, more housing for the dollar are all made possible because of Cardinal's commitment to a standardized, yet versatile product manufactured in volume. Those are the keys to Cardinal's success as the nation's leading producer of modular housing.

The Products

Cardinal Industries has five major product lines. Each is briefly described in the following sections. Exhibit 24.4 contains representative photographs of each general product category.

Apartments

Cardinal offers a one-bedroom, one-bathroom apartment; a completely furnished studio apartment; a two-bedroom, one-bathroom apartment; and a two-bedroom, two-bathroom apartment. Inside each apartment, residents benefit from features not usually found in apartments: a built-in bookcase, plush carpeting, one-piece tub and shower unit, Wall-Tex (a vinyl-covered fabric wall covering developed by The Borden Company), and General Electric heating and cooling units. Quality engineering and construction also produce an energy-efficient, sound-controlled environment, while double-wall construction puts two walls between units, providing excellent fire protection. Attention to detail yields tight-fitting doors and windows and perfectly hung cabinets.

Any of these apartments may be furnished through Cardinal's furniture leasing business. The company often syndicates an apartment development; investors, as limited partners, share in the investment and tax advantages of ownership in a ratio based on their equity contribution, with Cardinal being the general partner. These products have now been used in more than 600 developments.

Motels

By the end of 1986, the rapidly expanding Knights Inn chain will contain over 11,000 rooms in 100 motels. Its wide variety of room types and its consistent quality, cleanliness, and service at moderate rates help to maintain the chain's higher-than-averge occupancy rates. Ownership and management of Knights Inns are typically retained within the company. The Inns are occasionally franchised.

Cardinal's motel chain earned its AAA-rated cleanliness status by paying constant attention to meeting each customer's needs. Like offering a choice of rooms for nonsmoking guests and training innkeepers in life-saving cardiopulmonary resuscitation (CPR). The more than 8,440 motel rooms currently available in a twelve-state area maintain an occupancy rate up to 15 percent higher than a comparable motel chain.

Each Knights Inn is constructed from the basic Cardinal modular unit. The double-wall construction method means that every Knights Inn offers extra sound-proofing while limiting the hazard of fires. Cardinal Industries monitors closely the service offered at each Knights Inn. Besides employing service auditors who travel regularly to motels in the chain, Cardinal encourages guest comments via a postage-paid card available in each room. Every comment is given prompt personal attention and a response.

Retail Products — Condominiums and Homes

Cardinal's first retail product, the condominium, features cathedral ceilings, skylights, and walled courtyards. The company is presently expanding this line with several condominium communities in Florida. They are marketed through on-site sales centers staffed by Cardinal employees. "Courtyard Homes," the name for Cardinal's one and two-bedroom condominiums, feature the same quality construction found in every Cardinal unit, and creative exterior and interior design gives each unit a distinctive appearance. Courtyard Homes can also

Exhibit 24.4   Photographs of Cardinal's Basic Product Categories

be purchased as investment properties to provide investors with both tax shelters and rental income.

The company's "expandable home" allows a family's residence to grow as income and family size increase. The home is sold to individuals who own their own lots. After purchase of the basic two-bedroom home with one bath, floor space can more than double with the addition of a master bedroom suite and family room or other additions. Each home is designed so that additional modules can be added with a minimum of interior refitting. A new room can be moved into the same day the module is placed on its foundation.

Retirement Communities

Cardinal introduced its first retirement community—Cardinal Village—in 1982. The company has plans to add several more of these developments. Each will consist of 70 to 120 apartments, connected by hallways to a central common area.

Each development features community living without sacrificing privacy or security. Double-walled construction minimizes sound from neighboring units, while single-story design and screened-in porches offer "villagers" convenient living. Cardinal Villages also offer numerous services to residents, including an evening meal, a "Village Square" for relaxing or meeting guests, a library, an exercise room, and other expanded living facilities. The congregate developments are marked to investors in the form of limited partnerships or directly to individuals or groups who manage their own properties.

Commercial Buildings

Cardinal units can be combined in a variety of configurations suitable for branch banks, savings and loan offices, doctors' offices, shops, and so on. The individual offices or shops can open to a common hallway or can have their own outside entrances. The buildings may include conference rooms, kitchens, garages, and atrium-style reception areas. They are marketed to business-people, professionals seeking office space, and developers.

Commercial use of the Cardinal module is nearly unlimited. Through use of a connecting atrium and reception area, with offices extending off the center, the module can become professional offices and dormitories. As new designs evolve, expanded uses will be possible. As with each Cardinal product, substantial testing and research and design work continue to make new applications of the module practical, feasible, and likely.

Module housing - housing almost completed (pre-fabricated)

Cooperative - operation is run by a corporation
Units are sold to stockholders if they wish to live there.

Case 24 Analysis Form

Cardinal Industries, Inc.: Manufactured Modular Housing

1. What do you see as the "real product" being produced and marketed by Cardinal Industries?

_____

_____

_____

_____

_____

_____

_____

_____

_____

2. What types of marketing problems might Cardinal Industries face in the future?

_____

_____

_____

_____

_____

_____

_____

_____

_____

_____

3. Discuss how each of the following components of the business environment relates to the success of Cardinal's products.

Social-Cultural: _____

_____

_____

_____

_____

_____

_____

Economic: _____

_____

_____

_____

_____

_____

Legal-Political: _____

_____

_____

_____

_____

_____

Competitive: _____

_____

_____

_____

_____

_____

_____

4.   Describe the demographic (socio-economic) and psychographic (lifestyle) characteristics of the likely market target for a Cardinal home.

Demographic: _____

_____

_____

_____

_____

_____

_____

_____

Psychographic: _____

_____

_____

_____

_____

_____

_____

_____

5.   What other applications do you see as possible markets for Cardinal's commercial buildings?

_____

_____

_____

_____

_____

_____

_____

_____

_____

6. What types of market research would be helpful to Cardinal Industries in further developing its product strategy?

_____

_____

_____

_____

_____

_____

_____

_____

_____

_____

7. Based on your analysis of the case and your response to Question 2, what specific recommendations do you have for Cardinal Industries in the area of product strategy?

_____

_____

_____

_____

_____

_____

_____

_____

_____

_____

People Express Airlines, Inc.: Low-Priced Airline Travel

Case 25

In an era of recession, deregulation of the airline industry, and the bankruptcy of some airlines, and in a geographic area of the United States generally stagnant in population growth, a new airline, People Express, was formed. By early 1986, the company had experienced many ups and downs, but with two major acquisitions under its belt and 1985 sales of almost $1 billion, People Express introduced sale prices on its already low airfares.

Company History

People Express Airlines, Inc., operating under the name of People Express or its service mark, PEOPLExpress, began operations on April 30, 1981, with three aircraft serving four cities. It rapidly grew to a major carrier providing short- and medium-haul jet passenger service to 16 airports in the eastern United States using 21 Boeing 737 aircraft. It operated from a hub at Newark International Airport, which serves the New York/New Jersey metropolitan area.

From the beginning, People Express adopted a simple pricing policy for each of its routes. Two prices, peak and off-peak, were offered. The company's price levels were substantially lower than the standard coach fares other airlines charged prior to the announcement of the People Express service. However, competitors did match its prices on some of the routes. By 1983, People Express was carrying several million passengers annually. It had agreed to acquire up to 37 used Boeing 727-300 aircraft and leased a 747-200 aircraft from a bankrupt airline for use in international flights to London, England.

People Express began operations by offering service between Newark International Airport and Buffalo/Niagara Falls; Columbus, Ohio; and Norfolk/Virginia Beach, Virginia. The inaugural cities for People Express routes were selected on the basis of their market size, transportation needs, and competitive airline prices. All of the original cities were large metropolitan areas with strong commercial ties to the New York/New Jersey area; none of the cities were receiving a level of nonstop service sufficient to meet passenger demand. Until People Express entered these cities, all experienced high airline fares to the New York metropolitan area.

Source: Adapted from Blackwell, Engel, and Talarzyk, *Contemporary Cases in Consumer Behavior,* 2d ed. Hinsdale, Ill.: Dryden Press, 1985, with updated information from "Up, Up and Away?" *Business Week,* November 25, 1985, p. 80 and "Super Savings in the Skies," *Time,* January 13, 1986, p. 40.

The company was formed by three former executives of Texas International Airlines who raised $800,000 among themselves and another $200,000 from venture capitalists. Between 1981 and early 1983, the price of the company's stock as quoted on NASDAQ more than tripled, and it doubled during 1983, following a stock split and a new public issue.

As the company expanded its fleet of jets and its route systems, its business performance became more and more uneven. Between October 1984 and March 1985, People Express suffered operating losses of $21 million. In the following six months the airline did recover to earn $58 million. Its stock dropped from the 1983 high of almost $26 per share to less than $10 per share.

In October 1985, People Express acquired Frontier Airlines for $305 million. Based in Denver, Frontier added 80 cities to the market already served by People Express. In December 1985, People Express agreed to buy Britt Airways, the third-largest regional commuter line in the country, which serves 29 midwestern cities. When these mergers are complete, People Express will have flights to 133 airports. In some five years, People Express has grown to serving over 1 million passengers a month, making it the fifth largest U. S. airline, behind United, American, Delta, and Eastern.

Personnel Policies

People Express has implemented some of the most innovative personnel policies to be found in any firm. Each full-time employee, from the beginning of employment, must be a stockholder of the company. Donald C. Burr, founder and president of the company and a graduate of the Harvard Business School, has indicated that he would rather reward his employees with a piece of the action than a big salary. He says that, "Salaries are costs and expenses, dividends and high stock prices are the rewards of ownership." His full-time managers collectively own a third of the airline. Every new employee must buy and hold 100 shares of stock, offered at a 70 percent discount. The purchase can be financed through a payroll deduction and cannot be sold on the open market until after employment of six years or more. Profit sharing can add up to 27 percent to an employee's pay.

The company emphasizes individual decision-making, supervision of oneself and one's own work patterns, and the flexibility to find better ways of achieving results, rather than routinely following work rules developed years earlier. Employees are divided into three groups:

☐   Customer service managers (ticket counter agents and flight attendants)
☐   Maintenance managers (who supervise the upkeep of the planes)
☐   Flight managers (pilots)

People Express hires independent firms to provide other services such as taking telephone reservations and doing mechanical work on the airplanes. The employees are divided into groups of 20, each with two team leaders and a team manager. Above the team managers are only two levels of command: 20 general managers, who supervise groups of about 250, and 11 managing officers. Employees regularly switch jobs, and all have a say in who does what. A customer service manager may be a flight attendant one week and run a ticket counter the next. Pilots sometimes work in accounting or scheduling. Basically, the company's organization charts give the same clout to flight managers as to customer service managers.

The stock offerings, profit sharing, and democratic trappings are also designed to help People Express make up for low base salaries. The company's pilots earn $60,000 to $90,000 per year, while captains at United can make $150,000 or more. Burr's total compensation was nearly $114,000 in 1984, while the top person at United received about $425,000.

The company believes that its personnel policies substantially enhance the efficiencies attainable with its simplified operating procedures and thereby contribute to its ability to provide service at low cost. Pilots fly about 70 hours a month, in contrast to the industry average of 45, but they also work as dispatchers, instructors, and schedulers. Customer service managers work a normal management work week rather than the hours of flight attendants, which at other airlines are governed by FAA rules that relate to flying times.

In 1983, the starting salary of a customer service manager was $17,500, more than starting salaries at other airlines. However, because most other airlines had not grown enough to require any new employees for years, it was not uncommon for a $17,500 customer service manager at People Express to be compared in cost to a flight attendant at other airlines who might, due to seniority and union representation, be earning $30,000 or more. All full-time employees are part of management and are not subject to hourly wages and overtime payments. The company is nonunion.

Product Procedures

People Express is sometimes described in the media as a "no-frills" airline. It hopes to attract passengers not only from competing airlines, but from the roads and the rails with advertising slogans that read, "Flying that costs less than driving." The airline attracts a wide range of customers, including celebrities such as Senator Ted Kennedy and his family, Christopher Reeves (the star of the Superman movies), and some business travelers in blue pinstripe suits. Briefcases and pinstripes are blended on the planes, however, with a far larger quantity of backpacks and blue jeans.

The policy that is descibed as "no frills"by many observers is called "flying smart" by People Express. This policy has eliminated many services that are granted or optional on other airlines. No hot meals are served, although passengers can purchase "snack packs" for about $2, which include items such as granola bars, summer sausage or beef jerky, nuts, cheese and crackers, and cookies or a brownie. Coffee or soft drinks are sold for $.50 rather than given free as on other airlines.

The service includes an approach to baggage that is somewhat unique. It is based on the principle that the passenger and his baggage need never be separated. Newly designed oversized storage bins have been installed above each seat. Passengers are allowed to carry on two pieces of baggage that can fit in the overhead compartments or under the seat. All additional luggage costs $3 each piece to check as baggage. These policies are designed to eliminate the time-consuming, irritating wait for luggage at the end of a flight and the possibility of a passenger's luggage being in Boston while he is in Buffalo.

The ticketing procedure for People Express is also innovative. There is no check-in counter since the issuing and payment of tickets is done on board. Reservations can be made either in advance through a travel agent or directly by calling the People Express reservations phone number. All major credit cards are accepted by People Express. Travel agents may book flights with a People Express-devised ticketing program that is unique in the industry. This program gives agents greater incentives for encouraging the use of People Express. Listings of scheduled flights for People Express are available through a travel agent or by calling People Express directly. People Express does not participate in interline ticketing agreements, nor does it participate in interline baggage handling.

Through a high frequency "turnaround" system, People Express effectively increases the number of flights in and out of each city. Acting much like a mass transportation line, People Express jets run from the New York/New Jersey metropolitan area via the uncongested Newark International Airport to each city served and back again, fine-tuning airline operations for the needs of each particular market. People Express believes this back and forth service more directly meets the needs of the passengers since it allows time-sensitive scheduling. Instead of Syracuse (or any other People Express city) being a stopover to another city, it is the city itself that counts, as it becomes the only city on the run. Flights are divided between peak and off-peak hours.

Operations

People Express has achieved total costs per available seat-mile that are substantially below those of other airlines. These efficiencies are born of innovations in operations and acquisition of capital goods.

People Express uses Boeing 737-100 and 737-200 aircraft in single class configurations, with seating capacities of 118 and 130, respectively. These capacities are approximately 30 percent greater than those of standard airline configurations for such equipment, which include a first-class section and a larger galley. The company also acquired up to 37 used Boeing 727-200 aircraft and leased a Boeing 747-200 for international operations. The 737 planes were acquired from Lufthansa for $3.7 million each, compared to the $17 million cost of a new 737. A People Express 737 flies between 10 and 11 hours a day, 3 or 4 more than the industry average. The additional 28 seats added when the Lufthansa planes were retrofitted and the additional flying time more than double the planes' productivity without adding to capital costs.

The company has searched for ways to increase productivity wherever possible: routes were planned to minimize the number of overnight layovers by flight personnel; the Newark hub of operations provided fewer delays than more congested airports, and the simplified ticketing procedures by themselves eliminated about $18 of costs per ticket incurred by other airlines. Industry analysts estimated that all of these efforts have provided People Express with a cost per seat-mile of about 5.38 cents, compared with Continental's 6.19 cents, American's 7.61 cents, or United's 7.98 cents. Compared to the industry average, People Express costs per seat-mile are nearly 30 percent less. But because the fares are so low, the company had to fill more seats (67.8 percent) than the industry average (59.9 percent) in order to break even last year.

Pricing Strategy

The airport video screens for People Express do not display just departure and arrival times, they also list prices. Although competitors frequently match People Express' fares on many routes, such low rates are generally available only on a restricted basis. People Express owes much of its popularity to its practice of putting virtually no restrictions on its fares and using rules that are simple enough for someone without a computer to understand.

A two-tier pricing structure is offered for most of the company's routes. On short-haul routes, peak prices (generally applying to daytime and early evening flights on weekdays) can range from approximately 45 to 60 percent of the standard coach fares in effect for other airlines prior to the announcement of the People Express service. Off-peak prices (usually charged on late-night and weekend flights) vary between approximately 25 and 35 percent of standard fares. The company's peak and off-peak prices on medium-haul routes are also substantially below the standard coach fares in effect for other airlines prior to the announcement of service by People Express.

In 1985, the peak fare from Newark to Chicago, for example was $99, while the off-peak fare was $79. On most People Express flights, every seat has the same price. The exceptions are transcontinental and transatlantic flights on the firm's Boeing 747s, which offer a premium-class section for a higher fare. For example, flights at peak times from Newark to Los Angeles in 1985 offered a premium-class seat for $325 compared to $735 for a first-class seat on United or American. A regular seat on the Newark to Los Angeles People Express flight was priced at $149.

People Express' pricing policy has not been successful in every city. For example, People Express opened operations between Newark and Indianapolis with a fare of $79 in peak hours and $59 in off-peak hours. TWA and USAir, which previously were charging about $150, matched People's prices. People Express was unable to obtain enough volume to justify operations in the market and withdrew from Indianapolis. The president of People Express commented, "We got blasted out of there." Following the departure of People Express, TWA and USAir lifted their fares to $162.

In early 1986, People Express slashed many of its fares by 30 to 60 percent as a special "sale". Passengers could fly from the carrier's Newark base to Miami, Fort Lauderdale, and other Florida cities for $69, to Los Angeles or San Francisco for $99, to Minneapolis for $49, and to Greensboro or Raleigh, N. C. for $29. By changing planes in Newark, passengers can fly on People Express from Chicago to Florida or from Boston to Houston for $99. The airline's biggest bargain was a nonstop flight from San Francisco to Brussels for $99.

Advertising

Initially, People Express carefully planned its offer and found it so successful that the primary challenge was to take care of overwhelming numbers of customers that bought the offer. Newspaper advertising featured high amounts of information, mostly prices for the market to Newark, Florida, or some other cities. Some slogans were also used such as "Easy come, easy go," and "Flying that can cost less than phoning." The company developed extensive contact with the media, which often published stories about the pricing and other policies of People Express. Customer service managers often selected the marketing staff function in their rotation plan of assignments. The company also placed some advertising on television in key markets.

Today People Express is advertising in a variety of publications including *Time, U. S. News & World Report,* and even *The New Yorker.* Selected headlines for the advertisements include: "If you won't fly us for our prices, fly us for our frills," "The first airline that's smart enough to respect your intelligence," "This year we'll save the American flyer a billion dollars. How much of that will your company save?" and "We know we have to offer a sophisticated flyer like you a lot to overcome our low prices." The basic tag line on all the advertisements is "PEOPLExpress, Fly Smart."

Case 25 Analysis Form

People Express Airlines, Inc.: Low-Priced Airline Travel

1. What do you see as the two major customer segments in the airline market? What is the relative importance of various factors that cause each segment to select one airline over another?

Segment 1 _____

    Important Selection Factors: _____

_____

_____

_____

    Important Selection Factors: _____

_____

_____

_____

_____

2. What expenses do you have to take into account in determining prices for an airline?

_____

_____

_____

_____

_____

_____

_____

_____

_____

3.   How have the following environmental elements influenced People Express in its pricing strategy?

Social-Cultural Environment: _____

_____

_____

_____

_____

_____

_____

Legal-Political Environment: _____

_____

_____

_____

_____

_____

_____

Competitive Environment: _____

_____

_____

_____

_____

Economic Environment: _____

_____

_____

_____

_____

_____

4. What do you see as the advantages and disadvantages of People Express offering a frequent-flyer program to provide special or free travel to flyers who use the airline a lot? Should the firm implement such a program? Please support your response.

Advantages: _____

_____

_____

Disadvantages: _____

_____

_____

Implement a Program?_____

_____

_____

_____

5. What are the relative advantages and disadvantages to an airline like People Express in running a sale?

Advantages: _____

_____

_____

Disadvantages: _____

_____

_____

Implement a program?_____

_____

_____

_____

_____

_____

_____

6.   How would you respond to the pricing strategy of People Express if you were one of its competitors?

_____

_____

_____

_____

_____

_____

_____

_____

7.   What is your overall evaluation of the pricing strategy of People Express? What changes, if any, would you recommend. Please provide the rationale for your recommendations.

Evaluation: _____

_____

_____

_____

Recommendations: _____

_____

_____

_____

_____

Rationale: _____

_____

_____

_____

_____

G. D. Ritzy's, Inc.: Pricing Food and Ice Cream

Case 26

The company owns, operates, and franchises a distinctive style of quick-service food and ice cream restaurant under the name of G. D. Ritzy's Luxury Grill & Ice Creams. The restaurants offer a limited menu featuring natural casing hot dogs, freshly grilled hamburgers, chili served seven different ways and super-premium ice cream. As of December 1985, there were 18 company-owned restaurants open. The company has entered into agreements with franchisees requiring them to open or have under construction 468 restaurants during the next 12 years, 54 of which were open and three of which were under construction as of December 1985, with an additional 19 to be opened or under construction during 1986.

Background Development

Graydon D. Webb, president and founder of G. D. Ritzy's, first recognized the need for a quick-service, quality food and ice cream restaurant in 1979 when he made the following observations concerning the restaurant industry:

☐ Consumer demand for premium ice creams was more than a trend, but rather indicated a shift in consumer priorities favoring quality over price.
☐ No quick-service national restaurant chain featured both quality food and premium ice creams.
☐ "Cincinnati Chili," never seriously marketed outside of Cincinnati, Ohio, was earning restaurant owners attractive profits with a unique style chili cooked without beans and served with toppings such as diced onions, beans, and cheese, with the option of being served over spaghetti.

At the same time, Mr. Webb noticed a strong nostalgic appreciation for the 1930s and 1940s as evidenced by: intense public interest in movies and entertainers of this glamorous age, radio stations playing Big Band formats, Art Deco architecture, the return of ballroom dancing, and the normal human tendency to remember "the good old days." He also was aware that other factors, such as the popularity of artist Norman Rockwell, have played a significant role in attracting today's consumer to the style and quality of the 1940s.

"Ritzy's is a compilation of my growing-up experiences," says Webb. "We've taken the quick service and quality food of the 1940s soda fountain and placed them in a 1980s format." Webb's experience base includes an in depth contact with food service. He spent more than ten years with Wendy's International, originally working part-time at the first Wendy's unit during his college days. He advanced with Wendy's, becoming vice president of franchise sales.

During the 1950s, Webb had been introduced to another food service legend when his father signed one of the first Kentucky Fried Chicken franchise agreements. Even prior to that, Webb had worked in his family's dairy bar in Portsmouth, Ohio for three years and then at a root beer stand that they opened. Webb traces G. D. Ritzy's roots back even farther, to his grandmother's kitchen. He developed many of Ritzy's ice creams from her basic recipe and flavor ideas.

With all of this as a food-service background, Webb opened the first G. D. Ritzy's Restaurant in Columbus, Ohio in May 1980. The guiding statement for the restaurant chain can be described as follows:

> G. D. Ritzy's Luxury Grill and Ice Cream is a quick-service, theme restaurant chain with emphasis on premium quality food and ice creams, ultraclean dining and service areas, unique menu items not readily available in other restaurants, and maximum utilization of leased space. It is the intent of G. D. Ritzy's to maintain strict, yet reasonable, product quality standards for all franchised and company-owned stores.

Operations

All G. D. Ritzy's restaurants are built to company specifications as to interior and exterior decor. The free-standing, image restaurants are substantially uniform in design and appearance, generally contain approximately 1,500 to 2,400 square feet, and are constructed on approximately 15,000 to 20,000 square-foot sites with parking for 15 to 25 cars. The free-standing, image restaurant seats approximately 60 people and utilizes a pick-up window for in-car service. Approximately 35 percent of the business of the company's free-standing, image restaurants is generated from such in-car service. The cost to construct a free-standing, image restaurant has been approximately $180,000 for the building and $125,000 for equipment. Land, if purchased, has cost approximately $150,000 to $200,000 per restaurant. Once a site has been selected, it generally takes from 60 to 90 days before a free-standing restaurant can be constructed and opened for business. Exhibit 26.1 shows the exterior of a free-standing unit.

In-line restaurants vary in appearance and dimensions from location to location due to the differences in available space, but generally retain the overall image and color scheme of white, green, silver, and red. The cost for an in-line restaurant generally ranges from approximately $100,000 to $150,000 for leasehold improvements (the cost variance is dependent upon the improvements

Exhibit 26.1   Exterior Photograph of G. D. Ritzy's

needed) and $85,000 to $100,000 for equipment. In-line restaurants generally are ready to open after a shorter period of time, which varies depending upon the extent of the improvements needed.

Due to the small property size requirements (15,000 to 20,000 square feet) for construction of a standard free-standing, image restaurant, the company is able to select from sites which ordinarily would not be large enough for construction of the restaurants of many other quick-service chains. The building site requirements also enable the company to convert or remodel former gas stations, car washes, hamburger stands, and other commercial outlets typically found on smaller property sites, thereby enhancing the company's ability to meet its expansion plans.

The standardized interior decor features burnished aluminum surfaces, highlighted with rich, dark green carpeting, unique Art Deco period lighting fixtures, and white, hexagonal floor tile. The wall surfaces are appointed with pictures of products, period graphics, and 1930s and 1940s-style merchandising signs.

G. D. Ritzy's restaurants depend upon a large customer base with a heavy repeat business and are generally located in urban or heavily populated suburban areas. Based on the company's experience to date, sales in its restaurants have tended to increase during the summer months, primarily due to ice cream sales. However, sales of its non-ice cream food products are not substantially dependent upon seasonal changes. Popularity of the ice cream does result in some overall traffic declines in the winter months. Recently opened company-owned restaurants have experienced more rapid sales growth and higher initial sales levels than the company's initial restaurants because of increased consumer awareness of the company's products.

G. D. Ritzy's restaurants generally open for lunch at 10:30 a.m., and remain open for business until 11:30 p.m. Sunday through Thursday, and until 12:30 a.m. Friday and Saturday nights in the summer. During winter months, closing times are 10:30 p.m. on weekdays, and 11:30 p.m. on weekends. The presence of super-premium ice cream together with its other high-quality menu selections has enabled G. D. Ritzy's restaurants to draw customer traffic during four distinct day parts, as opposed to the three peak meal periods usual for those quick-service restaurants offering a breakfast menu, and the two peak meal periods for those quick-service restaurants which do not offer breakfast menus. The company has found the sales generally break down as follows:

Opening — 2:00 (Lunch)	35 percent
2:00 — 5:00	15 percent
5:00 — 8:00 (Dinner)	30 percent
8:00 — Closing	20 percent

The Product Offering

Attracting the thirst and appetite of today's public is a keenly competitive business. In the quick-service category alone, there is no shortage of restaurants offering everything from chicken to hamburgers to pizza in every variety imaginable. G. D. Ritzy's does not intend to be all things to all people. The following menu items as described by company literature have been designed to provide a product mix with moderate food cost, wide appeal, readily attainable ingredients, and authenticity of the soda shop theme. A complete listing of the menu items with prices is presented in Exhibit 26.2.

☐   CHILI — served up to seven ways, cooked daily in the store using our own special recipe. Customers order according to individual preferences: plain or with any combination of cheese, onions, beans, tomatoes, green peppers, or all together served atop tender spaghetti.

☐ CONEY DOGS — either an "old style" 100 percent juicy beef frankfurter in a natural casing that pops with every mouth-watering bite, or in the "all American" skinless style. Served plain or covered with tangy coney sauce just juicy enough to flavor the warm bakery bun.

☐ LIGHT MENU — consisting of an unbreaded chicken breast sandwich, frashly prepared salads, and steamed vegetables.

☐ HAMBURGER — once again, soda shop authenticity calls for pure beef, customers' choice of condiments, and a special method of cooking that involves shaping the meat into patty form after it is placed on the grill.

☐ WORLD'S GREATEST PB & J — A meal in itself, Peanut Butter and Jelly sandwich made with:
a. Rich, creamy peanut butter
b. Strawberry preserves
c. Fresh sliced strawberries
d. Crushed peanuts sprinkled generously
e. Delicious, thick-sliced bread

☐ FRENCH FRIES — Ultra-thin, sliced shoestring style.

☐ Our own all-natural "LUXURY ICE CREAMS" manufactured by G. D. Ritzy's exceed all industry standards, both written and implied, for premium ice cream. G. D. Ritzy's overrun specification (content of air) is especially impressive, at less than half that of commercial ice cream. Our butterfat content, the most talked about statistic by ice cream lovers, is a whopping 16 percent.

Exhibit 26.2   Price List for G. D. Ritzy's

Hot Dog (all American)	$ .89	Chili-Cheese	.40
Coney (old style)	.99	Chili-Beans	.15
Sauce	.15 extra	Small Drink	.50
Cheese	.15 extra	Med. Drink	.65
Hamburgers	1.15	Large Drink	.69
Dbl. Hamburgers	2.09	Milk	.55
Cheeseburgers	1.35	Small Coffee	.35
Dbl. Cheeseburgers	2.29	Large Coffee	.50
Chili-Spaghetti	1.44	Hot Tea	.35
3-Way	1.79	Iced Tea	.50
4-Way	1.94	Flavor for Drink	.15
5-Way	2.09	Hot Chocolate	.40
7-Way	2.39	Basket[a]	.75 extra
Chili	1.29	Shake	1.39
P.B.&J.	1.79	Soda	1.29
Fries	.69	Float	1.19
Slaw (al carte)	.45	Sm. Sundae	1.15
Sauerkraut	.15	Lg. Sundae	2.19
Hamburger-Tom.	.15	Scoop	.79
Chili-Grn. Pepper	.15	Pints	2.49
Chili-Tom.	.15	Quarts	4.25
Chili-Onions	.15	Nuts, M&Ms, etc.	.25

[a]Includes slaw and french fries

Advertising and Promotion

The company advertises for company-owned restaurants on an ongoing basis through television, radio, newspapers, and other varied media. The company keeps its franchisees informed of current advertising techniques and effective promotions through direct contact and periodic mailings. The company's advertising materials are made available to franchisees at bulk-rate costs. The company's franchise agreements require franchisees to spend a minimum of 5.5 percent of their gross sales (as defined) for advertising and promotions. Further, such agreements require that, at such time as a national advertising cooperative is formed, 2 percent of this 5.5 percent commitment will be allocated to such national advertising cooperative. Selected advertisements with emphasis on the product offering are shown in Exhibits 26.3 through 26.5.

Exhibit 26.3   Print Advertisement for Ice Cream

Exhibit 26.4   Print Advertisement for Hot Dogs

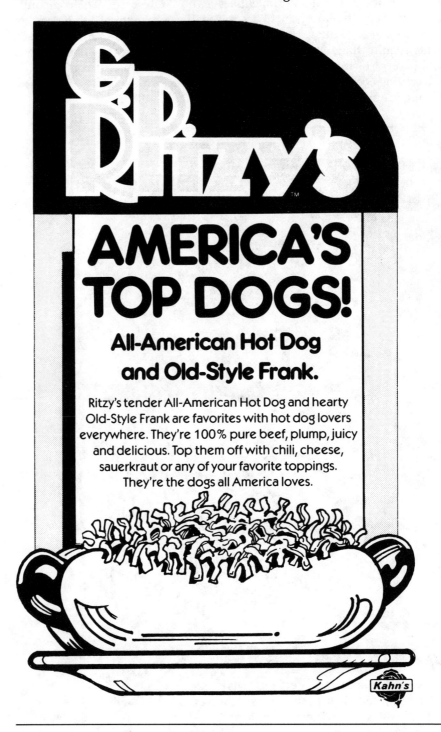

Exhibit 26.5   Print Advertisement for Hamburgers

Nobody else builds a better burger! Two pure beef patties hand-shaped and grilled to order for old-time goodness. Seared to lock in the flavor. Thin on the edges, thick and tender in the middle. Served in a bakery-fresh bun with your choice of toppings. Try one. They don't taste any better than this!

Case 26 *Analysis Form*

G. D. Ritzy's: Pricing Food and Ice Cream

1. In terms of consumer behavior, how would you describe the "real business" of G. D. Ritzy's?

    _____

    _____

    _____

    _____

    _____

    _____

    _____

    _____

    _____

    _____

2. How price-sensitive or price-conscious would you say that G. D. Ritzy's customers are? Why?

    _____

    _____

    _____

    _____

    _____

    _____

    _____

    _____

    _____

    _____

    _____

    _____

3. If you were going to use a full-costing approach to the pricing of products at G. D. Ritzy's, what would be the fixed costs and the variable costs that you would have to take into account?

Fixed Costs:_____

_____

_____

_____

_____

_____

Variable Costs: _____

_____

_____

_____

_____

_____

4. Explain how G. D. Ritzy's might use the concept of "psychological pricing" for its various products.

_____

_____

_____

_____

_____

_____

_____

_____

5.   G. D. Ritzy's currently charges nine cents less for the second dip of ice cream on a double-dip order. Should the firm have the same price for the second dip or an even lower price? Please support your logic.

_____

_____

_____

_____

_____

_____

6.   What are the relative advantages and disadvantages of coupon price promotions for a firm like G. D. Ritzy's?

Advantages:

Disadvantages:

7.   What kinds of marketing research would be helpful to G. D. Ritzy's in the area of pricing?

_____

_____

_____

_____

_____

_____

_____

_____

_____

_____

8.   Based on your overall analysis of the case, what recommendations would you make to G. D. Ritzy's in terms of pricing?

_____

_____

_____

_____

_____

_____

_____

_____

_____

_____

Haire Brothers Funeral Chapel: Pricing Funeral Services

On Wednesday, March 14, 1984, Volume 49, Number 51 of *The Federal Register* carried the Federal Trade Commission's 16 CFR Part 453 Trade Regulation Rule dealing with Funeral Industry Practices. A major portion of that FTC regulation dealt with pricing approaches of funeral firms. The regulation, known as the "Funeral Rule," was not unexpected. In August 1975, the FTC issued a series of proposed rules for the funeral industry. A long series of hearings, proposals, and counterproposals finally led to the 1984 Funeral Rule. Exhibit 27.1 provides an abbreviated summary of the FTC's Funeral Rule.

Current Approach to Pricing

Ever since the firm's founding in 1895, Haire Brothers Funeral Chapel, currently located in a medium-sized town in Georgia, has used what is known as the unit pricing system. Under this approach to pricing, the consumer is quoted a single price that includes the funeral director's professional services, the use of the firm's physical facilities and automotive equipment, and a casket. Prices for a complete funeral are established by applying a multiplier to the wholesale cost of the casket. The multiplier at Haire Brothers varies from 5.2 down to 3.2 with the higher values being applied to the lower-cost caskets. This approach to pricing yields a range of complete funeral services priced from $795 to $4,950.

Alternative Approaches to Pricing

Prior to the enactment of the FTC's Funeral Rule, most funeral directors used one of three methods of pricing their services. Most used the unit approach like Haire Brothers. The industry direction, however, was toward the use of either the professional pricing system or the itemized method, which is similar to that specified by the FTC's Funeral Rule. The following sections briefly describe each of these methods.

Unit

One price covers all the costs of the funeral except cash advances and optional extras. This is the most widely used method at the present time and is frequently based on some multiple times the funeral director's cost of the casket. Some funeral homes vary the value of the multiple, using a higher multiple for lower-cost caskets than for more expensive ones. Other funeral directors compute their overhead structure and add this to a reasonable markup on a given casket to arrive at the total unit price.

The unit price usually includes such items as:

1. Removal of remains to mortuary
2. Complete preparation and dressing of remains
3. Securing of necessary certificates and permits
4. Use of mortuary facilities
5. Assistance of the mortuary staff
6. Transportation of the remains to the cemetery
7. Fixed amount of additional transportation to cemetery
8. Acknowledgment cards and memorial register
9. Casket selected

Exhibit 27.1   Abbreviated Summary of FTC Rule

PART 453 — FUNERAL INDUSTRY PRACTICES

SEC. 453.1   DEFINITIONS

SEC. 453.2   PRICE DISCLOSURES

SEC. 453.3   MISREPRESENTATIONS

SEC. 453.4   REQUIRED PURCHASE OF FUNERAL GOODS OR SERVICES

SEC. 453.5   SERVICES PROVIDED WITHOUT PRIOR APPROVAL

SEC. 453.6   RETENTION OF DOCUMENTS

SEC. 453.7   COMPREHENSION OF DISCLOSURES

SEC. 453.8   DECLARATION OF INTENT

SEC. 453.9   STATE EXEMPTIONS

SEC. 453.10 MANDATORY REVIEW

SEC. 453.1 — DEFINITIONS

(b) **ALTERNATIVE CONTAINER** — is a non-metal receptacle or enclosure without ornamentation or a fixed interior lining, which is designed for the encasement of human remains and which is made of cardboard, pressed wood, composition materials (with or without an outside covering) or pouches of canvas or other materials.

(d) **CASKET** — is a rigid container which is designed for the encasement of human remains and which is usually constructed of wood, metal, or like material, and ornamented and lined with fabric.

(j) **FUNERAL PROVIDER** — is any person, partnership, or corporation that sells or offers to sell funeral goods and funeral services to the public.

(m) **OUTER BURIAL CONTAINER** — is any container which is designed for placement in the grave around the casket including, but not limited to, containers commonly known as burial vaults, grave boxes, and grave liners.

continued

Exhibit 27.1 *continued*

(p) **UNFINISHED WOOD BOX**—is an unornamented casket made of wood which does not have a fixed interior lining.

SEC. 453.2—PRICE DISCLOSURES

(a) UNFAIR OR DECEPTIVE ACTS OR PRACTICES.

. . . To fail to furnish price information disclosing the cost to the purchaser for each of the specific funeral goods and funeral services used in connection with the disposition of deceased human bodies, including at least the price of embalming, transportation of remains, use of facilities, caskets, outer burial containers, immediate burials, or direct cremations, to persons inquiring about the purchase of funerals.

(b) PREVENTATIVE REQUIREMENTS. To prevent these unfair or deceptive acts or practices . . . the funeral provider must:

(1) TELEPHONE PRICE DISCLOSURES. Tell persons who call the funeral provider's place of business and ask about terms, conditions, or prices . . . that such information is available over the telephone.

Tell persons who ask by telephone . . . any accurate information from the price lists and any other information which reasonably answers the question and which is readily available.

(2) CASKET PRICE LIST. Give a printed price list to people who inquire in person about the offerings or prices of caskets or alternative containers.

. . . The funeral provider must offer the list upon beginning discussion of, but in any event, before showing caskets.

The list must contain at least the retail prices of all caskets and alternative containers offered which do not require special ordering, enough information to identify each, and the effective date of the price list.

In lieu of a written list, other formats, such as notebooks, brochures, or charts may be used if they contain the same information . . .

Must place on the list . . . the name of the funeral provider's place of business and a caption describing the list as a "Casket Price List."

(3) OUTER BURIAL CONTAINER PRICE LIST (Same parameters as above).

(4) GENERAL PRICE LIST. Give a price list for retention . . .

When people inquire in person about funeral arrangements or the prices of goods or services, the funeral provider must offer them the list upon beginning discussion of either arrangements or selection of goods and services.

(5) STATEMENT OF FUNERAL GOODS AND SERVICES SELECTED. Must be given for retention to each person at conclusion of arrangements discussion.

SEC. 453.2 (b) (4) (ii)—GENERAL PRICE LIST

Include on the price list, in any order, the retail prices and other information specified below for at least each of the following items . . .

continued

Exhibit 27.1 *continued*

(A)   Forwarding of remains to another funeral home, together with a list of the services provided for any quoted price.

(B)   Receiving remains from another funeral home, together with . . .

(C)   Price range for the direct cremations offered, together with . . .
    (1) Separate price where purchaser provides the container.
    (2) Separate prices for each direct cremation offering including an unfinished wood box or alternative container.
    (3) Description of services and container included in each price.

(D)   Price range for immediate burials offered, together with . . .
    (1) Separate price where purchaser provides the casket.
    (2) Separate prices for each direct burial offered including casket or alternative container.
    (3) Description of services and container included in each price.

(E)   Transfer of remains to funeral home.

(F)   Embalming.

(G)   Other preparation of the body.

(H)   Use of facilities for viewing.

(I)   Use of facilities for funeral ceremony.

(J)   Other use of facilities, together with list of facilities here and price.

(K)   Hearse.

(L)   Limousine.

(M)   Other automotive equipment together with description and price.

(N)   Acknowledgment cards.

(iii)   (A) Price range of caskets offered together with statement that a complete price list will be provided — or — casket price list.

    (B) Price range of outer burial containers together with . . . (same)

    (C) Price for the services of the funeral director and staff, together with a list of the principal services provided for any quoted price, and if the charges cannot be declined, the statement, "This fee for our services will be added to the total cost of the funeral arrangements you select."

OR

"Please note that a fee for the use of our services is included in the price of our caskets. Our services include (specify)."

SEC. 453.3 — MISREPRESENTATIONS

(a) EMBALMING PROVISIONS.

    (1) Deceptive act or practic to:

      (i)   represent that law requires embalming when such is not the case.

      (ii) fail to disclose that embalming is not required by law except in certain cases.

continued

Exhibit 27.1 *continued*

(2) Preventive requirements. To prevent deceptive act, the provider must . . .

    (i) not present that a deceased person is required to be embalmed for direct cremation, immediate burial, a funeral using a sealed casket . . .

    (ii) place disclosure " . . . " on general price list in area of embalming price

(b) CASKET FOR CREMATION PROVISIONS.

(1) Deceptive act or practice to:

    (i) represent that law requires a casket for direct cremation.

    (ii) represent that a casket (other than unfinished wood box) is required for direct cremation.

(2) Preventive requirements. To prevent deceptive act, the provider must place the following disclosure in conjunction with cremation prices:

> "If you want to arrange a direct cremation, you can use an unfinished wood box or alternative container. Alternative containers can be made of materials like heavy cardboard, or composition materials, or pouches of canvas."

(c) OUTER BURIAL CONTAINER PROVISIONS (same outline as above).

(d) GENERAL PROVISIONS ON LEGAL AND CEMETERY REQUIREMENTS. Funeral director must provide in writing any legal, cemetery or crematory requirement compelling the purchase of funeral goods or funeral services if such is the case.

(e) PROVISIONS ON PRESERVATIVE AND PROTECTIVE VALUE CLAIMS. It is a deceptive act or practice for the funeral provider to:

(1) Represent that funeral goods or funeral services will delay the natural decomposition of human remains for a long term or indefinite time.

(2) Represent that funeral goods have protective features or will protect the body from graveside substances, when such is not the case.

(f) CASH ADVANCE PROVISIONS. Deceptive act or practice to:

    (i) represent that the price charged for cash advance item is the same as the cost to funeral provider when such is not the case.

    (ii) fail to disclose that the price being charged for a cash advance item is not the same as the cost to the funeral provider.

SEC. 453.4 — REQUIRED PURCHASE OF FUNERAL GOODS AND FUNERAL SERVICES

(a) CASKET FOR CREMATION PROVISIONS (detail as previously covered)

(b) OTHER REQUIRED PURCHASES OF FUNERAL GOODS OR SERVICES (detail as previously covered such as legal, cemetery requirements)

continued

Exhibit 27.1   *continued*

Preventive requirements: Required statements on "Menu Approach" and "Included Service Charges" at the head of general price list:

"The goods and services shown below are those we can provide to our customers. You may choose only the items you desire. If legal or other requirements mean you must buy any items you did not specifically ask for, we will explain the reason in writing on the statement we provide describing the funeral goods and services you selected."

"However, any funeral arrangements you selected will include a charge for our services." Should be inserted between the second and third sentences of above if such services cannot be declined.

FUNERAL PROVIDER WILL NOT BE IN VIOLATION BY FAILING TO COMPLY WITH A REQUEST FOR A COMBINATION WHICH WOULD BE IMPOSSIBLE, IMPRACTICAL, OR EXCESSIVELY BURDENSOME TO PROVIDE.

SEC. 453.5 — SERVICES PROVIDED WITHOUT PRIOR APPROVAL

Deals mainly with embalming without permission and when this is allowed.

SEC. 453.6 — RETENTION OF DOCUMENTS

Funeral providers must retain and make available for inspection by the commission officials true and accurate copies of the price lists required in previous paragraphs for at least one year after the date of their last distribution to customers, and a copy of each statement of funeral goods and services selected for a period of one year from the date the statement was signed.

SEC. 453.7 — COMPREHENSION OF DISCLOSURES

Funeral providers must make all disclosures required in the rule in a clear and conspicuous manner.

SEC. 453.8 — DECLARATION OF INTENT

If any provision of the rule is determined to be invalid, the remaining provisions shall continue in effect.

This rule shall not apply to the business of insurance or to acts in the conduct thereof.

SEC. 453.9 — STATE EXEMPTIONS

The commission will determine if state rules on these practices are equal or greater in protection and will grant exemptions for those provisions covered in state rules approved by the commission as long as the state rule exists.

SEC. 453.10 — MANDATORY REVIEW

No later than four years after the effective date of this rule, the commission shall initiate a rule making amendment to determine whether the rule should be amended or terminated. Final determination will be made no later than 18 months after initiation of the proceeding.

Complete Itemized

This method goes to the other extreme in breaking out a separate price for each element of the funeral service. Certain states have passed legislation requiring all funeral homes to use this pricing method. The logic is that if consumers know what they are paying for, they will be better able to select exactly what they need and want.

The complete itemized method provides a separate price for each of the following:

1. Removal of remains
2. Embalming
3. Dressing, casketing, and cosmetizing
4. Use of chapel
5. Use of other mortuary facilities and equipment
6. Staff assistance
7. Funeral coach
8. Additional vehicles
9. Casket
10. Memorial register
11. Acknowledgment cards
12. Usually continues on with all other items that are considered as extras in all other pricing methods.

Professional

The professional pricing system, sometimes called the functional approach, has a separate fee for the professional services of the funeral director rather than just including them with the merchandise he sells. Under the professional system, the funeral director charges for his services in the same manner as a doctor or lawyer. The casket is then sold separately with a normal markup.

Two to five separate categories may be used with this method. Together, they cover the cost of the funeral except any cash advances or optional extras. Various categories that may be used in different combinations are:

1. Professional services
2. Preparation for burial
3. Use of facilities and equipment
4. Motor vehicles
5. Cost of the casket

Pricing Considerations

Roger Haire, manager of the firm and grandson of one of the founders, is concerned about how to determine his prices to be fair to his consumers and to himself and to be in compliance with the FTC's Funeral Rule. In researching ways to determine prices in the funeral industry he located a manual, *The Return-on-Investment Approach to Professional Funeral Pricing* by Roger D. Blackwell and W. Wayne Talarzyk. The authors suggested that, regardless of the method of *price quotation* (unit, itemized, or professional), a funeral director's approach to *price determination* should take into account a fair return-on-investment.

The following sections indicate the four basic stages involved in implementing an ROI pricing system.[1]

Stage 1 — Determining Fixed and Variable Expenses.   The first stage in applying ROI procedures to pricing is a determination of fixed and variable expenses of the funeral firm. This determination should be based upon accurate information in as detailed a form as possible. A lack of detailed accounting information concerning fixed and variable costs is not the obstacle that might be assumed. It is probable that most funeral firm managers, because of the personal nature and size of the firm, can make usable estimates of the proportion of costs which are fixed and variable. As use of the system develops, based upon the preliminary estimates by management, the accounting system can gradually be modified as appropriate to provide more refined information concerning fixed and variable costs.

Stage 2 — Programming Desired Profitability.   The programmed profit is then added to the fixed costs of the firm, to be recovered from the sales of service and merchandise. Frequently, pricing systems currently used by funeral firms fail to include the "expense" of capital in the calculation of total fixed costs, thus understating true overhead of the firm.

Stage 3 — Determining Merchandise Contribution.   The third stage in ROI pricing is the determination of contribution to overhead to be derived from the sale of merchandise. In addition to covering the wholesale cost of the merchandise (such as caskets, vaults, and clothing), the merchandise will normally be priced to contribute some amount to the overhead that must be recovered from each family served. For example, if a firm's average merchandise sale were $600 and the average wholesale cost of that merchandise were $300, an average contribution of $300 per family would be derived from the sale of merchandise.

The pricing methods currently used in the funeral service field frequently fail to deduct the contribution of merchandise from the overhead of the firm. Unless the merchandise is sold at cost, however, a contribution is made to the overhead of the firm and should be subtracted from the amount to be recovered in the prices for services and facilities.

Stage 4 — Determining Prices for Services and Facilities.   The fourth stage in ROI pricing is to allocate the remainder of overhead costs from Stage 3 and the variable costs to services and facilities provided to families. The allocation should be based upon the costs associated with each component, moderated by the relative values perceived by consumers.

The fourth stage may be extended to three forms, influenced by the final method of price quotation to be used.

a.   Unit Pricing. The total amount from Stage 3 still to be recovered is divided by the anticipated number of standard services to yield the price charged to consumers for services and facilities. To this amount is added variable costs and the casket charge to yield the total unit price.

b.   Functional Pricing. The total amount from Stage 3 still to be recovered is allocated to the major functions to be performed. After this allocation the total amount of costs for each function is divided by the anticipated number of times

[1]From Roger D. Blackwell and W. Wayne Talarzyk, *A Manual for the Return-on-Investment Approach to Professional Funeral Pricing*, rev. ed. Batesville, Ind.: Batesville Management Services, 1985.

that function is to be performed. To this amount is added the variable costs for each function to yield the price to be quoted to the consumer.

c. Itemized Pricing. The process described for functional pricing is repeated, except that the allocation is performed for each component which is to be itemized in the price quotation to the consumer.

Financial Data

Mr. Haire decided that it would be appropriate for him to work through the basics of the ROI approach to pricing as a first step in determining the prices he would charge under the FTC's Funeral Rule. To that end, he began to assemble the necessary data to begin to implement the ROI system. Exhibits 27.2 and 27.3 are the firm's most recent balance sheet and income statement, respectively.

In analyzing the operating expenses for 1984, Haire determined that $233,432 represented fixed expenses with the remaining $23,779 being variable. Based on 160 families served during 1984, the variable costs per case then came out to be $149.

Haire was somewhat uncertain as to what would be the appropriate rate of return-on-investment for his funeral home. He also wondered what markup should be used for such merchandise items as caskets, vaults, and clothing. He did ascertain that while not all families purchased all three types of merchandise, the average family during 1984 purchased merchandise items with the following wholesale costs: caskets — $486; vaults — $180, clothing — $25.

Mr. Hair heard about some informational leaflets published by the Ohio Funeral Directors that could be distributed by funeral directors to help people understand more about funeral costs. He ordered a sample set and was trying to decide if he should distribute them in quantity. A copy of the leaflet is presented in Exhibit 27.4.

Pre-Need Funeral Arrangements

In recent years, there has been an increased emphasis on preplanning of funeral services. Part of this has been due to the efforts of funeral directors, while in other cases consumers have shown a desire to take care of their own funeral arrangements. In a study conducted for the Casket Manufacturers Association in 1974, 54.0 percent of respondents agreed at least somewhat that it would be good for them to make their own funeral arrangements in advance instead of leaving them to someone else. Some 25.5 percent disagreed at least somewhat with this idea, and 21.4 percent were undecided or had no opinion.

A study conducted by the Center for Marketing Sciences in 1982 found that attitudes toward preplanning became generally more positive as one moved from the East to the West. For example, 16.7 percent of those from the West reported having already made funeral arrangements versus only 4.4 percent of those from the East. In the South, 10.2 percent have made arrangements, and in the Midwest, 7.0 percent. Some 32.7 percent of those from the West, 35.3 percent from the South, 32.1 percent from the Midwest, and 23.5 percent from the East indicated that they "should and probably will" make arrangements.

Of those who were either positive or neutral toward making prearrangements for their funerals, 65.2 percent were not willing to make any prepayment for such prearrangements. The remaining 34.8 percent were willing to make some prepayment ranging from 10 percent to 100 percent of the costs for the funeral.

Over half (52.5 percent) were not aware that local funeral homes offered preplanning arrangements. Of the remaining respondents, 15.8 percent said they had heard a lot about preplanning and 31.8 percent said that they had heard a little about this.

Exhibit 27.2   Balance Sheet for Haire Brothers Funeral Chapel (December 31, 1984)

Assets

Current Assets			
Cash or equivalent	20,186		
Accounts receivable	63,102		
Inventory	26,751		
Other	2,212		
Total Current Assets		112,251	
Fixed Assets			
Physical facilities (depreciated)	279,821		
Automotive (depreciated)	40,899		
Total Fixed Assets		320,720	
Total Assets			$432,971

Liabilities and Owner's Equity

Current Liabilities			
Accounts payable	24,457		
Notes payable	30,200		
Other	17,755		
Total Current Liabilities: Liabilities		72,412	
Fixed Liabilities		194,496	
Total Liabilities			266,908
Owner's Equity (net worth)			166,063
Total Liabilities and Owner's Equity			$432,971

Exhibit 27.3   Income Statement for Haire Brothers Funeral Chapel (Year Ending December 31, 1984)

Total Revenues	$387,489
Cost of Sales	110,516
Gross Margin	276,973
Operating Expenses	257,211
Net Profit (before taxes)	19,762
Income Taxes	6,233
Net Profit (after taxes)	$ 13,539

Exhibit 27.4   OFDA Leaflet Describing Funeral Costs

FUNERAL COSTS

What should a funeral cost? It is difficult to state the exact cost of a funeral because the requests and needs of every family are different.

This leaflet outlines the major charges comprising the cost of the funeral. Any funeral director is willing to explain the specific charges for providing a funeral and final disposition to meet the family's needs.

FACILITIES AND EQUIPMENT must:

- Be appropriately located for public use;
- Make adequate space available for visitation and the funeral service;
- Provide facilities for care of the deceased;
- Keep an inventory of caskets and other merchandise.
- Maintain automotive equipment.

PROFESSIONAL STAFF

The funeral firm must retain professional personnel trained in embalming and funeral directing and licensed by the state. Professional services are available regardless of the time death occurs.

Labor costs represent approximately 30 percent of the funeral bill; the most expensive item charged.

PROFESSIONAL SERVICES

The services of the licensed funeral director as determined by the survivor's requests may include:

- Arrangement conference with family: Discussion of services available; Explanation of prices;
- Scheduling of funeral with clergy;
- Advising media of death;
- Coordinating the funeral ceremony;
- Communicating with the cemetery or crematory regarding final disposition;
- Pre-arrangement advice;
- Post-counseling services.

OTHER COSTS involved in a funeral and final disposition of the deceased which are not in the control of the funeral director. These expenses include:

- Charges by the cemetery or crematory for internment or inurnment;
- A monument or marker;
- Newspaper fees for death notices;
- Legal documents;
- Out-of-town transportation of the deceased where necessary;
- Clergy honorarium.

AVERAGE COST in 1981 of an adult funeral in the United States was $1,949 as reported in a survey by the National Funeral Directors Association. This average excludes charges for the vault, cemetery or crematory expenses, monuments or markers, or other items.

A service of the Ohio Funeral Directors Association.

Case 27 *Analysis Form*

Haire Brothers Funeral Chapel: Pricing Funeral Services

1. Using the model of profitability given in Worksheet 27.1, compute the return-of-net-worth (RONW) before taxes for Haire Brothers Funeral Chapel in 1984. What are the various ways which could be used to improve this RONW?

    _____

    _____

    _____

    _____

    _____

    _____

    _____

    _____

    _____

    _____

2. Do you think Haire Brothers should distribute the Funeral Costs leaflet? Why?

    _____

    _____

    _____

    _____

    _____

    _____

    _____

    _____

    _____

Worksheet 27.1   A Model of Profitability

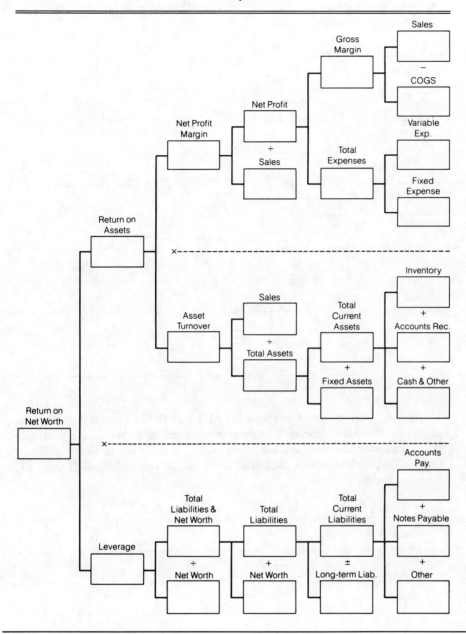

3.   Discuss what you believe would be an appropriate ROI before taxes and an appropriate markup for funeral merchandise such as caskets, vaults, and clothing.

_____

_____

_____

_____

_____

_____

_____

_____

_____

4.   Using your responses to Questions 2 and 3 and the information in the case, complete the ROI approach to determining prices as shown in Worksheet 27.2. Indicate the methodology you would use to break down the price determined in Worksheet 27.2 into more detail to comply with the FTC's Funeral Rule.

_____

_____

_____

_____

_____

_____

_____

_____

_____

Worksheet 27.2   Determining Charges for Professional Services, Facilities, and Automotive Collectively

Needed Information:

Investment in firm (owner's equity) $ _____

Appropriate return-on-investment (ROI)   _____ %

Total fixed costs $ _____

Variable costs per average case $ _____

Number of adult cases   _____ cases

Average markup on caskets   _____ %

Average markup on vaults   _____ %

Average markup on clothing   _____ %

Average selling price of caskets (per case) $ _____

Average selling price of vaults (per case) $ _____

Average selling price of clothing (per case) $ _____

I.   Amount Needed to Recover during Year:

    Appropriate RONW _____ % ($\times$) Investment $ _____ $ _____

      Total fixed costs $ _____ (+)

        Need to recover $ _____

II. Contribution from Sale of Merchandise:

    Contribution from average case:

    Selling price of casket $ _____ ($\times$) Casket markup   _____ % $ _____

    Selling price of vault $ _____ ($\times$) Vault markup   _____ % $ _____(+)

    Selling price of clothing $ _____ ($\times$) Clothing markup   _____ % $ _____(+)

      Total contribution per case $ _____

      Number of cases   _____ ($\times$)

        Total contribution from merchandise $ _____

III. Amount Still Needed to Be Recovered:

      Need to recover (from I) $ _____

      Total contribution from merchandise (from II) $ _____ ($-$)

        Still need to recover $ _____

IV. Charge for Professional Services and Facilities and Automotive

      Still need to recover (from III) $ _____

      Number of cases   _____ ($\div$)

      Amount recovered per case $ _____

      Variable costs per average case $ _____ (+)

        Charge for professional services, facilities, and automotive $ _____

5. Do you believe the proposed FTC rule concerning price disclosure should be put into effect? Why or why not?

_____

_____

_____

_____

_____

_____

_____

_____

_____

_____

6. Do you think Haire Brothers should offer pre-need funeral plans? Why or why not?

_____

_____

_____

_____

_____

_____

_____

_____

_____

_____

_____

Baskin-Robbins 31 Ice Cream Stores: Promoting Ice Cream

Case 28

In December 1976, Baskin-Robbins celebrated its thirty-first birthday. This organization, a nationwide manufacturer and distributor of high-quality ice cream through franchised outlets, represents one of the outstanding marketing success stories in North America.

When the firm reached 500 stores in 1967, the original partners merged with United Brands. In 1973, United Brands sold Baskin-Robbins to J. Lyons Company of London,[1] owners of Tetley Tea, for $37 million, and paid another $8 million to a separate group of stockholders.

By 1985, there were over 3,000 stores, serving over 1,400 cities in every major market from coast to coast and in Europe an Asia. In recent years, a new store has opened approximately every three days.

The company illustrates how promotional philosophy is a direct cause in successful marketing. Baskin-Robbins is unique in that its philosophy has been more closely related to products and product distribution than to formal mass-communication efforts. From the outset the company has exhibited both sensitivity and flexibility in promotional activities and has relied heavily on in-store promotions for mass exposure.

The overall nature of Baskin-Robbins today can best be illustrated by the description given in Exhibit 28.1, which was written by Professor Warren Schmidt, UCLA Graduate School of Business Administration and a special consultant to Baskin-Robbins.

Background Orientation

Company Development

In 1945, the trend in ice cream marketing was to prepackaged, self-service sales primarily in supermarkets. It was in this year that Burton Baskin and Irvine Robbins entered the ice cream business. Their concept was to offer sparkling, attractive stores that would feature only hand-packed ice cream of the highest quality

---

[1]Baskin-Robbins is now a wholly owned subsidiary of Allied U. S. Holdings, Inc., which is a subsidiary of Allied Breweries, Ltd. of London, England.

Exhibit 28.1   A Description of Baskin-Robbins

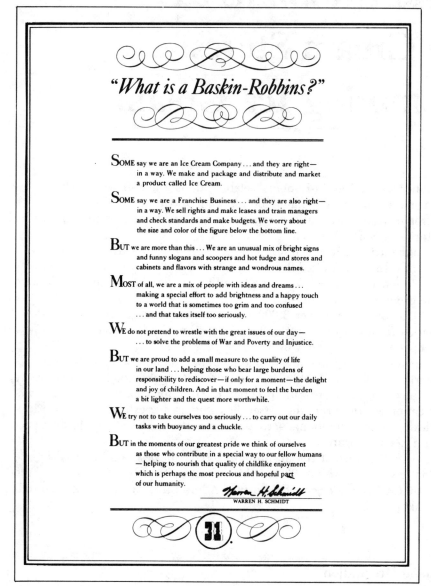

"What is a Baskin-Robbins?"

SOME say we are an Ice Cream Company . . . and they are right—in a way. We make and package and distribute and market a product called Ice Cream.

SOME say we are a Franchise Business . . . and they are also right—in a way. We sell rights and make leases and train managers and check standards and make budgets. We worry about the size and color of the figure below the bottom line.

BUT we are more than this . . . We are an unusual mix of bright signs and funny slogans and scoopers and hot fudge and stores and cabinets and flavors with strange and wondrous names.

MOST of all, we are a mix of people with ideas and dreams . . . making a special effort to add brightness and a happy touch to a world that is sometimes too grim and too confused . . . and that takes itself too seriously.

WE do not pretend to wrestle with the great issues of our day—. . . to solve the problems of War and Poverty and Injustice.

BUT we are proud to add a small measure to the quality of life in our land . . . helping those who bear large burdens of responsibility to rediscover—if only for a moment—the delight and joy of children. And in that moment to feel the burden a bit lighter and the quest more worthwhile.

WE try not to take ourselves too seriously . . . to carry out our daily tasks with buoyancy and a chuckle.

BUT in the moments of our greatest pride we think of ourselves as those who contribute in a special way to our fellow humans — helping to nourish that quality of childlike enjoyment which is perhaps the most precious and hopeful part of our humanity.

WARREN H. SCHMIDT

and, because of more costly ingredients, priced higher than the supermarket ice cream product. Prior to that time, the corner drugstore with its soda fountain service and strategic location had dominated retail ice cream distribution.

The supermarkets based their appeal on price and shopping convenience and ignored ice cream sodas, sundaes, cones, hand-packing, and all forms of personal service. When Baskin-Robbins entered the field, the basic marketing promise was to make the product and the stores so attractive to the public that the buyer would seek out and purchase the unique product — even though it meant extra effort. An essential ingredient in establishing demand was the creation of an unprecedented variety of unusual ice cream flavors. The initial marketing efforts were carried out by stores in Pasadena and Glendale, California. In these outlets, the marketing theory was put to test. These stores were an immediate success. They proved the public was flavor conscious. The buyer was happy to shop for top quality ice cream in immaculate stores that featured personalized service.

A Uniform Identification

In 1948, Baskin-Robbins made a significant marketing decision that was to shape the total company image. It selected Carson-Roberts Inc. as its advertising agency. Then in an embryonic stage, Carson-Roberts is today a division of Ogilvy & Mather, the third largest advertising agency in the world. Among the other Horatio Alger type companies guided by Carson-Roberts is Mattel Toys. A close rapport between client and agency has resulted in what agency principal Ralph Carson refers to as total involvement in advertising-merchandising efforts.

Baskin-Robbins had sought out the agency to create advertisements to run in the *Los Angeles Times*. The total budget was $500. At that time the ice cream stores had two separate identities: some of the stores were known as *Snowbird Ice Cream Stores*, and the remainder were called *Burton's Ice Cream Stores*. Both sets of stores sold identical products and held the same basic philosophy.

Carson-Roberts's recommendation — unorthodox considering that their primary purpose was to create and place advertisements — was *not to run any advertisements*. The agency counseled that a new name was needed to effect a uniform identification. The dual image of *Snowbird and Burton's* was to be consolidated under the trade name "Baskin-Robbins." To aid customer brand recognition, the numeral 31 was added (other classic examples of numeric trademarks are Heinz 57 Varieties and Union 76 oil products). Trademark design and truck-trademark identification were also recommended. The agency felt that the marketing theory was sound and that uniform identification would aid in promotion.

The image consolidation was successful. Within two years, an advertising budget of $5,000 had been established for a radio campaign in the Los Angeles market. The ensuing years brought a media mixture of local spot radio and local newspaper display advertising. At the writing of this case study, Baskin-Robbins had shifted the emphasis from newspaper to television and magazines, although newspaper display advertising and radio are used at the local level.

Marketing Information

Chairman of the board Irvine Robbins has stated the firm's philosophy: "We don't sell ice cream, we sell fun." From the outset, Baskin-Robbins has marketed its brand of "fun" in a very creative manner.

Creating and Naming

Baskin-Robbins is pledged to the highest possible quality, and it has received Gold Medal Awards periodically at state and county fairs in competitive judging over a number of years. The company features the most complete assortment of ice cream products available anywhere in America and has been listed in the *Guinness Book of Records* as marketing a world record 600-plus flavors. As can be seen from the partial list of Baskin-Robbins flavors in Exhibit 28.2, every effort is made to tempt the public appetite with exotically created and named flavors. Vanilla, for example, becomes *Pennant Winning Vanilla* when combined with *Umpire Style Razzberries* and *Nutty Cashews* in *Baseball Nut Ice Cream*.

With a reputation for being a master at the game, Baskin-Robbins applies a timely twist of events of the day in naming and creating products. *Beatnut* was in-

Exhibit 28.2   A Partial List of Baskin-Robbins Flavors

100 & 31 FLAVORS

(And more are being created each month)

APRICOT BRANDY SHERBET	CHOCOLATE MARSHMALLOW RIBBON	ORANGE SHERBET
APRICOT MARMALADE	CHOCOLATE MINT	OREGON BLACKBERRY
APRICOT-ORANGE ICE	CHOCOLATE RIBBON	PARIS PARFAIT
APPLE PIE	CHOPPED CHOCOLATE	FRESH PEACH
APPLE STRUDEL	FRESH COCONUT	PEACH CHIFFON
FRESH BANANA	COCONUT ALMOND FUDGE	PEACHES MELBA
BANANA ALMOND FUDGE	COCONUT STRAWBERRY	PEACHES 'N CREAM
BANANA BERRY	COCO 'N FUDGE	PEANUT BUTTER 'N JELLY
BANANA COCONUT	CRANBERRY SHERBET	PEPPERMINT
BANANA DAIQUIRI ICE	CREME DE CARAMEL	PEPPERMINT FUDGE RIBBON
BANANA MARSHMALLOW	CREME DE MENTHE	PINEAPPLE CHEESECAKE
BANANA ROCKY ROAD	DAIQUIRI ICE	PINEAPPLE ICE
BANANAS 'N STRAWBERRY	DAIQUIRI ALMOND ICE	PINEAPPLE NUT
BASEBALL NUT	DATE KRUNCH	PINEAPPLE UPSIDE DOWN CAKE
BAVARIAN CHOCOLATE MINT	DEVILS FOOD CAKE	PINK GRAPEFRUIT ICE
BLACK RASPBERRY	EGG NOG	PISTACHIO ALMOND
BLACK WALNUT	ENGLISH TOFFEE	PISTACHIO ALMOND FUDGE
BLUEBERRY CHEESECAKE	ESPRESSO	PLUM NUTS
BLUEBERRY MARSHMALLOW	FRENCH VANILLA	PRALINES 'N CREAM
BLUEBERRIES 'N CREAM	FUDGE BROWNIE	PUMPKIN PIE
BOYSENBERRY CHEESECAKE	GERMAN CHOCOLATE CAKE	RAINBOW SHERBET
BOYSENBERRIES 'N CREAM	GOOSEBERRY SHERBET	R·SPBERRIES 'N CREAM
BOYSENBERRY SHERBET	GRAHAM CRACKER	RASPBERRY SHERBET
BITTERSWEET CHOCOLATE	GRAPE ICE	RED APPLE JACK ICE
BURGUNDY CHERRY	HERE COMES THE FUDGE	RED, WHITE & BLUEBERRY
SPARKLING BURGUNDY ICE	JAMOCA	R.S.V.P.
BUTTER PECAN	JAMOCA ALMOND FUDGE	ROCKY ROAD
CAFÉ OLÉ	JACK LEMMON	RUM RAISIN
CARAMEL ALMOND CRUNCH	LEMON CHIFFON	SARSAPARILLA
CARAMEL BRITTLE	LEMON CUSTARD	SPUMONI
CARAMEL ROCKY ROAD	LEMON SHERBET	SHIBUI GINGER
CARAMEL WALNUT	LEMON LIME SHERBET	FRESH STRAWBERRY
CHAMPAGNE GRAPE ICE	LEMON PEEL SHERBET	STRAWBERRY CHEESECAKE
CHERRY CHEESECAKE	LICORICE	STRAWBERRY DAIQUIRI ICE
CHERRY PIE	LIME ICE	STRAWBERRY ICE
CHERRIES ROMANOFF	MACADAMIA NUT	STRAWBERRY RHUBARB SHERBET
CHERRY VANILLA	MANDARIN CHOCOLATE SHERBET	STRAWBERRY SHORTCAKE
CHARLEY BROWNIE	MANGO SHERBET	TANGANILLA
CHOCOLATE	MINT ON MINT	TANGERINE SHERBET
CHOCOLATE ALMOND	NEW ENGLAND MAPLE NUT	TIN ROOF
CHOCOLATE CHEESECAKE	NUTCRACKER SWEET	VANILLA
CHOCOLATE CHIP	NUTS TO YOU	WATERMELON ICE
CHOCOLATE ECLAIR	NUTTY COCONUT	32ND FLAVOR
CHOCOLATE FUDGE	ORANGE CUSTARD	

© 1972 BASKIN-ROBBINS, INC.   PRINTED IN U.S.A.

troduced in the early 1960s to catch the flavor of the "Beatniks," and *Astro-nut* honored the first astronaut put into orbit. A zany concoction of almonds, cherries, toffee, and caramel called *Would You Believe?* was created to tie in with the phrase made popular by Don Adams, the bumbling star of the television show, *Get Smart*. As skirts went up, *Mod Mini-Mint* ice cream was created to show approval of the trend in women's fashion. Well-known characters and television shows brought more flavors such as *Charley Brownie, Steverino, Bewitched, My Three Sons' All American Flavor Chocolate Mint*, and *Jack Lemmon Ice Cream*.

To celebrate the bicentennial, Baskin-Robbins introduced such flavors as *Yankee Doodle Strudel* (with cherries and strudel crumbs), *Valley Forge Fudge* (chocolate fudge ice cream with brownie pieces), *Concord Grape*, and *Minute Man Mint* (green peppermint ice cream with peppermint candy and marshmallow ribbons).

Performance Record

Americans have traditionally led the world in ice cream consumption (the annual consumption rate, now at thirty pints of ice cream per year per person, is still growing). Baskin-Robbins has contributed to this growth in consumption, especially in recent years. In 1962 the firm sold ice cream enough to fill 50 million cones; by 1975 annual sales exceeded the equivalent of 800 million cones. During 1976 the chain sold about 28 million gallons of ice cream, with almost $75 million in gross sales and revenues. By 1982, sales were up to almost 33 million gallons.

Custom-made Products

Custom-made ice cream desserts are an important part of Baskin-Robbins's product line. Standard or special-order custom-made desserts of ice cream or ice cream combined with cakes are made in the stores. Franchisees and their employees are trained to make approximately twenty standard items, which they display in a specially designed ice cream dessert display case. Many franchisees merchandise special items of their own creation. High-profit products that lend themselves well to advertising and promotional opportunities, especially during holiday seasons, ice cream desserts comprise approximately 12 percent of the average store's business. Illustrations of such products are shown in Exhibit 28.3, taken from a franchise bulletin. Exhibit 28.4 shows some of the items on display for immediate sale in the case.

Special Merchandising

Baskin-Robbins utilizes many different types of special merchandising efforts for its products. As shown in Exhibit 28.5, Baskin-Robbins illustrates a different way of eating ice cream—in a pie—by offering a wide variety of ice cream pies. Seasonal promotions include such products as beach balls, book covers, and other items given with various purchases. Exhibit 28.5 also shows an example of a special for Father's Day—a monogrammed shirt decoration on a cake-and-ice cream cake and a free ice cream cone for father on Father's Day. Also featured in Exhibit 28.5 are two additional examples of special merchandising—one supporting Baskin-Robbins's offer of sample tastes and the other promoting the ice cream sodas available in any of the ice cream flavors.

Promotional Strategy

National Advertising

The first national advertising campaign, paid for jointly by Baskin-Robbins and franchised operators, took place in May-June 1970. Using a tongue-in-cheek concept, the company introduced its Top Secret 32d Flavor with full-color ads in *Life* and *Look* magazines and in the Sunday supplements of selected newspapers throughout the country.

Exhibit 28.3   Illustrations of Holiday, Custom-made Products

National advertising was supported by a promotion at the store level featuring television star Jonathan Winters as the president of B.R.U.C.E. (Baskin-Robbins United Closet Eaters), "a society dedicated to eating the Top Secret 32d Flavor in a closet or other secret places." Membership cards carrying Jonathan Winters's photo and signature were distributed in stores and through publicity and promotional channels. Stickers, window posters, and point-of-sale display material supported the campaign, as did local newspaper ads, radio spots, and publicity releases. National publicity was obtained with the B.R.U.C.E. press party given by Winters.

Since 1970, Baskin-Robbins has made regular use of national advertising. It has advertised during television coverage of the Rose Parade and on such network programs as *The Waltons, Little House on the Prairie, The Jeffersons, Wonderful World of Disney, Tom Sawyer Special, Bionic Woman, Donnie and Marie,* and others. Televison advertising has featured a thirty-second spot with the theme "Get That 31derful Feeling."

As part of its national promotion campaign, Baskin-Robbins regularly uses its ice cream as prizes to contestants and participants on television quiz and game

Exhibit 28.4   Specially Designed Ice Cream Dessert Display Case

shows. Some of the shows involving Baskin-Robbins have included *The Price Is Right, Hot Seat, Let's Make a Deal, The Gong Show,* and *Wheel of Fortune.*

Baskin-Robbins has selected women eighteen to forty-nine years of age with children as its target market for television communications. This market segment is perceived to represent the firm's best customers.

Reseller Support Activities

Kits of in-store displays, special promotions, and tie-ins with national advertising are provided to each franchisee every month. Local franchisees are also encouraged to place advertisements in their local advertising media. Baskin-Robbins supplies support materials which include newspaper mats, radio scripts and jingle transcriptions, layout and copy suggestions, and publicity releases.

Each store also has a Birthday Club for all children. Each child registered is offered an ice cream cone on his or her birthday each year until the age of thirteen. The redemption card, which is sent to the home shortly before the child's birthday, also features a message just for Mom abut ice cream desserts.

Publicity and Merchandising

Since its beginning, Baskin-Robbin's management has been publicity-oriented, and its activities and merchandising in this area have been numerous. Several of the most eventful publicity and merchandising events are described below.

Here Comes the Fudge.   One of the most successful promotions Baskin-Robbins has had was a tie-in with the television show *Laugh-in* for a *Here Comes the Fudge Ice Cream* flavor. Before the flavor was introduced in the stores, it was

Exhibit 28.5   Examples of Advertisements Supporting Special Merchandising

continued

Exhibit 28.5 *continued*

served at a Chamber of Commerce luncheon for over 700 guests in "Beautiful Downtown Burbank," honoring the show's cast, producers, and crew. Resulting publicity swept the country, and when the flavor went on sale it zoomed to a top seller in the first few weeks. Stickers, printed pullover shirts, special window posters, counter display cards, and advertising mats were added to the regular merchandising support material. The campaign was so successful that it was extended for a month, and the flavor was so popular that it has periodically been returned to the flavor list by popular demand.

Lunar Cheesecake.   When the Apollo 11 astronauts landed on the moon, Baskin-Robbins had *Lunar Cheesecake Ice Cream* in all of the stores within hours after the landing. This entailed considerable planning and timing. The product, all merchandising, and publicity material were produced in advance, delivered to the stores, and held until the men landed on the moon. Warning was issued to stores that should any disaster befall the return flight, all products and signs should be pulled immediately from the stores. This promotion received wide national coverage in the press and on radio. UPI, food editors, radio commentators, and columnists publicized the promotion.

Herbie Goes to Monte Carlo.   In another campaign, Baskin-Robbins and Walt Disney joined promotional efforts around the Disney movie, *Herbie Goes to Monte Carlo.* For the tie-in campaign, Baskin-Robbins created a new flavor, *Monte Carlo Strip,* a fruit-flavored ice cream combining orange-pineapple and peach flavorings with a red raspberry ribbon. A thirty-second television commercial, four radio commercials, a series of print advertisements, and a variety of point-of-purchase materials were developed to promote the ice cream flavor and a special Monte Carlo Sweepstakes.

Other Tie-ins.   Baskin-Robbins also urges local stores to develop individual tie-in promotions. Exhibit 28.6 displays information about some successful local promotion between banks and Baskin-Robbins stores.

Public Relations

Baskin-Robbins has also successfully incorporated the public relations function into its marketing mix. Their Public Relations Department acts as the official company spokesperson, handles all media inquiries, and keeps Baskin-Robbins before the public through press releases, food editor releases, and publicity events.

Recipe Contest.   One of the most successful campaigns is the Baskin-Robbins "Ice Cream Show-Off" Recipe Contest. The contest, which is held biannually, has several objectives: to build hand-packed ice cream sales and repeat sales, to generate national food publicity, to develop a recipe "bank" for future publicity opportunities, and to promote Baskin-Robbins's consumer involvement. Entries are divided into four categories: drinks, individual treats, sundaes, and ice cream spectaculars.

Professional home economists, food editors, and ice cream connoisseurs from all over the United States judge the recipes and select the top prize winners. More than 15,000 contestants have entered ice cream recipes which have generated thousands of column inches of publicity in the food sections of major metropolitan and suburban newspapers plus radio and TV coverage.

In addition, "Tasting Parties" are held for the media in Dallas, Chicago, and New York, where the press samples desserts and interviews winners. The winning recipes (131 in all) provide a source of recipes for future seasonal food editor releases and in-store flavor-list recipes.

Exhibit 28.6   Information about Local Tie-in Promotional Campaigns

Local Promotions...

Bank Tie-Ins Spell Money in Your Bank

A DEPOSIT TODAY BRINGS SOME ICE CREAM YOUR WAY

A grand total of 20,000 single-scoop-cone certificates were distributed by the Central Du Page Federal Savings for deposits made by all customers during a given month. The certificates were redeemable at any one of four Baskin-Robbins' stores: in Carol Stream, Glen Ellyn, Lombard and Villa Park, Illinois.

Customers were invited to, "Enjoy a cone yourself, or, if you like, you can give your ice cream certificate back to us, and treat kids in pediatrics at Central Du-Page Hospital."

B-R store owners received additional publicity through the bank's advertising which encouraged depositors to drop their names into the Baskin-Robbins' ice cream tub — one at each of their six bank branches — for a weekly drawing. (This added up to a total of 30 drawings). Winners received a National Gift of Joy Certificate — worth $17.00 each.

Store owners submitted the coupons to Central Du Page Federal Savings for reimbursement at the rate of 18¢ per certificate; the reimbursement for the Gift of Joy Certificates was in the amount of $10.00.

This promotion was an effective way to stimulate bank deposits and focus customer awareness on Baskin-Robbins over a concentrated period of time.

FREE!

Just for the fun of it . . . have an ice cream cone on us!

Everytime you make a savings deposit of any size between June 14 and July 17 we'll give you a certificate for a Baskin-Robbins ice cream cone. Enjoy it yourself, or if you like, you can give your ice cream certificate back to us, to treat the kids in pediatrics at Central DuPage hospital.

WIN $17.76
WORTH OF BASKIN-ROBBINS

ICE CREAM!

30 DRAWINGS . . . NO SAVINGS DEPOSIT REQUIRED . . . ANY ONE CAN WIN!

Tie-in, or reciprocal promotions are something many Baskin-Robbins store owners find working well in their Merchandising Areas.

In each case illustrated here, sales volume has been increased by a significant percentage during the period of the tie-in; perhaps more important, the store involved is tapping new customers who are potentials for strong repeat business.

Just drop your name in the Baskin-Robbins ice cream tub, at any of our six offices. A drawing will be held every Saturday through July 17 in each office. That's 30 drawings . . . 30 opportunities for someone to win $17.76 worth of Baskin-Robbins ice cream. That's enough to throw the most delicious ice cream social your block has ever seen. Enter as often as you like at all six offices. You could win!

Note: Local laws on promotional advertising may differ. You can get guidance from from your B-R area or division office.

BASKIN-ROBBINS ICE CREAM

Baskin-Robbins Employee Championship.   The B-R Employee Championship Awards is a six-month program designed to recognize employee excellence in customer service, product handling, and overall Baskin-Robbins team spirit.

Each store-level winner receives an award certificate from his or her employer and the opportunity to compete for the Baskin-Robbins District Blue Ribbon Team. District-level winners are chosen by district representatives, based on achievement levels and an evaluation. These winners receive a Baskin-Robbins 31 Flavors watch and the chance to contend for the highest International Gold Medal Team, members of which are chosen by division managers and regional directors at district meetings in March.

The finalists of the International Gold Medal Team, representing each division and region, are named in late spring. The entire team is flown to Disney World for a rally and all-expense-paid vacation. Exciting work shops and programs featuring top communications experts, a Baskin-Robbins Championship T-shirt, engraved Cross pen and pencil set, Disney World passes, a side trip, and more are all included in this employee recognition program.

Other PR Activities.

- 31st Birthday Party—Baskin-Robbins's first major New York City press party was held in 1976 in honor of its 31st Birthday.
- Rocky & Rhoda—Baskin-Robbins clowns are used for store birthdays or grand openings.
- Poster Contest (1974 and 1976)—31st Birthday poster contest asked people of all ages to create an "ice cream birthday fantasy" on paper. Winning posters toured shopping malls across the United States.
- Women's Opportunity—A series of seminars are designed to "reach out" to entrepreneurial women and spread the story of franchising as an opportunity for women who are ready to move up or re-enter the business world.

Consumer Relations.   An important function of the Public Relations Department is consumer relations. In this age of increasing consumer awareness, Baskin-Robbins takes special care in monitoring and answering the mail it receives. Every month, 200–400 letters are sent to international headquarters concerning everything from complaints, compliments, flavor requests, or suggestions to requests for nutritional/ingredients information. Each letter is investigated and answered. Consumer mail provides valuable feedback because the information received may point to a potential problem in the system or act as a tool to measure the popularity of a flavor.

Case 28 Anaysis Form

Baskin-Robbins 31 Ice Cream Stores: Promoting Ice Cream

1. What is your overall evaluation of Baskin-Robbins's marketing strategy?

Strengths: _____

_____

_____

_____

_____

_____

_____

Weaknesses: _____

_____

_____

_____

_____

_____

_____

2. What effectiveness do you attribute to the firm's publicity efforts?

_____

_____

_____

_____

_____

_____

_____

3.   What should be the established objectives for the advertising and promotion of Baskin-Robbins ice cream?

_____

_____

_____

_____

_____

_____

_____

_____

_____

_____

4.   How would you measure the effectiveness of Baskin-Robbins advertising and promotion?

_____

_____

_____

_____

_____

_____

_____

_____

_____

5. What message strategy, media strategy, and creative strategy do you recommend for future Baskin-Robbins advertising?

Message Strategy: _____

_____

_____

_____

_____

_____

_____

Media Strategy: _____

_____

_____

_____

_____

_____

_____

Creative Strategy: _____

_____

_____

_____

_____

_____

_____

_____

6.   What specific recommendation do you have for Baskin-Robbins in the following areas?

Reseller Support: _____

_____

_____

_____

_____

_____

_____

Publicity and Merchandising: _____

_____

_____

_____

_____

_____

_____

Public Relations: _____

_____

_____

_____

_____

_____

_____

_____

Bounce-a-Roo, Inc.: New Product Advertising

Hi! My family and I are very proud to be introducing Bounce-a-Roos to the United States. They have been part of almost every baby's early life in Australia for many years. When our first baby was born, my mother, who lives in Australia, sent us one and we found it almost indispensable. As people saw our babies enjoying it they wanted one, and what started as my mother sending Bounce-a-Roos one at a time has grown to the point that we are now starting to market them on a wide scale in the United States.

This was the note, included with a product brochure, that Judyth Box, M. D. sent to people who inquired about purchasing a Bounce-a-Roo.

Product Description

First invented in Chicago about 20 years ago, the Bounce-a-Roo patent was sold to an Australian. In that country, the seats have been considered a necessity for babies for years. Bounce-a-Roos are very simple in design and consist of a spring steel frame with a cotton net. The gentle bouncing motion of the Bounce-a-Roo, brought about by baby's own movements or by someone else, is very soothing to a fussy baby and is also pleasing to a happy one. Bounce-a-Roos weigh only three pounds and slip over the arm for easy portability.

The net slips off to go into the washing machine and is available in many colors. The Bounce-a-Roo can be used for babies from birth to about one year old, depending on the nature of the baby. It is especially nice in hot weather. Mothers of babies who have used the Bounce-a-Roos are beginning to report a new use for the seats. According to several mothers, toddlers of 18 months to three years are using them as toys. "Christina sits on her Bounce-a-Roo and bounces, almost like it's a trampoline." says Melinda Newsome. Other mothers report older children using Bounce-a-Roos as backrests for watching television. While all these uses prolong the useful life of the Bounce-a-Roo, Judyth Box advises turning the net upside down so children won't catch a foot in the baby strap.

Similar products are appearing on the market now, but they do not compare in quality with the Bounce-a-Roo. "We have been trying to have the frames made here in the United States, but our standard is that a ten-pound baby must be at a 45 degree angle to the floor when sitting on the Bounce-a-Roo. U.S. prototypes produced so far have a ten-pound baby lying flat, and so do the competitive products on the market," Box explained. Another feature of the Bounce-a-Roo not seen on the competing models is the netting. A ten-pound baby sinks into the netting and is kept in place by his or her own weight. Many of the competitive products have a denim seat cover and the baby is held in by, or hung up on, a strap. There is a strap on the Bounce-a-Roo for safety's sake, but it is not essential. "The Bounce-a-Roo will remain the Rolls Royce of baby seats for some time yet," says Box.

Exhibit 29.1   Portions of Brochure for Bounce-a-Roo

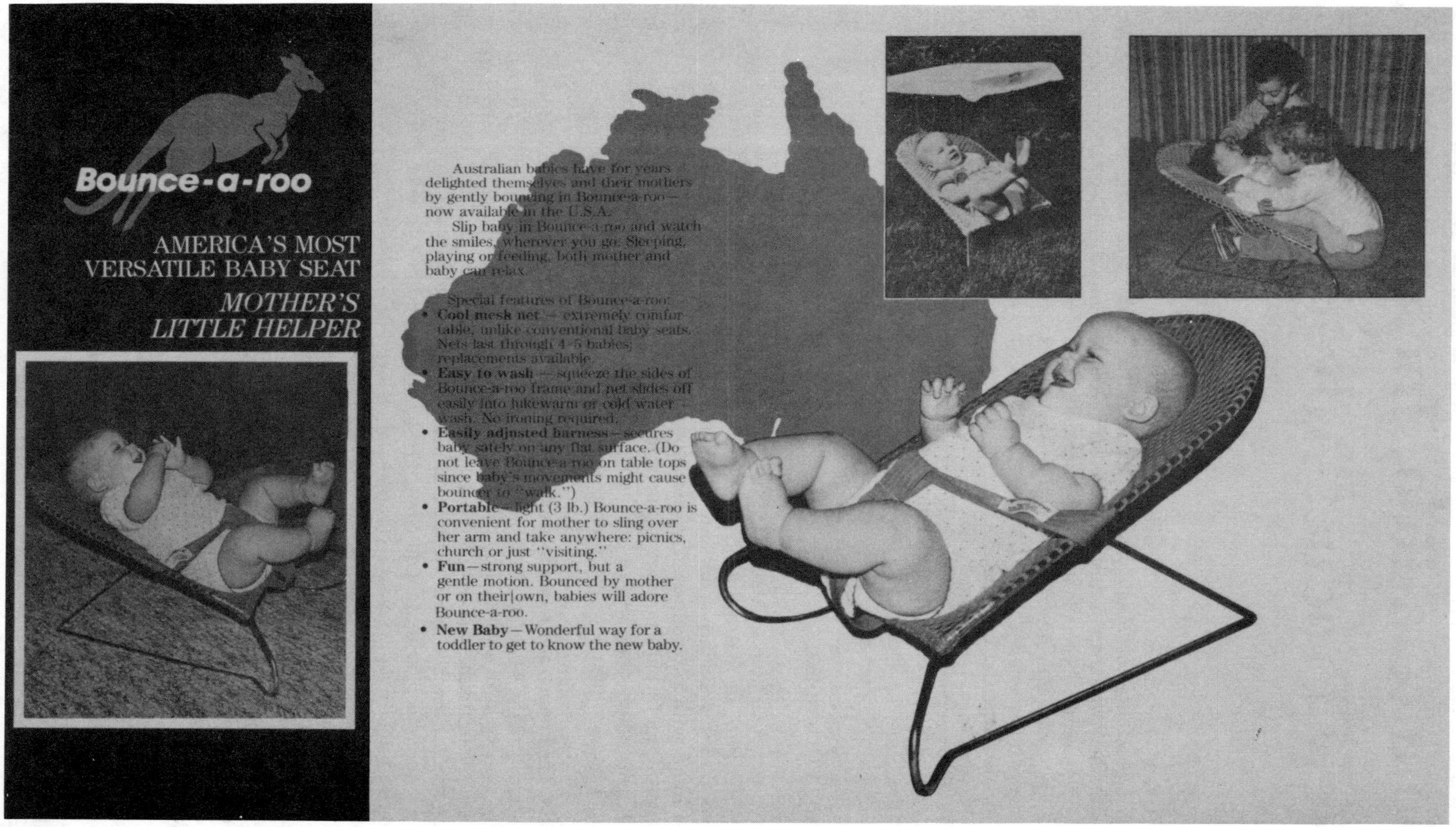

Bounce-a-roo

AMERICA'S MOST VERSATILE BABY SEAT

MOTHER'S LITTLE HELPER

Australian babies have for years delighted themselves and their mothers by gently bouncing in Bounce-a-roo—now available in the U.S.A.

Slip baby in Bounce-a-roo and watch the smiles. Whenever you go. Sleeping, playing or resting, both mother and baby can relax.

Special features of Bounce-a-roo:

• **Cool mesh net** – extremely comfortable, unlike conventional baby seats. Nets last through 4-5 babies (replacements available).

• **Easy to wash** – squeeze the sides of Bounce-a-roo frame and baby slides off easily into lukewarm or cold water wash. No ironing required.

• **Easily adjusted harness** secures baby safely on any flat surface. (Do not leave Bounce-a-roo on table tops since baby's movements might cause bouncing and a fall.)

• **Portable** weight (3 lb.) Bounce-a-roo is convenient for mother to sling over her arm and take anywhere: picnics, church or just "visiting."

• **Fun**—strong support, but a gentle motion. Bounced by mother or on their[own], babies will adore Bounce-a-roo.

• **New Baby**— Wonderful way for a toddler to get to know the new baby.

Bounce-a-Roos cost $29 each and are available in nine colors: pink, red, green, gold, yellow, brown, royal blue, light blue, and white. There is no charge for shipping anywhere in the continental United States. The sunshade, in white or light blue, is available at a cost of $18. The company accepts checks or money orders and Visa or MasterCard for purchases. A brochure describing the product is shown in Exhibit 29.1.

Sales Patterns

Sales for Bounce-a-Roos have been showing a steady increase overall since their introduction to the United States in April 1982. "There must be more babies born in the fall than at any other time of the year," says Box. "Or else people see our Bounce-a-Roos in campgrounds and at picnics during the summer and want one for the baby in their life. At any rate, we at Bounce-a-Roo notice a build-up in sales over the summer and early fall, then a tapering off for a brief period—and the Christmas rush hits."

Box notes that it seems popular for expectant grandparents and aunts to send a Bounce-a-Roo for a shower or baby gift. These types of customers especially appreciate the convenience of simply calling Bounce-a-Roo and having their gift shipped out of town or out of state. "As women are having their first baby at an older age today, friends and relatives seem even more excited," Box observes. "We often hear, 'She's having her first baby at 32, and she deserves something extra—a Bounce-a-Roo!' A new mother who receives a Bounce-a-Roo as a gift is frequently so excited about it that she buys them for her friends who have babies after her. The record so far is held by one young mother who gave five Bounce-a-Roos to friends within eight months of receiving her own at a baby shower.

Advertising Possibilities

Most of the sales of Bounce-a-Roos to date have come from new purchases by and referrals from previous customers. The company is currently considering ways in which it can effectively advertise to expand the market for Bounce-a-Roos. One alternative the company is exploring is advertising in a special section of the Saturday edition of a local newspaper. The following information describes this advertising opportunity.

> These "People, Products, and Business" pages are a very effective advertising medium for distributors, dealers, manufacturers, contractors, consultants, agencies, and other businesses that sell or service commercial accounts, as well as retail establishments. Businesses on these pages run a small advertisement each week for a period of one year. During that year, they receive free write-ups on a request basis. The write-ups appear similar to a news story and usually include a photograph. Each write-up is about one-sixteenth of a page in size. The smallest one-inch advertisement costs $20.95 weekly ($1,089.40 yearly) and entitles the advertiser to a maximum of three write-ups. A two-inch advertisement costs $40.70 weekly ($2,116.40 yearly) and entitles the advertiser to a maximum of five write-ups. The paper has a readership of approximately 400,000 people. Write-ups on a business may

emphasize its services, product line, personnel, newly introduced products, special capabilities, location changes or expansions, awards or recognitions, or any other aspect of the operation that the advertiser wishes to stress. An account executive can assist in the writing of the final draft of the story and a newspaper photographer can take any pictures necessary, all free of additional charge.

Case 29 Analysis Form

Bounce-a-Roo, Inc.: New Product Advertising

1. From an advertising perspective, what do you see as the basic problems facing Bounce-a-Roo?

2. What types of market research would be helpful to the firm at this time?

    The bounce-a-Roo has had much success in Australia, and appears to be liked in the United States. However geographic research, # of babies, etc should be considered in the mrkt research for the U.S., before further expenditures are drawn on the Bounce-a-Roo

3. How would you segment the market for a product like this?

    -By the number of babies, new borns across the nation. Income of families with new borns, and price (economical) of the bounce-a-Roo.

4.   Discuss the strengths and weaknesses of the following media for Bounce-a-Roo's advertising.

Radio
Strengths: _Many mothers with new born babies will listen to radio,_

Weaknesses: _It is a difficult product to describe over the radio._

Television
Strengths: _Excellent way to show what the product is, and what it can do._

Weaknesses: _Expensive, and difficult to find an ideal time the targeted market will view T.V._

Print
Strengths: _- Reach a wide audience_
- Describe product in full
- Many readers out there
- Pictorial (photographs) can be used.

Weaknesses: _May_

Direct Mail
Strengths: _____

Weaknesses: _____

5. If you were going to use direct mail, who would you want to mail to and why?

Mothers families who have children or are considering having children. Also grandparents who possibly have grand kids - Particularly those living in warm climate wheather due to the product's usability outdoors. But the product does not have to be limited there

6. Do you think that Bounce-a-Roo would be better off to use newspapers, magazines, or both as a print medium for its advertising?

yes, I feel Bounce-a-Roo is best advertised (economically and effectivly) in print media.

7.   Please answer the following questions regarding advertising in the "People, Products, and Business" section of the local newspaper.

a.   What copy would you put in the one- or two-inch weekly advertisement?

_____

_____

_____

_____

_____

_____

b.   What copy and photographs would you want to feature in the write-ups on Bounce-a-Roo?

_____

_____

_____

_____

_____

_____

c.   What is your recommendation concerning the use or non-use of this type of advertising? Please provide your rationale.

Recommendations: _____

_____

_____

_____

Rationale: _____

_____

_____

_____

_____

_____

The Timken Company: Advertising Specialty Alloy Steel

Case 30

mixture (alloy) of steel [handwritten]

The Timken Company has always been well-known for its tapered roller bearings. Among prime prospects, some 74 percent have instant unaided recall of Timken tapered roller bearings. In 1974, however, only 3 percent had an unaided recall of the company as a steel manufacturer. At this time the energy crisis was starting, a recession was in the making, employment was down, and The Timken Company's sales had declined.

It was decided that in order to increase sales in a declining market, the firm had to improve market penetration. To help increase market penetration, the firm established an advertising objective to improve the awareness level of The Timken Company's specialty alloy steel line.

Company Profile

By the very nature of its products and processes, The Timken Company is highly dependent upon technology. Most of the worldwide industrial applications for the company's products are themselves quite specialized and complex. Timken products fall into two major classifications: the first includes tapered roller bearings, the company's priorized products, and percussion rock bits; the second classification is alloy steels.

— roller bearings [handwritten]
— alloy steel [handwritten]

The Timken Company produces two classifications of seamless steel tubing as part of its alloy steel product mix. Mechanical tubing is used in such industries as automotive, aircraft, missiles, ordnance, railroad, textiles, mining, anti-friction bearing, oil and gas well drilling, construction and heavy road machinery, electrical equipment, farm machinery, machine tool, and hand tool. Pressure tubing is used to convey fluids or gases under pressure in such industries as oil and gas, steam power, nuclear power, and chemical.

Other alloy steel products include hot rolled bars and billets used in aircraft, anti-friction bearings, gun quality steel, missiles, and steel with high transverse mechanical properties. Cold finished alloy steel bars are also produced for similar applications.

Description of Advertising Campaign[1]

Believing that awareness levels among buying influences signal share of mind, and share of mind facilitates brand awareness and preference; it follows that our advertising objective was to increase awareness levels of our specialty alloy steel

---

[1]This section is based on comments made by R. L. Bohmer, Manager—Advertising for The Timken Company.

line among prospects located in markets of greatest potential. With the increased share of mind added to an existing strong marketing strategy and sales team, our market penetration had to improve and counter the declining market. Planning sessions with our advertising agency, Batten, Barton, Durstine & Osborn, put into action the application of an advertising discipline. The key word, of course, is discipline. We believe that to "create" consistently effective advertising, we must follow a discipline which utilizes the knowledge, experience, and innovative thinking that both we and our agency can collectively apply to solving the problem.

Two Basic Considerations

A disciplined approach to advertising requires us to cover the basic considerations—strategy and execution. Our strategy is built upon the answers to three questions:

1.   Who is the prime prospect?

2.   What is the prime prospect's problem?

3.   How does our product or service solve the prime prospect's problem?

These three points are the essential elements that go into our advertising strategy. They are so fundamental to both our thinking and our system that they deserve some amplification.

It's been our experience that for every category of goods and services there is a *prime prospect*—a small percentage of people who account for the lion's share of volume in the category. Finding out who this group is, reaching them with our advertising, and converting them to our product is by far the most effective way to help the sales team increase sales through greater market penetration.

Our experience has shown that the best way of winning a brand decision is not to seek out desired benefits, but rather to solve a problem the prospect is currently experiencing in a specific product category. We have found customers to be very articulate in specifying the problems and frustrations that plague them in their use of specialty alloy steel.

Once we know all about our prime prospects and know what their problems are, we can turn to our product. We approach the product with the knowledge of what major problems our prime prospects are currently experiencing, and we examine, question, and probe the product to discover what *major* prospect's problems it solves.

This then forms our basic advertising strategy: communication to our prime prospects on how *our* product can best solve *their* problems. But the strategy is only "what" we seek to communicate. It is the function of "execution" to accomplish this communication. It is "how" we communicate.

However, it is the first three disciplines of "what" that go toward establishing the strategies. So now that strategies are established, let's address ourselves to the "how's" of execution. Who is the prime prospect for specialty alloy steel?

Through market research, we found that our key buying influence for this kind of steel were professional/managerial persons with individual incomes of $35,000 + employed by an industrial company with 500 or more employees. These prime prospects functioned as operating and production management, metallurgists, purchasing management, and top management. It's important to note that advertising does not sell steel; sales engineers do. But it is extremely necessary to gain a share of mind and a favorable attitude among customer management toward a company and the company's product before a switch in a steel supplier can be considered. And, here is were advertising can help.

Media Approach

To reach these prime prospects, we developed a two-tiered media approach. We traditionally used a "flat" media approach which had only targeted in on our prospects by function demographically throughout the country. But it did not differentiate them geographically.

The tiered approach provided the way to place national support behind specialty alloy steel through advertisements in selective business publications. And it provided additional support behind steel in twelve high-potential markets to bolster both product awareness and preference among prime prospects.

Basically, we use *Business Week*, *Fortune*, and *Dun's Review* for frequent reach of our management prospect. We rounded off our corporate print campaign with *The Wall Street Journal* for a broad national reach of audience. In twelve local markets, which account for a large percent of sales, we used televison and radio to "heavy up" our message. In other instances, we reached selective audiences of national news magazines on a market-by-market basis through Magazine Network, Inc. Totally, the effect worked and continues to work for us today.

The Market's Problems

Now that we know how to effectively reach our prime prospect, the next step in our advertising discipline is: Know you prime prospect's problems. We found "that *advanced technology* makes it imperative for customers to seek a steel manufacturer who can *continually provide* specialty alloy steels of a *consistent quality* that will meet their *changing requirements*." On the surface, this sounds rather mundane. But these key words—"advanced technology," "continually provide," "consistent quality," and "changing requirements"—tell the story.

Here is the execution of the third step of the advertising discipline: Know the product (how the product solves the prospect's problems). We realized we had the production capabilities and the technical expertise to produce specialty alloy steel with the characteristics the customer requires. It's that simple: "A steel source that could continually supply quality alloy steels for changing needs would solve our prospect problems."

Creative Strategy

What happened next is what this case history is all about. We set in place our creative strategy which has not deviated even unto today. It is:

1.   Position The Timken Company as a small steel company.
2.   Show The Timken Company's ability to tailor-make specialty alloy steel to fill a customer's exact needs.

Exhibit 30.1 illustrates two of the advertisements used in the print campaign. Other basic themes included "It's Amazing What Big Things a Small Steel Com-

Exhibit 30.1 Print Advertisements for The Timken Company

SPECIALTY STEEL IS OUR STRONG SUIT.

If you can get your job done with ready-made steel, great. There are plenty of steel companies that can deal out all the ready-made product you want.

But if your job needs special steel, The Timken Company could be your ace in the hole. We deal only in custom steel, selected and made precisely to your order.

From the very beginning we leave nothing to chance.

Our sales engineer — most likely a graduate metallurgist — will sit down with your people to find out exactly what you want your steel to do. Then he'll help pick the best Timken® alloy steel for the job.

We'll tailor a production sequence for your steel and your steel alone. A meticulously detailed program that will cover every step from the first shovelful of alloys to the wrappings on your finished steel.

So there are no slip-ups, we'll test your steel again and again — up to 30 times in all. Before we ship, we'll even spark-test each piece individually to make double-sure the steel you ordered is the steel you get.

When you need special steel, make our strong suit your strong suit. Steel the way you like it is the only way we make it.

The Timken Company, Steel Division, Canton, Ohio 44706.

Steel. As you like it.

TIMKEN®
REGISTERED TRADEMARK

Exhibit 30.1 *continued*

OUR LITTLE ACT IS GETTING GREAT REVIEWS.

When our steel company made its debut back in 1916, the only audience was The Timken Company family. We started making steel ourselves — so we'd always have quality alloys for our bearings.

We kept working on our routine — getting every step right every time. And we kept getting better.

It wasn't long before other companies heard about the quality o Timken® Steel. They invited us to perform for them. Perform we did, and today we make specialty alloy steel for hundreds of companies besides our own.

Our little steel act has gotten a lot more sophisticated over the years. But there's one way it hasn't changed. We've never stopped polishing our routine.

We still test every heat of Timken steel every step of the way — up to 30 times in all — to see that the steel you get is just the steel you specify. Order after order.

We figure that's why our little steel act keeps getting such great reviews. And why companies keep inviting us back for repeat performances.

The Timken Company, Steel Division, Canton, Ohio 44706.

Steel. As you like it.

TIMKEN

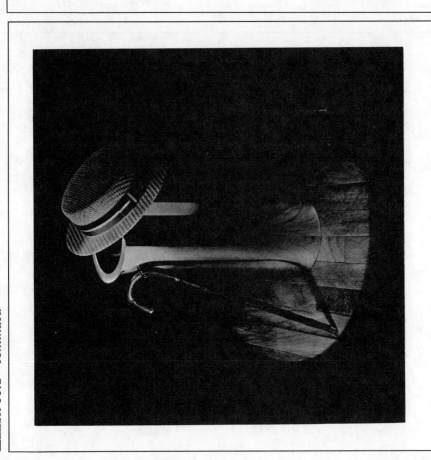

pany Can Do," "Is There a Place for a Small Steel Company in an Age of Steelmaking Giants?" and "If the Steel You Need Isn't on Our Menu We'll Cook up a New Recipe."

Campaign Results

The Timken Company was the first American bearing manufacturer to produce its own steel. Now we have become *one* of the leading sources for specialty alloy steel in the United States. As shown in Exhibit 30.2, what happened was this: Unaided brand awareness went from 3 percent in 1974 to 27 percent. Our unaided brand awareness is right there with the leaders in specialty steel making. Total awareness reached 89 percent, putting us up with other major steel producers.

Most importantly, prospects are hearing our message and reacting favorably to it. We have increased our sales through increased market penetration. In a nutshell, we found steel customers had a problem and we went out and told them The Timken Company could solve that problem. It worked!

Exhibit 30.2   Awareness Levels of The Timken Company and Other Steel Producers

	Unaided Awareness	Total Awareness
Company A	31%	98%
The Timken Company	27	89
Company B	20	89
Company C	13	87
Company D	10	86

Case 30 *Analysis Form*

The Timken Company: Advertising Specialty Alloy Steel

1.   What is the "real business" of The Timken Company in the area of specialty alloy steel?

Real business — solving the customer's problems through the use of their product(s). Listening, to the customers — Hopefully providing for their needs/wants

2.   Discuss how industrial advertising is similar and dissimilar compared to consumer advertising.

Similarities: Advertising is geared to a market. Both markets have a need to be satisfied (filled)

Dissimilarities: One is for consumer use, the other for industrial use.
- Thought of as a raw material (industrial)
- Thought of as a finished product (consumer)

3.   Discuss the ways one could pretest and posttest the effectiveness of The Timken Company's advertising program.

Pretest: _____

_____

_____

_____

Posttest: _____

_____

_____

_____

4.   Discuss the relative advantages of the following media for The Timken Company's specialty alloy steel advertising.

Print: _____

_____

_____

_____

Radio: _____

_____

_____

_____

Direct Mail: _____

_____

_____

_____

Television: _____

_____

_____

_____

5. Indicate how The Timken Company's advertising campaign meets each of the following possible objectives for a promotional program.

Objective	How The Timken Company's Campaign Meets the Objective
Provide Information	*their print ads provide information tremendously well.*
Stimulate Demand	*↑ Awarness goes up. Demand tends to follow*
Differentiate the Product	
Accentuate the Value of the Product	
Stabilize Sales	

6.   Based upon your analysis of the case, what specific recommendations would you make to The Timken Company in the following areas?

Other Themes:_____

_____

_____

_____

_____

_____

Media Choice:_____

_____

_____

_____

_____

_____

Research: _____

_____

_____

_____

_____

_____

Other:_____

_____

_____

_____

_____

_____

Wolverine Brass Works: Exclusive Distribution Strategy

Case 31

Wolverine Brass Works, a division of The Citation Companies, sells plumbers' brass goods to over 20,000 quality-conscious builders and contractors. The firm is the only company in its field to sell directly and exclusively to plumbing contractors and other professionals. Its products cannot be bought at retail, nor does the company market through distributors.

The Citation Companies

Individual divisions of The Citation Companies are engaged in various activities related to the home. Its largest operation, Wolverine Brass Works, markets a complete plumbing products line including over 2,000 stock items.

Another division, H. B. Sherman, is one of the top two makers of nationally sold lawn sprinklers, hose nozzles, and related accessories. The company sells through manufacturers' representatives. Retail customers include leading hardware chains and co-ops, mass merchandisers, and garden supply outlets.

Handy Things Manufacturing Company, another consumer division, is one of the nation's largest manufacturers of Christmas tree stands. The company also manufactures household utensils such as potato ricers, kitchen tongs, and fruit presses and a line of housewares including towel racks, soap dishes, and clothesline reels.

In the area of builders' hardware, The Newell Manufacturing Division markets pneumatic door closers, door latches, and accessories to retail outlets, mill supply houses, and storm door manufacturers. The firm recently introduced "Weather All," a do-it-yourself plastic storm window kit in the retail market.

Glynn-Johnson, another builders' hardware division, specializes in architect-specified products for commercial and industrial construction. Its high-styled products, designed to appeal to architects and designers, include overhead door holders, invisible door latches, door catches, bumpers, and special builders' hardware items. The company sells to jobbers through commissioned sales representatives; its retail marketing is insignificant.

Exhibit 31.1 presents a five-year summary of The Citation Companies' operating and financial staistics. A summary of sales and earnings by line of business is shown in Exhibit 31.2.

Wolverine Brass Works

Wolverine Brass Works is over 80 years old. Its lines of faucets, tubular traps, bronze valves, compression stops, and related specialty items are among the broadest in the industry. Some companies may produce more of a single item, but

Exhibit 31.1   Five-Year Summary of the Citation Companies' Financial Statistics

Operating Results	1977	1976	1975	1974	1973
Total revenues	$48,669,260	$44,253,409	$37,002,707	$41,873,770	$44,075,095
Operating expenses	43,335,606	40,090,670	35,124,554	38,662,585	40,135,622
Operating income	5,333,654	4,162,739	1,878,153	3,251,185	3,939,473
Interest expense	749,864	703,342	831,337	1,170,384	985,611
Write-off of goodwill	—	—	1,589,417	—	—
Income (loss) before income taxes	4,583,790	3,459,397	(542,601)	2,080,801	2,953,862
Income taxes	2,090,000	1,283,000	549,000	995,000	1,487,000
Net income (loss)	2,493,790	2,176,397	(1,091,601)	1,085,801	1,466,862
Depreciation and amortization of property and equipment	1,239,427	1,043,163	1,006,310	1,036,681	972,700
Capital expenditures, including leased equipment under capital leased	2,011,481	1,561,033	667,824	672,850	1,204,753
Balance Sheet Data					
Current assets	20,889,584	19,871,228	17,874,314	19,931,542	22,652,294
Net property and equipment and leased equipment	9,996,649	9,590,973	9,099,074	9,456,959	9,841,803
Total assets	32,409,320	30,748,981	28,492,722	32,553,215	35,736,855
Current liabilities	7,102,469	7,332,253	5,654,090	7,001,019	11,774,589
Long-term debt, including obligations under capital leases	7,467,607	7,452,500	8,506,500	9,624,422	8,769,809
Stockholders' equity	16,930,691	15,111,908	13,506,593	15,181,306	14,507,460
Working capital	13,797,115	12,538,975	12,220,224	12,930,523	10,877,705

continued

Exhibit 31.1 *continued*

Ratio analysis					
Return on sales	5.1	4.9	(3.0)	2.6	3.3
Revenues per $ of assets	1.50	1.43	1.3	1.29	1.23
Assets per $ of equity	1.91	2.03	2.11	2.14	2.46
Return on assets	7.7	7.1	(3.8)	3.3	4.1
Return on average equity	15.6	15.2	—	7.3	10.5
Current assets to current liabilities	2.9 to 1	2.7 to 1	3.2 to 1	2.8 to 1	1.9 to 1
Debt to equity	.44	.49	.63	.63	.60
Per Share					
Net income (loss)[a]	1.63	1.44	(.71)	.71	.95
Dividends[a]	.43	.34	.32	.26	.25
Payout percentage	26%	23%	—	38%	26%
Stockholders' equity[b]	11.30	11.08	11.35	12.53	11.97
Average shares outstanding[a]	1,532,788	1,516,319	1,530,751	1,539,355	1,542,226

Notes: (a) Restated for stock dividends in 1976 and 1977.
(b) Based on actual number of shares outstanding at the end of each year.

Exhibit 31.2   Sales and Earnings by Line of Business

Year	Plumbing Products	Consumer Hardware	Builders' Hardware	Other[a]
1977 Net Sales	56.9%	30.4%	12.7%	— %
1977 Earnings	49.3	36.1	12.9	1.7
1976 Net Sales	54.3	29.9	14.4	1.4
1976 Earnings	52.8	32.3	16.2	(1.3)
1975 Net Sales	54.7	28.7	15.3	1.3
1975 Earnings	53.4	28.3	21.5	(3.2)
1974 Net Sales	53.7	29,7	14.2	2.4
1974 Earnings	52.9	39.4	13.0	(5.3)
1973 Net Sales	48.9	26.4	15.6	9.1
1973 Earnings	68.2	29.9	6.1	(4.2)

[a]Mobile Home Products discontinued in 1976

no competitor serves the plumber's needs with as wide a variety of supplies. Wolverine employs seventy-five full-time salesmen and selected sales agents who sell to 20,000 contractors in all parts of the country.

The fact that Wolverine Brass Works is the only company in its field to market directly and exclusively to plumbing contractors and other professionals attracts loyal customers. This is one of the firm's principal reasons for staying with this form of distribution. In management's opinion, plumbers' loyalty means reliable sales, an advantage that outweighs the potential sales which might be realized by competing with others in the retail market.

A computerized order entry system enables the company to move with unusual speed, efficiency, accuracy, and low cost. The goal is to fill orders within 24 to 36 hours of receipt. This goal is designed not only to win customer satisfaction, but also to aid production scheduling, inventory control, and trouble shooting in various areas. Management believes its order entry system is a key to profitability and a major reason for success with such a diversified product line and so many individual customers.

The division also makes service fixtures for hospitals and scientific laboratories, including foot-operated and gooseneck faucets, service turrets for controlling and transmitting gases, needle valves, and gas shut-off valves. These products are sold to laboratory furniture manufacturers and scientific apparatus jobbers.

Wolverine Brass's sales historically have been stable despite the varying pace of new home construction because, management conjectures, a high percentage of its products are used for remodeling or replacement of plumbing fixtures in existing homes.

Product Areas

Wolverine Brass products are designed and manufactured to assure quality, quick installation, and minimum service. The firm's product offering is divided into six basic areas:

1. Faucets, including necessary accessories, for sinks, showers, tubs, lavatories, laundry, and lawn;

2. Valves of all types, including gate, ball, globe, check, relief, and regulating, and valve repair kits;

3. Water closet and tank accessories;

4. Tubular and cast drainage products;

5. Supplies, such as flexible and rigid supply lines and supply valves, tubes, and connections; and

6. Miscellaneous plumbing products, including waste disposals, sump pumps, sinks, nuts, bolts, screws, washers, gaskets, and plumbers' supplies and tools.

Advertising

Consistent with its distribution strategy, Wolverine Brass directs its advertising to contractors. Exhibit 31.3 shows two typical advertisements used in trade publications. The firm also utilizes a series of mailings from the "Wolverine Brass Tacks Department" to inform customers of new products and services. Exhibit 31.4 gives two examples of such mailings. Advertising specialties such as memo pads, key chains, and coin holders are widely distributed to supplement other advertising efforts.

Current Plans

Wolverine Brass Works sell most heavily to plumbing contractors engaged in repair/remodeling work and builders of custom homes, where quality and service are usually as important as or more important than price. As part of the program implemented to attain a stronger position in the larger brass market — especially in speculative multi- and single-family dwellings — Wolverine introduced the competitively priced Encore line of faucets in 1977, planning to add other inexpensive brass products to its line in 1978, keeping cost down by designing simpler products, and still retaining some premium features.

Robert J. MacIntyre, president of Wolverine Brass Works, states:

> Wolverine's most important objective, far and away, has been additional strength in the competitively priced field. Our successful introduction of the Encore faucet line now moves us in that direction. Furthermore, sales of higher-priced lines have continued to move ahead, indicating that we're not sacrificing profits in one direction to gain them in another. I should also emphasize that there is a substantial difference between competitive pricing of quality products, which is our program, and the marketing of cheap merchandise on which price is everything and quality means nothing. We'll stay away from the field.

service
customer loyalty

Exhibit 31.3   Typical Trade Advertisements for Wolverine Brass

When a Plumbing Contractor has something to say to us, we get the message...

through 75 on-the-spot full-time representatives

Wolverine Brass products are sold directly to Plumbing Contractors. The full-time WB man in each marketing area establishes company-to-Contractor communication. He's a customer-oriented man who keeps us sensitive to product and service requirements.

Valves for homes and institutions

 WOLVERINE BRASS WORKS
Grand Rapids, Michigan 49502

PRODUCTS THAT GIVE AN EXTRA MEASURE OF VALUE

At Wolverine Brass, it's a total effort in behalf of the Plumbing Contractor

Every year we look for new ways to serve our customers

For more than 70 years, our products have been sold exclusively through the Plumbing Contractor, a distribution policy which reflects a company attitude of support for the role of the Plumbing Contractor. Wolverine Brass helps to strengthen the Plumbing Contractor's "complete service" to customers by enabling him to stock and install, with confidence, a recognized quality line of products no other market source can offer.

Wolverine Brass Concealed Fixtures

 WOLVERINE BRASS WORKS
Grand Rapids, Michigan 49502

PRODUCTS THAT GIVE AN EXTRA MEASURE OF VALUE

Exhibit 31.4   Sample Wolverine Brass Tacks Department Mailings

From the Wolverine
Brass Tacks Department:

LAVATORY CENTER SET

This new twist for the bathroom ends dripping once and for all. The polished ceramic seats in its Finale cartridge "slice" off water instead of "pinching" it, turn water flow from full-off to full-on with an easy one-quarter twist. Won't drip, won't wear, won't corrode. Eliminate the need for bibb washers and conventional packing. You can install it and forget it.

One-piece center set design has integral cast brass body, spout and threaded shanks. Available with crystal-clear acrylic handles (a special N.A.S. acrylic that resists household chemicals) or chrome plated metal handles. Pop-up drain optional.

From the Wolverine
Brass Tacks Department:

NEW AQUA-FLO WATER FILTER
for removing rust and sediment
or unpleasant tastes and odors

Here's a new profit maker for you that *keeps on* making profits. One you can quickly and easily install. And give your customers positive removal of rust and sediment or taste and odor from household water. The new Wolverine Aqua-Flo Water Filter has replaceable filter elements for removing either rust and sediment or taste and odor. Elements last from one to six months, depending on conditions, and can be easily replaced by the homeowner (and bought from you, of course). The perfect answer for clearing up discolored, sediment-laden water from private systems. For removing offensive tastes and odors from chemically treated municipal systems, as well. And for making continuous profits for you.

Case 31 Analysis Form

Wolverine Brass Works: Exclusive Distribution Strategy

1. What do you see as the basic problems facing Wolverine Brass Works relative to its distribution strategy?

    Its distribution strategy
    is a good one: marketing exclusively
    to plumbing contractors in order to
    get customer loyalty. However,
    the company should learn to sell
    its products to other available
    markets out there if it wants
    to grow.

2. Why would a plumbing contractor select one line of plumbing supplies over another?

3. How do alternative price lines (some high-priced lines, some low-priced ones) relate to a firm's distribution strategies?

_____

_____

_____

_____

_____

_____

_____

_____

_____

4. How should Wolverine promote its products to best reach the plumbing contractor?

_____

_____

_____

_____

_____

_____

_____

_____

_____

5.   Please discuss the relative advantages and disadvantages to Wolverine in distributing its products through each of the following channels.

Plumbing Contractors
Advantages: _____

_____

_____

Disadvantages: _____

_____

_____

Hardware Stores
Advantages: _____

_____

_____

Disadvantages: _____

_____

_____

Discount Stores
Advantages: _____

_____

_____

Disadvantages: _____

_____

_____

Building Supply Home Centers
Advantages: _____

_____

_____

Disadvantages: _____

_____

_____

6.   What marketing recommendations would you make to Wolverine's management based on your total analysis of the case? Please be specific in terms of distribution, product strategy, pricing, and advertising.

Distribution: _____

_____

_____

_____

_____

Product Strategy:_____

_____

_____

_____

_____

Pricing:_____

_____

_____

_____

_____

Advertising: _____

_____

_____

_____

_____

Hyde-Phillip Chemical Company: Alternative Forms of Sales Representation

Case 32

Michael Claxton, a recent marketing graduate of a well-known college, has been assigned the task of evaluating Hyde-Phillip Chemical Company's methods of selling the firm's products. Hyde-Phillip currently utilizes a mix of company salespersons, merchant wholesalers, and agent wholesalers to present its products to present and potential users. While this combination of selling forces is somewhat unusual, it reflects the orientation of management over time to the relative values of alternative forms of sales representation. Claxton's challenge is to review the data that has been gathered on the three types of sales efforts, determine if additional information is needed, and make recommendations as to what changes, if any, should be made in the firm's approach to sales representation.

Information on the Company

Hyde-Phillip was formed in the early 1960s through the merger of Hyde Industrial Chemicals and Phillip Laboratories. Both firms had a broad range of experience in the development and production of certain types of chemicals and related supplies for a variety of industrial users. While the two firms had a few overlapping product lines, each brought to the merger some exclusive product offerings. The resulting combination of the two firms yielded a new organization capable of marketing a complete line of chemicals for industrial use.

Prior to the merger, Hyde Industrial Chemicals had utilized a group of industrial distributors (merchant wholesalers) to market its products. Phillip Laboratories, on the other hand, had several manufacturers' agents (agent wholesalers) who sold its product offering. The new firm, after the merger, retained some of the industrial distributors and some of the manufacturing agents and then began to develop its own salesforce.

Today, Hyde-Phillip serves 30 sales territories in states east of the Mississippi through its own salesforce of 50 individuals (six women and 44 men), nine industrial distributors, and nine manufacturers' agents. The 50 salespeople are about evenly allocated across twelve of the sales territories. Each of the industrial distributors and manufacturers' agents has exclusive selling rights in one of the 18 remaining sales territories. Individual distributors and agents have from five to 30 people working for them and many represent other noncompeting manufacturers. The 30 sales territories were originally established to represent areas of approximately equal sales potential for Hyde-Phillip's products.

Many types of sales support are made available to each sales territory by the company. Individual managers of the territories have the option of using or not using each type of sales support. Sales support items currently available include (1) a variety of descriptive brochures to supplement the information given in the firm's product catalog, (2) study programs with cassette tapes to enable sales representatives to be more familiar with the firm's products and current market situations and developments, (3) a program to provide generous product samples to potential customers for test purposes, and (4) direct-mail programs aimed at prospective customers to solicit inquiries for descriptive materials and product samples.

Data on Sales Territories

As a first step in beginning his analysis, Claxton asked his assistant to compile the available information on each of the 30 sales territories. This information is presented in coded form in Exhibit 32.1.

In terms of level of sales, 9 territories have annual sales in excess of $2 million, 15 have sales between $1 and $2 million, and 6 have sales less than $1 million. As already indicated, in 12 of the territories, the firm is represented by its own salesforce, and industrial distributors and manufacturers' agents each represent the company in 9 territories.

Based on estimates provided by the sales support department, 12 of the territories make extensive use of the available sales support programs, 12 are moderate users, and 6 are light users. Each of the firm's sales territories is also divided into one of three geographic divisions, Northern, Southern, or Eastern. As indicated in Exhibit 32.1, each of these geographic locations includes ten sales territories.

Initial Analysis

Using the information in Exhibit 32.1, Claxton constructed the cross-tabulation of sales versus type of representation as shown in that exhibit. He first set up the cross-tabulation using raw numbers and then calculated the conditional probabilities for each row and column.

As seen in Part B of Exhibit 32.2, 55.6 percent of Hyde-Phillip's territories with sales more than $2 million were ones served by industrial distributors. Only 11.1 percent of the largest sales territories were represented by manufacturers' agents and 33.3 percent were served by the company salesforce. Stated differently, as shown in Part C of Exhibit 32.2, 25.0 percent of territories served by the company's salesforce had sales more than $2 million, while 55.6 percent of the industrial distributors and 11.1 percent of the manufacturers' agents served territories with sales more than $2 million.

Claxton's initial reaction was that the firm should consider replacing part of its own salesforce and the manufacturers' agents with more industrial distributors. He was concerned, however, with what other variables should be taken into account to more fully analyze and evaluate Hyde-Phillip's current approach to sales representation.

Exhibit 32.1   Available Data on Sales Territories

Territory Number	Level of Sales	Type of Representation	Use of Sales Support	Geographic Location
1	2	1	2	3
2	3	1	3	3
3	2	2	1	1
4	1	1	1	1
5	2	3	1	1
6	2	1	2	1
7	3	3	2	3
8	1	2	1	2
9	2	1	2	2
10	2	1	2	3
11	1	2	1	1
12	1	1	1	2
13	2	2	2	2
14	2	3	2	1
15	1	1	2	3
16	2	3	2	2
17	2	1	3	1
18	1	2	1	2
19	2	3	2	2
20	3	1	3	2
21	1	3	1	3
22	2	2	1	3
23	3	3	1	1
24	3	1	3	2
25	3	2	3	1
26	1	2	1	2
27	2	1	2	2
28	1	2	1	3
29	2	3	3	3
30	2	3	2	3

Codes: Level of sales: 1 = more than $2 million; 2 = $1–2 million; 3 = less than $1 million
Type of representation: 1 = company salesforce; 2 = industrial distributor; 3 = manufacturers' agent
Use of sales support 1 = extensive user; 2 = moderate user; 3 = light user
Geographic location: 1 = Norther; 2 = Southern; 3 = Eastern

New Marketing Approach

At a recent conference on improving productivity in marketing activities, Claxton learned about a new marketing approach, developed by AT&T Communications, called Telemarketing. The following information is from an AT&T Communications publication titled, 'Telemarketing: Marketing System for the 80s."

Introduction to Telemarketing

Telemarketing: Solution for the 80s.   Telemarketing—a new marketing system—is a synthesis of telecommunications technology with management systems for planned, controlled sales and service programs.

Telemarketing is a component of the marketing communications mix. It can

Exhibit 32.2   Cross Tabulation of Level of Sales versus Type of Representation

			Company Salesforce (1)	Industrial Distributor (2)	Manufacturers' Agent (3)	Totals	
Level	More than $2 million	(1)	3	5	1	9	
of	$1—2 million	(2)	6	3	6	15	A
Sales	Less than $1 million	(3)	3	1	2	6	
		Totals	12	9	9		

			Company Salesforce (1)	Industrial Distributor (2)	Manufacturers' Agent (3)	Totals	
Level	More than $2 million	(1)	33.3	55.6	11.1	100.0	
of	$1—2 million	(2)	40.0	20.0	40.0	100.0	B
Sales	Less than $1 million	(3)	50.0	16.7	33.3	100.0	
		Totals	40.0	30.0	30.0	100.0	

			Company Salesforce (1)	Industrial Distributor (2)	Manufacturers' Agent (3)	Totals	
Level	More than $2 million	(1)	25.0	55.6	11.1	30.0	
of	$1—2 million	(2)	50.0	33.3	66.7	50.0	C
Sales	Less than $1 million	(3)	25.0	11.1	22.2	20.0	
		Totals	100.0	100.0	100.0		

Code: A = raw numbers
B = row conditional probabilities
C = column conditional probabilities

be used solely or in combination with media advertising, direct mail, catalog selling, face-to-face selling, and other communication modes—efficiently and cost effectively.

Telemarketing can be applied at any and all functions in the marketing spectrum—from order taking to full account management. It can be used to respond to inquiries, supplement (and sometimes replace) personal selling, qualify leads, sell to marginal accounts profitably, trade-up orders, increase advertising effectiveness, replace traditional retail shopping and render instant and cost-effective personal service to customers when they need it most.

By conducting conventional marketing and service activities in innovative ways, telemarking is a new communications channel—delivering high impact at low cost—for critical marketing/service roles. That is why it must be integrated into the total marketing mix.

In essence, then, telemarketing is a system—with a special facility, staffed by specially trained professionals, supported by special management information and telecommunications systems—that allows businesses to execute and implement well-defined sales and service programs to identified target markets.

Because telemarketing is results-oriented, it adds a new dimension and flexibility to the marketing operation—quick, responsive, manageable, *measurable* fulfillment of the selling and servicing roles.

Therefore, telemarketing is recognized as the means for achieving such key objectives as deeper market penetration and greater market share, controlling sales and service costs, and making advertising more accountable to cost-and-results analysis.

While telemarketing is demanding, it is also highly productive. As such, this new system can assist the progressive marketer through the turbulent economic weather of the 1980s.

Benefits of Telemarketing

Telemarketing Increases Sales.   Telemarketing is a low-cost means of contacting many customers and prospects—over a broad geographic area—in a short period of time. Because the communication is two-way, it allows sales personnel to persuasively and efficienty move customers and prospects to a buying decision. Sales volumes can be increased with the expert use of such techniques as upgrade selling, cross-selling, and turning service calls into sales.

Telemarketing Supports Field Sales.   Once a customer relationship has been established, repeat visits do not always have to be made face-to-face. The combination of telemarketing's personalized contact with face-to-face selling can raise sales productivity to new levels.

Also, through Telemarketing, leads from promotion campaigns can be skillfully qualified. By preconditioning the prospect over the phone, the follow-up face-to-face visit can result in a truly productive sales call. Dead-end sales visits can be almost eliminated.

Telemarketing Expands Market Share, Deepens Market Penetration.   You can expand your market without expanding your field salesforce. Your telemarketing system can conveniently match your advertising's geographic reach. So you can coordinate promotion with extended sales territory coverage to enlarge your market share.

Telemarketing permits you to intensify your selling activities in geographic areas and market segments that are low in sales volume, and to support the selling and promotional programs of your distributors.

Telemarketing Cuts Sales Costs.   The need for highly-skilled, well-trained salespeople, coupled with the skyrocketing increase in travel and other sales expenses, have almost tripled the cost of sales calls in the past ten years.

But, an equally skilled and trained—but smaller—telemarketing staff can cover an even larger territory, with dramatic results. And, there are no travel or mileage allowances or hotel, lunch, or entertainment expenses to contend with. So productivity is high while the cost per-sales-contact drops sharply.

Telemarketing Enhances Customer Service.   With telemarketing, your customers can get quick answers to product problems and service needs. Convenient, available service prevents problems from developing into deep-seated dissatisfactions. They can also obtain information on product usage, when they need it the most.

As a side benefit, product and distribution difficulties are easily recognized and can be promptly rectified. And it can all be done cost effectively.

Telemarketing Increases Advertising Effectiveness.   Ad response rates can be improved by inviting customers to place orders through an 800 number. Thus, instead of completing an order card or coupon and having to mail it, your customer makes a simple toll-free call. The advantages are: prospects make the purchase while the idea is strong; it is more convenient to telephone than to fill in and mail a coupon; a telemarketing specialist can influence the customer's decision to close a sale; and since communication is two-way, there are additional opportunities to upgrade, cross-sell, and sell substitute high-inventory items.

You will find, as many other businesses have, that you close more sales with telemarketing.

Telemarketing Increases Profits.   Put all of the above together—more sales, lower sales costs, greater market share, deeper market penetration, improved advertising effectiveness, and enhanced customer service—and what do you get? Greater efficiency. Greater productivity. And greater profitability.

In addition to the telemarketing benefits just reviewed, there are significant beneficial results that telemarketing provides.

☐   *Timely cost/benefit analysis:* Prompt data—on number of inquiries, number of sales, income per sale, cost per sale, for example—can help you measure effectiveness.

☐   *Fast feedback:* Prompt response helps you test the pulling power of direct mail or advertising. Changes can be made before you make an irreversible commitment to a promotion.

☐   *Season extension:* Time available for selling during seasons and holidays—such as for Christmas—is limited when orders are placed by mail. Since calls to a telemarketing center speed the receipt of orders, the selling period can be extended by up to an additional week.

☐   *Improved cash flow:* Customers are encouraged to act quickly. And you can ship and bill the same day. So you can coordinate sales promotion activity with inventories to convert heavily stocked goods into cash.

☐   *Targeting the market:* Effective selling is targeted to specific markets—e.g., men aged 30–40 earning $20,000–$30,000 and living in the Southeast. Quickly and inexpensively, you can determine the effectiveness of a promotional program to selected telemarketing targets, because responses arrive more quickly by telephone than by mail, and management systems can give rapid analysis of program performance.

Case 32 Analysis Form

Hyde-Phillip Chemical Company: Alternative
Forms of Sales Representation

1. Using the following matrix, discuss the general advantages and disadvantages associated with each of the given forms of sales representation.

Company Sales Force

Advantages:

Disadvantages:

Merchant Wholesaler

Advantages:

Disadvantages:

Agent Wholesaler

Advantages:

Disadvantages:

---

2.   After filling in the following cross tabulation form, discuss the relationship between level of sales and geographic location.

Geographic Location

	Raw Numbers				Row Conditional Probabilities					Column Conditional Probabilities		
	(1)	(2)	(3)		(1)	(2)	(3)			(1)	(2)	(3)
Level of Sales (1)				(1)				100.0	(1)			
(2)				(2)				100.0	(2)			
(3)				(3)				100.0	(3)			
								100.0		100.0	100.0	100.0 100.0

Relationship: _____

_____

_____

_____

_____

_____

_____

_____

_____

_____

_____

_____

_____

_____

_____

_____

_____

_____

3.   After filling in the following two cross tabulation forms, discuss the relationship between use of sales support and type of distribution and sales.

Use of Sales Support

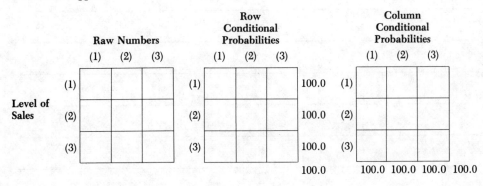

Use of Sales Support

Relationship: _____

_____

_____

_____

_____

_____

_____

_____

_____

_____

_____

4.   Do you think that telemarketing has any potential for Hyde-Phillip?

_____

_____

_____

_____

_____

_____

_____

5.   Based on your total analysis of the case, what would be your specific recommendations to Hyde-Phillip at this time?

_____

_____

_____

_____

_____

_____

_____

_____

_____

_____

_____

_____

_____

_____

_____

HomeOwners Warehouse — Mr. How: Marketing to the Do-It-Yourselfer

When HomeOwners Warehouse, also known as "HOW," was acquired by Service Merchandise Corporation in May 1983, eyes and ears in the industry concentrated on the Margate, Florida-based retailer. HOW had been a weighty figure in the market on its own. With the substantial resources of Service Merchandise behind it, the firm looked as though it could quickly become a real powerhouse. Surprisingly, little happened for some time. The company, which had changed its name to Mr. HOW Warehouse, quietly operated three stores in Florida and Georgia.

Expansion Takes Place

Then the dam broke. Early last year, the company began signing leases for store sites at a stunning pace, and by November had locked in 21 locations. Stores began sprouting almost before the ink was dry on the leases. Mr. HOW finished 1984 with 12 stores in place and plans to add 23 in the next year. "We were preparing for the expansion by gathering our resources, building a management staff, organizing, and developing plans," says Mr. HOW Marketing Director Mark Clark. "When that was ready, we made our move. Our objective is simple: We intend to be a $1 billion company within five years."

Also of note is where the company plans to expand. Although many of the new stores are in Mr. HOW's native Sunbelt, the company is also moving into northern cities. "Service Merchandise is a national company, and it thinks in terms of nationwide operations," Clark notes. "There are no boundaries for Mr. HOW."

Nor is Mr. HOW apparently concerned about the highly competitive environment that's a fact of life in many of the new locations. Two stores, for instance, opened in the Philadelphia area in November, where they're going toe-to-toe with solidly in-place heavyweights like Hechlinger, Channel, Grossman's, Rickel, 84 Lumber, Wickes, and Mr. Goodbuys. Four stores were recently opened in Cincinnati, also a beehive of building-supply home-center activity.

Entering the Chicago Market

Next, the company invaded the Chicago area, already the arena for a fierce struggle among Handy Andy Home Improvement Centers, the recently formed Builders Square, and several strong, well-entrenched local firms, including Courtesy Home Centers, Gee Lumber, and Edward Hines Lumber.

Exhibit 33.1   Pictures of Mr. HOW Stores

Its opening volley in the Windy City was the opening of a 70,000-square-foot store in early January. (See Exhibit 33.1 for photographs of Mr. HOW Warehouses.) Later that month, it bought five Forest City stores that had been a major force in the Chicago market. These units were then converted to the Mr. HOW format, and the first went on line in late May. "Sure, there's competition," says Clark, "but the demographics are still right. Big northern cities have heavy concentrations of people to support the stores. In Chicago, there may be as many people living within five miles of our store as there are within 25 miles of a store in another part of the country."

Consumer Services

But Mr. HOW isn't relying on demographics alone. The company is prepared for any competition. "We offer size, selection, low price, and — most important — excellent service," says Clark. He notes such free services as cutting wire, lumber, and window shades, along with custom paint tinting. There are regular clinics and 50 free how-to pamphlets. Three major credit cards are accepted and delivery is available. For customers who'd rather take home a large load themselves, Mr. HOW has car-top carriers and tie-down twine and clearance flags for long loads. Parking-lot employees help load purchases.

But the backbone of the company's service is well-trained personnel, exemplified at each store by the highly qualified customer adviser, called "Mr. HOW," who is capable of aiding customers in need of help for nearly any do-it-yourself project. "All employees take our training program," says Clark. "It was developed by Dick Nunn, an acknowledged industry expert and author of numerous how-to books. Although the training involves some salesmanship, it concentrates on product knowledge, so our employees can give customers the information and advice they need. Mr. HOW is not a 'self-service' store — it's a 'self-selection' store. Our people are trained to assist customers in making their selections." The Mr. HOW experts are a company trademark and have established a laudable image and reputation. "In a broad sense, Mr. HOW, the adviser, symbolizes the commitment to service of Mr. HOW, the company," Clark explains. "On a practical basis, he is an invaluable aid to customers."

Each store has at least one Mr. HOW always on duty at the Mr. HOW booth. During peak periods at busy stores, two or three may man the booth at once. They are aided by a computer programmed with detailed information and specifications on more than 100 common do-it-yourself projects. Mr. HOW feeds in the variables from a customer's particular project, and the computer provides data specifically for that project. A customer building a deck, for instance, relates its size and other pertinent information, and the computer prints out everything from the quantity and dimensions of lumber needed to the type of nails required. It also shows if the items are in stock, their locations, the price of each item, and the total cost of the project. The Mr. HOW adviser also conducts clinics and serves as a backup source of information for other store sales personnel, although employees are discouraged from using him as a crutch.

Store Design and Layout

Mr. HOW booths are centrally situated and highly visible in the stores, all of which have a similar layout and merchandising style, although there are differences at each location. The new 70,000-square-foot Chicago store is fairly typical. Traffic is guided by a semi-racetrack, and department placement is often determined by the importance of a product category, creating a layout somewhat unusual among warehouse stores. For one notable example, the single main entrance feeds customers into the plumbing department. Many stores greet customers with lighting fixtures, ceiling fans, or other products particularly conducive to dazzling display. Plumbing is, however, one of Mr. HOW's key product categories, and although many retailers consider it difficult to display well, Mr. HOW presents it very attractively.

The plumbing department leads to the beginning of the main power aisle, which runs the entire width of the store and features imposing island displays. Eye-catching four- and six-foot endcaps effectively draw customers into the side aisles that branch from this main aisle. "Store design was considered carefully prior to our expansion," says Clark. "We wanted everything to be just right."

Future Directions

Although a relative newcomer to the industry, Mr. HOW has already made its presence felt and is well on the way to its $1 billion goal. A basic question is, how does Mr. HOW plan to grow so quickly? To help answer that question, *Building Supply Home Centers* interviewed Raymond Zimmerman, Chairman and President of Service Merchandise. The questions and his comments are presented in Exhibit 33.2.

Exhibit 33.2   Interview with Mr. HOW's Chairman of the Board

What prompted your purchase of Mr. HOW?

The circumstances were opportune. We were in a strong cash and management position, and Mr. HOW was a powerful vehicle to put them to use.

Last year, Mr. HOW lost more than $4 million. What caused this, and when do you expect it to become profitable?

The losses were mainly due to heavy store-opening expenses. Last year, we opened 10 stores. This year, we've already opened 12, plan to open 12 more, and may have another 20–25 in 1986.

Mr. HOW will break even this year and generate substantial profits in 1986. We predicted it would be a $1 billion company in five years. We're ahead of schedule. I think we'll do it in four.

What drew you to the building supply home center industry?

After seeing Home Depot's success, we looked into the market and decided there was room for another player.

Is there really *room? Isn't this market getting a little crowded?*

An operation like ours expands a market, creates greater demand. Home Depot's Atlanta stores do $100 million a year. Their competition is still there—and Atlanta wasn't a $100 million market when Home Depot opened.

A rising tide raises all ships?

Yes—and when things get too crowded, some of them get banged up and sink.

It sounds like you expect to see some casualties.

There will be casualties. But not us. We understand what's happening. The same business mentality occurred in the catalog showroom business in the sixties. We're taking an industry that's used to high margins and low sales and flip-flopping it—making it a big-volume, low-margin market. Also, we have resources in money, management, and physical plant to sustain us.

And we've got excellent controls and systems. Service Merchandise is strongly centrally controlled, and we're implanting this into Mr. HOW.

What's the biggest advantage of this?

Experts in the home office do the day-to-day buying and make certain the stores are in stock. All the people at the stores have to do is make sure customers who come into our stores—which we call "our home"—are happy.

Store personnel must maintain accurate inventory records. But we're highly automated. So, they have the tools to do that well and still be free to concentrate on the primary job of keeping the store neat and clean and giving customers first-rate service. Their job is to move goods as fast as they can.

Building supply home centers have roughly the same brick-and-mortar cost, payroll cost, and about the same prices. It's the neat, clean store that's always well stocked and has well-trained people to serve the customer that will survive.

You mention people a lot. How important are they to you, and where are you getting managers for the large number of stores you're opening?

People are our most important asset. Without good people, your company goes down the tube.

The managers come from a good, solid cadre of them that we built up before we began our expansion, and are still building up. They're drawn mainly from Service Merchandise, managers who have gone as far as they can in our showrooms but are still capable of handling more. A typical showroom has 50 people, maybe 200–250 in the peak season. The average warehouse home center starts at about 125 people. So, we promoted these showroom managers to Mr. HOW stores, giving them the positions of greater responsibility they deserve but were unavailable to them.

The reason for doing this, aside from rewarding good people, is that we're talking about a $20 million store. That requires a professional manager, not just someone knowledgeable about products. These managers know our systems, know how to manage people, and are experts in store operations. They have general managers beneath them to run the departments. They're the ones with product knowledge.

Mr. HOW and other large, resource-rich operations seem to be holding all the aces. Where does that leave the small independents?

All this may work against them. On the other hand, a good, strong independent can wreak havoc on a chain. In the showroom business, we worry more about the solid independents than we do other chains. They're flexible and can do anything creative they want. They can quickly change prices and displays and policies. And it's like a family. Their people are charged up and excited and greet customers by their first names.

And, you know, that's the real fun of retailing—being innovative, dealing with people. That's where I cut my teeth, and, frankly, I miss it. It's exciting.

You're the boss. Why don't you just do it?

Because I'd step on toes, and that's not a good idea. You have to respect your people. You put them in responsible positions and delegate authority to them. If you override their decisions, you don't need them and they don't need you. You have to bring in young, aggressive people and let them run.

How do you get them motivated and loyal and charged up?

You give them a fun place to work, make it exciting. You promote them before they're ready. What they lack in experience and knowledge, they'll make up for in heart. We give them enough responsibility to go out and do their thing and get worked up about it. Our strong systems and controls tell us if there's a problem, and we catch them before they go too far down the wrong path. We give them enough rope to maneuver, but we don't let them hang themselves.

Case 33 Analysis Form

HomeOwners Warehouse—Mr. How: Marketing to the Do-It-Yourselfer

1. To what do you attribute the retailing success of Mr. HOW?

_____

_____

_____

_____

_____

_____

_____

_____

_____

2. What do you see as the potential marketing problems facing Mr. HOW in
    the future?

_____

_____

_____

_____

_____

_____

_____

_____

_____

_____

3.   Please discuss the impact that each of the following environmental factors is having on the traditional hardware store today.

Factor	Impact upon Hardware Stores
Cultural and Social Environment	
Competitive Environment	
Economic Environment	

4.   What are the basic criteria that consumers use to choose one building-supply store over another?

_____

_____

_____

_____

_____

_____

_____

5.   What are the basic consumer reasons behind the increase in do-it-yourself (D-I-Y) activities? Do you expect the trend to continue? Why or why not?

Reasons for Increase in D-I-Y:_____

_____

_____

_____

_____

_____

Will Trend Continue? _____

_____

_____

_____

_____

_____

6.   What types of consumer research would be helpful to Mr. HOW at this time?

_____

_____

_____

_____

_____

_____

_____

_____

_____

7. As the building supply warehouse field becomes more crowded, what will determine the survivors and casualties?

_____

_____

_____

_____

_____

_____

_____

_____

_____

_____

8. What sorts of new technologies will assist firms like Mr. HOW in better serving their customers?

_____

_____

_____

_____

_____

_____

_____

_____

_____

_____

_____

_____

Comprehensive Cases

Part III

The ten cases in this part of the book provide an opportunity to apply the cumulative analytical skills developed through the cases in the previous parts. A variety of companies and organizations as well as different types of goods and services are presented in these ten cases.

Instructors may wish to assign specific questions to students based on materials in the *Instructor's Manual.* The alternative involves the analytical approach.

With the analytical approach, once the problem has been isolated, the decision-making process continues with (a) the identification of problem-solving alternatives open to the organization, (b) a detailed evaluation of each alternative as it relates to the problem and to the organization's objectives and constraints, and (c) specific recommendations about which plan of action the organization should take to solve the problem.

Although there are many different approaches to these steps, certain questions always should be considered in connection with the process, among them:

1. the market and its influence on the problem and decision, including present and potential size and any special characteristics, such as geographic location and seasonality;

2. the ultimate consumer, including needs, buying habits, motivations, and key classifications;

3. the channels of distribution for the product and their influence on the problem and ultimate decision;

4. the types of competition, their present and anticipated future position in the market, and their likely reactions to the various plans of action; and

5. the legal and political environment and its implications for problem solutions.

Other factors should be evaluated simultaneously. They include the present and future state of the economy, the seriousness and urgency of the problem, the financial position of the organization, the potential risk of the decision, and the effects of the proposed plan of action on key personnel in the company, other product lines, and the company's image.

Wendy's International, Inc.: Wendy's Old Fashioned Hamburgers

Case 34

"Does America need another hamburger chain?" was the question being asked as R. David Thomas opened the doors to his first Wendy's Old Fashioned Hamburgers restaurant at 257 East Broad Street in downtown Columbus, Ohio on November 15, 1969. At that time many food industry experts and some skeptical observers had commented that the fast-food growth curve had already peaked during the late 1960s and that the rapid expansion of the industry was over.

On March 21, 1978, after only eight years and four months, the thousandth restaurant in the Wendy's chain opened at 1000 Memorial Boulevard in Springfield, Tennessee. Never before had such an accomplishment been achieved in such a short period of time. During 1985, the company opened over 400 new units to bring the number of Wendy's Old Fashioned Hamburgers restaurants to approximately 3,400 at year end.

Company Background

Wendy's was founded by R. David Thomas, who was previously associated with Kentucky Fried Chicken and Arthur Treacher's Fish and Chips. Thomas presently serves as Senior Chairman of the Board. Robert L. Barney, currently Chairman and Chief Executive Officer, joined Wendy's in 1970. He started in the fast-food business in 1962, when he became an owner of a Kentucky Fried Chicken franchise, later becoming a regional vice president in charge of 135 restaurants. For a short period of time before joining Wendy's, he was vice president of operations at Arthur Treacher's Fish and Chips. Ronald P. Fay is President and Chief Operating Officer. He was in charge of W. T. Grant's food service operations, one of the few profitable divisions for the company, until 1975 when he became a partner in a Wendy's franchise in Virginia Beach, Virginia. In December 1979, he sold his restaurants to Wendy's International and joined the corporation.

Much of Wendy's phenomenal success can be attributed to its large, well-run franchise organization and its low costs of operation along with quality and speed of service and upscale ambience. As a relative latecomer to the fast-food scene, Wendy's had a big advantage over the predecessor chains. But competition had a head start on restaurant development. McDonald's had started 14 years before Wendy's which gave it an advantage in market penetration. While McDonald's, Burger King, Burger Chef (now owned by Hardees), and many of the other fast-food pioneers had to build their franchise business from scratch, training managers with little or no restaurant experience, Wendy's drew from the ranks of former chain operators who were well acquainted with the business. Using a territorial franchise approach, the company emphasized those franchisees who could finance and manage their own "minichain" of five, ten, or more units. Franchisees pay a continuing 4 percent of sales franchise royalty, paid monthly to the parent company.

The second key to Wendy's success is its efficient operation. Initially the typical Wendy's building was about 30 × 76 feet, seating 90 to 100 people, with parking for 30 to 45 cars. Most units are built on half- to three-quarter-acre lots as opposed to a McDonald's or Burger King, which usually occupy an acre or more. Wendy's typically needs less land than the other two operations because a drive-in window accounts for 40 to 45 percent of a unit's total sales. Those customers who use the pick-up window obviously do not require parking spaces or inside eating areas. Exhibit 34.1 shows the new-image restaurant.

Exhibit 34.1   Picture of Wendy's New-Image Restaurant

In 1984, 120 new Wendy's and 151 existing restaurants adopted the latest design change—the addition of a "greenhouse" at the front of the restaurant, or in some cases, along one or both sides. With more natural light, higher seating capacity, and more attractive ambience, studies show that restaurants with greenhouses have higher sales than those without.

An average investment of $770,000 is required to construct a Wendy's unit. Of this total, about 50 percet goes for the building, another 30 percent for real estate, and the remaining 20 percent for equipment. The typical Wendy's outlet averaged $861,000 in annual sales in 1984. Selected financial data is presented in Exhibit 34.2.

In recent years, Wendy's has continued to focus attention toward opening company-owned outlets. This is being accomplished in two ways—either by buying back existing franchises or by constructing its own company-owned units. Of the 1,057 company-operated restaurants at the close of 1984, 15 were acquired from franchise owners during the year. In 1984, 120 new company-operated restaurants were built. The company also operates a number of Sisters Chicken & Biscuits restaurants, through a wholly-owned subsidiary, Sisters International. Most of the present 76 restaurants are company owned and operated with the rest being franchised.

Exhibit 34.2 Selected Financial Data — A Five-Year Financial Review

Selected Financial Data—A five year financial review

	1984	1983	1982	1981	1980
	(Dollars in thousands except per share data)				
Operations					
Retail sales	$ 877,269	$ 665,591	$ 560,516	$ 446,800	$ 310,067
Revenues	944,768	720,383	606,964	488,825	348,391
Company restaurant operating profit	166,383	126,367	101,717	74,832	54,385
Income before income taxes	126,882	99,476	80,031	64,897	54,804
Net income	68,707	55,220	44,102	36,852	30,096
Per share data:					
Net income	1.25	1.01	.84	.76	.67
Cash dividends	.25	.20	.15	.14	.13
Pro forma per share data:*					
Net income	.93	.76	.63	.57	.50
Cash dividends	.19	.15	.11	.11	.10
Cash flow from operations	135,850	97,885	75,985	66,857	58,345
Company restaurant operating profit margin	19.0%	19.0%	18.1%	16.7%	17.5%
Pre-tax profit margin	13.4%	13.8%	13.2%	13.3%	15.7%
Return on average assets	14.3%	14.0%	14.1%	15.2%	18.2%
Return on average equity	20.4%	19.3%	19.5%	22.0%	26.6%
Systemwide Wendy's sales	$2,423,000	$1,922,913	$1,632,440	$1,424,215	$1,209,314
Average sales per Wendy's restaurant:					
Company	869	754	706	702	665
Franchise	857	762	701	662	615
Systemwide	861	759	703	674	627
Financial position					
Total assets	$ 613,636	$ 506,713	$ 453,561	$ 375,469	$ 218,718
Property and equipment, net	498,593	377,911	327,442	281,008	174,235
Long-term obligations	105,005	86,671	103,070	97,956	42,418
Shareholders' equity	364,466	308,282	264,733	201,738	125,596
Shareholders' equity per share	6.63	5.67	4.87	3.95	2.80
Current ratio	.53	.65	.80	.58	.55
Ratio of debt to equity	29%	28%	39%	49%	34%
Ratio of debt to total capitalization	22%	22%	28%	33%	25%
Restaurant data (number open at year end)					
Domestic Wendy's:					
Company	1,014	887	802	734	502
Franchise	1,801	1,633	1,503	1,386	1,450
International Wendy's:					
Company	43	35	25	14	4
Franchise	134	118	100	95	78
Total Wendy's	2,992	2,673	2,430	2,229	2,034
Sisters:					
Company	26	21	17	10	4
Franchise	50	28	8	4	
Total Sisters	76	49	25	14	4
Other data					
Weighted average shares outstanding (000)	55,142	54,701	52,220	48,594	45,031
Number of shareholders at year end	31,000	25,000	20,000	19,000	18,000
Number of employees at year end	47,000	36,000	29,000	26,000	18,000

*Reflects the effects of a 4-for-3 stock split declared in February, 1985

International Expansion

In 1984, Wendy's continued to build on a base of international operations, with a focus on the long-term potentials of those markets. The top priority was one of improved penetration of existing franchised and company-operated markets. The firm opened eight company-operated restaurants in 1984, including four in Munich. The concentration of units in England, Spain, and West Germany enables Wendy's to advertise effectively in those company markets. Exhibit 34.3 provides a variety of data about Wendy's international operations.

Exhibit 34.3   Fact Sheet: International Development, 1984-1985

1984

☐ Signed development agreements in Taiwan, Korea, New Zealand, and the Netherlands

☐ Opened 24 new restaurants outside the United States: 8 company-operated restaurants and 16 franchise-operated restaurants.

☐ At year-end, 177 restaurants served markets outside the United States.

International Restaurants

Australia	9	Philippines	2
Bahamas	1	Puerto Rico	13
Canada	71	Singapore	1
Hong Kong	1	Spain	11
Italy	3	Switzerland	4
Japan	24	United Kingdom	13
Korea	1	West Germany	2
Malaysia	4	Total	177

1985

☐ April: Acquired Wendy's Restaurants of Canada, Inc., formerly a franchisee. Purchase included 71 existing restaurants.

☐ Opened five more restaurants in Canada, for a total of 76 at year-end.

Restaurants Opened YTD 1985

Australia	2	Puerto Rico	2
Canada	5	Spain	2
Italy	1	Taiwan[a]	4[a]
Japan	1	Netherlands[a]	1[a]
Korea	3	United Kingdom[a]	1[a]
New Zealand[a]	1	West Germany	2
Philippines	1	Total	26

[a]First Wendy's in the country.

1986

☐ Plan approximately 30 new restaurants in Canada as a result of an aggressive franchising program there.

☐ Plan approximately 33 new restaurants elsewhere outside United States.

☐ 1986 total: over 60 international restaurants.

Product Offering

Wendy's places primary emphasis upon consistent quality in all areas of food preparation and presentation. The firm uses 100 percent pure beef, which is delivered in bulk and pattied fresh every morning in each of its restaurants. The patties are cooked slowly to retain their natural juices and flavors. Whether the customer orders the quarter-pound single, the half-pound double, or the three-quarter-pound triple, the hamburger is served directly from the grill. By mixing and matching the nine available condiments, a Wendy's customer can specify one of 1,024 different ways to have his or her hamburger served. Hamburgers account for about 40 percent of all sales and of these approximately 65 percent are singles, 33 percent doubles, and 2 percent triples.

Chili is also on the menu. In addition to being popular with customers, this product serves a unique secondary purpose. To keep the hamburgers fresh for customers, no cooked patties are kept on the grill for more than four minutes. In order to eliminate this potential meat waste factor, hamburgers not served within the four-minute time period are steamed in a kettle and used for the next day's chili. French fries, Frosties, coffee, tea, milk, and soft drinks round out the basic menu. The Frosty, a Wendy's exclusive, is a thick, creamy blend of chocolate and vanilla (much like a very thick milkshake) served with a spoon.

Addition of Salad Bars

In 1979, seeking ways to improve customer traffic, Wendy's turned to a strategy that had worked fairly well for other food service organizations — an expanded menu. The company's desire to diffuse its dependence on beef products and yet not interfere with its extremely efficient in-store operating setup led to salad bars as the first menu addition.

Salads represented a logical extension of the menu by being compatible with Wendy's operational system while enhancing the company's adult image. The salad bar also widened Wendy's appeal to families and increased its lunch and dinner business. Salads also helped attract the health- and weight-conscious and smaller-appetite consumers, both of which are growing market segments.

Other Menu Items

Wendy's also began testing a breakfast menu in May 1979 that included omelette and scrambled egg platters, bacon, sausage, biscuits, hashbrown potatoes, and french toast. Breakfast is prepared primarily on the grill, with relatively minor additions to kitchen equipment, and is compatible with Wendy's system. It is designed to utilize the restaurants from 7:00 to 10:30 a.m., before the lunch day part begins. Breakfast represents an attractive opportunity to increase sales and utilization of the restaurants. Customers view Wendy's offering as a superior product. By late 1983 the breakfast menu, narrowed down to omelets, breakfast sandwiches, and french toast was offered in about 200 restaurants. Breakfast was implemented systemwide in June 1985.

Other significant developments evolving from changing strategies were three systemwide menu additions. First, a breaded filet of chicken breast sandwich, started in test in January 1980, was rolled out in most company and franchise stores. The second item was Wendy's Kids' Meal, a child-oriented meal. It consists of a smaller hamburger, smaller order of french fries, and a small Frosty or a small soft drink.

The third item was the Taco Salad, which incorporated several existing ingredients with no additional capital investment and minimal food preparation training: Wendy's uses lettuce, tomatoes, and cheese from the salad bar, plus the chili—the only new ingredients are taco chips and a special dressing. All of these product additions helped Wendy's sales volume by attracting new market segments and increasing the visit frequency of present customers. "Hot Stuffed" baked potatoes were introduced in late 1983 and became the most successful new product introduction to date. Exhibit 34.4 shows a television storyboard for Wendy's baked potatoes.

Testing of a full dinner menu began in 1982 in 29 Wendy's in Cincinnati. A successful dinner program has significant profit potential for the system. The test menu consists of five entrees, each competitively priced for family dinner business. Some of the dinner entrees are chopped beef and mushroom sauce, chicken parmesan, and country beef and gravy. The entrees include a side salad and dinner potatoes to provide a balanced meal. Entrees are based, for the most part, on products already in the restaurants. To date, customer feedback has been very favorable and testing is still in process.

Exhibit 34.4

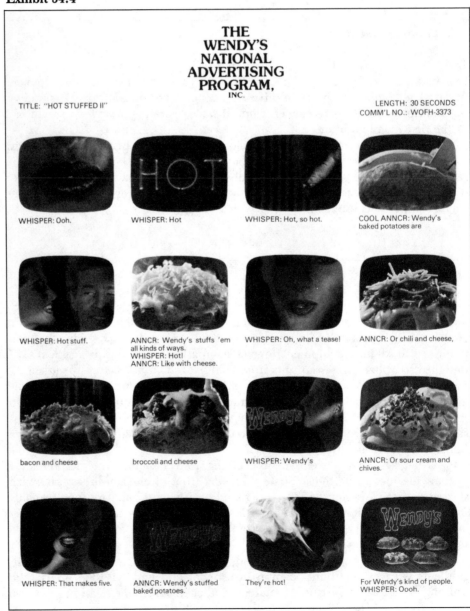

Advertising and Promotion

To utilize the media to build overall awareness of Wendy's among potential as well as current customers (particularly adults from 18 through 34 years of age) Wendy's titled its 1982 advertising campaign "WKOP" ("Wendy's Kind of People"). The campaign goals were to create excitement, to generate increased store traffic, and to get consumers to try Wendy's products. Exhibit 34.5 presents some of the basic objectives and strategies for this campaign.

Wendy's uses coupons as a promotional device to increase sales and to heighten awareness on a short-term basis (a phenomenon which the firm hopes will retain some residual benefit in return customers). Coupons provide an opportunity for consumers to save money and also may encourage them to try new menu items. Coupons used by Wendy's generally offer a free item with the purchase of another one, or two menu items at the regular price of one, or a discount off the regular price of an item. From test situations, Wendy's has found that coupons distributed through newspaper inserts and direct mail are most frequently redeemed and are most effective for Wendy's because of the greater selectivity of saturation per dollar spent.

Wendy's also focuses on cultivating a good relationship with the public in each store's market. Local restaurants are encouraged to take part in public activities and community programs. Examples of such participation include fund raising for local charities, crime prevention programs, and sponsoring civic and cultural events.

Exhibit 34.5   Media Objectives and Strategies for 1982

I.   **National/Local Media Objectives**

During this crucial introductory period and the fall hamburger emphasis period, we recommend that local market media planning be guided by the following objectives:

1.   To make strategic and creative use of media at the local level (and in conjuction with Wendy's national advertising) to generate both broad and rapid as well as sustained awareness of Wendy's new "You're Wendy's Kind of People" campaign.

2.   To utilize media to build overal awareness of Wendy's among potential as well as current customers — particularly adults 18–34 — to create excitement, generate increased store traffic trial of Wendy's products, and visit frequency during this important marketing period.

II.   **Media Strategy**

A.   Local Television

In order to execute these objectives, we are recommending that in all markets where affordable, spot television should serve as the primary local medium in support of this introduction. Spot television is recommended for several key reasons:

1.   Its proven ability to generate broad reach quickly is essential to the successful introduction of "You're Wendy's Kind of People" campaign.

continued

Exhibit 34.5   *continued*

2. Television provides an excellent opportunity to present the strong people- and food-oriented visual messages which characterize the new campaign.

3. When spot television is used selectively and in combination with the network television schedule, the investment in both media is optimized to build awareness.

B. Local Radio

Radio is recommended as an effective local complement to the local spot television activity (in most markets) and as the primary medium only in those markets where spot television is not affordable for several reasons:

1. Radio's strength as a frequency medium can be instrumental in reinforcing the new visual elements of Wendy's campaign as well as establishing in the consumer's mind the various musical executions of "Wendy's Kind of People."

2. Radio provides an excellent opportunity to deliver long-copy messages to the consumer.

3. Radio can be an effective reach-extender by reaching light TV viewers including the out-of-home audience, which can be an important target for our inside as well as Pick-Up Window business.

C. Local Newpapers

Where affordable, markets should also consider using newspapers, particularly where their use can be particularly effective in generating unusual interest or excitement in the new campaign. (See special "Teaser" campaign recommendations later.)

D. Other Media

While a number of other media options may be available locally, we would recommend that their local use in the introductory plan be governed by the following:

1. The relative speed with which the medium's messages accumulate against the consumer, i.e., the more quickly a medium's audience builds over time, the more suitable it may be for introductory use.

2. The relative cost of using the medium and the degree to which its use would divert dollars from our primary media, i.e., spot television and radio.

III. **National Advertising Plan**

A. New Campaign Introduction Flight

1. Prime-time Television

This network emphasis period will be supported on network television with 80 prime-time target (adults

continued

Exhibit 34.5 *continued*

> 18–34) GRPs per week for six consecutive weeks, highlighted by a Wendy's participation in the highest-rated program of the summer months—the Baseball All-Star game (and the pre-game program) on ABC, July 12, 1982. (A schedule of all Wendy's network appearances during the entire flight has been sent to all agencies.)

2. Network Radio

> For six consecutive weekends, Wendy's will deliver 20 target GRPs/week through its ¼ sponsorship of Mutual's Dick Clark National Music Survey.

B. Hamburger Emphasis Period

1. Prime-time Television

> This network emphasis period will be supported with 100 Prime-Time Target GRPs per week for each week of this six-week flight.

2. Network Radio

> During this six-week flight, Wendy's will again deliver 20 Target points per week via Mutual's Dick Clark National Music Survey.

"Where's the Beef?"

Since 1982, the major hamburger fast-service chains have been fighting what the media dubbed the "Burger Wars." Wendy's, the world's third-largest hamburger chain, is outspent in advertising eight to one by its major competitors, McDonald's and Burger King. Accordingly, the company has been compelled to communicate using creative treatments and media extension techniques that break through the clutter and dramatize product benefits in a unique, often humorous and exaggerated manner.

At the start of 1984, when the Burger Wars began anew, the company again found itself in this position. McDonald's attacked with 39-cent hamburgers. Burger King came out swinging with its "flame-broiling versus frying" campaign. At the same time, research showed that consumers perceived McDonald's and Burger King's hamburgers to be larger, although in reality Wendy's Single contains more beef.

Seizing its size advantage, Wendy's created the "Where's the Beef?" campaign, spots for which first aired January 9, 1984. Its goal was to create consumer awareness of its larger-size hamburger and leverage a comparatively small ad budget to extend the reach and frequency of the ad message beyond purchased media impressions. In other words, use public relations to do more with less: Bring the advertising theme into the American vernacular, create awareness of Wendy's larger hamburger, and underscore the inherent value of all Wendy's menu items.

Objectives

Wendy's sought a unified marketing and public relations plan to create excitement and awareness for the campaign and the slogan. The public relations objectives for the campaign became to (1) build national and local media and consumer awareness and involvement in the campaign by making the slogan a news item and (2) persuade consumers that Wendy's offers them more beef in its hamburgers than other major competitors.

Once the initial objectives were achieved and "Where's the Beef?" took America by storm, Wendy's produced a sequel to satisfy the public's demand. Public relations objectives continued to focus efforts on extending the widespread awareness and impact of "Where's the Beef?"

Then, after a five-month leave of absence from the airwaves, "Where's the Beef?" was revived with a third campaign. Public relations activities paved the way for a triumphant return. The company added two elements — the promotion of licensed "Where's the Beef?" products and an NFL "Where's the Beef?" Monday Night Football sweepstakes. Public relations plans supported these elements, as well. Exhibit 34.6 provides some additional information about this campaign and its results. A television storyboard for one of the later commercials is shown in Exhibit 34.7.

Exhibit 34.6   Information on "Where's the Beef?" Campaign

Execution (Techniques and Materials)

Imagine receiving a plain box, marked "Perishable — Open Immediately!" that is filled with a large fluffy sesame seed bun. That is how the media first learned about "Where's the Beef?" The press materials, not the beef, were tucked between the 12-inch buns, along with a large magnifying glass.

While the teaser press kit was the key to gain media support, Wendy's created a fictional character and story to generate additional awareness. The character, Sheerluck Homes, helped media and customers solve "The Case of the Missing Beef" in key major markets.

Once the commercial ran, Wendy's focused efforts on maximizing exposure by using the slogan and the commercial's star, Clara Peller. Wendy's seized an opportunity for major news coverage with the filming of the second commercial at the Chicago studio of Director Joe Sedelmaier. Press were invited to view the last day of filming and to interview Clara and Wendy's spokespeople. One crew, trying for an exclusive, camped outside Sedelmaier's door for seven hours the previous day. Clara was ushered out a back entrance into a waiting car. On the evening news, the station covered the fact that its reporter had been duped by Wendy's "Where's the Beef?" people.

Public relations efforts focused heaviy on national placements. Because of the popularity of Clara's photo, placed from the commercial's filming, AP had to run it three times to meet requests from its member newspapers. *Newsweek* ran an exclusive on its "Newsmakers" page. Subsequent photos of Clara with Muhammed Ali, with a "Where's the Beef?" cartoon caption, up to her waist in buns, and in front of the 1949 DeSoto used in the third commercial were placed with the wire services and national publications.

Video news releases and interviews with major national shows were arranged through careful planning. The result was coverage on

continued

Exhibit 34.6   *continued*

news shows nationwide and interviews for Clara with scores of television hosts. Syndicated radio releases carried still more coverage.

Media events heralded more activity when "Where's the Beef?" returned, including the filming of the third campaign, Clara's Nashville recording debut as the "Where's the Beef?" record star, and the kickoff of the NFL Monday Night Football promotion.

Publicity manuals with how-to instructions and locally adaptable materials were distributed to the entire Wendy's system for each effort. These activities were designed to expand the national plan to the grassroots level. Licensees were kept informed through biweekly "Where's the Beef?" updates about the merchandising effort.

Results/Measurements

"Where's the Beef?" did more to raise Wendy's awareness and market share, and increase Wendy's sales and profit value, than any campaign in the company's history. Sales for 1984 increased 26 percent to $2.4 billion, compared with 1983 sales of $1.9 billion. Profits also rose 24 percent over 1983. Wendy's market share in the restaurant sandwich category increased 20 percent during the campaign's first four months, while restaurant name awareness rose 48 percent during the year. These results were achieved despite the company's being outspent by its major competitors.

Publicity efforts yielded more than 3.6 billion consumer impressions, which means each American was exposed to media coverage 16 times. The campaign accumulated more than 26,000 press clippings, more than 9,000 radio news stories and more than 1,200 television news stories. The campaign also made news throughout Europe and the Far East.

The commercial garnered three Clio Awards and was named the top commercial of 1984 by Video Storyboard Tests, Inc.

"Fresh" Campaign Overview

Based on Wendy's most extensive research ever, which determined that five out of the top ten fast-service attributes most valued by consumers had to do with freshness, Wendy's developed the campaign line, "Choose Fresh. Choose Wendy's." in 1985. After advertising freshness for over 16 years, Wendy's decided to put a more vigorous effort behind letting consumers know about its "unfair competitive advantage." More than 1,200 consumers (ages 18–49) were interviewed on their expectations of fast-service restaurants. Five of the top ten points included:

□   Food served piping hot
□   Food not precooked or reheated
□   Food prepared the way I like it
□   Food is fresh
□   Food prepared with great care

Wendy's ranked significantly higher on these points. The top three hamburger chains rated similarly on the still-important categories of "fast, friendly service," "reasonable prices," and "clean, comfortable environment."

Exhibit 34.7

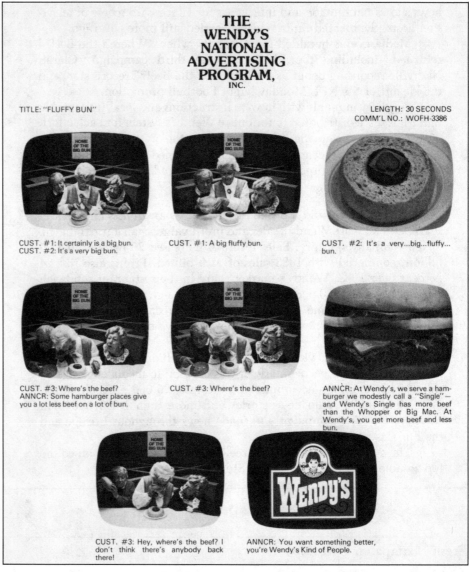

THE WENDY'S NATIONAL ADVERTISING PROGRAM, INC.

TITLE: "FLUFFY BUN"

LENGTH: 30 SECONDS
COMM'L NO.: WOFH-3386

CUST. #1: It certainly is a big bun.
CUST. #2: It's a very big bun.

CUST. #1: A big fluffy bun.

CUST. #2: It's a very...big...fluffy...bun.

CUST. #3: Where's the beef?
ANNCR: Some hamburger places give you a lot less beef on a lot of bun.

CUST. #3: Where's the beef?

ANNCR: At Wendy's, we serve a hamburger we modestly call a "Single"— and Wendy's Single has more beef than the Whopper or Big Mac. At Wendy's, you get more beef and less bun.

CUST. #3: Hey, where's the beef? I don't think there's anybody back there!

ANNCR: You want something better, you're Wendy's Kind of People.

Two television commercials created for this campaign include "Lamps," (Exhibit 34.8) a spot contrasting Wendy's freshly prepared salads, toppings, and sandwiches with prepackaged varieties at those "other" hamburger restaurants, and "Birthday", which questions the uncertain age of hamburgers at "other" restaurants (Exhibit 34.9).

Two additional spots were developed. "Onions" tells the story of a man faced with a choice of "rehydrated" onions at the "other" hamburger restaurant, or fresh onions at Wendy's. "Express" laments the poor local hamburger, which stops before reaching its destination, the holding bin. The Wendy's Express, on the other hand, tells the story of speed.

A 30-second television advertisement aimed at blacks was called "The Will." It depicted a nephew who lost out on an inheritance because he took his uncle to restaurants that made hamburgers in advance and then put them in plastic boxes under heat lamps. Two Hispanic-oriented spots carried through with Wendy's theme of offering freshly prepared sandwiches that are not made from frozen beef or prepackaged and held under heat lamps. Both starred Don Cucufato, who tested well with Wendy's consumers and proved to be an effective spokesperson for Hispanic consumers.

Exhibit 34.8

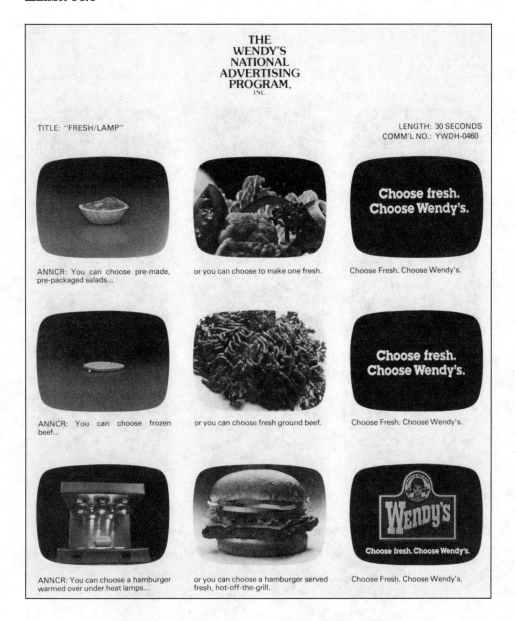

National Tracking Study

The Wendy's National Tracking Study is an on-going probability-sampling telephone survey of U. S. consumers. Exhibit 34.10 presents some selected results from the first quarter, 1985 study. Approximately 1,500 interviews are conducted each quarter among consumers aged 16–70 who have visited a restaurant serving mainly hamburgers at least once in the past month. The major objectives of the study are to:

- Define Wendy's market position relative to major competition.
- Monitor changes in the market position resulting from Wendy's advertising and sales promotion programs, competitive activity, economic conditions, etc.
- Detect and/or anticipate potential problem and opportunity areas.

Exhibit 34.9

Exhibit 34.10   Selected Results from Wendy's National Tracking Study (First Quarter, 1985)

Marketing Activity

□   Wendy's emphasized baked potatoes on network television during the first quarter of 1985 (1/7–2/3). This was followed by a video coupon in 85 percent of company markets (2/7–2/24) and a network television "Fresh Emphasis" (2/25–4/14). Wendy's emphasized the chicken sandwich during late fourth quarter of 1984 (11/19–12/23).

□   During the first quarter, the major competitive activities included:
—McDonald's: Double cheeseburger, "Hot Hand Warmin'," Filet-O-Fish emphasis, breakfast, 99¢ Big Mac
—Burger King: Croissanwich (2:1 preference over Egg McMuffin), 39¢ Hamburgers, 49¢ Cheeseburgers, 99¢ Whoppers
—Hardee's: Fisherman's Filet, Roast Beef Combo Meal

Unaided Advertising Awareness

| | | | | Point Change (percent) | |
| | | | | 1st Qtr. '85 vs. 4th Qtr. '84 | 1st Qtr. '85 vs. 1st Qtr. '84 |
	1st Qtr. '84	4th Qtr. '84	1st Qtr. '85		
Wendy's	45.9%	50.2%	44.3%	−5.9	−1.6
Burger King	60.9	52.7	52.2	−0.5	−8.7
McDonald's	68.3	66.8	69.9	+3.1	+1.6
Hardee's	11.7	12.6	13.5	+0.9	+1.8

| | | | | Point Change (percent) | |
| | | | | 1st Qtr. '85 vs. 4th Qtr. '84 | 1st Qtr. '85 vs. 1st Qtr. '84 |
	1st Qtr. '84	4th Qtr. '84	1st Qtr. '85		
"Where's the Beef?"	71.2%	84.8%	83.0%	−1.8	+11.8
"You Want Something Better, You're Wendy's Kind of People"	45.1	43.8	37.0	−6.8	−8.1
"Aren't You Hungry for Burger King now?"	77.3	77.2	77.1	−0.1	−0.2
"It's a Good Time for the Great Taste at McDonald's"	N.A.	65.3	74.5	+9.2	N.A.
"It's all Here at Hardee's"	N.A.	23.0	27.3	+4.3	N.A.

| | | | | Point Change (percent) | |
| | | | | 1st Qtr. '85 vs. 4th Qtr. '84 | 1st Qtr. '85 vs. 1st Qtr. '84 |
	1st Qtr. '84	4th Qtr. '84	1st Qtr. '85		
Number of interviews	1,541	1,537	1,497		
Breakfast	18.4%	34.2%	46.7%	+12.5	+28.3
Chicken sandwich	43.5	48.0	56.5	+8.5	+13.0
Hot stuffed baked potatoes	70.5	75.5	82.0	+6.5	+11.5

Exhibit 34.10   *continued*

Ever Tried Wendy's Products (Among Total Customers)

	1st Qtr. '84	4th Qtr. '84	1st Qtr. '85	Point Change (percent)	
				1st Qtr. '85 vs. 4th Qtr. '84	1st Qtr. '85 vs. 1st Qtr. '84
Number of interviews	1,541	1,537	1,497		
Single hamburgers	N.A.	72.2%	75.7%	+3.5	N.A.
Chicken sandwich	18.0	21.5	23.4	+1.9	+ 5.4
Frosty	48.2	47.4	49.0	+1.6	+ 0.8
Breakfast	2.7	6.6	8.0	+1.4	+ 5.3
Apple dumplings	N.A.	7.8	9.0	+1.2	N.A.
Hot stuffed baked potatoes	25.2	34.7	35.8	+1.1	+10.6

Reasons for Going/Not Going to Wendy's

☐   Food quality was cited most often (52.1 percent) during the first quarter of 1985 as the main reason for going to Wendy's. This was followed by convenience (30.4 percent).

☐   Convenience was also cited most often (49.9 percent) as the main reason for not going to Wendy's more often. Cost was mentioned second most frequently (9.7 percent).

Ten Most Important Attributes
(10 = highest importance; 1 = lowest importance)

Rank	Attribute	Importance Rating
1	Hamburgers served fresh	9.18
2	Quality of food	9.08
3	Clean dining room	9.03
4	Fresh food	8.96
5	Taste of hamburgers	8.88
6	Food piping hot	8.86
7	Hamburgers served hot off the grill	8.86
8	Value for the money	8.57
9	Accuracy of order inside	8.53
10	Friendly service	8.53

Ratings on Ten Most Important Attributes (10 = Excellent; 1 = Poor)

Importance Rank	Attribute	Attribute Ratings		
		Wendy's	Burger King	McDonald's
1	Hamburgers served fresh	8.66*	8.09	7.40
2	Quality of food	8.17*	7.73	7.23
3	Clean dining room	8.51	8.19	8.29
4	Fresh food	8.34*	7.82	7.41
5	Taste of hamburgers	8.07*	7.76	6.82
6	Food piping hot	8.57*	8.00	7.70
7	Hamburgers served hot off the grill	8.51*	7.91	6.96
8	Value for the money	7.91	7.85	7.81
9	Accuracy of order inside	8.73*	8.49	8.33
10	Friendly service	8.25*	8.01	8.01

* = Wendy's significantly preferred over competition.   ***continued***

Exhibit 34.10   *continued*

Ratings on Other Attributes (10 = Excellent; 1 = Poor)

Importance Rank	Attribute	Attribute Ratings		
		Wendy's	Burger King	McDonald's
11	Clean restrooms	8.28*	8.05	8.05
12	Food not precooked or reheated	8.20*	7.62	7.03
13	Convenient location	7.07**	7.55	8.53
14	Accuracy of drive-through window	8.36	8.19	8.01
15	Order speed inside restaurant	8.27*	7.81	7.98
16	Taste of french fries	7.57†	7.46	8.19
17	Drive-through order speed	7.59	7.63	7.26
18	Appealing menu selection	8.19*	7.68	7.38
19	Overall menu prices	7.29**	7.68	8.11
20	Dining atmosphere	8.13*	7.61	7.66
21	Menu variety	8.14*	7.59	7.50
22	Nutritional food	7.94*	7.40	6.89
23	Roomy seating accommodations	7.93**	8.21	8.27
24	Suitable facilities for dining with children	7.75**	8.10	8.78
25	Hamburgers that are flame broiled	N.A.	N.A.	N.A.
26	Quality of salad bar	8.41*	7.50	N.A.
27	Price specials or discounts	6.45**	7.61	7.23
28	Restaurant appealing to children	6.77**	7.52	9.11
29	Community involvement	7.04	7.12	8.33

* = Wendy's significantly more acceptable than both competitors

** = Wendy's significantly less acceptable than both competitors

† = Wendy's significantly less acceptable than McDonald's, but comparable to Burger King

Agriplex: The Future of Agrimarketing

Case 35

Agribusiness: The Industry

One out of every five workers in the United States is employed in agriculture—from growing to selling at market. Farming alone employs 4.4 million on 2.8 million farms. The agricultural industry has assets of $671 billion. Cash receipts were $110 billion in 1978 and have grown at 10 to 15 percent per year since then.

Worldwide, 46 percent of the economically active population is involved in agricultural production. The agricultural economy of the world totals $14.8 trillion.

The real basis for agricultural productivity is cheap, abundant energy. Marketing has been a big cost component in agriculture.

For the first time, the world's agribuyers and agrisellers will be coming together in one spectacular 7 million-square-foot trade center. It's Agriplex, an $800 million project that showcases a complete range of agricultural goods and services.

Form its huge exhibition facility to permanent manufacturers' displays to hotel and meeting facilities, Agriplex is designed to create a uniquely favorable sales and business environment. It will do this by making product comparison easier for the customer, and by bringing real prospects directly to the manufacturers.

Purpose of Agriplex

Agriplex is not a luxury—it is a necessity in an industry progressing as rapidly as world agriculture. In just 50 years, the world population will double and every year more and more land is given up to development, making the need to squeeze every ounce of food out of each acre even more critical than it is today.

As inefficiency and inflation continue to eat into profits, customers will become more and more selective in their purchases. They will have less time available to make them. Agriplex gives agribusinesspeople one place to compare products, gather information from experts, and make intelligent buying decisions.

Internationally, the implications are even greater. Agriplex gives international customers the unique opportunity to evaluate state-of-the-art technology in every agribusiness area. For instance, a foreign customer setting up a new livestock operation will find everything he needs under one roof—from breeds to buildings to feed, storage, heating, and cooling—even the computers and software to manage the whole operation. According to the U. S. Department of Commerce, it takes an average of 25 months from when a country makes the decision

Source: The material in this case has been extracted from promotional and descriptive brochures provided by the organization.

to start an industry to when the product is available for consumption. By providing a central location where potential buyers can review at one site most of the components needed to improve, increase, or develop productivity in a previously unexplored area, the length of the cycle from decision to product will be reduced 9–11 months.

Of course, all these benefits to the customer are also benefits to the manufacturer, because they mean that Agriplex will attract serious prospects; the kind that, in today's domestic economy, would cost hundreds of dollars to reach with a sales call. The same kind of contact with international prospects could cost thousands of dollars.

The hosting of a continuous variety of agricultural trade association events guarantees a cross section of prequalified buyers who are in regular attendance at Agriplex. This environment delivers prequalified customers to the manufactureres and suppliers at a direct sales call cost far less than presently being incurred within the industry. This same concept has been the key to the success of the various merchandise marts throughout the world.

Agriplex is a forum for manufacturers to combine their most qualified technical and marketing talents to promote products — and respond to inquiries from qualified prospective customers. Since Agriplex combines the attractions of an agribusiness mart with complete convention and exhibition facilities, it's the logical location for successful trade association events.

This dynamic project is being developed in one of the most vibrant, appealing, and accessible areas in the world, Orlando, Florida. Orlando is the world's number one destination spot, home of Walt Disney World and Epcot Center which draw more than 22 million national and international visitors a year. Most importantly, Orlando enjoys a temperate year-round climate, a necessity for a year-round facility. Beautiful weather, travel convenience, hotel accommodations, family attractions . . . they all combine to make Orlando the perfect location for Agriplex.

Inside Agriplex

Agriplex is 7 million square feet of flexibility and advanced design. Latest building systems technology will be implemented to combine maximum tenant and visitor comfort with operating efficiency. Exhibit 35.1 shows an artist's rendition of the project while Exhibit 35.2 provides a summary description of Agriplex.

A small "city" in itself, Agriplex will be equipped with its own trasportation system, hotels, offices, and entertainment center, all supporting the heart of Agriplex — its permanent display mart and its exhibition center. Visitors to the permanent display mart will enter through a half-mile, S-shaped enclosed central mall, 250 feet wide, six stories high, and punctuated by four magnificent atrium areas. A full range of agriproducts and services will be showcased in this 3 million-square-foot mart.

The 900,000 (ultimately 1.8 million) square-foot Exhibition Center is capable of housing agribusiness exhibits of every conceivable type and size. In fact, its unique design permits several trade shows and conventions to be effectively run at the same time — without interruption. A full complement of support facilities is designed to make Agriplex run like a well-oiled machine. An elevated monorail system, for example, will quickly move people from landscaped parking areas to key points inside the complex.

Located on a lake's edge, Agriplex's internationally-oriented facilities will provide tenants and visitors with all essential services, including auditoriums with combined seating for up to 5,000. An incredible array of entertainment options is also available — outstanding hotels, a wide variety of fine restaurants, shops and boutiques, theaters, and many family-oriented recreational activities.

Exhibit 35.1   Artist's Rendition of Agriplex

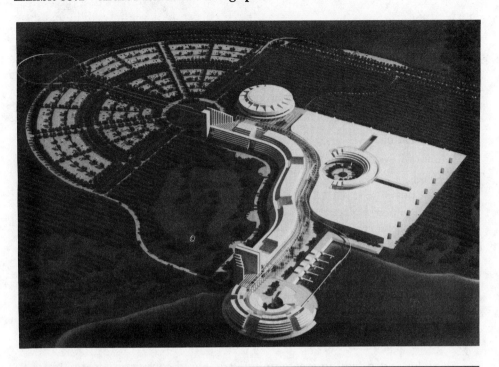

Exhibit 35.2   Data Description of Agriplex

Type of Development:
International agribusiness trade mart showcasing farm machinery and equipment, horticulture, animal husbandry, and other agricultural products and services.

Location:
Orlando, Florida. Eight miles north of Walt Disney World and EPCOT. Ten miles northwest of new Orlando Airport and two miles north of proposed MCA Universal City.

Size:
Agriplex will utilize 400 acres within a 1,600 acre tract. Total building area will cover more than 7 million square feet.

Features:

Merchanidse Mart/Mall	3 million square feet of permanent display area, 250 feet wide, six stories high, and punctuated by four magnificent atrium areas. Visitors to the permanent display mart will enter through a half-mile S-shaped enclosed central mall.
Exhibit Hall	1.8 million square feet
Arena	Total seating capacity 8,000 to 10,000 (as determined by market demand)

continued

Exhibit 35.2 *continued*

Three Amphitheaters	Total seating capacity 1,500 to 5,000 (as determined by market demand)
Retail/Commercial	100,000 square feet
Office & Marketing Support Facilities	500,000 square feet
Parking	6,000 cars and transit vehicles
Three Hotels	2,200 Rooms
Monorail System/People Mover	Elevated to transport visitors to all Agriplex facilities
Amenities	18-hole championship golf course, tennis courts, and small nonpower boat marina included within complex
Utilities	Agriplex will be totally self-sufficient, with its own utilities distribution system, electrical cogeneration plant, wastewater treatment, fire, and security protection. In all these areas, including energy management, the accent is on advanced technology.

Agriplex is designed to create unique trade and consumer benefits by bringing qualified national and international agribuyers and agrisellers to a trade center where both permanent and temporary tenants will present their products through exhibits, meetings, forums, and trade shows. The complex will showcase a complete range of agricultural goods, service, and technology on a scale heretofore unavailable to the international agricultural industry.

Near the entrance to Agriplex, an 8,000 seat arena will be used to host a variety of agriculture-related activities from rodeos and tractor pulls to auctions and livestock shows. Agriplex will be totally self-sufficient, with its own utilities distribution system, waste disposal, fire, and security protection. In all these areas, including energy management, the accent is on advanced technology. Exhibit 35.3 shows part of a brochure aimed at agrimarketers.

Marketing Facilities

Agriplex's potential market is identified as the entire food chain, from growers, distributors, processors, and manufacturers to associations who will hold their meetings at Agriplex and companies who sell agriculturally related products from seed to fences, from fertilizer to computerized milking machines, and export trading companies. Also included are countries selling agricultural information, who will interface with countries who are buying information.

Exhibit 35.3   Page from Promotional Brochure Aimed at Agrimarketers

The Future Begins Now

For the agribusiness executive, that means making the decisions now that will best benefit your marketing effort in the next decade — and the next century.

One of them is a commitment to AGRIPLEX. Because it's a local extension of present marketing methods.

AGRIPLEX will create an international agribusiness forum, solving export and international financing problems. And giving international customers one place to evaluate the full range of state-of-the-art agricultural technology. Domestically, it helps solve the "which trade shows should we sink our money into" dilemma. Manufacturers can now be much more selective, since AGRIPLEX gives them the opportunity to reach more and better-qualified customers than any other single marketing medium.

And since AGRIPLEX primarily plays a decision-prompting role, it supports rather than disrupts a company's marketing network.

Companies displaying in the AGRIPLEX permanent mart will also have the benefit of being in very good company — alongside the most aggressive, forward-thinking agribusinesses in the world.

Make the decision now to take part in a project that will be an agrimarketing landmark, the beginning of a whole new efficient method of doing business both domestically and internationally.

Commit now, plan to join the most progressive companies and trade organizations in a venture that will create a new dimension in world agribusiness.

Think about it. AGRIPLEX really *is* the future of agrimarketing. Make sure you're part of that future.

Everything about Agriplex is carefully planned to create the best possible marketing environment. Permanent mart residents should stand to benefit the most from the 5,000 agribusiness buyers expected to visit the center each day, since they will be working through a unique and efficient sales medium.

Each permanent showroom in the six-story mart area will be designed to tenant specifications. Virtually any size and shape is available, to help suppliers best highlight their products and competitive advantages. Because these showrooms are permanent, they will not have that "quickly assembled" look. They will enhance the quality image of the companies, as well as their products. They will be manned by marketing and technical experts fully equipped to answer customer questions, and present products and services in their most favorable light.

With the buyers that the mart itself attracts, plus the constant flow of visitors from Agriplex trade shows and conventions, attendance is expected to top 1.5 million each year. For convenient access, showrooms will be grouped in general product and service categories, including machinery and equipment, agronomy, livestock science, and support services. This allows a company to dramatize its competitive advantages by presenting them in an environment where a customer can actually compare with alternatives.

Agriplex adds another dimension to agribusiness marketing with its educational facilities. Multimedia auditoriums and meeting rooms are available to tenants for customer education and sales presentations. On the upper levels of the mart area, 500,000 square feet of office space will be occupied by both tenant offices and support groups such as insurance, finance, and education. Foreign trade missions and international banking representatives will be on the spot to cut export red tape—and help make international selling and financing as easy as domestic.

Alternative office space will also be available to tenants in spearate buildings adjacent to the markt. In addition, diversified agriculture in the fertile central Florida region provides ample opportunity for actual product demonstration. Both tenants and mart visitors can easily take advantage of the luxury hotels at each end of Agriplex. Geared toward making business a pleasure, these hotels feature hospitality rooms, suites, conference areas, specialty restaurants, and boutiques. All these facilities and services are backed by the total commitment of Agriplex management. That means tenants' needs will be quickly and professionally met. It also means Agriplex will provide a consistent worldwide marketing effort to solicit prequalified agribuyers—including dealers, various trade associations, and national and international buyer groups seeking agribusiness products.

Meeting Facilities

Agriplex will be the world's largest and busiest agribusiness forum, making it a natural environment for trade shows and conventions. Association executives and meeting planners will find that Agriplex is equipped to handle virtually all of their needs. It has the most sophisticated facilities and services anywhere. With the adjacent permanent mart displays and central Florida's recreational appeal, it has the ability to attract bigger crowds. With its outstanding support facilities, it can accommodate them without confusion or inconvenience.

The Exhibition Center is designed to house exhibits of any shape or size, and still allow trade show traffic to flow quickly and comfortably. Show size is no problem—in fact, the center is large enough to easily handle several conventions and shows simultaneously. That means several associations from related industries can now meet at the same time, with each show benefiting from the other. Surrounding support facilities are just as accommodating as the Exhibition Center. The entrance area to the Center is an open-air court and surge space, designed for large assemblies. Inside, a multimedia auditorium seats 850, and will be used for everything from lectures to films to symposiums. It is just one aspect of a total audio-visual capability, including state-of-the-art satellite telecommunications. This sophisticated technology allows trade show groups to project and record show activities, as well as communicate to any point in Agriplex—or around the world.

A flexible group of meeting, conference, and office facilities is available to fill any association need—and these facilities are located next to the Exhibition Center. A professional staff is available to help engineer the total operation of any show, convention, or meeting. From determining the number of exhibit spaces, meeting rooms, and offices needed, to the type of food service, to light and sound systems, even display or decorating services—all will be expertly and efficiently arranged. Exhibit 35.4 shows part of a brochure aimed at meeting planners.

Exhibit 35.4   Page from Promotional Brochure Aimed at Meeting Planners

The Future Begins Now

For the trade association executive or meeting planner, it means choosing the best-equipped, and most profitable environment for your organization's meetings.

AGRIPLEX is that environment. With exhibit space to spare, education facilities, hotels, recreation, professional management—AGRIPLEX has all the ingredients that insure a smooth-running show or meeting. Including the exciting features of a one-of-a-kind agribusiness mart.

Make the decision now to take part in a project that will be an agrimarketing landmark, the beginning of a whole new efficient method of doing business—both domestically and internationally.

Commit now, plan to join the most progressive companies and trade organizations in a venture that will create a vigorous new dimension in world agribusiness.

Think about it. AGRIPLEX really *is* the future of agrimarketing. Make sure your organization is part of that future.

Additional Information

The following information has been provided by Charles Brennan, president of Agriplex, through various interviews with the media:

- Agriplex is positioned to serve emerging marketing needs. It is not a panacea, but rather part of the solution that brings about more efficient marketing.
- Agriplex is on the cutting edge of the marketing evolution that will take place in world agribusiness.
- The price for renting permanent exhibit space at Agriplex will range from $65 to $120 per square foot per year.
- It costs a manufacturer from $150 to $200 (based on 1981 data) to make an industrial sales call. We are going to deliver that same prequalified call to the manufacturer's door for $20 to $30.
- It looks like there are 400 national agricultural associations, with a membership based of 14 million people. There are probably another 2,000 state and regional associations. In addition, there are international associations. Agriplex expects to have a potential customer base of associations somewhere between 3,000 and 5,000 worldwide.
- If 10 percent of the one million visitors to Agriplex each year were potential tractor customers, those 100,000 prequalified customers would represent a fixed cost to a tractor exhibitor of $9 apiece. That is based on a permanent exhibit of 10,000 square feet at a typical Agriplex rental rate of $90 a foot.

Conversations with Brennan

When members of the Georgia Farm Equipment Dealers Association (GFEDA) got their chance to examine plans for Agriplex, one of the first questions put to President Charles Brennan was, "Can a farmer visiting Orlando purchase a tractor while at Agriplex and eliminate the local dealer in the farmer's home town?" Brennan replied,

No, Agriplex is intended to be a facility where manufacturers present their products in an ultimate marketing environment in a "support" role to the local dealer network. Agribusinessmen depend a great deal on the availability and quality of service given by their local dealer when purchasing equipment and this element of the buyer's decision process is not expected to change.

A GFEDA member asked, "How is Agriplex going to help me, a local dealer, sell more tractors?" Brennan answered,

Manufacturers will utilize direct product displays and audio/visual presentations to showcase the complete line of products available through their networks. Few, if any, dealers have the financial resources to maintain a complete inventory of products available from the manufactureres they represent. It is anticipated that local dealers will encourage their respective customers to visit the manufacturer displays at Agriplex to obtain a more comprehensive understanding of existing and future products available from their manufacturers.

A member of the GFEDA asked, "Will a manufacturer need to increase the selling price of his product to cover the increased costs resulting from a showroom staffed with professional marketing personnel at Agriplex?" Brennan replied,

No, Agriplex is attractive to manufacturers because of the efficiency realized in the unit cost of each marketing or sales contact. The cost of making an industrial sales call has risen sharply in recent years to about $200. A trade show delivers a prequalified customer to an exhibitor for about $55 and that figure will be substantially less through Agriplex. It's more cost effective to display in a market center than in a show which will last only a week . . . and we know the trade show is more cost effective than making direct sales calls.

And with either a trade show or a trade mart, the seller has psychology on his side. The client has come to you. It is the reverse of you going to the client, and psychologically it is far more effective.

Developing Nations

Many of the developing nations have placed increased emphasis on improving their agricultural infrastructure. These countries have been the primary focus of our current activities.

The appeal of Agriplex to developing nations is that it will offer the unique opportunity to monitor food production technology available in the world markets.

I have recently returned from my second trip to the People's Republic of China where discussions are continuing toward formalizing China's central and provincial governments' participation at Agriplex. Such a country's presence within the facility will benefit U. S. agriculturists by providing access to new markets.

We certainly do not portray Agriplex to be the ultimate solution to agriculture's global problems, however, it will provide a forum to present technological progress.

Exportation

The world will always be faced with disasters (such as the Ethiopian famine brought about by drought) that create the need for food relief programs. We are not criticizing the current relief efforts in Ethiopia, but recognize the underlying problem to be the existence of a type government which does not allow a free enterprise system to operate in the farming community.

The Soviet Union, prior to the Bolshevik Revolution, was the world's leading exporter of grains. Since the communist system has taken over, the Soviet Union has now become a major importer of grains, beef, and pork. Although there will continue to be the demand for exporting commodities well on into the next century, the real opportunity is the exportation of agriculture systems, technology, and know-how.

Agriplex is intended to be a platform to showcase American and Western agriculture in a free-market environment. There is a need to increase both the scale and effectiveness of international programs to increase food production, especially in third-world countries.

People's Republic of China

China is planning to make major capital expenditures in future years for agricultural infrastructure to incrase domestic food production. Agriplex has the potential to become a primary purchasing point for these capital expenditures.

The Agriplex offers a unique opportunity to monitor food production technology available in the world markets. Jointly, we will establish an exchange program where selected farmers from China will be trained in the United States in order to elevate them to their next level of production capability.

Through the Agriplex exchange program, a production and technology transfer will be arranged and a working relationship will be established with areas in the United States that have similar climatic conditions to those in the People's Republic of China.

CompuServe:
Videotex Services

CompuServe, a wholly owned subsidiary of H & R Block, is a major computer services company based in Columbus, Ohio. The company operates large mainframe computers and a growing communications network that covers over 150 cities in the United States and Canada.

CompuServe has served both government and industry since 1969 and has earned an enviable reputation for reliability and performance in providing remote computing and information services. In addition, the company is a leading supplier of electronic mail to large corporations and government agencies and recently announced entry into the value-added network business. CompuServe now sells the use of that network to large corporations that wish to connect their own terminals.

Having attained a leading position in the computer services industry by the late 1970s, CompuServe turned its attention and expertise to personal computing services. By combining its history of reliability and innovation with its desire to utilize off-peak hours of computer power, the company created the Consumer Information Service (CIS), an information utility designed for use by the hobbyist, the professional, and the home computer user.

CIS Availability and Pricing

The Consumer Information Service is available to persons who own or have access to a personal computer or terminal. CIS is sold in computer stores across the United States and in Canada and is also available through various manufacturers of computer software and equipment. Exhibit 36.1 indicates some of the systems and requirements for accessing the CompuServe Information Service. A new CIS customer can purchase a subscription for $39.95, which includes a special access number, a secret password, the CIS User's Guide, and $25 usage credit. Also included with the service is a free subscription to *Online Today* magazine, a monthly CompuServe publication that keeps the user up to date on videotex industry trends, and a monthly newsletter that lists the latest innovations and additions to the service. Users can access CIS for $6.25 (plus a 25¢ communications charge) per standard hour (6 p.m.–5 a.m.) and $12.50 per prime-time hour at the 300 baud rate. At the faster speed of 1,200 baud, rates are $12.50 for standard and $15.00 per hour for prime time. Additional charges may be incurred if certain premium-priced products are used.

The CIS computer and common carrier networks provide access to the service through a local telephone call in over 300 cities in the United States and Canada. Users in cities not reached by CompuServe may be able to access CIS through the TYMNET system, a common carrier network, for an additional $2.00/hour communication surcharge.

By successfully integrating the use of microcomputers with large data processing mainframe computers, the firm has rapidly established a leadership

Exhibit 36.1   Selected Systems and Requirements for Accessing the CompuServe
Information Service

Equipment, Compatibility and Requirements

The following list of computers, data terminals, communication hardware and communication software represent a few of the many different devices that will allow you to access the CompuServe Information Service.

Personal Computer/Data Terminal	Communication Hardware/ Software Necessary
APPLE II and II Plus	Micromodem II® or a modem with a communications card, and terminal software.
APPLE III	Modem and terminal software.
ATARI 400 and 800	Interface module, modem and Telelink I.
COMMODORE PET	IEEE interface module, modem and terminal software.
COMMODORE VIC	VICMODEM and terminal software.
COMMODORE 64	VICMODEM and terminal software.
EXIDY Sorcerer	Modem and terminal software.
HEATH/ZENITH computers	Serial port, modem and terminal software.
IBM PC	Async. card, modem and VIDTEX software.
I/O INDUSTRIES Terminal	Nothing else required.
OSBORNE I	Modem and terminal software.
PANASONIC Hand Held Computer	Communications module and modem.
QUASAR Hand Held Computer	Communications module and modem.
RCA 3300 Series Terminal	Modem.
RCA 3501 Terminal	Nothing else required.
TEXAS INSTRUMENTS 99/4 and 99/4A	RS-232 interface, modem and terminal emulator I or II.
TRS-80 Model I/III	RS-232 board, modem and VIDTEX software.
TRS-80 Model II	Modem and VIDTEX software.
TRS-80 Color Computer	Modem and Videotex cartridge or terminal software.
TRS-80 DT-1 Terminal	Modem.
TRS-80 Videotex	Nothing else required.
XEROX – Sam 820	Modem and communications software.
ZENITH ZTA-1 Terminal	Nothing else required.

position in the steadily evolving computer information services industry. It currently provides services to more than 250,000 microcomputer users, and its consumer and commercial customer base is growing at the rate of 8,000 new subsribers per month.

Selected Product Offerings

CIS combines menu-choice and word-search technology to provide its users with a versatile means of obtaining information. The menu-choice approach, which requires no special programming or computer language knowledge, allows the novice user to "go" anywhere on the service by simply pushing a button and entering a number into the terminal. The word-search approach, especially popular with more experienced users, allows the user to enter a word or topic into designated areas of CIS; the computer then looks for related information.

CIS has a broad data base that offers a variety of information services to its customers. For example, CIS gives users access to a world of financial information with news reports, reference sources, and electronic mail capabilities. These include figures on more than 9,000 securities updated throughout each trading day; current and historical information on more than 40,000 stocks, bonds, and options; and specialized reports on commodities, today's economy, and implications for the future. CIS provides its users with personal financial services as well, which include basic financial tools for figuring mortgage loans, depreciation, and other financial categories.

With CIS, research on a multitude of subjects is as easy as the touch of a button. The contents of the CIS reference library (which includes Grolier's Academic American Encyclopedia), combined with the resources found in other CIS service areas (financial, newspapers, newsletters, special interest groups, etc.) comprise a vast wealth of information available instantly.

CIS offers transaction services such as shopping and banking at home. CIS shopping allows users to scan the pages of the ultimate electronic catalog and pick and choose from over 50,000 items—from cookware to clothing—available at discounted prices. Regular monthly bills can be paid via CIS Bank-at-Home, after entering and verifying information displayed on the user's terminal screen. Current information on individual checking accounts is available, including a running balance and a list of all checks and deposits received by the bank each day. Shopping and banking at home on CIS offers convenience, with product and personal financial information available at the user's fingertips.

National and international newswires give users a rundown of events as they occur, and electronic editions of many of the nation's major newspapers let CIS users know what is happening all over the country through detailed news reports, critical commentary, and sports reports. CIS offers electronic editions of popular consumer magazines featuring articles on a wide variety of topics.

Game playing is popular with CIS users who can compete against other players across the country or with just the computer. CIS has electronic versions of familiar games—blackjack, backgammon, football, etc.—as well as computerized creations, such as MegaWars, that provide users with hours of enjoyment and entertainment. MegaWars allows up to eight players from any part of the country to compete with each other in an "inter-galactic shootout." In a joint venture with Hallmark, a new game has been developed called "You Guessed It." Similar to the television show "Family Feud," players in teams play in real time answering trivia questions.

Communications possibilities are expanded dramatically with CIS. Users can send messages, electronically, to other CIS customers nationwide using any of several methods. EasyPlex electronic mail, a person-to-person message delivery system, allows users to privately communicate with one another. Less costly than a telephone call and faster than the postal service, the EMAIL system is especially applicable to business use. CB is CompuServe's unique simulation of Citizen's Band radio; it puts users "on channel" so they can talk directly with one or more persons who are also tuned in. The National Bulletin Board system on CIS allows users to post messages for all CIS customers to read. Notices of club meetings, items for sale, and requests for information from other CIS customers are some examples of how users can communicate via the computerized bulletin board.

Other Selected Services on CIS

Aviation.   CompuServe supports the private pilot with over a dozen aviation-related on-line offerings. Three sophisticated interactive programs provide flight support. Two return computer-generated routes for RNAV- or VOR-direct flights. A third supports pilots who choose to specify a prepared flight route along selected Navaids. Pilot briefings pertinent to the specific flight plan automatically accompany route information, including weather briefings from the NWS along with reports from FAA data networks. A CompuServe Aviation Weather service complements flight planning, providing Hourly Weather Reports, Terminal Forecasts, Winds Aloft, Pilot Reports, Notices to Airmen, Area Forecasts, Radar Summaries, and other resources.

Shopping.   The Electronic Mail is the most ambitious electronic shopping service ever launched on a videotex system. A service of CompuServe and L. M. Berry & Company, one of the nation's largest Yellow Pages directory publishing companies, the mall is home for dozens of businesses, providing one-stop shopping at a single keyboard. New merchants are setting up shop here every week.

Selected merchants include Sears, Bloomingdales, Waldenbooks, American Express, Buick, Record World, Kodak, and many others. The service offers special sales, discount prices, and convenient selection and ordering procedures.

Financial Services.   Several banks offer on-line financial and information systems where customers can review transactions, transfer funds, pay bills, compare current interest rates, and even exchange electronic mail with bank officers. Quick & Reilly, Inc., the nation's third-largest discount brokerage firm, offers brokerage services that include on-line purchases and sales of securities 24 hours a day, current stock and option prices, portfolio management, and automatic tax-record keeping. Tickerscreen is a financial information service of the discount brokerage Max Ule & Co. It offers closing NYSE prices, commission comparisons, and direct order entry of buy and sell orders for clients of Max Ule.

Clipping Service.   CompuServe's Executive News Service is an electronic clipping service that puts the power and scope of the Associated Press state and national news wires at subscribers' fingertips. Words or phrases of interest are entered and the Executive News Service scans the AP wires around the clock, filing appropriate stories in electronic folders to be read at the subscriber's convenience.

Travel.   With TWA Travelshopper, a subscriber can check flight schedules and fares for virtually any airline in the world; book flights electronically; and arrange for tickets to be either mailed directly, issued by a travel agent, or held at an airline counter. The A–Z Worldwide Hotel Index provides complete reservation information and lodging descriptions for over 25,000 hotels worldwide. Travelers can shop for accommodations by a variety of criteria: price range, specific hotel name, hotel chain name, hotel location, and other factors. Once a particular hotel is selected, the index provides an address and telephone number, location description (city, suburb, airport, etc.), current rates, credit cards accepted, and an overview of meeting, health, and restaurant facilities.

USA Today **Update.**   Each day, *USA Today* Update streamlines information from a variety of business and industrial sources for quick analysis by busy executives. *USA Today*'s editors and researchers monitor hundreds of news sources, including the entire *USA Today* network, major wire services, top metropolitan newspapers, magazines, trade publications, and newsletters. General news reports are summarized hourly. Reports for specific industries, such as telecommunications, appear in concise executive summary format once each day.

Forums.   Forum message boards present inquiries and responses for individuals or small groups within the forum's audience. On-line conferences, similar to CB Simulator, generate lively forum discussion on timely issues. Also, forum libraries are maintained to save contributions for later reference both by forum veterans and newcomers who want to discover the history of a discussion. There are literally hundreds of special-interest groups who meet on-line to discuss topics of mutual interest. They draw from over 250,000 subscribers nationwide, more than any similar service. When all the military veterans, firefighters, science teachers, pilots, organic farmers, lawyers, veterinarians, trivia purists, or science fiction buffs put their heads together on-line, it generates quite a brain trust. Forums that unite the owners and users of specific computers and software are among the most popular. These groups are a great source for tips about getting the most out of a computer and often include direct contact with the customer service staffs of computer manufacturers and software firms.

Promotional Campaigns

In 1982, CompuServe launched an advertising theme pointing out the fact that the computer information age, long dreamed of by scientists and science fiction writers, has arrived with the CompuServe Information Service. The "Welcome to Someday" campaign emphasized that the imagined "technology of the future" is a reality today and can make everyday events such as banking, reading the newspaper, and shopping take on exciting new dimensions. To carry out the "Someday" theme, four-color advertisements were developed along with an educational brochure which was displayed in many computer stores across the country. Exhibit 36.2 shows the cover of this brochure. The brochure was designed to introduce potential customers to CIS offerings and highlight the various services discussed above. The brochure also served to heighten consumer awareness regarding the many ways in which CIS can enhance and dramatically increase the capabilities of personal computers. The color advertisements were placed in computer-related publications and were designed to appeal to the technically oriented hobbyist, CIS's initial target market. Exhibit 36.3 shows a more recent two-page advertisement describing the services.

The number of CIS users grew steadily, as did the diversity of the subscriber base. No longer a hobbyist-dominated service, CIS began attracting users from both the business and home consumer markets. CIS management found that the needs of each of these market segments could be satisfied through the variety of services available on CompuServe's data base. CIS's objective was to develop advertisements that would appeal to all three market segments (business, home consumer, and hobbyist). Due to the newness of the technology, consumer awareness of videotex, and CIS, initial usage was minimal.

In order to attract attention to their product, CIS conducted a promotional campaign for MegaWars, one of its computerized games. As shown in Exhibit 36.4, one free hour of play was offered to all entrants, and an invitation was extended to potential users to learn more about the CompuServe videotex service.

Exhibit 36.2   Cover of "Welcome to Someday" Brochure

CompuServe has also developed advertisements, as presented in Exhibit 36.5, that are directed toward the computer retailer who sells the CIS subscription and Vidtex software to consumers. CompuServe has positioned its product as a sale-closer and profit-maker for computer salesmen. A modem (a device that enables computer signals to be transmitted over telephone lines) is required for users to access the CompuServe data base; therefore, a purchase of CIS software by a consumer means a modem sale to the dealer. CIS has obviously appealed to the dealer's need to sell equipment by providing a reason for consumers to buy computers and peripheral devices.

Exhibit 36.3 Informational Advertisement for CompuServe

Exhibit 36.4   Magazine Advertisement for MegaWars

Exhibits 36.6 and 36.7 are recent print advertisements for CompuServe featuring EasyPlex electronic mail and investment information. Each CIS advertisement invites interested persons to contact the company by mail or toll-free number if they wish to receive further information about the videotex service and the procedure for becoming a CIS subscriber.

Despite an increase in its advertising and promotion budget, CompuServe's management is hesitant to use electronic media (*e.g.*, television) for mass promotion purposes. They have identified the home consumer as a market in which they

Exhibit 36.5   CIS Advertisement Directed at Computer Retailers

are interested, but feel that in the future CIS may direct its efforts toward smaller segments of that huge market in order to attain their intended level of success. The firm is testing television, however, in four markets. Both 30- and 60-second commercials are being used to solicit direct responses from potential CIS customers.

Exhibit 36.8 shows selected results from a 1985 research study of CompuServe Subscribers. A total of 400 respondents completed the survey. The company recognized that growing competition in the videotex industry may require modification in their marketing strategy. However, management feels it is too early to predict what the nature of such a change might be. CIS is quite happy with the current scheme of things.

Exhibit 36.6   Print Advertisement for CompuServe

Exhibit 36.7   Print Advertisement for CompuServe

Exhibit 36.8   Selected Information from CompuServe User Profile

Length of Time User Has Subscribed to CompuServe

Response Categories	
Less than 3 months	14%
3–6 months	28
6–12 months	18
1–2 years	25
More than 2 years	16

How User First Found Out about CompuServe

Response Categories	
Advertisement in business magazine	2%
Advertisement in computer magazine	42
Retail store	11
Referral	18
Came free with hardware	22
Other	4
No response	3

Ages of Subscribers

Age	
12–17	7%
18–24	9
25–34	34
35–44	29
45–54	14
55 +	7

Subscribers' Levels of Education

Education	
High school or less	7%
High school graduate	15
Some college	28
College graduate	26
Some graduate	4
Graduate degree	18
No response	2

Subscribers' Genders

Sex	
Female	5%
Male	95

continued

Exhibit 36.8   *continued*

Subscribers' Occupations

Occupation	
Professional/technical	45%
Managers/administrators/proprietors	15
Sales workers	4
Clerical workers	7
Foremen/craftsmen	10
Operatives/transportation	1
Service workers	3
Military	3
Student	1
Homemaker	1
No response	3

Subscribers' Income Levels

Income	
Under $25,000	12%
$25,000–$34,999	21
$35,000–$44,999	23
$45,000–$54,999	14
$55,000–$74,999	14
$75,000 +	7
No response	10

Bank One of Columbus: Financial Services Marketing

Case 37

During the last two decades, Banc One Corporation in Columbus, Ohio, has built one of the most impressive records of growth and profitability of any bank in the nation. It has accomplished this by imaginative and aggressive policies and programs designed to serve its various customer bases better. As executive management pondered the future, they recognized that banking would become a much more deregulated business, and that they would have to become even more aggressive if they were to continue to be a major national factor in financial service delivery systems.

Background

Bank One, Columbus, NA (formerly known as City National Bank) has served the residents and businesses in central Ohio since 1868. As a result of several consolidations in the early 1920s, the bank became the third-largest in central Ohio.

In 1968, City National applied for and received permission to establish First Banc Group of Ohio, a registered bank holding company. The spelling of "Banc" was dictated by a regulation prohibiting nonbanking institutions from including the designation "Bank" in their names. During its first decade, the corporation grew to include 16 banks throughout the state, with total assets exceeding $2 million.

Up until the mid-1970s, banking was a highly regulated and protected business. However, management realized early that by the end of the decade, major changes would be underway that would eventually almost completely deregulate the banking business. Therefore, it was essential to map out a strategy that would direct the corporation into a wider range of income-producing businesses, other than just providing routine banking services.

In addition, in the late 1970s it was felt that it would be beneficial if all the corporation's member banks had the same name throughout the state. Even though member banks were part of First Banc Group, they retained their original names after affiliation. Therefore, in 1979 First Banc Group changed its name to Banc One Corporation. At that time all bank names were changed to Bank One.

Banc One Corporation was able to acquire a number of profitable and very well managed affiliate banks because of its unusual philosophy of running the corporation. For a list, see Exhibit 37.1. The philosophy is called an "Uncommon Partnership" since member banks continue to operate relatively autonomously in their communities. The corporation consolidated data processing and marketing functions, but left management of the human factors up to each bank. In addition, each bank maintained its board of directors on an active basis and also made almost all decisions on lending. Therefore, member banks enjoy the economies of

Exhibit 37.1   Information on Banc One Corporation

Bank Affiliates

BANK ONE, AKRON, NA
BANK ONE, ALLIANCE, NA
BANK ONE, ASHLAND
BANK ONE, ATHENS, NA
BANK ONE, CAMBRIDGE, NA
BANK ONE, CLEVELAND, NA
BANK ONE, COLUMBUS, NA
BANK ONE, COSHOCTON, NA
BANK ONE, DAYTON, NA
BANK ONE, DOVER, NA
BANK ONE, EASTERN OHIO, NA
BANK ONE, FREMONT, NA
BANK ONE, LIMA, NA
BANK ONE, MANSFIELD
BANK ONE, MARION
BANK ONE, MIDDLETOWN
BANK ONE, MILFORD, NA
BANK ONE, PORTSMOUTH, NA
BANK ONE, SIDNEY, NA
BANK ONE, WAPAKONETA, NA
BANK ONE, WOOSTER, NA

BANK ONE, TRUST COMPANY, NA

Other Affiliates

BANC ONE LEASING CORPORATION
BANC ONE LIFE INSURANCE COMPANY
BANC ONE MORTGAGE CORPORATION
BANC ONE REALTY CORPORATION
BANC ONE CAPITAL CORPORATION
BANC ONE CREDIT CORPORATION

Stock Transfer Agent & Registrar

Common and Series A Preferred
BANK ONE, DAYTON, NA
Corporate Trust Department
Kettering Tower
Dayton, Ohio 45401
(513) 449-8796
In Ohio (Toll Free)
1-800-848-0191

Dividend Reinvestment Agent

BANK ONE, DAYTON, NA
Corporate Trust Department
Kettering Tower
Dayton, Ohio 45401
(513) 449-8722

Stock Listings

Common:
  New York Stock Exchange: BncOne
  Ticker Symbol: ONE
Series A Preferred:
  NASDAQ: Banc One pf A
  Ticker Symbol: BONEP.

10-K Report

Shareholders may receive a copy of BANC ONE's 1984 10-K Annual Report as filed with The Securities and Exchange Commission upon submission of an appropriate written request to George R.L. Meiling at the corporate offices. The report will be available after April 1, 1985.

scale of a national banking organization, but still maintain the ability to operate on a relatively independent basis. By mid-1985, Banc One Corporation had grown to become the largest banking organization in Ohio, with over 24 member banks and assets of almost $10 billion. In addition, the corporation is acquiring affiliate banks in Indiana, Kentucky, and Michigan, and plans to add affiliates in other surrounding states as new regulations permit.

Since 1970, Banc One Corporation has been consistently among the ten most profitable banking organizations in the nation. Net operating income before taxes for Banc One Corporation increased from about $15.5 million in 1968 to over $100 million in 1984. Exhibit 37.2 provides a financial summary of Banc One Corporation for 1984.

Objectives

In 1960, executive management started to develop a new concept in banking. They determined that paying a great deal more attention to the consumer segment of the market would not only permit the bank to grow rapidly, but it would be a very profitable venture. The primary reason for this assumption was that major competition was either concentrating on business or trust customer relationships. No one was really trying to develop better banking services for regular customers.

Exhibit 37.2   Financial Statements

BANC ONE CORPORATION and Subsidiaries

Consolidated Balance Sheet
$(thousands)

	December 31, 1984	December 31, 1983
Assets:		
Cash and due from banks (Note 14)	$ 614,845	$ 433,481
Deposits in other banks, interest bearing (including Eurodollar placements and negotiable certificates of deposit of $527,500 and $871,900 at December 31, 1984 and 1983)	531,710	874,561
Short-term investments	217,914	154,406
Securities (market value approximates $1,395,200 and $1,047,900 at December 31, 1984 and 1983) (Notes 1 and 14)		
United States government obligations	499,793	293,073
Obligations of federal agencies	138,085	155,093
Obligations of states and political subdivisions	704,108	568,564
Other securities	63,175	47,973
Total securities	1,405,161	1,064,703
Loans and leases (Notes 1 and 4):		
Commercial, financial and agricultural	2,159,966	1,670,652
Real estate, construction	94,003	66,219
Real estate, mortgage	941,739	885,992
Consumer	2,334,148	1,547,326
Tax exempt	446,362	296,946
Leases	180,294	154,710
Gross loans and leases	6,156,512	4,621,845
Unearned loan and lease interest (Note 1)	291,139	264,661
Total loans and leases	5,865,373	4,357,184
Reserve for possible loan and lease losses (Notes 1 and 3)	73,590	50,764
Net loans and leases	5,791,783	4,306,420
Other assets:		
Bank premises and equipment, net (Notes 1 and 10)	181,758	164,993
Interest earned not collected	110,306	90,553
Other real estate owned (Note 1)	8,546	10,182
Excess of cost over net assets of affiliates purchased (Notes 1 and 2)	125,070	110,161
Other	119,000	61,021
Total other assets	544,680	436,910
Total assets	$9,106,093	$7,270,481

The accompanying notes are an integral part of the financial statements.

	December 31, 1984	December 31, 1983
Liabilities:		
Deposits:		
Demand—non-interest bearing	$1,470,630	$1,215,128
Demand—interest bearing	634,383	565,309
Savings	721,160	702,084
Money market accounts	898,427	810,130
Time	3,682,638	2,644,418
Total deposits	7,407,238	5,937,069
Short-term borrowings (Note 6):		
Federal funds purchased and repurchase agreements	651,626	512,672
Other	80,470	38,287
Total short-term borrowings	732,096	550,959
Long-term borrowings (Note 7)	96,980	100,077
Other liabilities:		
Accrued interest payable	94,857	70,793
Other	106,135	54,567
Total other liabilities	200,992	125,360
Total liabilities	8,437,306	6,713,465
Commitments and contingencies (Notes 5 and 14)		
Preferred stock, Series A convertible, no par value, 5,000,000 shares authorized, 996,732 and 996,989 shares issued, respectively (Note 12)	49,837	49,849
Common stockholders' equity (Notes 2, 7 and 12):		
Common stock, no par value, $5 stated value, 50,000,000 shares authorized, 36,380,869 and 34,359,134 shares issued, respectively (December 31, 1983 shares reflect the 10% stock dividend effective February 3, 1984)	181,905	171,796
Capital in excess of aggregate stated value of common stock	295,085	260,167
Undivided profits	145,123	77,675
Total common stockholders' equity before treasury shares	622,113	509,638
Less 135,000 and 101,200 treasury shares, respectively, at cost (December 31, 1983 shares reflect the 10% stock dividend effective February 3, 1984)	(3,163)	(2,471)
Total common stockholders' equity	618,950	507,167
Total capital	668,787	557,016
Total liabilities and capital	$9,106,093	$7,270,481

The accompanying notes are an integral part of the financial statements.

BANC ONE CORPORATION and Subsidiaries

Consolidated Statement of Income
for the three years ended December 31, 1984
$(thousands, except per share data)

	1984	1983	1982
Interest income (Note 1):			
Interest and fees on loans and leases	$727,446	$480,317	$374,933
Interest and dividends on:			
Obligations of U.S. government and federal agencies and other securities	72,420	54,592	41,433
Obligations of states and political subdivisions	56,195	39,977	29,797
Other interest income, including interest on Eurodollar placements and negotiable certificates of deposit of $66,000, $73,154 and $73,840 in 1984, 1983 and 1982	77,093	83,478	97,989
Total interest income	933,154	658,364	544,152
Interest expense:			
Interest on deposits:			
Demand and savings deposits	143,377	111,068	39,840
Time deposits	329,984	232,051	240,634
Other borrowings	80,754	53,143	69,261
Total interest expense	554,115	396,262	349,735
Net interest income	379,039	262,102	194,417
Provision for loan and lease losses (Note 3)	64,347	23,451	19,175
Net interest income after provision for loan and lease losses	314,692	238,651	175,242
Other income (Note 1):			
Income from fiduciary activities	21,480	17,828	8,027
Service charges on deposit accounts	33,702	26,375	17,214
Financial card services income	41,077	31,586	27,038
Securities losses	(681)	(4,229)	(14,504)
Other	20,725	13,226	8,866
Total other income	116,303	84,786	46,641
Other expenses:			
Salaries and related costs	146,174	114,123	79,885
Net occupancy expense, exclusive of depreciation	18,491	13,457	6,368
Depreciation and amortization (Note 1)	23,289	15,884	10,234
Professional fees and services	26,889	24,299	14,830
Other	91,021	63,964	52,968
Total other expenses	305,864	231,727	164,285
Income before federal income taxes	125,131	91,710	57,598
Federal income tax (provision) benefit (Note 8):			
Income excluding securities transactions	(18,152)	(12,099)	(9,956)
Securities transactions	994	3,667	9,879
Net income	$107,973	$83,278	$57,521
Net income per common share after preferred dividend requirements (data restated to reflect the 3-for-2 stock split effective August 9, 1983 and the 10% stock dividend effective February 3, 1984)	$2.88	$2.55	$2.18
Weighted average common shares outstanding	35,632,974	31,422,095	26,327,955

The accompanying notes are an integral part of the financial statements.

This strategic decision caused a number of major changes in the organization. Management had to develop a staff who were knowledgeable in data processing and marketing as well as familiar with the brokerage, insurance, and retailing businesses. It was felt that in order to maximize return on stockholders' equity, the corporation would certainly have to consider entering these other financially related business opportunities.

It was also obvious to management that significant financial support would need to be given to this new direction. Therefore, a decision was made to allocate up to 3 percent of net earnings each year for research and development of new products and services. Bank One became one of very few banks in the country to actually have money earmarked for research and development programs. Under these guidelines, management had easy access to funds to try out new ideas and services. This philosophy worked well. The corporation soon generated a reputation as being one of the most innovative new service developers in the country.

Marketing

Executive management realized early on that they would have to recruit and develop a fully functioning marketing department if they were to achieve their goals. Prior to 1960, few banks in the country had even considered the importance of marketing in their total operations. Several had a person designated as advertising manager, and even fewer performed any of the other major marketing functions.

A marketing staff was hired, and the division was initially charged with two main responsibilities. First, the staff was to develop advanced services for all potential market segments. This included not only primary customers, but also services that could be sold to other financially related businesses. Second, they were to develop the most advanced delivery systems for those services. There were no restrictions placed on these developments other than that they should concentrate the development effort on programs that could be immediately offered within existing regulatory framework.

Advertising

One of the first steps in the development of a marketing function was to hire an advertising manager who could create a new and distinctive image of the bank. The resulting advertising and promotional effort soon became recognized as being among the most successful bank promotional efforts in the country. An example of this advertising is included in Exhibit 37.3.

Branching and Affiliation

If the bank was going to serve the consumer market, it had to have locations convenient to where consumers lived and worked. Therefore, the bank undertook an aggressive branching program throughout Columbus suburbs. In 1960, Bank One, Columbus, had seven branches. By 1984, it had 33 full-service branches and 9 mini-branch facilities called AutoBanks.

Exhibit 37.3   Promotional Brochure for Bank One Services

THERE'S NEVER BEEN ANYTHING LIKE IT!

This year, if you pay taxes on any interest from a savings plan, you should consider a BANK ONE Tax Free All-Savers Certificate as part of your regular savings program. The All-Savers Certificate lets you earn tax free interest* with a minimum of only $500 and a one year maturity. The program provides individuals up to $1,000 and those filing a joint return up to $2,000 in tax free interest. This Tax Free All-Savers Certificate could give you the highest after-tax yield you've ever earned, and it's insured by an agency of the federal government. Savers have never had this opportunity before, so stop by any BANK ONE office and sign up today.

YOU CAN BENEFIT FROM AN ALL-SAVERS PROGRAM

IF the tax rate on your taxable income is over 22%.

Because interest you're now earning on other savings is taxable, you would have to earn much higher rates on those savings to better the net interest you earn from an All-Savers Certificate. The higher your tax bracket, the more interest you would have to earn on an alternative investment.

IF you have a six-month money market CD.

If you have a BANK ONE six-month Super T Certificate, you can convert your investment to an All-Savers Certificate without any interest penalty and earn tax free rather than taxable interest. Just bring your Super T Certificate to any BANK ONE office and we'll convert it for you.

IF you have funds in a taxable money market fund.

If you have money in a money market fund, you should probably shift at least a portion of your investment to a Tax Free All-Savers Certificate at BANK ONE, since the interest is tax free rather than taxable. The rate is fixed for a full year and insured by an agency of the federal government.

*Tax free interest means free from Federal and Ohio State Income Tax.
There is a substantial interest penalty for early withdrawal.

BANK ONE ™ ®

Earn insured, high Money Market Rates.

Now that BANK ONE has an investment vehicle for all kinds of investors, there's no reason for you to invest your money anywhere else . . . whether it's $100 or $10,000. You can invest your funds for as short as three months or as long as three-and-a-half years, and always earn high money market interest rates.

When interest rates are high and your investment needs change, we can satisfy those changing needs with a wide choice of options. BANK ONE has many Money Market Investor Services to choose from, including tax-saver Investor Services. So, whenever you're investing your money . . . now, put it back in the bank.

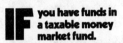
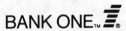

Choose from these Money Market Investor Services depending on how much you want to invest and how long you want to invest it.

INVESTOR SERVICE THAT'S BEST FOR YOU	HOW LONG YOU WANT TO INVEST	HOW MUCH YOU HAVE TO INVEST
3-Month SUPER T*	3 Months	$7,500+
6-Month SUPER T*	6 Months	$10,000+
Small Saver SUPER T	2½ Years to 41 Months	$100+
SUPER CERTIFICATE	3½ Years or More	$500+
BANK ONE also has these tax-saver investments		
Tax-Free All Savers Certificate	1 year	$500+
Individual Retirement Account (Fixed Rate)	Until Retirement	$500
Individual Retirement Account (Variable Rate)	Until Retirement	$100

*Federal regulations prohibit the compounding of interest during the term of the deposit.
There is a substantial interest penalty for early withdrawal.
The effective yield on U.S. Treasury securities is higher than the quoted discount rate.

MONEY MARKET INVESTOR SERVICES

BANK ONE ™
Member FDIC

At the same time Bank One was aggressively growing, Banc One Corporation was acquiring a large number of well-managed affiliates throughout the state. By 1985, Banc One Corporation member banks had over 300 banking offices located all over Ohio, which made it the ninth-largest branch banking system in the United States.

At the same time the corporation was growing, there were tremendous advances taking place in the computer technology used to support the operational areas of banking.

Central Data File

In the early 1970s, the marketing division decided that the first step in the product development effort was to thoroughly understand the structure of the business relationships that customers had with the bank.

This determination was very difficult, since most banks keep their computer files in account rather than customer sequence. Therefore, it was impossible to determine how much business each customer did with the bank since there was no ability to cross-reference accounts on a total bank basis.

The Marketing Research Department was charged with the responsibility of developing a central information file concept for the bank. This system was to be designed to cross-reference all account information so that it would be relatively easy to determine a customer's total relationship with the bank. In addition, this system was to include other socio-economic information that could be used in determining which customers would likely be candidates for additional banking services.

Toward this end, Banc One began to plan for the total reprogramming of all computer applications so that the bank could move into a completely automated customer information file system (CIF). The new computer files were designed to contain all usable information about the accounts that the customer has with the bank. In addition, the files permit inclusion of many items of external data. A small sampling of the information available for consumer research follows:

- Sex
- Birthdays of family
- Children (number, ages)
- Home ownership or rental
- Marital status
- Transaction history (all accounts)
- Credit rating
- Reason accounts closed
- Occupation
- Dun and Bradstreet rating
- Zip code
- Income range
- Census tract
- Interest paid last year
- Opening officer
- Real estate taxes paid last year

A computer program was available with a complete set of management report options with which the bank could cross-classify the segments of its business by any variable in the CIF. For example, if Bank One, Columbus, wanted to know the age distribution of its Passbook Savings accounts, it could place an inquiry in the computer and receive such a report. If it wanted to determine those accounts with large demand deposit accounts but no other relationships, that could easily be reported. The CIF allows for the design of a highly specific direct mail campaign to Bank One customers by census tract, effective direct increase business, and cross-selling existing customers on new banking services. Another feature of the CIF is the capacity to treat a customer as a "net account." That is, the balance and profitability of a customer could be accessed rather than the balance and profitability of an account, which typically is only a fractional representation of the customer.

Account Structure

The central information file data, coupled with other primary research information, led to the development of a number of new banking services, several of which are discussed below.

Visa

One of the most significant new services offered by Bank One was the Visa Credit Card (formerly BankAmericard). This comprehensive credit card program was originally developed and introduced by Bank of America in California. Bank One's management went to the Bank of America and "convinced" their top management to franchise the service to other banks across the country. Bank One was successful and became the first bank in the nation to offer the Visa Credit Card to customers outside California.

Acceptance of the Visa card in Columbus was excellent, and management quickly realized that plastic card services were going to play a very important role in future financial service delivery systems. By the end of the second year of operation, over 100,000 customers carried and used the Visa Credit Card in the 8,000 merchant outlets in central Ohio.

Bank One refranchised the Visa program throughout the Midwest, and it now processes the credit cards for over 200 banks, savings and loans, and credit unions. The Visa Credit Card is accepted by hundreds of thousands of merchants across the country and around the world.

VISA Checking Account Card

In 1975, Bank One was the first bank to introduce the Visa Debit Card (formerly called Entree), which looked just like a credit card, but worked like a check. Therefore, customers could have the convenience of using a credit card, but could use money on deposit rather than charging to a credit card account. In introducing the debit card, the bank's target was the so-called "convenience user," who charged purchases not so much for deferred payment, but as a substitute for cash. Since debit card transactions are withdrawn from funds on deposit, the bank was not funding an outstanding balance on a credit card account.

From a customer's point of view, the VISA debit card offered limited advantages over the credit card, as long as the credit card was free. Therefore, for the first two years of the VISA debit card program, few customers signed up for the service. Then Bank One introduced a yearly fee of $20 on the Visa credit card, while it still offered the VISA debit card at no charge. This stimulated a large number of convenience credit card users to switch to the VISA debit program.

Line O' Credit

In addition, Bank One expanded the credit card program to include overdraft checking account protection for customers who had both a credit card and a checking account. This program was introduced to help take the hassle out of "bouncing a check." It proved to be a very valuable service and one which saved time, money, and embarrassment for customers.

Account Relationships

Comprehensive research and use of the new central information file indicated that about half of the bank's customers only had one account with the bank. Financial analysis of these accounts found that many of the customers with one account represented unprofitable business.

Therefore, it was considered essential to make a concerted effort to cross-sell additional services to present customers. Basic research indicated that customers wanted to receive one statement encompassing their entire banking relationship, rather than a savings statement for each savings account, a checking statement for each checking account, and so forth. This led to the introduction of the "Total Account Bank Statement," which lists the monthly details for all accounts owned by a customer on one monthly statement. These may be checking and savings accounts, loans, and certificates of deposit. Exhibit 37.4 describes the total account bank statement in more detail.

Cash Management Account

The bank then included some advanced features in its credit card processing system so that other types of financially related businesses could issue credit cards to their customers. This included finance companies and brokers. Bank One soon developed into the major processor for cash management type accounts by providing the service to the nine largest stock brokerage companies in the country. Within a few years, more than a million broker customers carried and used a Bank One, Columbus, Visa credit card as part of their CMA service.

Cash management accounts permit customers to earn money market interest rates on all their funds, plus have access to cash and a line of credit through both checks and credit/debit cards. It also typically offers full brokerage transaction capability. Minimum opening amounts for these accounts range from $1,000 to $20,000. Yearly fees range from $60 to over $200.

This type of account has been very popular around the country. Over 2 million high-income individuals signed up for cash management account service within the first few years after introduction.

The checking accounts and Visa cards issued to almost all cash management type accounts are provided and processed by Bank One. All check and credit card transactions are cleared through Bank One, which then provides individual account information to the brokers to be used in monthly statements to customers.

Exhibit 37.4   Description of Total Account Bank Statement

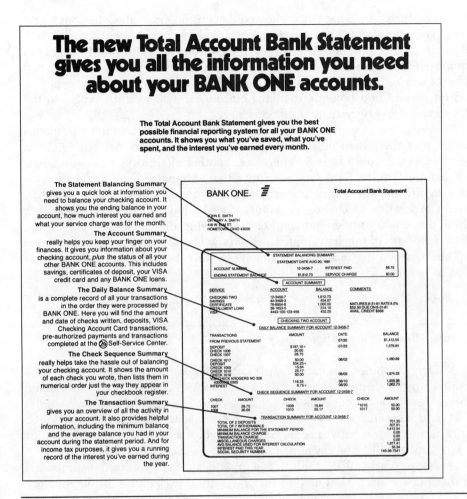

In addition, Bank One developed a new "joint issue" type of credit card program. This service permitted the bank to issue cards in conjunction with a wide range of major nonbank businesses across the country. The first joint issue program was developed for a national electronic catalog service called Comp-U-Card. During the first two years of operation, Bank One issued over a million cards to members of the Comp-U-Card service. Other joint issue programs are planned with major airlines, automobile manufacturers, retailers, and insurance companies.

Computer Services

Bank One is a leader is computerizing bank services. Beginning in 1962, the bank viewed computerization as a means to "separate the paper work from the people work." In 1975 and in 1981, two major additions augmented its computer center operations, and new IBM equipment was installed. Bank management has a strong commitment to seeking new computerized decision-making tools for management and those that would assist customers in managing their accounts.

Service Delivery Systems

Research conducted by Bank One indicated that customers of all Columbus banks had two basic complaints about service. First, banks were not open during convenient hours, and second, once inside the bank, customers had to wait in long lines to complete their transactions. It was obvious to management that a definite and significant service differential could be achieved if these two problems could be solved for present and potential banking customers. This meant changes in the bank's service delivery systems were necessary.

An evaluation of expanded branch operating hours to solve these problems indicated that the return on investment based on the additional business that could be expected would be low. Therefore, another alternative was considered.

After much study, Bank One concluded that automated banking facilities offered a significant alternative for expanded branch operating hours. In 1970, Docutel Corporation in Dallas, Texas introduced an automated cash-dispensing machine that could provide banking services around the clock every day of the week. On the basis of much evaluation, the Marketing Department recommended to top management that automated banking facilities be installed in all branches as soon as possible.

Automated Banking Facilities

Cash 'N Carry machines, the nation's first automatic cash vending machines, were introduced to the United States by Bank One in 1970. The more sophisticated machines were brought out in late 1971 under the name Bank24. With a special Bank24 card, consumers are able to activate the machine and transact deposits, withdrawals, transfers between checking and savings accounts, and payments for Visa bills, utility bills, and installment or mortgage loans, 24 hours a day.

During the early 1980s, there was a great deal of activity in the automated teller machine business. Most major financial institutions had installed equipment for customer use. In addition, many had banned together to provide regional and national interchange programs so that customers could have access to their accounts even while out of town. In addition, major retailers began planning to install automatic banking machines in their financial services locations.

At the same time, both the Visa and MasterCard national card programs announced plans to install automatic banking machines on a national basis so that cardholders of either program would have access to their bank accounts around the country. They introduced new technology which would permit member bank cards to be used both in automated teller machines and point-of-sale terminals located at major retailing outlets.

Bank One became the first bank in the country to introduce the new Electron Visa card to its customers. This was done in the fall of 1983. These cards could be used in any participating Visa interchange banking machines, in Bank One's own statewide banking machine network, and in point-of-sale terminals for the authorization of purchases. The new program was called Jubilee throughout the Banc One affiliate network to differentiate it from all the other programs which had banker type names. Exhibit 37.5 describes the machines and their operation.

In 1974, BANK ONE opened the first of two Bank24 branch facilities using both live and automated tellers to provide all routine banking services, 24 hours a day, seven days a week. These unique Bank24 branches allow customers to carry on virtually all of their banking business at their convenience, without ever going

Exhibit 37.5   Description of Bank One's Self-Service Centers

inside the bank. Exhibit 37.6 shows alternative architectural schemes for these branches.

Autobank

An analysis of the Bank24 branches indicated that they had been over-built and that a smaller facility could be developed to provide essentially the same services at a much lower cost.

Bank One then developed and introduced the AutoBank in 1978. The AutoBank provided the same services as the older Bank24 branches, yet it was only 96 square feet in size and cost less than $15,000. The building was small enough to be placed on self-service gas station sites or in shopping center parking lots. Therefore, the bank could place many of the AutoBanks in convenient locations around town at minimal cost. This convenience factor attracted many new customers to the bank.

Point-of-Sale Transaction Terminals

Bank One's advanced computer capabilities permitted it to become a lead bank in all automated services, including the experiment with point-of-sale terminals in stores. The bank's terminals directly transferred money from a customer's account to a merchant's account when the sale was made. Bank One was the first bank in the country to test such a system. It installed 60 terminals in 30 stores in a suburb of Columbus. Over 250 banks from every free country in the world sent representatives to Columbus to view and analyze the experiment.

While over 10 million transactions were completed on these terminals, Bank One terminated the service because no future profit potential was anticipated. The equipment was too expensive to maintain and install, and grocery stores were unwilling to pay a high enough fee to enable Bank One to recover its investment.

By the mid-1980s, Bank One hoped to provide a similar transaction guarantee service in grocery stores. The stores have been installing their own inventory control computers and automated check registers. Bank One intends to develop a way to tap into these computer systems to provide the transactions guarantee, but will avoid the large fixed cost of installing the hardware.

Home Information Systems

The bank's management continually felt that in order to be competitive, the corporation would have to develop the most sophisticated, yet easiest-to-use electronic banking programs in the country.

The Marketing Division carefully watched the development of the home computer market and the resultant increase in consumer awareness of use of the technology in the home. In early 1980, the decision was made to introduce a home banking system on an experimental basis. This was not to be a pay-by-phone program, which had been introduced by about 250 banks and savings and loans.

Exhibit 37.6   Examples of Architectural Schemes for Bank24 Branch Facilities

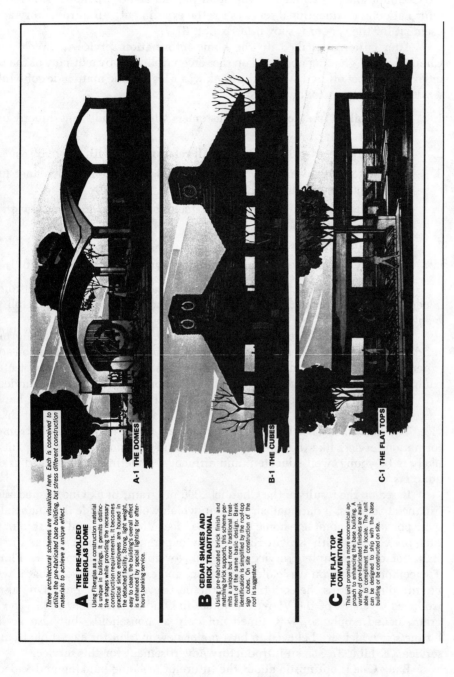

Three architectural schemes are visualized here. Each is conceived to utilize the pre-fabricated base building, but stress different construction materials to achieve a unique effect.

A THE PRE-MOLDED FIBERGLAS DOME

Using Fiberglas as a construction material is unique in buildings. It permits distinctive shapes while providing the necessary construction requirements. It becomes practical since employees are housed in the detached facility. Strong, light weight, easy to clean, the building's overall effect is enhanced by special lighting for after-hours banking service.

A-1 THE DOMES

B CEDAR SHAKES AND BRICK TRADITIONAL

Using pre-fabricated brick finish and matching brick supports, this scheme permits a unique but more traditional treatment of the same basic design. Bank identification is simplified by the roof-top sign cubes. On site construction of the roof is suggested.

B-1 THE CUBES

C THE FLAT TOP CONVENTIONAL

This unit promises a more economical approach to enhancing the base building. A variety of pre-fabricated finishes are available to compliment the locale. The unit can be designed to ship with the base building or be constructed on site.

C-1 THE FLAT TOPS

Rather it was to be a system which would connect a telephone line to a customer's home TV set so that a wide range of information and transaction services could be provided.

The home banking program, called Channel 2000, was generically known as a Videotex throughout the industry. Bank One's role in this jointly sponsored project was to provide the financial service delivery capability to about 200 homes in the Columbus area. In addition, the other partner could provide a wide range of information and educational services for the experiment. An introductory advertisement for the system is shown in Exhibit 37.7.

After customers called up the home information service, a "Welcome to Channel 2000" greeting appeared on the screen, followed by a display of the main index for services offered. When the bank was selected, the main index of banking services appeared as follows:

1. Display bill, a function used by customers who have bills sent directly to the bank

2. Account balances, which included all relationships with the bank

3. Bank statement this month, which provided transaction and balance information on a month-to-date basis

4. Bank statement last month, which included all the information on last month's bank statement

5. Current interest rates

6. Enter a bill, used by customers to make payments on preselected bills

Three types of financial information were available to the sample customers: general financial information, account status, and the two methods of bill payment shown above.

The Channel 2000 experiment allowed the test participants to form attitudes, opinions, and perceptions about in-home banking services based on actual experience. Bank One completed a great deal of research after the project was completed to determine what participants liked or disliked about the service.

The results of the experiment showed that nearly 80 percent of the banking customers in the test were willing to pay more than $7.50 per month for the service. The experiment also helped define the likely target market for electronic information services like those tested. It was found that potential participants are likely to be young, well-educated, and affluent—sometimes categorized as early adapters.

Based on the results of the Channel 2000 program, Bank One formed Video-Financial Services, a national corporation which would provide the financial services portion of a complete home delivery service. VideoFinancial's first joint venture project was with Knight-Ridder Newspapers in Miami, Florida. First installation of the complete service started in November 1983 in southern Florida. The complete program was called Viewtron, and expectations were that it would be introduced across the country over the next several years. Bank One also introduced a version of the Viewtron system in Ohio in December 1985. The program, called Applause, was aimed not only at households, but also at small businesses, which are believed to be a major new market for electronic financial services. Exhibit 37.8 is an introductory advertisement for this service.

Bank One is optimistic about the future of in-home banking and Videotex, predicting that in five years at least 30 percent of American households will be using some form of in-home information systems. It also predicts that in ten years, at least 60 percent of American households will be using some form of this system.

Exhibit 37.7   Newspaper Advertisement for Channel 2000 Introduction

BANK ONE ⧨

This week BANK ONE and 100 pioneering customers are launching the first major test of delivering banking services directly to the home.

This is an historic week for 100 bank customers who have become participants in BANK ONE's Channel 2000 program...a brand new way of delivering banking services directly to the home by linking the telephone to the standard television set. They're helping BANK ONE develop better services for banking customers all over the country. This project was jointly developed by BANK ONE and OCLC, Inc., the nation's leading provider of computerized library services. Channel 2000 is the first major test of its kind in the United States.

Channel 2000 will let customers pay bills, check on account balances, and get current interest rates and other general financial information. All information will be displayed on the TV screen in the customer's home. In addition to banking use, Channel 2000 will provide access to other valuable community and educational information.

With the cost of transportation and postage getting higher and higher, customers will want more convenient ways to pay bills and complete routine banking transactions. BANK ONE is testing the Channel 2000 now to help make banking more convenient in the future.

BANK ONE ⧨
BANK ONE OF COLUMBUS

Member FDIC

Exhibit 37.8   Introductory Advertisement for Bank One's Home Banking

Financial Centers

Bank One has been very successful in convincing customers to use electronic bank-ing machines. By the end of 1985, 28 percent of all the transactions in the Colum-bus bank were being completed through an automated teller machine. Expecta-tions are that this percentage could increase to about 50 percent by 1990. As a result, a continually decreasing number of customers enter a branch lobby to com-plete a banking transaction. Therefore, physical banking facilities are considered to be underutilized. As a result, Bank One is experimenting with combining other types of financially related services in its existing branches. They have converted a major branch bank into a financial service center by decreasing the amount of space used to provide regular banking services, and by including insurance, brokerage, travel, and real estate agents in the facility. These agents pay rent for the space, and therefore generate additional income for the branch. If this experiment is successful, the bank plans to install similar operations in other Bank One offices throughout the state.

Deregulation

It is predicted that the decade of the 1980s will usher in many changes for the financial services industry. Banks will follow airline, trucking, and telephone company deregulation set by Congress. These changes will certainly allow interstate branching, removal of interest rate ceilings, and the ability to introduce a wide range of new products. Bank One is considering the possibility of offering the following services:

☐ Insurance services, including brokerage and underwriting
☐ Stock brokerage services, both discount and full service
☐ Securities underwriting
☐ Real estate services, including investment and brokerage
☐ Data processing and telecommunication services
☐ Management consulting services to other banks and customers
☐ Mutual fund management
☐ Retail-oriented lease financing

The question uppermost in senior management's mind is what will be the services Bank One should introduce during the coming years to provide profitable growth through the decade of the 1990s.

Beef Industry Council:
Marketing Beef

Case 38

Beef's Lead Over Its Competitors Could Decrease in 1986, say the food editors of America's daily newspapers. This view emerges from data reported by *Progressive Grocer* magazine in its January 1986 edition. The magazine asked 90 leading food editors to predict consumer food shopping behavior in 1986. When asked how consumer usage of beef will change in 1986, 68 percent of the editors predict consumers will use beef "a little bit less" and 14 percent predict "much less." In total, 82 percent predict consumers will be using less beef. Similar predictions are made for pork, lamb, and veal. In contrast, 71 percent predict consumers will use fish and seafood "much more" and 29 percent predict "a little bit more." Add it up and the prediction is unanimous: consumers will use more fish and seafood in 1986. As for poultry, 98 percent of the editors predict usage will be "much more" or "a little bit more"; none think it will be less. Other trends predicted by the food editors are more switching to low-calorie items and more comparing of nutrition information on labels. They also predict that consumers will show increasing interest in recipes that emphasize low-calorie content, convenience, and low-cholesterol content.

In reporting the above information in the January 10, 1986 issue of its *The Beef Promotion Bullhorn*, the Beef Industry Council also provided the following information on beef consumption.

Beef's Position as "King of the Perishables" should be kept in mind when considering current predictions of declining consumption. *Supermarket Business* magazine's annual report on consumer food expenditures shows beef's overwhelming dominance of other perishables.

Americans spent more than $21 billion on fresh beef in 1984. Compare that with expenditures of less than $6.5 billion on fresh poultry and less than $2.5 billion on fresh fish and other seafood. Every year consumers spend more money on fresh beef than they do on all baked goods, on all dairy products, even on all frozen foods. Sales of fresh beef exceed sales of either fresh vegetables or fresh fruits. Beef's "Number One" position appears unassailable.

Organizational Background

In the mid-1950s, the National Beef Council was formed. In 1962, a merger was effected between that council and the National Livestock and Meat Board, and the board's Beef Committee was renamed the Beef Industry Council (BIC). The following sections are a brief review of the National Livestock and Meat Board and its BIC.

National Livestock and Meat Board

The idea that developed into the Meat Board was first presented by Thomas E. Wilson, then president of Wilson & Co., at the annual meeting of the Kansas Livestock Association at Hutchinson, Kansas in February 1919. Livestock prices at the time had benefited from wartime inflation, but cattle slaughter, especially, was at a cyclical peak and prices were unsatisfactory despite the war. The packers were blamed by the producers, but Wilson, a packer, did not see the problems in the same light and went to Hutchinson at the invitation of the Kansas ranchers to discuss the situation.

He suggested an organization in which producers and packers might work together on their mutual problems. Over a period of three years, various groups with related problems and interests met and discussed ways in which they might effectively join forces "to take steps to promote increased consumption of meat and to counteract the widespread propaganda against meat." On March 16, 1922, the National Livestock and Meat Board was formally organized. Its 17 directors represented 12 supporting organizations. Of the 17, 11 represented livestock producers, 2 spoke for the terminal markets, 2 were meat packers, and 2 represented retail distribution.

The primary fact that first brought the industry together and that proved the focus for joint discussions was the prevalent belief that a high level of meat consumption was adverse to health. The Meat Board set out to counteract this belief by accumulating and disseminating nutritional information about meat. The purpose of the Meat Board, as set forth in its constitution, were:

1. To initiate and encourage research and education in regard to livestock and meat products.

2. To disseminate correct information about meat in the diet and its relation to health.

3. To do all things necessary to promote the interest of the livestock and meat industry.

To these broad purposes the Meat Board has adhered through the years, and to these purposes the otherwise diverse interests represented in the Meat Board have given common allegiance. All the groups have worked together in recognition of the basic fact that any one kind of meat cannot fully succeed in the market if red meat, in general, is under a cloud of adverse public attitude.

Through changing times, and to meet the responsibilities of a business organization serving its constituent industries and the public in the more consumer-oriented society that began to evolve in the 1960s, the Meat Board reached its half-century mark in 1972 with its purposes much the same, but more specifically described. The Meat Board now speaks for meat and the industry through the design and execution of central programs:

1. To strengthen the market for cattle, hogs, and sheep by creating and maintaining a strong consumer dollar demand for meat.

2. To initiate, encourage, generate, and finance research about livestock and meat products.

3. To keep the American public informed about the health-giving qualities of meat on the basis of such scientific research.

4. To keep the American public informed of the contribution of the livestock and meat industry to the economic well-being of the country.

5. To help guide the industry itself toward better understanding and recognition of the consumers' needs and preferences.

Meat Board Activities

The activities of the National Livestock and Meat Board can be divided into several organizational categories: Meat Science and Nutritional Research, Consumer Information and Communications, Education and Meat Merchandising, Beef Industry Council, Pork Industry Group, and Lamb Committee.

Meat Science and Nutritional Research

The Meat Board itself is not set up to carry on research. Its research contributions have been made as grants to scholars who are interested in meat and who submit (or are invited to submit) significant research proposals with requests for grants-in-aid. Thus, the Meat Board has seldom had to pay the full cost of research projects in which it is interested and it has also drawn upon much broader and more varied talent than could possibly be hired within the limitations of its budget.

Over the years, the Meat Board has allocated as much as 10 percent of its annual expenditures to research grants. Over 450 projects have been assisted by board grants over the years. These have ranged widely. There have been many investigations of the role of meat in human nutrition and in relation to longevity and reproduction. Questions of blood regeneration have been considered, along with studies of fat in human health and nutrition. Similar studies have been undertaken in relation to protein, vitamins, and minerals furnished from meat. Studies of meat cookery have been designed to respond to the changing characteristics of meat and to radically changed consumer and industrial cooking equipment and utensils. Approaches to processing, distributing, and merchandising frozen meat have been developed. Studies have probed consumers' attitudes toward specific meats and cuts and toward marketing, and their knowledge of meat grading. The beliefs of physicians have also been studied.

Consumer Information and Communications

The Meat Board's Departments of Consumer Services, Communications, and Creative Services are in the information business, telling the red meat story to both consumers and industry people. Consumers have priority because they ultimately determine the success or failure of the industry's products in the marketplace. By talking directly to consumers, the Meat Board hopes to have an appreciable effect on their willingness to buy beef, pork, or lamb. Attempts are made to reach consumers through newspapers, magazines, radio, and television. Disseminating materials and other resources is a primary objective of the Meat Board's communications function.

Newspaper food editors across the country receive on a regular basis two publicity services offered by the Meat Board. *Meat Feature Service* is sent monthly to approximately 500 of the most important food editors in the country. Included in this service are articles on such topics as nutrition, purchasing beef subprimals, or cooking pork in microwave ovens, as well as a selection of kitchen-tested recipes and professionally photographed meat dishes. *Copy that Clicks* is a bimonthly publication sent to 4,200 smaller daily and weekly newspapers. It contains recipes, buying and storage tips, and other information suited to smaller newspapers.

Because of the diversity of the red meat industry, it is necessary for the Meat Board to also maintain a constant flow of information to various segments of the meat and livestock industries. *Meat Board Reports* is a monthly publication sent to 10,000 livestock and meat industry leaders. Each edition updates readers on current Meat Board programs and provides them with newly researched information on issues affecting the red meat industry.

Coordinating activities between the Beef Industry Council, the Pork Industry Group, and their respective state organizations is the purpose of *Beef Promotion Bullhorn* and the *Pork Industry Group Letter*, both semi-weekly newsletters. Filled with news of Meat Board activities or late-breaking news of concern to particular groups, these publications keep state managers well-informed of goings-on at the national level.

The Meat Board also spreads its messages via the electronic media. For example, Meat Board staffers can regularly be found on WGN-TV's "Top o' the Morning" show, giving a monthly talk on meat promotion, nutrition, cookery, or merchandising. This television program is broadcast via cable to 40 states and is seen by thousands of viewers. Also available is a service to radio broadcasters whereby agriculture reporters from around the country can call a toll-free telephone number to obtain live or taped "Meat Board Radio News." Trade publications receive much material in the form of news releases and special articles.

Education and Meat Merchandising

From the beginning, the Meat Board has emphasized the supplying of educational materials to schools. Since many companies, trade associations, and other special-interest groups are active in providing educational materials, educators are forced to look closely at supplemental teaching aids. In addition, several groups opposed to the consumption of meat have become active in schools.

Faced with these challenges, the Meat Board Education Department takes several steps to make sure its materials are used in the classrooms. First, ideas, opinions, and reactions are solicited from teachers in the field and from industry professionals. Their comments and suggestions are incorporated into the final versions of the materials. Second, a prototype of the finished item is tested on students to obtain their reactions to it and to measure its effectiveness. The third and final step is to let teachers know that it exists. This is accomplished through journals for teachers, catalog mailings to schools, and exhibits at teachers' conventions.

The annual *Catalog of Literature and Audio-Visual Aids* is designed to inform educators and others about the availability of the Meat Board's materials. The catalog is distributed widely to teachers, industry executives, news media personnel, government agencies, and other outlets of information about meat and food. The Meat Board also supports a series of meat judging contests for high school and college students. The board helped sponsor the 4-H and FFA Judging and Identification contest and assisted in several junior contests during the year. For college students, the Meat Board sponsored five events: the National Western, Southwestern, Eastern, American Royal, and International Meat Judging Contests.

Species Divisions

While it is important for the livestock industry to support the general work of the Meat Board in promoting the corporate family of red meats, there is also a need for more narrowly focused merchandising and promotion programs specifically designed to encourage the consumption of beef, pork, and lamb. It is believed that as highly individualized programs are developed for beef, pork, and lamb, each competing for a greater share of the total market, they collectively gain a greater share of the total market for the corporate red meat industry. In certain areas — such as research, formal education, public relations, and medical fields — the Meat Board's organizational resources and energies support the consumption of all red meat. These programs are administered and financed as a group. The board of directors and management of the Meat Board balance the total program with the specific programs, increasing each as new financial capability is gained. All investments for the Meat Board are identified by species source and the board of directors members representing each species are accountable for the allocation of those funds.

The Beef Industry Council

The Beef Industry Council (BIC) focuses specifically on beef. It works closely with various councils, commissions, boards, or groups at the individual state level to help support the marketing of beef. The BIC's primary role can be described as fulfilling the following functions:

1. Developing and carrying out marketing programs — including promotion, advertising and advertising services, public relations, and publicity — to encourage and strengthen the consumer's dollar demand for beef food products.

2. Acting as national coordinator, when appropriate, for state or regional programs originating with ranchers' or state beef council groups, thus facilitating the maximum concentration of both financial resources and effectiveness in the consumer market.

3. Participating with the full board of directors in guiding programs and supervising the expenditure of total Meat Board dollars, in addition to supervising specific budgets and programs of the council.

4. Working to strengthen industry investment in both the BIC and Meat Board programs.

   The specific mission statement of the BIC reads,

   Maintain and Build Demand for Beef Products that Satisfy Consumer Needs and Wants through Market Development Programs (Communications, Education, Promotion, and Research), thereby Increasing the Opportunity for All Segments of the Beef Industry to Earn an Adequate Return on Investment.

Marketing Environment

In 1983, the BIC completed and issued its first long-range plan. That plan covers a five-year period and is updated and revised every year. The major responsibilities of the committee developing the long-range plan include:

    ☐   Analyze the present status of the beef industry and review the factors responsible.

    ☐   Assess issues that shape the future environment that the industry and our products will face.

    ☐   Identify and analyze the products and firms against which beef does and will compete.

    ☐   Provide direction to the beef industry in marketing, BIC/state council organizational development, and funding for those marketing plans.

Appendix A includes the environmental analysis completed by the committee as part of the planning process. The prognosis stage of the planning process examined the outlook for the beef industry if it continues to do only the marketing activities that it has in the past. Appendix B shows the basic conclusions of the long-range planning committee in the areas of beef's market share, health and nutrition concerns, beef's image, trends in beef/beef product development, trends in industry size, and food safety.

Marketing Research

In-Home Consumption

Exhibit 38.1 summarizes the findings from a study analyzing the in-home consumption of beef. This report also profiles the heaviest beef user. As can be seen, beef consumption has declined since the earlier studies in the 1960s and 1970s. Another major change has been the increase in the serving of ground beef and the decreases in serving steaks and roasts. The BIC prepared an informational piece based on this research and provided copies to cattlemen around the country. That informational piece is reproduced in Exhibit 38.2.

Exhibit 38.1   In-Home Consumption of Beef: Summary of Findings

General Consumption Trends

    ☐   Improvement in the economy since 1981 has fueled growth in away-from-home eating occasions, causing a decline in the number of meals consumed in-home. On an individual household basis, in-home food consumption declined further as a result of trends towards smaller household size and downsizing of meals.

    ☐   On a per capita basis, beef is served an average of 4.4 times in an average two-week period. This level has remained relatively stable thus far through the 1980s, but represents a substantial decline from levels of 5.5–5.6 seen from the late 1960s through mid-1970s.

    ☐   Ninety percent of U. S. households serve beef at least once during an average two-week period, a level stable since 1981, but representing a gradual decline over time: penetration levels in 1967, 1972, and 1975 were 97 percent, 96 percent, and 95 percent, respectively.

continued

Exhibit 38.1 *continued*

Currently, beef's two-week penetration of 90 percent holds a considerable edge over those of chicken (72 percent), pork (72 percent), and seafood (64 percent). Segments with considerably smaller two-week user bases include turkey (22 percent), lamb (5 percent), and veal (3 percent).

□ Among those households serving beef, the average frequency with which it is served is 4.9 occasions within a two-week period, a level relatively stable throughout the 1980s, but a significant decline from levels of 5.7–5.9 seen between 1967 and 1975.

Beef maintains, however, substantial edges in frequency as compared with users of pork (4.2), chicken (2.5), seafood (2.5), turkey (2.5), lamb (1.4), and veal (1.4) during an average two-week period.

□ Beef currently accounts for 30 percent of all meat/fish/poultry eatings. Previously, beef's share had been as high as 39 percent in 1977. Since that time, poultry has made the largest inroads against beef, followed by pork, seafood, and processed meats.

	Distribution of Meat/Fish/Poultry Eatings	
	1977/78	1983/84
Beef	39%	30%
Pork	22	25
Poultry	10	14
Processed meat	21	22
Seafood	8	9
Total	100%	100%

□ Seventy percent of beef serving occasions occur at the evening meal, 24 percent occur at the midday meal. This profile has remained constant since 1975.

Beef's time-of-day profile is most directly competitive with that of chicken. Pork, lamb, and veal display much stronger evening skews, while ham, turkey, and seafood exhibit stronger tendencies towards the midday meal.

□ Beef is present in 31 percent of all evening meal eatings, and has remained virtually stable since 1981. Trailing are chicken and pork, which each account for 12 percent of evening meal eatings.

□ At the midday meal, 13 percent of all eatings include beef. This ties with meatless sandwiches (also at 13 percent) for the most popular midday meal items. Pork follows close behind at 11 percent, with the majority (9 percent) representing ham.

□ Slightly more than one-half (54 percent) of all beef is consumed as an end item in itself, with the 46 percent remaining constituting use as an ingredient in another dish. These ingredient uses break out as follows:

continued

Exhibit 38.1 *continued*

	Ingredient Eatings (Percent)	Beef Eatings (Percent)
Sandwiches	39%	18%
Combination dishes	36	17
Meat-based dishes	20	9
All other	5	2
Total ingredient eatings	**100%**	**46%**

Hamburgers represent 46 percent of all sandwich eatings, followed by sliced/roast beef at 24 percent. Spaghetti is the most frequently served combination dish, accounting for 26 percent of all eatings. Stew/Goulash follows, representing 15 percent of all combination dishes.

☐ Ground beef has risen substantially in importance over time. Steaks have displayed the greatest relative stability. Roasts have suffered large declines.

	Distribution of Beef Serving Occasions		
	1967/68	1975	1983/84
Ground beef	37%	45%	53%
Steaks	22	25	22
Roasts	25	20	15
All other	16	10	10
Total beef	**100%**	**100%**	**100%**

☐ As mentioned previously, 90 percent of all households serve some form of beef in an average two-week period. Most beef-using households will have occasion to use ground beef during two weeks' time, as household penetration of ground beef stands at 78 percent. Fifty percent report serving steak, and 33 percent report serving roasts.

Demographics of Beef Users

☐ The heaviest beef users are those who serve beef on six or more occasions during an average two-week period. These users, while representing only 32 percent of the household population, account for 61 percent of total beef eatings. The demographic characteristics of these heavy beef-using households are as follows:

Income:	$15,000–$30,000
Household size:	3+ members
Age of female head:	45–54 years
Occupation of household head:	Blue-collar
Market size:	50,000
Census Region:	West North Central
	West South Central
	East South Central

Exhibit 38.2   How Lifestyle and Attitudes Can Affect Beef Demand

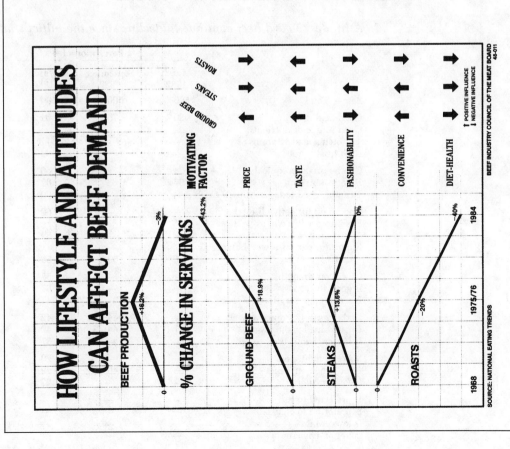

HOW CONSUMER HABITS INFLUENCE THE BEEF INDUSTRY

Walk through the accompanying charts.

As a cattleman, you certainly watch the beef production cycle. In 1976, beef production peaked at 127.5 pounds per capita (carcass weight). Most cattlemen didn't realize a profit in 1976 and would agree with economists that supply must come closer in alignment with demand. By 1983–84, the industry had dropped beef supply to 3% below 1968's production levels.

Have We Lowered "Supply" Enough?

During the 1980's, the answer may not only lie in supply, but also in how consumer lifestyles and attitudes are changing eating habits and, consequently, the selection of beef products.

Beef is purchased in three major forms: **ground beef, steaks,** and **roasts.** The accompanying charts reflect their change in "servings" since 1968. Along with beef supply, other factors like disposable income, the economy, etc., have changed since 1968. Note how the product categories for beef also changed.

Why is Ground Beef Climbing?

The first logical reaction might be that McDonalds, Burger King and Wendy's have contributed to ground beef's tremendous increase in servings. That is true, but this data is based on actual "at-home servings" . . . what is actually consumed at the family dinner table.

GROUND BEEF is the most frequently used fresh meat. It accounts for more than half of all beef servings at home. Its biggest positives are low price, ease of preparation, and great taste. Ground beef's weakness can be contributed to diet-health concerns.

What About Steaks and Roasts?

STEAKS rank well as beef's highest ticketed item. Steak's strong positioning comes from taste, ease of preparation, and great image. What's easier and more impressive than serving steaks for dinner? But price and perceived nutritional concerns hamper its growth.

Although the price of certain roast cuts are competitive, **ROASTS** generally don't fit into today's smaller households and convenience-oriented society. Changing the roast simply by repackaging, precooking, or a value-added product could rejuvenate this category.

How Can the Beef Industry Respond?

The Beef Industry's challenge will not only include better marketing and promotion programs of specific beef products, but also will include identifying those important issues and consumer trends that help keep beef marketing activities in tune and on target. The consumer of the 80's is concerned with health, fitness, convenience, and fashionability. The main thrust of the Beef Industry Council and state marketing programs is targeted toward the active lifestyle, health-conscious segment of the population, who are light users of beef.

The "Beef Give Strength" advertising program is targeted toward college-educated women between the ages of 25 and 44 with a household income of $30,000 plus. Steaks and roasts are emphasized due to their growth potential. Early results are exciting. A recent survey documents that 23% of consumers who looked at our magazine ads indicated it changed the way they think about beef. In addition, our advertising and in-store materials were shown to increase beef sales by 16%.

Are We Doing Enough?

We've got the marketing needs of the industry in sharper focus now than ever before. We've segmented and isolated the targets and developed programs to impact these markets. We simply have to "put more fuel on the fire if we want to heat up demand."

BEEF INDUSTRY COUNCIL OF THE MEAT BOARD

In early 1985, a national random telephone survey was conducted with 500 consumers who were the primary grocery shoppers in their households. The purpose of the study was to see if consumers were aware of beef industry advertising, in general, and the theme line "Beef Gives Strength," which had been featured in much of the industry's advertising and marketing communications. The study also explored consumers' perceptions of and attitudes toward beef. Exhibit 38.3 shows the attitudes toward beef over time and Exhibit 38.4 shows how attitudes of respondents aware of BIC's marketing activities compare to those of respondents with no awareness of BIC's marketing activities. Top-line conclusions from the research follows.

National Advertising Awareness

Advertising awareness and awareness of the theme line "Beef Gives Strength" have increased significantly.

1. Awareness of BIC advertising has significantly increased from 14 percent (March 1984) to 20 percent (February 1985).

2. Most of those aware of BIC advertising claim to have seen it on television.

3. Aided recall of the "Beef Gives Strength" theme line has increased significantly (from 17 percent in 1984 to 24 percent in 1985).

Exhibit 38.3   Consumer Attitudes toward Beef

Attitudes toward beef continue to decline since the initial studies.

	Perception of Beef in			
	March 1982	September 1982	March 1984	February 1985
Base — Total	500	500	500	501
Good tasting	80%	75%	81%[a]	75%
Good source of nutrients, proteins, and vitamins	—	—	71[a]	64
High-quality food	—	—	66	66
Can be prepared quickly	74	72[a]	66	—
High in nutrition	67	65	63	61
Tastes as good today as it used to	—	—	60	60
Good food for active lifestyles	—	—	60[a]	54
Fits into my lifestyle as well as it used to	—	—	59	54
Important part of a well-balanced diet	66[a]	59	58	54
Gives you strength	—	—	58	59
Is good for you	—	—	57	53
Is a contemporary food	—	—	47	44
Nothing satisfies quite as well	44	44	42	—
Good value for the money	47	44	42	44
Is leaner than it used to be	—	—	37	36
Makes a light meal	—	—	29	25
Good when on a diet	38	40	29	—
Is low in calories	—	—	23	24
Is preferred to fish	—	—	—	43
Is preferred to chicken	—	—	—	35
Is low in fat	—	—	—	23
Is low in cholesterol	—	—	—	16

[a]Significantly different at 95 percent level of confidence

Exhibit 38.4   Consumer Attitudes toward Beef

Respondents aware of the BIC advertising, theme line, or in-store materials have significantly better attitudes toward beef in the area of lifestyle/contemporary than those not aware of these elements.

	Perception of Beef by Awareness of Marketing Mix February 1985	
	Aware of Marketing Mix[a]	Not Aware of Marketing Mix
Base — Total	311	190
Good tasting	79[b]	68
Good source of nutrients, proteins, and vitamins	67	60
High-quality food	69	62
Can be prepared quickly	—	—
High in nutrition	64	57
Tastes as good today as it used to	65[b]	53
Good food for active lifestyles	57[b]	48
Fits into my lifestyle as well as it used to	55	51
Important part of a well-balanced diet	60[b]	44
Gives you strength	63[b]	54
Is good for you	56	48
Is a contemporary food	50[b]	34
Nothing satisfies quite as well	—	—
Good value for the money	46	39
Is leaner than it used to be	38	33
Makes a light meal	24	27
Good when on a diet	—	—
Is low in calories	25	24
Is preferred to chicken	37	33
Is low in fat	24	22
Is low in cholesterol	15	18
Is preferred to fish	44	42

[a]Aware of BIC advertising *or* theme line "Beef Gives Strength" *or* in-store materials
[b]Significantly higher at 95 percent level of confidence

National Attitudes

Attitudes toward beef continue to decline, mainly due to declining attitudes among light users. Such negative health/lifestyle perceptions of beef among light users, with attitudes stable among heavy and medium users, continue to confirm the correctness of the copy strategy and target audience. People exposed to the BIC advertising and in-store materials have significantly better attitudes toward beef in many strategic areas.

Industry Finding

In just five years, the Beef Industry has increased its market development programs almost threefold due to increased producer participation in state checkoff programs and to increased packer, processor, and purebred breeder investments.

This increase in investments has allowed the industry to increase its per capita investment per consumer from 3 cents in 1980 to 8 cents in 1985. Exhibit 38.5 shows the amounts contributed per head by each state in 1980 compared to 1985.

The 1985 Farm Bill included legislation that would permit the beef industry to establish a national, uniform $1-per-head checkoff for a national beef promotion program. The legislation followed action taken by the National Cattlemen's Association. In early 1985, cattlemen urged NCA to pursue the possibility of amending the current law. NCA state affiliates, board members, and committee members approved, and a study committee was appointed to research possible amendments. The study committee developed a list of amendments. Following approval by the NCA executive committee, the amendments were studied by cattlemen and then, in the form of new legislation, were introduced and passed by a House subcommittee. Key provisions of the proposal follow.

☐ *Title:* Change the name from Beef Research and Information Act to Beef Promotion and Research Act.

☐ *Referendum:* Provide for a delayed referendum approximately two years after the program is implemented.

☐ *Checkoff:* Establish a $1-per-head national checkoff rate on all cattle.

☐ *Coordination:* Give existing state beef promotion organizatoins responsibility for collecting the funds, and develop a credit system to allow state councils to receive credit for an amount equal to their existing checkoff, not to exceed 50 cents per head.

☐ *National Program:* Create a Cattleman's Beef Promotion Board, based on state cattle population, that would be responsible for (1) administering the checkoff collection program, (2) approving the final budget, and (3) electing ten people to serve on the Beef Promotion Operating Committee. The committee will include the ten members elected by the Cattlemen's Board plus ten members elected by the Beef Industry Council. The committee will be responsible for developing budgets and contracting with existing national organizations to conduct programs of beef promotion and research.

Without this legislation, the BIC was estimating total dollars available for state and national beef programs at around $22 million or 9.2 cents per capita. With the $1-per-head national checkoff, the total dollar amount should reach $76.2 million or 31.5 cents per capita. Assuming that 60 percent of this total fund could be coordinated through the BIC (with the remainder being invested at the state level) the total income to the BIC could increase from over $13 million to over $46 million as shown below:

BIC Income Projections from	Fiscal 1986	Fiscal 1987
Producers' checkoff	$12,360,000	$44,772,000
Purebred funding	300,000	300,000
Packer investments	550,000	650,000
Processor investments	35,000	50,000
Sales of literature and materials, plus interest	525,000	600,000
	$13,770,000	$46,372,000

Exhibit 38.5   Beef Investment Growth (State Checkoff Rates, 1980 and 1985)

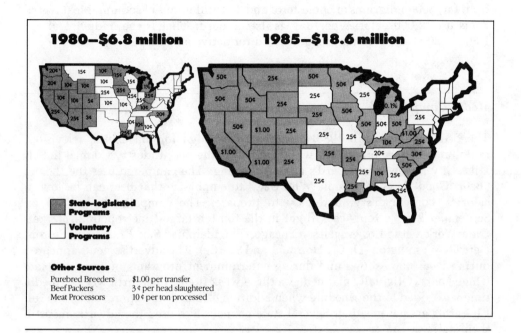

Advertising/Sales Promotions/Marketing

Meat Nutri-Facts

A revolutionary nutrition information program called Meat Nutri-Facts was announced in New York City in May 1985 to the national news media. The response so far has been overwhelming. For the first time, consumers are able to find nutrition information on a cut-by-cut basis at the supermarket meat case, and the information they find is more comprehensive than the information offered by any other food industry. After telling the press about the program, the Meat Board introduced the program to retailers at the Food Marketing Institute's annual convention. The program was developed jointly by the Meat Board, the Food Marketing Institute, and the American Meat Institute.

Within a few months of its introduction, the Nutri-Facts program was installed in several large retail chains, with many more planning to add the program by year's end. Meat Nutri-Facts uses the most recent U. S. Department of Agriculture nutrient composition research on beef, pork, and lamb, and presents the data graphically in a way that helps shoppers make informed decisions right at the meat case. The program is intended primarily for active-lifestyle and health-oriented consumers, or those shoppers who tend to let nutrition concerns govern their meat purchase decisions.

One interesting feature of the program is the use of stickers right on the packages to identify meat cuts with fewer than 200 calories per three-ounce cooked, trimmed serving. The cut-by-cut charts show protein, vitamins, and minerals as percentages of U. S. Recommended Daily Allowances (U. S. RDAs). Calories, fat, cholesterol, and sodium levels, all of which have no established U. S.

RDAs, are compared with standard daily limits established by the American Heart Association and the National Academy of Sciences: 30 percent of calories from fat, 300 milligrams of cholesterol and 330 milligrams of sodium. Meat Nutri-Facts uses 2,000 calories per day as its standard. That is the midpoint of the 1,800–2,200 calorie range recommended for active adult women.

Media Campaign

The beef industry's fall 1985 advertising campaign for magazines, television, radio, and in-store promotion was unveiled by the Beef Industry Council in Salt Lake City at the Meat Board's annual meeting. The campaign uses the theme, "Beef. Good News for People Who Eat," to emphasize that beef can be low in calories, contemporary, and easy to prepare. The campaign kicked off on September 2 for a four-week flight in the top ten largest metropolitan markets (New York City, Los Angeles, Chicago, Philadelphia, San Francisco, Boston, Detroit, Washington, D. C., Houston, and Seattle). The advertisements appeared during local news shows and during entertainment programs in early and late fringe hours. Originally planned as a three-week flight, the fourth week of media time was added to the schedule when additional funds were approved by the full BIC at its annual meeting. Several state councils also used the advertisement in their states.

The television advertisement drew enthusiastic responses from both inside and outside the industry. The advertisement includes shots of 16 different beef dishes and the music of Beethoven's "Ode to Joy" theme from his Ninth Symphony. Bob Talbert, a regular columnist for the Detroit *Free Press*, wrote in his September 23 column: "I tell you this: I can't watch that new 'Beef. Good News For People Who Eat' (with a maestro using a shish-ke-baton) without getting hungry. You, too? It could even make a vegetarian have second thoughts." The storyboard for the advertisement is shown in Exhibit 38.6.

The "Middle Management" advertisement shown in Exhibit 38.7 was the beef industry's fall 1985 print advertisement. It appeared in issues of nine consumer magazines. The tenderloin pictured weighed four ounces raw and yielded three ounces cooked. This advertisement also had a one-third page recipe for "Light and Luxurious Ten Minute Beef Saute" as an addition to the advertisement. The advertisement and recipe addressed the three issues of the BIC's active-lifestyle/health-oriented target: diet-health, fashionability, convenience. The advertisement, without the recipe, ran in two September issues of *Newsweek*.

Two radio commercials, in both 60- and 30-second versions were prepared for use by state beef councils in key market areas. More than 26,000 retail outlets across the country participated in the point-of-purchase promotion campaign, "Take It Along. It's Nutritious."

Exhibit 38.6   Television Storyboard

320   Case 38

Exhibit 38.7   Magazine Advertisement

Environmental
Analysis   38A

The focus of this section is an analysis of the environment in which the beef industry operates. Five environments are analyzed: social/cultural, competitive, technological, legal/political, and economic. From such analysis we gain insight as to how changes in the environment are likely to affect industry activities.

I. Social/Cultural Environment

    A. Short-Term Issues

        1. Family structure continues to change as two-thirds of women 25–44 years of age are employed outside the home, as are 57 percent of married women with children.

        2. Appearance, weight, and health-consciousness will continue to impact dietary patterns with emphasis upon calorie and fat content and portion size.

        3. Fitness awareness will continue with persons who exercise regularly reducing their intake of cigarettes, meat, and sugar.

        4. The language bond that unites the diverse Hispanic cultures of the United States influences advertising, marketing, and educational campaigns directed to this segment.

        5. The trend toward eating more meals away from home will continue, with ethnic foods, led by Mexican cuisine, becoming even more popular.

        6. Concern about fat, cholesterol, additives, preservatives, residues, and antibiotics will make consumers highly sensitive to these characteristics when deciding whether or not to buy beef.

        7. Media coverage of animal treatment in research laboratories and the growing effectiveness of animal welfare activists makes the animal welfare issue potentially explosive.

    B. Long-Term Issues

        1. Population changes will impact beef sales.

            a. The largest population segment will be between 25 and 44 years of age and have high education and discretionary income levels.

            b. The fastest growing segments will be 35–44 and over 65 years of age and population growth will be most rapid in Texas, California, and Florida.

            c. The nation's largest minority ethnic group, the Hispanic, will grow at 7 percent a year. They will be concentrated in the New York, San Antonio, Miami, Chicago, and Los Angeles areas.

2. Family structure will continue to evolve.

    a. The percentage of zero- and one-child families will increase and the average household size will decline.

    b. By 1990, married couples will head only 50 percent of households and only 14 percent of households will be supported by a single breadwinner.

    c. Such lifestyle and family structures will continue to stress convenience, diversity, nutrition, and "grazing" in their eating habits.

3. Concern for animal welfare will continue, with a focus on proper use of resources, vegetarianism, the rights of animals, antibiotics and chemical use, and diet/health issues.

4. Awareness of agriculture as a way of life will continue to fade, and as people move from the city to the country, rural areas will lose their distinct agricultural character.

II. Competitive Environment

A. Short-Term Issues

1. Beef is experiencing the largest reduction in servings of any product category at the food-service level.

    a. Poultry and main-dish salads are the fastest growing competition.

    b. Hamburger's share is steady, but beef entrees are losing share.

2. The fresh meat counter is receiving proportionately less attention at the retail level, as hot and cold take-out counters (delis) and prewrapped salad/vegetable/fruit servings are becoming more common.

3. In 1984, poultry consumption surpassed pork consumption and is projected to surpass beef by 1987.

    a. Aggressive poultry product development will continue.

    b. Consumers feel poultry out-performs beef in price/value and health areas and is equal in taste preference.

4. Food perceptions have changed.

    a. People are eating a wider variety of foods.

    b. Beef is no longer a fashionable food for today's lifestyles.

    c. Some health-care professionals and consumers regard beef as a heavy, unhealthful nutrient source.

5. Consumers are spending less on food (17 percent of income) and more on nonfood items like entertainment, automobiles, homes, and electronics.

6. Increasing consumer awareness of labeling, residues, government regulation, and other food safety issues may impact beef consumption.

B. Long-Term Issues

   1. Increased efficiency in poultry production, along with consumer acceptance and new product introductions are major forces impacting beef.

   2. With ongoing interest in nutrition, radical consumer groups will challenge beef's nutrition message.

   3. Beef merchandising has not changed significantly in two decades.

     a. Other meats are better meeting consumer demands.

     b. There is a need for new product-development efforts.

III. Technological Environment

A. Short-Term Issues

   1. A variety of value-added competitive products now on the market have not been met with comparable or better beef products.

     a. Available technology can be adapted.

     b. New technology can be developed.

   2. Public pressure against antibiotics used in beef production will increase significantly and non-human-usable substitutes are needed.

   3. UPC technology already in place will be more widely used.

   4. The trend toward centralized, tray-ready beef portioning at the packer level will increase.

   5. The importance of technical information as a consumer marketing tool will increase.

     a. Vacuum packaging and microwave cooking instructions are important.

     b. Video point-of-purchase materials and nutrient labeling are needed.

B. Long-Term Issues

   1. The existing research base is not communicated and utilized adequately throughout the industry to improve efficiency and create products that satisfy consumer demand.

   2. Economic pressures will necessitate the development of higher-value use of by-products.

   3. Responses to continuing concern over the total cost of production include:

     a. Genetic engineering

     b. Management techniques to develop product-specific carcasses

     c. Automation advances, including robotics, in packing and process phases.

4. Packaging modernizations will be necessary, including:

   a. Food-in-a-bag for food-service

   b. Retort pouches for extended at-home shelf life

   c. Irradiation

   d. Frozen beef

   e. Kitchen-ready packaging

5. Likely responses by the livestock and meat industries that have not participated in the technology of today's "information explosion" include:

   a. Electronic grading

   b. Electronic marketing

   c. Computerized national inventory of cattle on feed, carcass inventories, and the like

   d. Electronic consumer marketing

IV. Legal/Political Environment

A. Short-Term Issues

1. The food safety issue is gaining momentum, especially regarding:

   a. Antibiotics and residues

   b. Tainted and contaminated meat

   c. Additives and preservatives.

2. Consumer activism is increasing and big business, including the beef industry, will receive closer scrutiny.

3. The importance of lobbyists and special interest groups calls for:

   a. Better support of Washington-based industry allies

   b. Enhanced collateral materials for use in communication efforts.

4. The 1985 Farm Bill may impact the beef industry in a number of ways.

B. Long-Term Issues

1. Continued dialogue by the beef industry with health organizations will have a positive effect on the policies and recommendations of these organizations.

2. Increasing fractionalization within the beef industry decreases cohesiveness among larger organizations.

3. Import/export/tariff regulations will loosen, allowing more aggressive pursuit of overseas markets and increased competition from imports.

4. The legality of the industry's checkoff system may be challenged on a state by state basis.

5. Government deregulation, applied to the meat industry, could create negative perceptions in the minds of consumers regarding loosening of quality standards, inspection by private firms, labeling, and so on.

V. Economic Environment

    A. Short- and Long-Term Issues

        1. Both short- and long-term interest rates will trend slightly higher for the remainder of 1986 before beginning a gradual decline of 25–30 percent by 1990.

        2. The U. S. dollar will strengthen 10–15 percent over the next five years with inflation of 0–5 percent annually and declining energy prices.

        3. Farm-land values will continue to decline until they reach a level where the land will produce a positive cash flow.

        4. As the general business environment becomes more price competitive, all sectors of agribusiness will implement innovative means to become more cost efficient and productive, despite an archaic pricing system that will continue to hamper the efficiency of the beef industry.

        5. The trend toward fewer but larger farms and more vertical integration will continue while land once used as crop land will be increasingly used for pastures.

        6. Many state, local, and national institutions, particularly schools, will encounter financial difficulty, but government funded research will shrink with private industry attempting to make up the difference.

This section has presented events that could impact the beef industry during the planning period. The purpose of predicting possible future events is to allow the long-range plan sufficient flexibility to meet possible contingencies if future events do not occur exactly as predicted. In addition, prediction allows the development of a specific plan of action to confront these events as they occur.

Prognosis for the Beef Industry

If the beef industry only continues its present level of activity in the area of promotion, education, communications and research, the following conditions will be likely to occur.

A.   Beef's Market Share

Beef's competition (other meats and nonmeats) will have a larger share of the consumer's food dollar . . . beef's share will drop.

1.   There will be increasing competition from other meats, especially poultry, in all markets, including the ones where beef has been traditionally strong.

2.   There will be increasing competition from other foods, and nonfood items for the consumer dollar.

3.   Beef's share of the menu will continue to decline in all food-service segments.

4.   An increasing variety of food choices coupled with an aging population will continue to push the trend toward lighter beef usage in a growing number of households.

5.   Beef exports will continue to show slow growth and imports, and will continue to be regulated by the counter-cyclical meat import law.

B.   Health and Nutrition Concerns

Health and nutrition concerns will continue to impact all food choices with specific emphasis on beef.

1.   Competing products will continue to convince some segments of the market that beef is less nutritious or healthful than some other foods.

2.   Concerns over dietary fat intake and calories will become more important than dietary cholesterol.

3.   The trend of exercise and physical fitness will continue. The consumer will become more aware of "wellness" programs and combining good nutrition and lifestyle.

C.   Beef's Image

Beef's image as a fashionable or contemporary food will continue to decline.

1.   Eating will continue to be more of a social event to some consumer segments and we will continue to see trendy and elegant foods consumed and merchandised.

2.   The market segment gaining in affluence is also the group most concerned with physical fitness and eating light, low-caloric foods.

3. Consumers' perception of inconsistent beef quality attributes will continue to be an issue.

D. Trends in Beef/Beef Product Development

The lack of new product development will lead to decreased usage of beef as trends continue toward more precooked products or entrees with beef as an ingredient. This will lead to less demand for roasts, stews, etc.

1. Changing lifestyles will continue to demand products that are conveniently packaged, quick and easy to prepare.

2. Smaller core families will demand smaller, different portion sizes than are now in the case.

3. Microwave ovens will be in the majority of homes and consumers will continue to search for products that can be cooked in the appliance.

E. Trends in Industry Size

The industry trend toward a smaller beef industry and fewer but larger individual operations will continue.

1. This will lead to a numerically smaller resource base to actively support beef programs.

2. Economies of scale may work to lower or help production costs.

F. Food Safety

Food safety has been described as the consumer issue of the 1980s and it has potential to negatively affect beef demand.

1. Concern over the use of antibiotics, feed additives, growth stimulants, etc., will continue to be issues of public concern.

2. Microbiological contamination of meat and meat products has potential to become an explosive issue.

Other factors such as imports, exports, and efficiency of production will affect industry profitability. They have not been addressed in the report because the BIC has no direct responsibility in these areas. However, the factors that have been addressed all point to decreasing profit opportunities for the various segments of the beef industry if the industry continues only what it has been doing.

Christina Lane Cosmetics, Inc.: Natural Body Care Products

Case 39

In early 1985, Dan Brice, a southern California natural food retailer and nutritional counselor, approached Christina Lane Cosmetics about developing a personalized line of natural body care products. His plan was that he would bring the product development expertise and image to the product line and Christina Lane Cosmetics would provide the manufacturing, distribution, and marketing efforts necessary to ensure product success. The line would include a variety of products under the brand name Dan Brice Naturals and be distributed exclusively through health food stores.

Bill Wayne, vice president of marketing for Christina Lane Cosmetics was initially very interested in the concept and strongly supported it to top management. However, as industry and consumer research began to be completed and marketing strategies were being discussed and formulated, he started to have second thoughts. He wondered about the product name, the advisability of going through health food stores exclusively, the breadth of product mix, and, in a broader sense, whether or not a market really existed for an additional product entrant.

Background — Christina Lane Cosmetics

For almost a decade, Christina Lane had been one of North America's most sought-after fashion models. She appeared on the covers of many leading magazines and did a number of television commercials for major consumer companies. Around Christmas one year, two investors and a marketing executive for a large cosmetics firms approached Christina about forming a corporation to develop and distribute a full line of women's cosmetics bearing her name. While it seemed logical that her name recognition and position as a model would provide instant market exposure for such a cosmetics line, the decision was not an easy one for Christina to make. The prospects of being part of a company carrying her name seemed exciting and potentially rewarding, but it did mean that her modeling career would be severely limited as she went into competition with some of her former clients. After much personal evaluation and counsel from trusted friends and business associates, Christina decided to go ahead with the idea. Christina Lane Cosmetics, Inc. became a reality.

In many ways, the company was an overnight success. National sales distribution was achieved by developing a field salesforce that personally called on all of the major department and women's specialty stores that carried full lines of high-quality cosmetics. The company decided early in the development of its marketing strategy that the product line would not be distributed through drug stores, discount stores, or smaller department stores. A multimedia advertising and promotional campaign involving national television, most women's fashion and general interest magazines, and an extensive retailer cooperative program supported the Christina Lane line of cosmetics. Christina herself was highly visible in most of the company's advertising and frequently made guest appearances at trade shows and major fashion programs at leading retail stores. During the company's first five years, sales grew at an average annual rate of 125 percent and profits increased an average of 80 percent each year.

Background — Dan Brice

Dan Brice, a southern California natural food retailer and nutritional counselor, believes that sunscreening should be an all-year affair. He has seen too many of his customers complain of skin cancer and of prematurely aging skin. One out of every four to seven people is a victim of skin cancer. The most frightening aspect of skin cancer is not knowing whether you've already been overexposed to the sun. Skin cancer is cumulative. Sunshine actually alters the molecular structure of the skin, damaging the collagen, the skin's main supporting substance.

After researching skin cancer and how to prevent it, Dan saw a need for everyday skin and hair care products with a SPF of at least 8 to be used by everyone, regardless of skin type. Recent studies show that the UVA ray (tanning), as well as the UVB ray (burning), have been shown to cause premature aging and may also be implicated in skin cancer.

Dan met with cosmetic chemists and dermatologists to determine the best approach for developing natural products with broad spectrum sun protection and natural nutrients to condition and nourish the skin. He explained he wanted products with no fragrance, no artificial dyes, natural nutrients, a non-Paba sunscreen, and moisturizers suited to different humidity conditions. After developing some preliminary product plans, he went to people at Christina Lane Cosmetics with his ideas.

Research on Health Food Stores

Bill Wayne asked his director of marketing research, Mark Powell, to try and get a handle on the health food market. He was specifically interested in how the health food stores were doing. Mark prepared the review shown in Exhibit 39.1 from information in *Health Food Stores* magazine. The data was obtained from replies to questionnaires sent to 2,500 independent retailers throughout the nation. Major chains were not included, but were taken into account when projecting industry-wide totals. Supermarkets and other mass merchants were not included at all.

Of the retailers that responded, 88 percent operated just one store. The remainder operated an average of 3.4 stores. The average length of time in business was eight years per store. The main purpose for this annual survey was to give an indication of trends at what might be termed a typical retail operation. Because the sample was taken at random and because it varied in size and character from year to year, readers were cautioned not to take the results too literally. Some of the data are based on respondents' estimates or personal interpretations of questions. Some of the main conclusions from the survey include:

1. There were 580 fewer health food stores at the end of 1984 than at the end of 1982. This alone is a major cause of the decrease in overall industry sales.

Exhibit 39.1   *Health Food Stores* **Survey Results**

Total Industry Sales

In 1984, for the second straight year sales slipped in the health food industry. Estimated industry sales were not quite $1.7 billion, down from just over $2.0 billion in 1983. That's a drop of 16.3 percent. (Last year the decrease was approximately 17 percent.)

Average Sales per Store

Going along with the drop in overall sales was a 17 percent slip in average store volume, from $211,854 in 1983 to $175,748 in 1984. In 1985, however, the majority by far of the respondents expect to see a reverse of the downtrend. Some 84 percent of the survey respondents said that they expect sales this year to be up an average of 19 percent. However, even more of the respondents to the survey last year — almost 90 percent — predicted an upturn in 1984, and it failed to materialize.

Average Annual Net Profits per Store

For profits in 1984, the drop was not quite as bad as it was in sales, but it was, nonetheless, significant. Average net after taxes among the respondents was $15,152, 14.4 percent lower than the $17,697 reported for 1983. Also, 22 percent of the respondents in the 1984 survey reported a loss, compared to just 10 percent a year ago. Another important point is that the current survey appears to report on somewhat smaller stores than it did in recent years. In this year's survey, just 22 percent of the respondents said their sales were over $300,000; that compares with 34 percent at a similar level a year ago.

Average Sale per Customer

In 1984, the amount of an average sale for the retailers dropped to its lowest level since 1980 — $10.61, compared with $11.78 in 1983, $15.48 in 1982, and $10.80 in 1981. This could be another indication that the stores represented in this survey were smaller than those surveyed in recent years.

Average Square Footage of Stores

The average square footage of health stores dropped from almost 1,800 in 1983 to roughly 1,250 in 1984. Again, this may be attributed to the number of small stores in the sample.

Store Locations

Statistics on store location show some changes from the previous year, although not dramatic changes. An identical 10 percent operated out of shopping malls, while 37 percent operated from strip shopping centers (up from 33 percent in 1983) and 47 percent were located on business streets compared to 45 percent last year. The remainder of the stores were located on residential streets (8 percent).

continued

Exhibit 39.1   *continued*

Average Dollars Spent on Advertising per Store

The retailers in this year's survey averaged $4,530 on advertising compared to roughly $3,000 in 1983. The media they spent the most on were weekly newspaper, Yellow Pages, direct mail, daily newspaper, fliers and posters, and radio.

Buying Patterns

Direct buying by the retailer rose in 1984, with over 85 percent of the survey participants mentioning that they do at least some buying without the aid of distributors. Among that 85 percent, the percentage of goods bought directly was 28 percent. In other words, approximately one-quarter of all merchandise bought in the industry is bought direct from manufacturers (28 percent of 85 percent).

Average Density of Competition

In 1984, the number of other health food stores competing with survey respondents dropped significantly—from 2.9 in 1983 to 2.0. Perhaps this was an indication of the decrease in the overall number of stores in the industry.

Total Industry Sales of Body Care Products

Sales of body care products in the health food industry totaled $129.5 million compared to $185.6 million in 1982 and $150.6 million in 1983. This decline could be attributed to the number of manufacturers selling to the supermarkets and mass merchants. In turn, the mass merchants undersell the health food retailers, thus taking a large portion of their business.

Average Body Care Sales per Store

The average body care sales per store has followed the same path as the overall industry sales of body care products. In 1982, the average sales of body care products was just over $20,000. In 1983, it dropped to $16,000 and in 1984, to $13,500.

Body Care as a Percent of Store Sales

Since 1981, this trend has been relatively flat, and 1984 is no different. In 1984, body care as a percent of store sales was 7.7 percent, an increase of 1 percent over 1983, 1982, and 1981.

Average Markup of Body Care Products

Average 1984 markup on body care products was 53 percent. This figure is just 2 percent below the figure for 1983.

---

2.   This is a time of adjustments for independent health food retailers, as they must learn to cope with their new competition.

3.   More and more companies that once claimed they sold exclusively to health food stores are entering the mass merchandise stores. This is definitely taking away business from the health food retailer.

Marketing Research

To help ascertain the market for Dan Brice Naturals, Mark Powell contracted with a marketing research organization. The firm was asked to conduct interviews with selected manufacturers, distributors, members of the trade press, and health foods marketing consultants at various industry conferences. They were also asked to interview health food store owners, managers, and sales personnel in selected markets in Florida, California, and Arizona. In addition, several focused group interviews were held with customers of health food stores. The criteria for participants in the focused group interviews included:

- Women 18 to 49 years old
- Men 18 +, with about 50 percent over age 35
- Household income $30,000 + annually
- Must have purchased products in health food stores at least four times in the past 12 months and at least once in the past 30 days
- Regular users of cosmetics, skin care products, sun care products
- About one-half of participants purchase some body care products in health food stores
- About one-half shop in health food stores, but tend to purchase most body care products in other stores

Exhibit 39.2 provides some of the general conclusions from the consumer interviews. Critical issues identified from all of the research conducted by the firm are presented in the following sections.

Product Mix

Limited Depth of Line Recommended.   The overwhelming majority of health food stores lack the floor space, shelf space, and open-to-buy necessary for a line of some 30 skin care, sun care, and hair care products. The line should be narrowed to about 12 high-opportunity products.

Natural Ingredients Demanded.   Operators and shoppers, first and foremost, want *natural* ingredients. However, neither operators nor shoppers really understand which ingredients are natural and which are not.

Sun Protection Ingredients Important.   Shoppers and operators believe the sun is a major threat to healthy skin and a leading cause of skin cancer. Natural sun protection ingredients will be perceived as an effective differential advantage in skin care products.

Moisturizing Ingredients Wanted.   Female and male shoppers and store operators recognize the importance of natural skin moisturizing ingredients. Many are believed to nourish and heal the skin.

Products Sought for Specific Skin Problems.   Operators and shoppers seek products promising solutions to specific skin problems such as oily skin, dry skin, skin that is oily in spots, and acne.

Paba-Free Products May Provide a Differential Advantage.   Paba is perceived as a positive, natural ingredient, and is recognized as a common ingredient in body care products, but some awareness of negative publicity is beginning.

Skin Care Sales Should Exceed Hair Care Sales.   Shoppers feel that it is less important to buy shampoo than skin care products in health food stores. The ingredients in shampoos are thought to rinse out, anyway.

Exhibit 39.2   General Detail from Customer Interviews

Why People Shop Health Food Stores over Other Stores (Insights into what is sought in products):

☐ The healthy adventure—feeling that one can search out and discover wonderful, healthy things not available in other kinds of stores.

☐ Perception that many products in supermarkets and drug stores include harmful substances, including body care products with harmful substances that are, "absorbed into my body." Included are mineral oil, bees' wax, perfumes, dyes, etc.

☐ Attitude that products in health food stores feature wonderful but little understood ingredients, such as vitamins, especially vitamin E; Aloe Vera, believed to be a natural miracle healing substance, and other even more exotic natural ingredients.

☐ For solutions to specific problems—allergies, overly oily skin, high triglycerides, low energy, etc. Older women with real or perceived health problems tend to be heavy users of health food stores.

☐ For "natural" products, ingredients, foods, pet foods, body care products. Natural equals *good;* natural equals *quality;* natural equals *healthy;* natural equals *gentle.* (But nobody really knows what is natural and what is not.)

☐ For knowledgeable, helpful advice and personal service. Store operators *are* consultants.

☐ To demonstrate individuality; to be a part of something that, clearly, is not perceived to be for everybody.

Distribution Mix

Effective, Cost Efficient Distribution Is the Greatest Marketing Challenge Facing the New Line.   The overwhelming majority of stores, about 6,000 or 85 percent of all health food stores, are of the small, cramped variety. They offer limited shelf space and limited volume and turn opportunities, yet request frequent service. Channels of distribution to these stores are highly fragmented.

Additional Distribution Important.   In phase one of distribution efforts, additional distribution should be sought in health-related outlets such as large fitness centers, spas, tennis clubs, golf clubs, etc., to help offset upfront distribution investments.

Communications Mix

☐ Priority 1 must be to win awareness and loyalty of distributors and store owners and managers.
☐ Brand name awareness is low for health food store body care products.
☐ Public relations will be important to the marketing launch.
☐ Local advertising will be a helpful sell-in factor with larger, more professional retailers.

□   Sampling should be a major component of the marketing program. A simple, direct, no-nonsense approach to skin care and hair care will be effective with distributors, stores, women, and men.
□   The European mystique provides an effective marketing appeal.
□   The word *natural* must be featured in all communications. *Naturals* can be a highly productive part of the product name.

Preliminary Marketing Plan

Even though he was somewhat hesitant to move into the market, Bill Wayne worked with members of his marketing staff and Dan Brice to develop a preliminary marketing plan. The plan was prepared in the form of a series of questions to provide a basis for internal discussions as to how the company should proceed with this new product line.

1.   *What Do We Sell?*

Dan Brice Naturals Products.   We sell a range of natural skin care and hair care products that have been formulated to help prevent premature aging and skin cancer (See Exhibit 39.3). Protective cosmetics products can reduce the risk of long-term, in-depth skin damage caused by overexposure to daylight and can help preserve a young and healthy skin. The products will protect and nourish the skin and hair and prevent damage from within and without. They represent a simple, direct, no-nonsense approach to skin care and hair care. Special features include fragrance free, no artificial dyes, no mineral oil, Paba-free sunscreens, and UVA/UVB block giving broad spectrum protection.

2.   *To Whom Will We Sell?*

□   Health-concerned market segment
□   Natural food store customer profile
  □   Upper middle income ($25,000 +)
  □   Female
  □   25–44
  □   Single, divorced, widowed, separated
  □   College educated
  □   Lives in large metro area
  □   Geographic strength: (1) West, (2) Northeast, (3) South, (4) Central
  □   Health is the foremost consideration, but time and convenience are significant. The customer moisturizes regularly and eats a controlled diet. This person is more brand loyal, but remains an experimenter. They see themselves as intelligent, creative, amicable, self-assured. They are prone to allergies, fever, headaches, and stress. They are exercise enthusiasts.

Exhibit 39.3   Dan Brice Naturals Proposed Product Line

Skin and Hair Types

Line	Oily	Combination	Dry	Special (For All Skin and Hair Types)
Skin Care	1. Cleansing bar 2. Oil-free creme	1. Thorough cleansing wash 2. Preventive age creme	1. Gentle creme cleanser 2. Skin renewal creme	1. Bath and shower soap bar 2. Hand and body lotion 3. Special protection toner 4. Anti-wrinkle creme 5. Exfoliating creme mask 6. Bath oil 7. Outdoor bronzing creme 8. Skin repair
Hair Care	1. Oil control shampoo 2. Extra light conditioner	1. Daily shampoo 2. Instant conditioner	1. Extra body shampoo 2. Extra control conditioner	1. Hair strengthener 2. Extra body styling gel 3. Conditioning spray
Sun Care				1. Dark tanning oil 2. Moderate sun-screen lotion 3. Maximum sun-screen lotion 4. Solastick 5. After-sun moisturizer

- ☐ Natural food retailer
  - ☐ Number of stores: Approximately 7,700
  - ☐ Average store sales: $175,748
  - ☐ Total industry sales: $1.7 billion
  - ☐ Average size: 1,700 sq. ft.
  - ☐ Sales per sq. ft.: $146
  - ☐ Average daily traffic: 71
  - ☐ Average customer sale: $10.66
  - ☐ Average annual net profits: $15,000
  - ☐ Body care sales: $129.5 million industrywide; average store sales: $13,500

3.   *What Are We Trying to Accomplish?*

- ☐ Gain distribution in 17 percent of the health food outlets that support 75 percent of the market.
- ☐ Sales volume first year of $500,000–$1 million depending on final product mix.

□   Once final product mix is selected, a unit/volume forecast will be done.
□   Market share: To replace Rachael Perry Skin Care, gain number 2 position in hair care, and gain a 10 percent market share.

---

4.   What Techniques Will We Use?

□   Competitive pricing
□   Sales push strategy
□   Top chains are *A* accounts (1,500 stores) and targets of Phase 1 penetration; *B* accounts are targets of Phase 2
   □   Work on regional managers, who are responsible for brokers and detailers
   □   Establish a strong broker network among small markets and detailers/ merchandisers
   □   Establish an in-store consultant network, *i.e.*, by mail training/ diplomas/lab coats/birthday cards. Sampling and P. M. (push money) program.
□   Marketing theme—unique technical graphs and data to support claims. Establish M. Stowe as a credible spokesperson with script, publicity, book, video.
   □   Educational approach to skin and hair.
   □   Unique payment terms: Ninety-day dating to *A* credit-rating stores for launch. Not final yet.
   □   Telemarketing for B–C accounts

---

5.   How Will We Introduce the Product?

□   Free goods—foil packets samples.
□   Floor displays/shelf displays
□   Major account thrust
□   Dan Brice—visit market by market—Seek free publicity through press thrust (TV, radio, newspaper)
□   Regional managers—three initially for West, East, and Midwest.
□   Product announcement
□   Mass mailing with samples to all 7,700 stores
□   Trade advertising
□   Trade shows

---

6.   How Are We Going to Advertise?

□   Trade journals during launch period
□   Three trade journals (six times each)
□   Want to make noise—lots of noise
□   National sampling mailing
□   Consumer—call to action in small ads in March, April, May or through direct mailing to target audience. No ads in *Vogue, Mademoiselle, Self,* etc., but target advertising.

7. How Do We Educate the Consumer about Product Features and Benefits?

Objective: To effectively train key store personnel

Techniques

Consumer: In-store video, PR on damaging effects of sun. Consumer brochure, direct mail, consumer advertising, product manual

Retail
Stores:
☐   Product manuals
☐   Trade ad offering course
☐   Technical seminars
☐   Sales support

Inter-Varsity Christian Fellowship: Religious Organization Marketing Strategy

Case 40

Introduction

In 1984, a new Division of Marketing and Communications was being established to oversee all of IVCF's public relations, fund-raising, and marketing activities. As of 1984, the Marketing Communication Division, under the leadership of Ron Nicholas, was in the process of defining a strategy to ensure that IVCF would grow and prosper.

Ron Nicholas was working late in his office trying to formulate a marketing plan to market the Christian gospel on college and university campuses across the United States through IVCF's Campus Ministry Division. He recognized that this was a challenge because not-for-profit organizations such as IVCF, an interdenominational organization, traditionally have shunned marketing practices. He had to decide how IVCF could begin to apply marketing principles to communicate this gospel message to the college campus.

Marketing in Nontraditional Areas

Ron reflected on the fact that marketing management theory, concepts, and strategies are increasingly being applied in nontraditional areas, *i.e.*, in settings other than that of the business organization whose primary *raison d'etre* is to earn a profit for its owners. This is because it is now widely recognized that all organizations have products, as well as customers toward whom the marketing concept can be practiced.

This marketing concept states that the organization must first understand the consumer's unsatisfied needs and wants, and then create a product to satisfy those needs and wants better than the competition does. The marketer's next job is to deliver that product to the marketplace and to make potential customers aware of and want to try that product via marketing communications. It was Ron's task to take the "product" that IVCF offered to college campuses and to market it appropriately.

Source: Appreciation is expressed to Professor Geoffrey Lantos, Stonehill College, for permission to include his case in this text.

Inter-Varsity's Background and Organizational Environment

History

In order to better understand IVCF so as to begin writing his marketing plan, Ron reviewed IVCF's history. IVCF has its roots in a student movement that began at Cambridge University in England during the 1870s. Certain Christian students felt an awareness of their own and their friends' unmet spiritual needs, and consequently they began to meet daily for group prayer and Bible study. This movement later spread to Canada and the United States, where three Canadian staff workers helped students at the University of Michigan found the first United States IVCF chapter in 1939.

In 1941, IVCF was incorporated as a not-for-profit organization under the bylaws of Illinois, and since then it has been an interdenominational ministry among Christian students and faculty who wished to bring the gospel message of salvation through Christ (described below) to the ever-changing, ever-growing, and complex world of the university campus.

IVCF has grown impressively in the past 20 years, from a movement with 65 staff workers on 450 campuses in 1965 to a presence with over 400 campus staff and over 30,000 students on almost 1,000 college and university campuses and schools of nursing in 1984. IVCF has student groups on more campuses than any other interdenominational ministry. Consequently, more than 30,000 Inter-Varsity students today are actively talking to their friends about the difference Christ can make in one's life.

Inter-Varsity's Christian Fellowship Today

Next, Ron reflected on IVCF's position today. IVCF remains a voluntary movement of individuals, represents no particular Christian denomination (is interdenominational), and it is not a church. Instead it encourages staff members and students to cooperate with and get involved with the work of local churches.

One of the hallmarks of IVCF is that students generally lead and direct activities and are responsible for the operation of their student groups. IVCF staff members, in turn, bring guidance and motivation to student-led chapters across the country by teaching (discipling) young Christians, modeling a lifestyle of evangelistic[1] outreach to others, stimulating interest and participation in world missions, directing and encouraging students to plan and carry out hundreds of Christian activities, and providing encouragement and reassurance to students whose faith might otherwise crumble under the pressures of a busy college life.

Furthermore, IVCF members believe that the Bible is the inspired word of God, that it is the final authority in all matters of belief and practice, and that God uses students on faculty college campuses to spread the gospel message of salvation.

---

[1]Evangelism is the process of explaining the gospel message to others.

Inter-Varsity's Organizational Strategic Plan

Now Ron felt ready to begin writing his marketing plan. In order to do this, he reviewed IVCF's three-year strategic plan outlined in Exhibit 40.1. Its mission is evangelistic, *i.e.*, its purpose is to establish, assist, and encourage groups of students and faculty members of colleges, universities, nursing schools, and other comparable educational institutions to witness to college students of America with the gospel message. IVCF believes that God is calling students to be leaders and missionaries to the college campus, and that IVCF staff members can assist them in living victorious Christian lives.

In order to realize this purpose, IVCF has outlined three primary objectives: (1) Leading others to a personal faith in Jesus Christ as Savior and Lord (evangelism); (2) creating an environment to help Christian students (*i.e.*, those who have been led to a personal faith in Jesus) mature as disciples of Christ by Bible study, prayer, and Christian fellowship (Christian growth); and (3) challenging these students to go in the world where God directs (world missions). Exhibit 40.2 contains a more complete statement of IVCF's objectives.

Ron realized that his marketing plan must begin by outlining the organization's mission and objectives. In the plan, specific goals (quantitative standards) had to be formulated in order to measure IVCF's progress in achieving these objectives. Traditionally, most interdenominational Christian organizations have evaluated their progress by their financial statements, especially in terms of operating funds, *i.e.*, revenues less expenses (see Exhibit 40.3). This, rather than achieving the core mission and objectives, has formed the basis for adding programs and staff.

Exhibit 40.1   IVCF Strategic Plan—July 1, 1984–June 30, 1987

Central Priority

Spiritual Vitality: Our central goal is for every member of our fellowship to be godly in character and activity. The movement must exhibit spiritual vitality throughout the fellowship.

Purpose

The purpose of Inter-Varsity Christian Fellowship is to establish, assist, and encourage at colleges, universities, nursing schools, and other comparable educational institutions in the United States of America, groups of students and faculty members who witness to the Lord Jesus Christ as God Incarnate, and who have these major objectives:

1. To lead others to personal faith in Christ as Lord and Savior.
2. To help Christians grow toward maturity as disciples of Christ, by study of the Bible, by prayer, and by Christian fellowship.
3. To present the call of God to the world mission of the Church: to help students and faculty to discover God's role for them.

Primary Focus

The campus is our mission field and as such campus ministry is the central focus for our priorities, plan, and programs. All departmental plans are related to accomplishing our purpose.

Source: IVCF National Strategic Plan 1984–1987

Exhibit 40.2 IVCF Ministry Ojectives

These ministry objectives are the end results we plan to achieve year in and year out via the total ministry of IVCF.

I. In accordance with our Purpose, we desire to *establish new groups* at nearly all the colleges of this land.

We will also assist and encourage groups of students and faculty who give witness to Jesus and Christ as God Incarnate, who are in agreement with our Basis of Faith, and who:

II. *Evangelize Their Academic Community by*
   A. Demonstrating commitment to penetrate their entire campus with the gospel of Jesus Christ.
   B. Knowing how to verbalize the gospel message and how to respond to questions people ask concerning the gospel.
   C. Living a life of compassion and justice.
   D. Leading others to personal faith in Jesus Christ as Lord and Savior.
   E. Incorporating new believers into the Christian community.

III. *Join the World Mission of the Church by*
   A. Knowing the call of God and their roles in the world mission of the church.
   B. Praying for the needs of the world.
   C. Giving financially to world missionary endeavors.
   D. Participating in cross-cultural ministry projects.
   E. Reaching out to international students.

IV. *Grow as Disciples of the Lord Jesus Christ by*
   A. Studying and obeying the Bible.
   B. Praying individually and with others.
   C. Participating in a local church.
   D. Exercising biblical leadership and community.
   E. Demonstrating Christ's Lordship in relationships, possessions, academics, vocation, and all other aspects of life.

Source: IVCF National Strategic Plan 1984–1987

Ron also knew that currently IVCF is beginning to evaluate itself more in terms of meeting its mission and objectives. For example, the *IVCF 1983 Annual Report* informs the reader that during the previous year, 2,505 students decided to commit their lives to a personal relationship with Jesus Christ through the work of Inter-Varsity staff and students (Objective 1), and that 1,708 were being followed up directly on campus by IVCF staff (Objective 2). The *IVCF 1982 Annual Report* shows that during the previous year the number of students who dedicated their lives to Christ through IVCF grew 21 percent. The number receiving IVCF training expanded 20 percent, and 30 percent more students went on short-term mission projects. Twenty-one percent more were praying and giving money to missions and 18 percent more students were seriously considering missionary careers. In 1984, the first comprehensive one-year plan was submitted to the board of trustees. Its purpose is to spell out everyone's responsibilities and to measure progress against goals.

Exhibit 40.3   Inter-Varsity Financial Position:
Combined Statements of Revenue and Expenses

	Year ended June 30	
	1984	1983
Operating Funds		
Revenue		
General fund campus ministry	$12,957,713	$11,970,208
General fund camps ministry	1,023,820	999,566
Literature division	5,011,792	4,832,171
	$18,993,325	$17,801,945
Expenses		
Operating	$13,641,438	$12,601,619
Cost of sales	1,861,786	1,868,130
Administrative	1,130,429	915,209
Sales and sales promotion	650,091	547,255
Fund raising	932,481	1,019,188
Depreciation and amortization	396,069	410,235
Other	173,398	115,206
	$18,785,692	$17,476,842
Excess of revenue over expenses—		
Operating funds	$207,683	$325,103
Nonoperating and restricted funds		
Revenue		
Specified-purpose gifts	$1,822,499	$2,077,657
Registration fees	439,466	299,321
Interest and dividends	255,567	121,796
Other	44,355	50,413
	$2,561,887	$2,559,187
Expenses		
Operating	$1,134,948	$ 320,377
Fund raising	109,170	37,742
Specified-purpose gifts	442,592	839,424
	$1,686,710	$1,197,543
Excess (deficit) of revenue over expenses—		
nonoperating and restricted funds	$875,177	$1,361,644
Excess (deficit) of revenue over expenses	$1,082,860	$1,686,747

Source: IVCF National Strategic Plan 1984–1987

In addition, IVCF has objectives and a broad strategy for future growth outlined in its long-range strategic plan. One priority is to strengthen its campus ministry (area of service). Currently, Inter-Varsity exists on less than one-third of the over 3,200 institutions of higher learning in the United States. By 1986, they would like to be on 1,100 campuses, and ultimately they hope to reach 2,500 of these institutions. The *1984 Annual Report* states that a strategic priority for Inter-Varsity is to nurture ministries at 200 new schools over the next three years. In order to do this, they need a 15 percent growth rate in staff during each of those years.

Growth onto new campuses is of prime importance. Campuses are entered where at least two, and usually three or more students, express interest in and commitment to a ministry and evangelistic outreach on their college campus. This is in line with IVCF's philosophy of dependence on student initiative as change agents and on student leadership. However, IVCF maintains a cautious growth strategy, being unwilling to sacrifice quality (dedicated staff and students) for quantity.

Reaching new potential target markets is a priority. IVCF is currently working on recruiting black staff members for predominantly black campuses, as well
as Hispanic staff. Since by 1990 almost 10 percent of the university population will
be international students, part of IVCF's long-range strategy is effectively to
reach them also.

Organizational Structure

As Ron evaluated this information he wondered whether IVCF was properly
viewing its objectives. He also wondered whether their growth strategy was
realistic. Next, Ron thought about where his division fit in with IVCF as a whole.
IVCF consists of a Marketing Communication Division, Campus Ministry Division, Department of Human Resources and Planning, Division of Specialized
Ministries (including missions, evangelism, Nurses Christian Fellowship, etc.),
and Administrative Division. Ron's task was to focus on the Campus Ministry
Division.

One of IVCF's chief assets, Ron realized, is their campus ministry staff
members, who are intrinsically motivated, involved in their local community,
and take their ministries seriously. Staff are recruited primarily from college
chapters and secondarily from seminaries. Thus, most are young and presumably
relate well to students. The average staff person remains with IVCF for four or
five years and usually travels among and works on three campuses. Because IVCF
is student-led, few campuses have a staff worker in residence. The staff worker's
role is to provide advice and assistance to students.

Most of IVCF's budget is used to pay the salaries of campus staff and support
personnel. In August 1982, a new policy was enacted which mandates that 100
percent of a new staff member's support must be raised before he or she can begin
his or her campus work, so as to curb deficits and keep IVCF's student work
uninterrupted.

Inter-Varsity's External Environment

Ron knew that prior to formulating a marketing strategy for his division, he
would need to analyze the changing environment.

Other Interdenominational Campus Ministries

IVCF views itself as cooperative with, rather than competitive with, other
organizations that spread the Christian message. These consist primarily of other
interdenominational ministries. Although some campuses, such as Ohio State,
have as many as 40 to 50 religiously oriented groups, and others, such as the
University of Wisconsin, have up to 30 interdenominational groups, the big three
include IVCF, Campus Crusade for Christ (CCC), and Navigators.

CCC began exclusively as a college ministry in 1951, but has since expanded
to between 400 and 700 campuses internationally, as well as into other ministries
including lay, high school, military, and others. Whereas the average IVCF staff
member works on three campuses, CCC usually has a staff team of four to seven
people on one campus. This is because CCC groups are usually staff-led, whereas

IVCF chapters are student-led, and because CCC offers more structured programs than IVCF does. However, CCC is also moving in the direction of fostering development of student leadership and the flexibility in programs that IVCF offers. In fact, in 1983, CCC and IVCF began a cooperative program to reach campuses that currently do not have an interdenominational ministry.

One of CCC's competitive advantages is their heavy use of promotional materials. For example, *The Four Spiritual Laws* (see Exhibit 40.4) is a booklet which gives a clear presentation of the gospel message. It is usually explained on a person-to-person basis. CCC also uses its own mass media, publishing *Collegiate Challenge*, *Worldwide Challenge*, and *Athletes in Action* magazines. CCC also utilizes a direct-mail program, which generates leads to be followed up personally by CCC staff and students, as well as running regular evangelistic meetings on campus where students share their faiths and how God is working in their lives. Special events include films and magic presentations. Frequently, staff members or students speak to various groups on campus (*e.g.*, fraternities, athletic teams, etc.) challenging the group members to investigate personally the gospel message.

On the other hand, Navigators, founded in the U. S. Navy during the 1930s, is more involved with the military and with families than with college campus ministries. Its mission is directed more to discipleship (one-on-one teaching) than to evangelism. Campus ministries are restricted for the most part to large university campuses. One staff member is assigned to work on a given college campus, where weekly Bible studies are held. Like CCC, much of the Navigators' resources go to international ministries as well as to U. S. ministries.

Marketplace and Consumer Behavior

Ron realized that reaching the college market is important for the gospel message to be diffused throughout society, for he believed that today's college students are tomorrow's opinion leaders. But he faced another problem. He was convinced that the college campus is quite heterogeneous, and is becoming more so, and that there is no "typical" college student.

As far as Ron was concerned, the difficulty was complicated by several phenomona. Campuses consist of students of all ages and backgrounds as well as of faculty and staff. Today there are more two-year colleges and technical schools. The average age of students is going up because high school students delay entry into college, and because working people over 21 are returning to college or entering for the first time. Today's typical student lives in a campus dorm during his first year at college and in a nearby apartment with fellow students thereafter. More of today's students are commuters with more outside commitments to a job, family, civic organizations, and other personal interests. Moreover, today's students are more politically conservative, less sexually free, and more likely to be involved in fraternities and sororities.

Observers also report that today's typical students may best be described as "pragmatic," being more concerned with personal career, money, and success, *i.e.*, "looking out for number one." They are less involved with social and political causes, and less concerned with the values and meaningful philosophies of life that were important during the late 1960s and early 1970s. Students view education as a means of attaining "the good life."

Such attitudes are seen by some observers as coping mechanisms, ways of dealing with personal circumstances and a world that seems to be even more out of control. They insist that many of today's students face life with a sense of powerlessness, especially to influence national and world events. They feel reluctant to invest much of themselves in bettering a world that could go up in smoke at

Exhibit 40.4   Have You Heard of the Four Spiritual Laws

Just as there are physical laws that govern the physical universe, so are there spiritual laws which govern your relationship with God.

1

LAW ONE

GOD **LOVES** YOU, AND OFFERS A WONDERFUL **PLAN** FOR YOUR LIFE.

(References contained in this booklet should be read in context from the Bible wherever possible.)

Written by Bill Bright. Copyright © Campus Crusade for Christ, Inc., 1965. All rights reserved.
Manufactured in the United States of America.

2

God's Love

"For God so loved the world, that He gave His only begotten Son, that whoever believes in Him should not perish, but have eternal life" (John 3:16).

God's Plan

(Christ speaking) "I came that they might have life, and might have it abundantly" (that it might be full and meaningful) (John 10:10).

Why is it that most people are not experiencing the abundant life?
Because . . . 3

2

LAW TWO

MAN IS **SINFUL** AND **SEPARATED** FROM GOD. THEREFORE, HE CANNOT KNOW AND EXPERIENCE GOD'S LOVE AND PLAN FOR HIS LIFE.

Man Is Sinful

"For all have sinned and fall short of the glory of God" (Romans 3:23).

Man was created to have fellowship with God; but, because of his stubborn self-will, he chose to go his own independent way and fellowship with God was broken. This self-will, characterized by an attitude of active rebellion or passive indifference, is evidence of what the Bible calls sin.

4

Man Is Separated

"For the wages of sin is death" (spiritual separation from God) (Romans 6:23).

This diagram illustrates that God is holy and man is sinful. A great gulf separates the two. The arrows illustrate that man is continually trying to reach God and the abundant life through his own efforts, such as a good life, philosophy or religion.

The third law explains the only way to bridge this gulf . . . 5

3

LAW THREE

JESUS CHRIST IS GOD'S **ONLY** PROVISION FOR MAN'S SIN. THROUGH HIM YOU CAN KNOW AND EXPERIENCE GOD'S LOVE AND PLAN FOR YOUR LIFE.

He Died in Our Place

"But God demonstrates His own love toward us, in that while we were yet sinners, Christ died for us" (Romans 5:8).

He Rose from the Dead

"Christ died for our sins . . . He was buried . . . He was raised on the third day, according to the Scriptures . . . He appeared to Peter, then to the twelve. After that He appeared to more than five hundred . . ." (I Corinthians 15:3-6).

6

He Is the Only Way to God

"Jesus said to him, 'I am the way, and the truth, and the life; no one comes to the Father, but through Me' " (John 14:6).

This diagram illustrates that God has bridged the gulf which separates us from Him by sending His Son, Jesus Christ, to die on the cross in our place to pay the penalty for our sins.

It is not enough just to know these three laws . . . 7

4

LAW FOUR

WE MUST INDIVIDUALLY **RECEIVE** JESUS CHRIST AS SAVIOR AND LORD; THEN WE CAN KNOW AND EXPERIENCE GOD'S LOVE AND PLAN FOR OUR LIVES.

We Must Receive Christ

"But as many as received Him, to them He gave the right to become children of God, even to those who believe in His name" (John 1:12).

We Receive Christ Through Faith

"For by grace you have been saved through faith; and that not of yourselves, it is the gift of God; not as a result of works, that no one should boast" (Ephesians 2:8,9).

When We Receive Christ, We Experience a New Birth. (Read John 3:1-8.)

8

We Receive Christ by Personal Invitation

(Christ is speaking): "Behold, I stand at the door and knock; if any one hears My voice and opens the door, I will come in to him" (Revelation 3:20). Receiving Christ involves turning to God from self (repentance) and trusting Christ to come into our lives to forgive our sins and to make us the kind of people He wants us to be. Just to agree intellectually that Jesus Christ is the Son of God and that He died on the cross for our sins is not enough. Nor is it enough to have an emotional experience. We receive Jesus Christ by faith, as an act of the will.

These two circles represent two kinds of lives:

SELF-DIRECTED LIFE
S — Self is on the throne
† — Christ is outside the life
● — Interests are directed by self, often resulting in discord and frustration

CHRIST-DIRECTED LIFE
† — Christ is in the life and on the throne
S — Self is yielding to Christ
● — Interests are directed by Christ, resulting in harmony with God's plan

Which circle best represents your life?
Which circle would you like to have represent your life?
The following explains how you can receive Christ: 9

YOU CAN RECEIVE CHRIST RIGHT NOW BY FAITH THROUGH PRAYER

(Prayer is talking with God)

God knows your heart and is not so concerned with your words as He is with the attitude of your heart. The following is a suggested prayer:

"Lord Jesus, I need You. Thank You for dying on the cross for my sins. I open the door of my life and receive You as my Savior and Lord. Thank You for forgiving my sins and giving me eternal life. Take control of the throne of my life. Make me the kind of person You want me to be."

Does this prayer express the desire of your heart?

If it does, pray this prayer right now, and Christ will come into your life, as He promised.

10

How to Know That Christ Is in Your Life

Did you receive Christ into your life? According to His promise in Revelation 3:20, where is Christ right now in relation to you? Christ said that He would come into your life. Would He mislead you? On what authority do you know that God has answered your prayer? (The trustworthiness of God Himself and His Word.)

The Bible Promises Eternal Life to All Who Receive Christ

"And the witness is this, that God has given us eternal life, and this life is in His Son. He who has the Son has the life; he who does not have the Son of God does not have the life. These things I have written to you who believe in the name of the Son of God, in order that you may know that you have eternal life" (I John 5:11-13).

Thank God often that Christ is in your life and that He will never leave you (Hebrews 13:5). You can know on the basis of His promise that Christ lives in you and that you have eternal life, from the very moment you invite Him in. He will not deceive you.

An important reminder . . . 11

DO NOT DEPEND UPON FEELINGS

The promise of God's Word, the Bible — not our feelings — is our authority. The Christian lives by faith (trust) in the trustworthiness of God Himself and His Word. This train diagram illustrates the relationship between **fact** (God and His Word), **faith** (our trust in God and His Word), and **feeling** (the result of our faith and obedience) (John 14:21).

FACT · FAITH · FEELING

The train will run with or without the caboose. However, it would be useless to attempt to pull the train by the caboose. In the same way, we, as Christians, do not depend on feelings or emotions, but we place our faith (trust) in the trustworthiness of God and the promises of His Word.

12

NOW THAT YOU HAVE RECEIVED CHRIST

The moment that you received Christ by faith, as an act of the will, many things happened, including the following:

1. Christ came into your life (Revelation 3:20 and Colossians 1:27).
2. Your sins were forgiven (Colossians 1:14).
3. You became a child of God (John 1:12).
4. You received eternal life (John 5:24).
5. You began the great adventure for which God created you (John 10:10; II Corinthians 5:17 and I Thessalonians 5:18).

Can you think of anything more wonderful that could happen to you than receiving Christ? Would you like to thank God in prayer right now for what He has done for you? By thanking God, you demonstrate your faith.

To enjoy your new life to the fullest . . . 13

SUGGESTIONS FOR CHRISTIAN GROWTH

Spiritual growth results from trusting Jesus Christ. "The righteous man shall live by faith" (Galatians 3:11). A life of faith will enable you to trust God increasingly with every detail of your life, and to practice the following:

G   Go to God in prayer daily (John 15:7).

R   Read God's Word daily (Acts 17:11)—begin with the Gospel of John.

O   Obey God moment by moment (John 14:21).

W   Witness for Christ by your life and words (Matthew 4:19; John 15:8).

T   Trust God for every detail of your life (I Peter 5:7).

H   Holy Spirit—allow Him to control and empower your daily life and witness (Galatians 5:16,17; Acts 1:8).

14

FELLOWSHIP IN A GOOD CHURCH

God's Word admonishes us not to forsake "the assembling of ourselves together . . ." (Hebrews 10:25). Several logs burn brightly together; but put one aside on the cold hearth and the fire goes out. So it is with your relationship to other Christians. If you do not belong to a church, do not wait to be invited. Take the initiative; call the pastor of a nearby church where Christ is honored and His Word is preached. Start this week, and make plans to attend regularly.

SPECIAL MATERIALS ARE AVAILABLE FOR CHRISTIAN GROWTH.

If you have come to know Christ personally through this presentation of the gospel, write for a free booklet especially written to assist you in your Christian growth.

A special Bible study series and an abundance of other helpful materials for Christian growth are also available. For additional information, please write Campus Crusade for Christ International, San Bernardino, CA 92414.

You will want to share this important discovery . . . 15

the drop of a nuclear bomb, and hence are reluctant to make political commitments. However, at the same time, casual observation by IVCF members as well as a 1983 Gallup poll suggest that there is among college students a renewed interest in and openness toward spiritual matters and the Christian message. However, much of this interest is spread all the way from Buddhism to fundamentalist cults. Also, some students see religion as nothing more than something that makes you feel warm and fuzzy, and many have no idea that it preaches that they're responsible toward a personal God, which is an important part of the Christian message and lifestyle.

There appears to be a growing need for stability in a society that continues to change at an accelerating pace. Students find it difficult to function in a society where more and more values are viewed as relative and changing rather than as absolute and certain. This lack of certainty over what is right and wrong also produces instability. Facing an uncertain world, students react by pursuing security and success in their personal lives.

In today's pluralistic society, many people believe that there are many kinds of ultimate reality, that truth is relative, and that no one possesses the whole truth. Each person is encouraged to "do his thing." Psychologically, however, this notion that nothing is right or wrong is confusing. It tends to cause a sense that life is meaningless, since meaning can be built only on certainties and convictions. Christianity offers these certainties, truths, and values to those seeking to find meaning in a hostile world. Surveys suggest that a majority of college students are seeking such meaning through a more personal religious faith. Also, in our age of high technology, many are seeking an element of humanness, love, and "high touch," all of which Christianity offers.

Our society has been described as the "age of secular man" or as the "post-Christian era." Secularization involves a shifting of focus from an afterlife to this life. Secular humanity tends to be pragmatic and preoccupied with the here and now. This characterizes many of today's career-oriented students.

Some of these students, being concerned more with the temporal than with the eternal, are also concerned with issues of human relations and world problems: race relations, war and peace, poverty, etc. However, because most people today believe in the inherent goodness and potential of humanity, many on the college campus are certain that the only solution to world problems is to change social institutions. Thus, they believe that if the environment, in the form of repressive social institutions, is changed, human beings will be able to live up to their full potential. This idea is often reinforced in secular psychology classes.

The Christian message that IVCF wishes to promote, on the other hand, says that the problem instead lies within humanity's inherent "sin nature" and that one must first undergo a spiritual change and renewal from within by entering into a personal relationship with God, and by allowing His Spirit to work within. They point to the changed lives of new Christians as powerful evidence of this.

Compounding the difficulty of persuading college students about the truth of the Christian message is the diversity found on the typical college campus. Students come from a variety of ethnic, geographic, and socioeconomic backgrounds. There are the "indies" versus the Greeks, jocks versus intellectuals, and engineers versus liberal arts students.

Moreover, members of the college community come from a wide variety of religious backgrounds and relationships to a supreme being. Most consider organized religion to be of little personal importance. Many reject anything to do with religion for reasons such as indifference, disbelief in God, rejection of childhood pressures to conform to their parents' faith, and unwillingness to accept religion's moral demands. Students also vary in their degree of interest in spiritual matters (be it faith in God, spiritual interest in the occult, or spiritual movements such as yoga and transcendental meditation). They also differ in their degree of conviction in their personal religious beliefs. Only a minority have an active faith that makes a difference in their daily lives. Nevertheless, campus religious organizations are growing in number and size as students are searching for something to believe in.

Reaching the college student via the media is a difficult task. Television and radio have proved disappointing in reaching out to college students. Their preoccupation with their studies, part-time jobs, and campus activities leaves little time for the electronic media. Direct marketing efforts, especially via the mail, have proved to be move effective. They can be reached individually by name, through cooperative mailings, or through resident mailings (*i.e.*, to dorms, fraternities, or sororities where a single mailing piece is often read by several roommates).

Other Publics

Another group that concerns IVCF is the local community. There are about 150 IVCF Local Committees across the United States in towns and cities where IVCF campuses are located. The Local Committee usually consists of a staff member, faculty member(s), local businesspeople (often IVCF alumni), and local churches and their pastors. Relations with the local community are especially important for the staff member, who is responsible for raising his or her own support.

IVCF also must consider the mass media. Most important here is the Christian media, as opposed to traditional secular media. Christian media include Christian newspapers (*e.g.*, *Christian Inquirer*) and magazines (*e.g.*, *Moody Monthly* and *Christianity Today*) as well as local Christian TV and radio stations and national Christian TV networks (*e.g.*, Christian Broadcasting Network and PTL).

Inter-Varsity Marketing Strategy

Target Markets

In view of the diversity described above, Ron knew that it would be a challenge to define IVCF's target market. IVCF broadly describes its potential customers as the "college community," since their strategy is to reach the entire campus. Sometimes the key person who is targeted in initial efforts to penetrate a given campus is an interested Christian faculty member who is willing to help establish and support an IVCF ministry. More often, however, the initial target market is a small core of three to seven concerned Christian students who are willing to take responsibility for and leadership of a campus chapter. In fact, these students often take the initiative in contacting IVCF headquarters. Permission is then obtained from the appropriate administrative channels on campus, and the newly founded local chapter of IVCF is able to use college facilities for meetings and activities and to promote these meetings and activities.

IVCF also targets its efforts to the Christian public in local communities and churches in order to raise funds to support the ministry. Donors tend to be quite loyal. Potential donors include leads from current contributors, as well as alumni of student chapters and parents of current student chapter members.

Marketing Objectives

The marketing and communications objective for IVCF, as stated in the *1984 IVCF Strategic Plan*, is "to present the ministry of IVCF to the Christian public and attract sufficient resources to accomplish our strategic plans." Ron was not sure that this was a clearly stated objective.

Marketing Budget

Ron knew that for the coming fiscal year, the Marketing and Communications Department had been granted $2 million. This money was to be allocated among staff salaries, literature to be distributed on college campuses, media, public relations, donor solicitation, headquarters staff, and on-campus services such as student training.

Marketing Research

IVCF has been able to document thoroughly campus activities via a semiannual field report by each staff member to his or her area director. The report contained a summary of activities on campus, with emphasis on evangelism. Also, in February 1984, the Management Information System (MIS) was begun. This was designed to provide national leadership with a measure of IVCF's activities and to compare them against the long-range strategic plan. Ron wondered whether this was sufficient.

Product

Ron considered the product offered by IVCF as multifaceted and as containing both hard and soft elements. These all offered help to the interested and concerned student, and they involved resources for Christian evangelism, discipleship, missions, and personal growth.

Included among hard elements would be books on the Christian faith and life. Inter-Varsity Press publishes books and booklets used in the student ministry. These publications often provide evangelistic information for both the Christian and non-Christian student, more in-depth information on doctrinal issues and on current topics than staff members can provide, as well as books that take a strong stand on a variety of social and religious issues. *HIS* magazine is designed for college students and is described by the *1983 Annual Report* as the "watchdog of current campus and societal trends." It helps students come to grips with current ethical and moral issues, and it provides useful advice on how to mature in the Christian faith. Issues covered include a Christian's views on war, sex, marriage, and divorce, and nuclear arms.

Another hard product is IVCF's media tools. Notable here is Twenty-One Hundred Productions, which produces multi-image shows that present Jesus Christ in terms that today's college students understand. For example, the show "Habakkuk" tours among campuses across the country presenting a contemporary look at the prophecies of the future by the Old Testament prophet Habakkuk. It also causes students to probe serious questions on the meaning of life. Another series of films has been designed to encourage students to get involved in missions and in evangelism.

Soft products include various training retreats and area conferences where students learn about the Christian life and evangelism. For example, during Bible and Life weekends, a small group of students and staff members meet, and students learn skills such as prayer and how to lead a Bible study. Each spring and summer, 12 evangelism training projects are held across the nation, where students receive in-depth training in evangelism and practical experience in sharing their faith. During summer camps, Christian students learn evangelistic skills from IVCF staff workers and hear speakers from top U. S. evangelical seminaries. In all of these events, students are trained to view their campus as a mission field. For many of these events, students are given half-price scholarships. Campus staff members are directed to spend 20 percent of their on-campus time training students.

The lifeblood of IVCF campus chapters is a weekly Bible study group where students study the scriptures and pray for one another. Emphasis is placed on building each person's personal relationship with God via a daily quiet time alone with Him in prayer and Bible reading. According to the *1981 IVCF Annual Report:*

> Many students go through "culture shock" when they head for college. The contrast between high school days of security, isolation, and a limited point of view and a world of new ideas, new experiences, and new freedoms can be devastating. Students in Inter-Varsity small groups learn they've got a group of friends who care about them by name. Such a group can often spell the difference between four years of stagnation and alienation and four years of personal and spiritual advancement.

The chapters are student-led and depend on student initiative. Each chapter is given the assistance, encouragement, and support of a staff member and sometimes of a faculty advisor. A primary purpose of the student chapters is to encourage students to evangelize and to serve the campus community, as well as to share their faith through their day-to-day living. In some schools, students also meet together for daily prayer gatherings. Thus, another purpose of the chapters is to provide Christian fellowship for the students.

IVCF also includes a Faculty Ministry. The *1982 IVCF Annual Report* asks:

> Where are students' values formed? Frequently, they take shape in the classroom where Christianity is often mocked by well-educated and highly influential professors. That's why Inter-Varsity's work with faculty is so crucial, and why staff make it a priority to spend time with the faculty on their campuses.

Faculty Ministries encourage Christian faculty to band together and grow in their faith.

Promotion

In reviewing IVCF's promotional strategy, Ron recognized that promotion of IVCF takes many forms. Mass media advertising is limited to point-of-purchase displays on Inter-Varsity Press book racks on college campuses and in Christian bookstores as well as direct-mail efforts from Inter-Varsity Press. Name recognition and an image of quality and depth are stressed in advertising copy. Direct-mail campaigns are also targeted toward churches, informing them of IVCF-sponsored activities on the local college campus. Advertising time and space is also purchased in the Christian media, primarily Christian publications and Christian TV and radio stations. Information on various IVCF activities described above is presented and IVCF's image is reinforced through the slogan "reaching tomorrow's leaders for Christ today."

Public relations is more important for IVCF than advertising. According to the *Inter-Varsity Strategic Plan 1984–1987:*

> The Public Relations Department is active in informing the public on Inter-Varsity's activities, policies, objectives, etc., and attempting to create favorable public opinions. It is an interpretive function: "telling Inter-Varsity's story" to its internal and external publics. As people have better understanding and appreciation of the purpose and program of Inter-Varsity they become supporters of Inter-Varsity in prayer, giving, and sending their young people into the ranks of Inter-Varsity's ministry. As more people know about Inter-Varsity more will have the opportunity of becoming a part of this ministry.

The Public Relations Department publishes the *Annual Report, View* magazine for IVCF employees, news releases, and public service announcements about IVCF and its activities. It coordinates IVCF's participation in denominational and associational conventions and provides media relations programs. It is responsible for getting information about IVCF into the Christian media. In the secular media, information is occasionally disemminated to writers of religious columns and of articles in local newspapers.

The most important public for public relations, Ron believed, is actual and potential donors, who are targeted via direct mail. Regular contributors receive *Inter-Varsity*, a quarterly informational magazine, as well as a prayer flyer called *Intercessor*. They are reached via mail, telephone solicitation, and on a person-to-person basis by staff members trying to raise their own support.

In fact, personal selling appeared to Ron to be the most fruitful way to communicate about IVCF not only to donors, but also to communicate the gospel to nonmember students. The local college chapter, he believed, was the vehicle through which to do this.

Bill Tiffin, Director of IVCF's Campus Ministries, had recently explained to Ron that, actually, promotion on the college campus is done at four levels. First is personal one-on-one communication with IVCF students' peers, known as "friendship evangelism." Of the four methods, this is the most effective, claimed Bill, because people tend to identify better with people rather than with an abstract idea or nebulous organization. One way this is done is when local chapters sponsor book tables in the college student union. Often a few select titles are displayed such as *Loneliness* or *Is there really a God?* Some of the literature, in the form of pamphlets or tracts, is given away free. Books are sold at cost.

Another method of personal communication, according to Bill, involves stationing Christian students in the dorms during freshman move-in at the beginning of the school year. The students identify themselves as IVCF members and offer to help the freshmen move in. Sometimes during orientation week, IVCF members invite the freshmen to a meal. Later the students will invite these new friends to one of their weekly IVCF meetings. This has proven effective, according to Bill, because during this time of stress and tension, the freshmen are more open to making new friends and have a need to be put at ease.

IVCF students sometimes reach out to their friends and get involved with them in non-Christian activities. A bridge of communication is built as the nonmember student learns to identify with his Christian friend. Many students believe that the best message is a changed life. Thus, the Christian student who has experienced an inner change has a powerful message to convey through his actions as well as through his words.

Eventually, the IVCF student can invite the non-IVCF student to the weekly Bible study or to an open house, which serves as a second level of communication. Another example is a small group discussion in a Christian student's room. Those who attend are offered snacks and a congenial atmosphere in which to learn more about Christianity.

Dorm Bible studies have been arranged in the various dormitories in some universities. IVCF members publicize and then hold regular studies in one of the dorm rooms. Often, emphasis is placed on evangelism during these studies.

At a third, large-group level, high-quality, well-known speakers are invited to speak on campus either in an auditorium or in the open air. For example, according to the *1982 Annual Report:*

> The chapter in Madison launched a mammoth evangelistic thrust from February 13–21, 1982. Well-known evangelist Luis Palau was brought in and addressed crowds of up to 950 for five nights. At the same time, 40 Inter-Varsity staff from around the country came together to penetrate the dorms. Through their tireless efforts, 110 students came to Christ while an additional 200 recommitted their lives.

The advantage of this approach, Bill told Ron, is that the non-Christian can simply remain an anonymous listener and, therefore, feel less threatened.

Finally, at the all-campus level, major events are staged, such as those produced by Twenty-One Hundred Productions. Preceding these events, publicity is generated in the local media, which results in mass reach to the community-at-large and high visibility for IVCF.

In fact, both Jimmy Locklear, Director of Public Relations, and Ron had agreed in a recent discussion that visibility and recognition seem to be key problems for IVCF. Ron explained to Jimmy,

> Creating more name recognition for IVCF so that it becomes better known among the Christian public is a key problem. One of the first things we'll have to do in the new department of marketing and communications is to formulate a clear statement on what it is we want to communicate. We'll have to decide how we view ourselves and what we want to say about where we're heading.

Visibility is also needed on the college campus. In his office, Ron wondered, "How can we use our established products to strengthen our presence on campus?" Ultimately, attracting students to the weekly meetings is important. This can be done through current members who must be motivated, first, to act as change agents in actively and credibly spreading the gospel on the campus, and, second, to encourage their peers to look into IVCF's campus activities. The key is to show people that IVCF's message of hope is a superior product that satisfies unmet needs.

Ron glanced at his watch. It was almost midnight. He had told his wife that he'd be home late, but he hoped she wasn't up waiting for him. Now that he had reviewed IVCF's Campus Ministry division, he knew that after a good night's sleep he'd be ready to tackle the job of writing its marketing plan.

Central Ohio Marketing Council: Marketing a Geographic Area

The following is a quote from a news release issued by the Central Ohio Marketing Council:

> With no strong negative image to overcome, Columbus will have many good opportunities over the next five years to promote itself as an excellent place to live, work, locate a business, and to visit. Two recently completed surveys among national business executives and consumers indicate that Columbus has no perceived major faults, which places it in a good position to buld upon existing strengths, according to representatives of the Central Ohio Marketing Council, the group that commissioned the surveys.

At the present time, the Central Ohio Marketing Council is reviewing its past activities with an eye toward what it should be doing in the future in terms of marketing.

The Central Ohio Marketing Council

The Central Ohio Marketing Council was formed for the express purpose of focusing and maximizing marketing efforts for the greater Columbus area. By combining the strengths of several organizations that had in the past individually marketed central Ohio, it was hoped that duplication of effort could be reduced and higher-quality messages could be communicated to various target markets. Additionally, the Central Ohio Marketing Council was put in place to assure a cohesive and consistent information flow, enabling each organization to utilize standardized statistical figures for various visitor and economic development needs.

Through preliminary planning for the Marketing Council, it was determined that the organization's mission would be to market the greater Columbus area locally, nationally, and internationally as one fo the finest areas in which to work, visit, and live. It was also determined that this mission would be accomplished with a thorough marketing plan that analyzed the best ways to communicate central Ohio's strengths. In September 1984, the City of Columbus, Columbus Area Chamber of Commerce, Greater Columbus Convention and Visitors Bureau, and the Franklin County Commissioners pledged their support to a cooperative marketing effort and announced their appointees to the Central Ohio Marketing Council. The board members were chosen for their business and civic leadership as well as their diversity of interests.

Central Ohio Profile

Stable, vital, and growing: all are accurate descriptions of the greater Columbus area. The area's recent steady growth pattern has propelled Columbus into the position of Ohio's largest city and the 19th largest city in the United States. However, regardless of its demonstrated vitality, Columbus remains one of America's best-kept secrets, with local experience and research showing that central Ohio is virtually unknown and unrecognized. Despite its lack of a clearly defined image, Columbus is one of the healthiest metropolitan areas in the country and is the only major city in the northeastern United States to demonstrate continued growth since 1970.

Columbus' centralized location has been quite beneficial to its economic development. Located within 500 miles of 60 percent of the country's population, central Ohio has the capability of accommodating extensive distribution needs. Additionally, the area's centralized location is attractive to convention planners and visitors, bolstering the increasingly lucrative travel and tourism industry. For more than 30 years, the city of Columbus has been one of America's most highly touted test markets for consumer as well as technological products. The area's diverse demographics, stable local economy, and superior distribution systems are prized possessions to companies looking to examine product acceptability. These same appealing market attributes have also attracted countless entrepreneurs to the area, keeping Columbus on the cutting edge of many fast-growth industries and services.

The educational base within central Ohio is excellent. Along with several strong public school systems and more than two dozen trade and technical schools, the area boasts eight universities and colleges. These invaluable community resources have contributed greatly to the advanced education level of the central Ohio population, which is among the most highly educated in the United States. Central Ohio's work force is extremely attractive to prospective employers. It offers nonskilled, semiskilled, and highly skilled employees who are productive, cooperative, and less costly than their counterparts in many other metropolitan areas. Several area medical education and research facilities contribute to the high level of health care available to central Ohio residents. Surprisingly, however, the expense for health care in the Columbus area is well below the national average.

The quality of life available in Columbus reflects the stability and vitality of the area. Often noted as a good place to raise a family, central Ohio offers a wide variety of housing, educational, and entertainment alternatives to complement any lifestyle. Additionally, the area is becoming increasingly recognized for its steadily maturing cultural arts community. The Columbus area thrives on its wealth of strengths and has the civic leadership necessary to address identified areas of improvement. However, before central Ohio can be appropriately recognized as one of the best areas in which to work, visit, or live, it must first dedicate itself to a far-reaching marketing effort. Exhibit 41.1, taken from a promotional brochure for the area, provides additional information about central Ohio.

Marketing Research

Several marketing research projects were undertaken to provide the information necessary to formulate a marketing strategy. Secondary research involved collecting existing data from numerous sources and compiling it in a manner that would meet short- and long-term needs of the marketing program. Primary research was

Exhibit 41.1   Information about Central Ohio

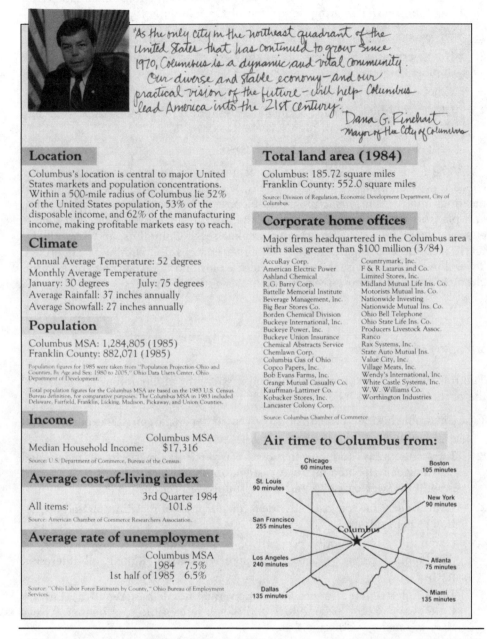

"As the only city in the northeast quadrant of the United States that has continued to grow since 1970, Columbus is a dynamic and vital community. Our diverse and stable economy—and our practical vision of the future—will help Columbus lead America into the 21st century."

Dana G. Rinehart
Mayor of the City of Columbus

Location

Columbus's location is central to major United States markets and population concentrations. Within a 500-mile radius of Columbus lie 52% of the United States population, 53% of the disposable income, and 62% of the manufacturing income, making profitable markets easy to reach.

Climate

Annual Average Temperature: 52 degrees
Monthly Average Temperature
January: 30 degrees   July: 75 degrees
Average Rainfall: 37 inches annually
Average Snowfall: 27 inches annually

Population

Columbus MSA: 1,284,805 (1985)
Franklin County: 882,071 (1985)

Population figures for 1985 were taken from "Population Projection-Ohio and Counties, By Age and Sex: 1980 to 2005," Ohio Data Users Center, Ohio Department of Development.

Total population figures for the Columbus MSA are based on the 1983 U.S. Census Bureau definition, for comparative purposes. The Columbus MSA in 1983 included Delaware, Fairfield, Franklin, Licking, Madison, Pickaway, and Union Counties.

Income

Columbus MSA
Median Household Income: $17,316

Source: U.S. Department of Commerce, Bureau of the Census.

Average cost-of-living index

3rd Quarter 1984
All items: 101.8

Source: American Chamber of Commerce Researchers Association.

Average rate of unemployment

Columbus MSA
1984   7.5%
1st half of 1985   6.5%

Source: "Ohio Labor Force Estimates by County," Ohio Bureau of Employment Services.

Total land area (1984)

Columbus: 185.72 square miles
Franklin County: 552.0 square miles

Source: Division of Regulation, Economic Development Department, City of Columbus.

Corporate home offices

Major firms headquartered in the Columbus area with sales greater than $100 million (3/84)

AccuRay Corp.	Countrymark, Inc.
American Electric Power	F & R Lazarus and Co.
Ashland Chemical	Limited Stores, Inc.
R.G. Barry Corp.	Midland Mutual Life Ins. Co.
Battelle Memorial Institute	Motorists Mutual Ins. Co.
Beverage Management, Inc.	Nationwide Investing
Big Bear Stores Co.	Nationwide Mutual Ins. Co.
Borden Chemical Division	Ohio Bell Telephone
Buckeye International, Inc.	Ohio State Life Ins. Co.
Buckeye Power, Inc.	Producers Livestock Assoc.
Buckeye Union Insurance	Ranco
Chemical Abstracts Service	Rax Systems, Inc.
Chemlawn Corp.	State Auto Mutual Ins.
Columbia Gas of Ohio	Value City, Inc.
Copco Papers, Inc.	Village Meats, Inc.
Bob Evans Farms, Inc.	Wendy's International, Inc.
Grange Mutual Casualty Co.	White Castle Systems, Inc.
Kauffman-Lattimer Co.	W.W. Williams Co.
Kobacker Stores, Inc.	Worthington Industries
Lancaster Colony Corp.	

Source: Columbus Chamber of Commerce

Air time to Columbus from:

Chicago 60 minutes
Boston 105 minutes
St. Louis 90 minutes
New York 90 minutes
San Francisco 255 minutes
Columbus
Los Angeles 240 minutes
Atlanta 75 minutes
Dallas 135 minutes
Miami 135 minutes

compiled through focus groups, extensive interviews, and surveys with local decision makers and with other key local, regional, and national meeting and convention planners and influencers. The following sections discuss some selected results of these research projects.

Focus Groups

Methodology

The purpose of the focused group approach was to provide a sampling of the elements that exist in opinions and beliefs about the city. Five groups were interviewed consisting of five to ten persons in a central location in Columbus. Each group was selected to be homogeneous in nature, to stimulate as much depth of thinking as possible on the issues facing Columbus and recommendations for resolving the issues. The groups consisted of the following types of individuals:

1.   Officers of real estate and development organizations

2.   Chief executive officers of established organizations employing large numbers of persons

3.   Chief executive officers of middle-sized organizations

4.   Chief executive officers of new, entrepreneurial organizations that had started in Columbus in the previous five years

5.   Officers of not-for-profit organizations

The focus group discussions were centered around the following six topics concerning Columbus: growth of firms, attraction of business, attraction of meetings and conventions, cultural development, comparisons with other cities, and plans/ideas for the future. During the interviews, several recurring themes emerged concerning the strengths and weaknesses of Columbus, and what the interviewees felt were the desirable development paths for Columbus to undertake. The following analysis is, therefore, structured around these positive and negative characteristics and their effects on the topics outlined above.

Strengths of Columbus

The following points summarize the major strengths of Columbus as viewed by the participants in the focus groups:

1.   Favorable business climate due to an entrepreneurial spirit, inexpensive land and buildings, and a low-cost, quality work force.

2.   Infrastructure is conducive to growth. In particular, participants mentioned a strategically located highway system, an abundance of low-cost land, and favorable sewer capacity and water supply projections.

3.   Central location is logistically ideal for purposes of distribution and attraction of conventions.

4.   Community is generally supportive, both financially and spiritually, of development projects through cooperative sharing among all interested parties.

5.   Light industrial and service orientation of economic base requires relatively little heavy capital expenditure and is less susceptible to economic swings than are many northern cities.

6.   People are warm and friendly, creating a stable, safe, and family-oriented society that is relatively open to newcomers.

7.   Low cost of living.

8.   Quality educational and medical facilities.

Weaknesses of Columbus

The following points summarize the major weaknesses of Columbus as viewed by the participants in the focus groups:

1. Cultural underdevelopment in the arts, tourist attractions, and food/ entertainment that is both a cause and effect of weak public support and involvement.

2. Downtown lacks cohesiveness and the related ability to support a high level of activity.

3. Citywide, retail shopping is generally unexciting.

4. Development efforts often are fragmented and misdirected. For example, existing businesses frequently are ignored and new development projects often underestimate the market.

5. Attraction of venture capital, both local and external, is difficult.

6. Negative media coverage often undermines the public support and success of development efforts.

National Research

The Central Ohio Marketing Council commissioned Market Group One, Inc., a Columbus-based marketing firm to conduct research that would assist the council to determine the image of Columbus nationally among business executives and the general public. Areas studied included: Columbus as a location for business, as a location for conventions/seminars, as a place to work/live, and as a place to visit. A telephone survey was conducted, with 500 business executives nationwide completing a survey. A mail panel was used to survey consumers. Approximately 1,400 questionnaires were returned out of 2,150 potential participants. Appendix A contains some of the major findings from this study.

Discover Columbus Campaign

The Central Ohio Marketing Council determined its overall mission statement to be, "To achieve worldwide recognition that the Greater Columbus Area is one of the best in which to work, visit, and live." It selected the following targets for its marketing activities:

Local
☐ Local business decision makers
☐ Local meeting planners
☐ Local public

National
☐ National business decision makers
☐ National meeting planners
☐ National traveling public

International
☐ International business
☐ International travelers

The Central Ohio Marketing Council, based on research results and target markets, decided on the following attributes on which to market the central Ohio area:

- Quality labor force
- High quality of life
- Favorable community environment
- Quality educational facilities
- Attractive business environment
- Low operating costs
- Good market accessibility
- Technology availability
- High-quality/low-cost health care
- Meeting and convention facilities

Marketing Objectives

Given its mission statement, the desired target markets, and the determination of the relevant attributes on which to market the area, the Central Ohio Marketing Council established the following marketing objectives:

- To identify and develop conditions in the greater Columbus area that work toward attracting firms and organizations considering location of new facilities.
- To identify and develop conditions in the greater Columbus area likely to contribute to growth in size and profitability of firms located in Columbus.
- To develop beliefs among businesses and other organizations that Columbus is an excellent host city for conventions, seminars, and other meetings.
- To develop beliefs among the general public that the greater Columbus area is an interesting and exciting destination to visit.
- To develop beliefs among American workers and Columbus-area citizens that Columbus offers thriving economic conditions.
- To identify the educational resources of the Columbus area and encourage their use as a business development tool.
- To develop a growing impact on the Columbus area through increased arts activities and attendance; increased use of Columbus-area cultural attractions in the tourism and convention industry, and an enhanced image nationally for the Columbus area cultural activities in order to aid in attracting and retaining businesses and their employees.
- To enhance the quality of life in the Columbus area by showcasing neighborhood and community-oriented activities and special events.

Marketing Message

Inherent in the role and expectations of the Central Ohio Marketing Council was the development of a marketing message that would visually and thematically unify the marketing efforts of the various agencies and organizations. In that spirit of collaboration, the following theme and logo were identified.

Slogan

"Discover Columbus" was the theme chosen by the Central Ohio Marketing Council as an appropriate starting point for a recognition campaign. This theme acknowledged the state of an unknown image, yet had a clear call to action that could highlight the positive aspects of the Columbus area (*i.e.*, Discover Columbus Schools, Discover Columbus Arts, etc.). Exhibit 41.2 provides a general overview of the marketing campaign.

The "Discover Columbus" slogan was planned for two-year life span (1985 and 1986). Then, because discovery is an active process, it is planned that the discovery marketing campaign will be changed to reflect the area's positive growth and accomplishments. "The Discovery of Columbus Goes On" may be the concept adopted as the second phase, "America Discovers Columbus" as the third phase, and by the year 1992, clearly a hallmark year for the city, the theme may be "America Celebrates Columbus."

Logo

The Central Ohio Marketing Council chose Roy Lichtenstein's "Brushstrokes in Flight" sculpture to graphically represent the Columbus area. The sculpture was selected to capture the spirit of central Ohio: contemporary, original, and progressive, yet undefined. The sculpture, with its bold upward strokes, can be viewed as a dynamic image of a city reaching for the future. Exhibit 41.3, featuring the sculpture, is from the cover of the "Quality of Life" brochure prepared as part of the Discover Columbus campaign.

"Brushstrokes in Flight" is on permanent display at the Port Columbus International Airport. The sculpture is site-specific, meaning that Lichtenstein designed it specially for the site where it now stands. "Brushstrokes in Flight" fits in beautifully at its current location drawing a direct parallel to the activity at the airport. Because of its strategic location, the city's dynamic new symbol welcomes national and international visitors to Columbus as they launch their discovery of the area.

Budgeting Process

The Central Ohio Marketing Council fulflls two very distinct functions. It is an initiator, taking the lead role in accomplishing defined projects, and it is a coordinating agency, helping to blend the overall marketing plans of organizations involved in the council and those organizations in the greater Columbus area that promote central Ohio on a local, national, or international basis. Funding for the marketing plan is also broken down into these two distinct areas, because funding sources are readily defined in this manner. Exhibit 41.4 shows the basic budgeting for the Central Ohio Marketing Council's programs.

Coordinated programs are funded in part through organizations that originally had those programs in their budgets, or that have agreed to take a lead role in bringing those projects to fruition. Coordinated programs do not have dollar amounts *budgeted;* rather they list dollar amounts as *values.* Although the Central Ohio Marketing Council will not be required to specifically fund these programs, value amounts will be included (and so indicated) in the marketing plan because they indicate the effective marketing values of the programs when implemented. Hundreds of programs will take place in coming years due to the coordinating efforts, business acumen, creative talents and enthusiasm made possible through the Central Ohio Marketing Council — programs that otherwise would have been only ideas.

Exhibit 41.2   Central Ohio Marketing Council Program Summary

CENTRAL OHIO MARKETING COUNCIL PROGRAM SUMMARY

RESEARCH
Local research activity including focus group studies and questionnaire surveys to identify target markets and a Columbus area market profile (attributes/weaknesses). National research project to determine perceptions of business decision makers and general consumers regarding Columbus as a place to live, work and visit.

COMMON MARKETING MESSAGE
Development of a logo and slogan to visually and thematically unify marketing efforts. The message is intended to acknowledge the state of an unknown image and make a progressive and contemporary statement.

QUALITY OF LIFE BROCHURE
Development of an all-encompassing brochure that presents the positive aspects of the Columbus area.

QUALITY OF LIFE AUDIO VISUAL
A companion piece to the Quality of Life Brochure that visually presents the positive aspects of the Columbus area.

THEME MERCHANDISE
Develop a line of merchandise that carrys the marketing message (logo and slogan) for businesses and organizations to use as premiums and for placement in retail outlets as souvenir items.

MARKETING PRODUCTS BROCHURE
A catalog that presents the line of theme merchandise and an inventory of marketing "tools" available for use by Columbus area businesses and organizations.

INFORMATION DIRECTORY/POINTS OF INTEREST PROGRAM
Support programs that provide stimulating information regarding Columbus area points of interest (high visibility signage/tourism packages).

DISPLAY BOOTH
Development of a visually dynamic display system for use at major trade fairs and conferences.

SPEAKER'S BUREAU
A program using public speakers with expertise on specific subjects as a way to communicate Columbus area attributes to target markets. Develop an inventory of subjects and speakers into a useful directory.

DIRECT MAIL
Establish a sequence of mailings to local, regional and national decision makers that provide information and stimulate interest in the developments of the greater Columbus area.

NATIONAL ADVERTISING
Increase visibility and awareness of the greater Columbus area through a national advertising campaign which utilizes the high reach medium of Fortune Magazine and USA Today to communicate business and quality of life attributes to national business decision makers and to the general population.

NATIONAL PUBLICITY
Editorial placements and national broadcast exposures that feature the greater Columbus area.

LOCAL MEDIA
Conduct an on-going information program with local media to encourage its enthusiasm and presentation of the Columbus area in a positive image.

INFORMATION SHARING
Develop a unifying information network between businesses, private organizations and civic agencies to interchange marketing programs.

FAMILIARIZATION TRIPS
Establish programs to bring targeted groups together for the purpose of showcasing the positive aspects of the Columbus area (of particular use with economic development prospects and convention planners).

INTERNATIONAL PROGRAMS
Develop support marketing materials in translated versions for use by the International Economic Development Program.

ANNUAL REPORT PAGES
Encourage Columbus-based companies and organizations to highlight marketable aspects of Columbus within their annual report.

LOCAL REALTORS
A program designed to reach-out to Columbus area realtors for cooperation in promoting positive and accurate information about the greater Columbus area.

SEMINARS
Coordination and production of a series of seminars targeted to key audiences to "spread the word" on the objectives of the Discover Columbus campaign and solicit community support and participation in the marketing process.

WALKING AMBASSADORS
Develop a lapel pin to be worn by the business community and general public to promote a positive and unified image.

SCHOOLS PROGRAM
Promote the educational resources of the Columbus area in marketing materials. Develop an out reach program with schools that contributes to a positive image at every education level.

HEALTH CARE PROGRAM
Promote the strengths of the health care facilites and the comparatively low costs of quality health care as a resource and positive attribute of the Columbus area.

VIP HOSPITALITY PROGRAM
Develop a pro-Columbus information package that would be used when distinguished visitors are in the Columbus area.

ARTS AWARENESS PROGRAM
A series of separate but integrated programs to bring the arts and business community into closer, more direct interaction and to heighten arts awareness and participation.

TECHNOLOGY AWARENESS
A series of programs to increase awareness of information processing, technology resources and facilities in the greater Columbus area.

AUXILIARY PRINT MATERIALS
Work as a liaison with businesses, private organizations and civic agencies to develop print communication pieces that are targeted to specific markets.

AUXILIARY AUDIO VISUAL PRESENTATIONS
Work as a liaison with businesses, private organizations and civic agencies to develop audio-visuals that are targeted to specific markets.

Exhibit 41.3   Cover from "Quality of Life" Brochure

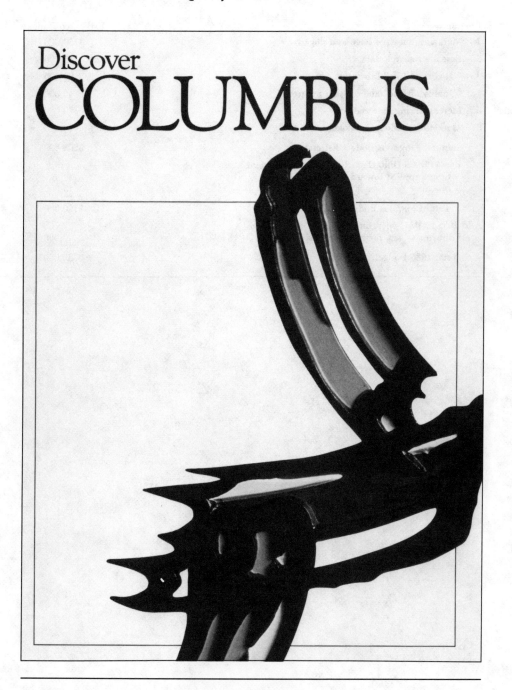

Exhibit 41.4   Central Ohio Marketing Council Basic Budget

Programs	Estimated Budget
1. Marketing message (logo and slogan)	$ 10,000
2. Baseline research data	35,000
3. "Quality of Life" brochure	90,000
4. "Quality of Life" audio-visual program	40,000
5. Merchandising materials	20,000
6. Marketing products catalogue	10,000
Subtotal Programs Budget Estimate	$205,000
Less $15,000 Ohio Department of Development Grant applied toward "Quality of Life" brochure	15,000
Total Programs Budget Estimate	$190,000
Add 1985 COMC operating costs (staff director salary, miscellaneous expenses)	40,000
Total 1985 Budget	$230,000

Results of Business and
General Population Studies 41A

Business Survey

Locating a Business

When asked to name three cities in which they would consider locating a business, business executives ranked Columbus among the top 20 (17th). Among Midwest cities, only Chicago was selected more often than Columbus. (Columbus tied with Indianapolis in number of unaided responses.) Business executives perceive Columbus as having a good geographic location in the country, with friendly people and state-of-the-art technology.

Columbus ranks low, however, in perceptions of available entertainment, cultural activities, and shopping.

When asked to compare the desirability of locating a business in Columbus to locating it in 15 other cities, Columbus ranked ninth, higher than any other Ohio city. Respondents indicated that a team of individuals within a company, rather than a single individual, are ultimately involved in deciding where to locate a business.

Conventions/Business Meetings

When asked to rate the importance of nine attributes with respect to holding a convention, respondents rated airline availability, hotel/meeting facilities, safety, and friendliness of people as most important. The three attributes Columbus rated highest on were: friendly people, airline availability, and safety. Columbus scored relatively low in perception of availability of hotel/meeting facilities.

In reality, Columbus has an above-average number of hotel rooms and meeting facilities available in comparison to cities of its size, and will need to communicate this fact to business executives.

When asked in an open-ended question to select the three most desirable cities in which to hold a business meeting, Columbus ranks 27th out of a possible 31. Chicago, Detroit, and Indianapolis were all selected more frequently than Columbus. However, when given a list of 15 other cities from which to chose, Columbus ranked higher than older industrial cities such as Baltimore, Cincinnati, Cleveland, Detroit, Indianapolis, and Pittsburgh, yet ranked lower than Boston, Chicago, and all South and West locations. In reality, in terms of number of convention delegates, Columbus ranks 13th. In number of conventions, Columbus ranks 5th.

Image of Columbus

Attributes business executives associate with Columbus are The Ohio State University (31 percent) and the state capital (12.6 percent). About one-fourth do not associate anything strongly with Columbus. A small percentage view Columbus as a declining industrial city. A couple of respondents mentioned Woody Hayes and Jack Nicklaus.

Awareness of Columbus-based Businesses

Of the 32 percent of respondents who indicated knowledge of Columbus-based businesses, most mentioned Nationwide, Borden, local banks, and Battelle Memorial Institute. Also mentioned were The Limited and Wendy's.

Reasons for Columbus' Growth

Over one-half of the respondents had no opinion as to what has been responsible for Columbus' growth. Of those who did give opinions, most mentioned opportunity, followed by OSU and location.

Visits to Columbus

Fifty-seven percent of the business executives in the sample had been to Columbus once and of that percentage, 71 percent had been there within the last year.

Profile of Respondents

The majority of respondents were from manufacturing (42 percent), followed by financial/insurance/real estate (38 percent). Nearly 55 percent indicated they were likely to locate a new facility in Columbus. Most respondents were from the Midwest and Northeast and were affiliated with companies having over 500 employees.

Comparisons of Local and National Perceptions of Columbus

In comparing this research with research conducted in 1984 among local business executives, the greatest disparity among opinions occurred in the following four attributes: quality of life (1.9 points), hotels/meeting facilities (1.8), availability of technology (1.8), and entertainment (1.6). Local people ranked all four higher than did national respondents.

General Population Survey

A Place to Live/Work/Visit

Consumers rated Columbus above average in quality of life, housing costs, and safety. Also ranked highly were friendliness of people, availability/costs of health facilities, safety, airline availability, parks and recreation facilities, and shopping. Entertainment and climate were rated as below average.

Relative to Other Cities to Visit/Live/Work

In comparison to 20 other cities, Columbus was rated higher than older, more heavily industrialized cities in the Midwest, with the exceptions of Baltimore and Chicago. It was rated lower than other cities, most notably in the South and West.

Columbus was rated higher as a place to live and work than as a place to visit.

Image of Columbus

Many respondents (41 percent) did not associate any one factor strongly with Columbus. Of those who did respond, 13 percent mentioned OSU sports and education, 8.3 percent mentioned relatives and friends, and 8 percent mentioned bad environment.

Reasons for Growth

Over half of the respondents were unable to cite specific reasons for Columbus' growth, however of those who did cite specifics, nearly 10 percent said good environment, 9.9 percent mentioned growth in industry and high technology, and 8.9 percent said job availability.

A Place to Visit

Over 70 percent of the respondents have never been to Columbus. Of those who have (28 percent), most visit less than once per year, most haven't been for over five years, and when they do visit, most come to visit families/friends (23 percent), on a business trip (22 percent), or to a convention (16 percent).

Events/Places Visited

Most Columbus visitors do no sightseeing, since they come to visit family/friends, on a business trip, or are passing through. However, of those who do, The Ohio State University, German Village, The Ohio State Fair, the State Capitol Tour, and the Columbus Zoo are major attractions.

Profile of Respondents

Most respondents were female (56 percent), and were between the ages of 20 and 39 (40 percent) and 40 and 59 (39 percent).

Comparison of Local and National Perceptions

When comparing this research with 1984 research, discrepancies between local and national consumers are not as dramatic as those between local and national business executives. Local consumers rated Columbus highest in terms of training and educational facilities, friendliness of people, and quality of life. National consumers rated Columbus highest in terms of availability/cost of health care facilities, airline availability, and training and educational facilities.

National and local consumers rated shopping and climate about the same and airline availability was rated better by national than local consumers.

In Conclusion

Generally, Columbus does not have a bad image. The most negative perceptions appear to arise from identification with other industrial cities experiencing the decline that is associated with failing industries, unions, and mundane cities of the Northeast and Midwest. Negatives also appear to stem from lack of knowledge about Columbus rather than from its major faults.

From the perspective of communications theory, this is an opportunity. It is much easier to create an image than to change one. Several strengths were identified in both surveys and should be used as the foundation on which to build a strong communications program. Strengths include accessibility by airline, available technology, good health care, training and education facilities, reasonable housing costs, a good quality of life, and friendliness of the people. Perceived weaknesses, such as lack of entertainment, shopping, and hotel/meeting facilities are areas that can be strengthened through a good communications program.

A well-planned, well-targeted, highly creative communications program will provide Columbus with an excellent opportunity to make a positive impact upon perceptions of business executives and consumers. However, to succeed, the communications programs must be carefully developed, implemented, and directed. There is a clear need for the Central Ohio Marketing Council to continue its efforts to coordinate these activities on behalf of the many organizations, businesses, and citizens who stand to benefit greatly from a stronger Columbus.

This research project was designed and executed to assist the COMC, its member organizations, and other interested parties in the central Ohio area in their decisions about how to accomplish the mission of achieving worldwide recognition that the greater Columbus area is one of the best in which to work, visit, and live.

Frederica's Restaurants: Restaurant Strategy in Japan

Background

On June 5, Toshio Hara, Osamu Ito, and Seiji Sasaki sat together solemnly at lunch in Frederica's Restaurant Number 7. Close friends since their college days at Sophia University, the three were partners in the 15th unit of Frederica's Restaurant Co. Ltd., Tokyo.

When all three graduated in 1970, they had taken jobs as management trainees with different family-type restaurant chains. They had been attracted to the restaurant industry as a result of their part-time jobs while students and believed that the restaurant industry could provide a fast track to success.

Although all three worked for different restaurant chains, they maintained their close friendship as well as they could, considering the long work hours at each company. When together, they often compared job experiences and discussed problems and opportunities at their respective firms. Before long, they realized that their pooled knowledge and experience and their observations of errors might be a strong basis for success in a firm of their own.

Once aware of the possibilities, they began to talk seriously and concretely. They lacked capital, however, and this was the drawback that delayed the fulfillment of their dream. But during the 1973 oil shock, the banker with whom they had been talking suddenly began to take more than polite interest in them. Excitedly, they enlisted the help of their own parents and that of their wives' parents, and with the cooperation of the banker, they launched Frederica's Number 1 in Tokyo.

In the 11 years that followed, 14 more stores were opened and the company showed a steady, although not excessive profit. The company owned all stores, none were franchises. Because of the pace of store openings and remodelling, the firm carried a heavy debt, but the three partners were always aware of the need to be financially prudent. They were proud of their progress and they worked well together. They talked all company matters over and came to studied and conservative decisions together. They worked hard, but they enjoyed life and provided above-average incomes for their families.

Source: Appreciation is expressed to Professor William H. Kaven, Cornell University, for permission to include his case in this text.

The Stores

All 15 stores were of the same style, although layout was adapted for each site. The stores offered table service only and mostly Western-style foods, though some Japanese items were also included, varying according to the season of the year. All stores had the same menu, which had changed little in 11 years. Per store sales volume was about at industry average for chain family-restaurants; per check average was Y800 (U.S.$3.46 at 231.1 exchange rate). No breakfast was served. Lunchtime revenue was 40 percent, dinnertime revenue 40 percent, and evening revenue 20 percent of overall business. None of the stores was losing money, but ten were only marginally profitable.

All 15 stores were at street level. Of the ten Tokyo area stores, half had no parking and were located within five minutes of a train or subway station; the other Tokyo stores had parking and sat on 400-tsubo lots,[1] the store itself occupying about 100 tsubo. The company's five other stores were in the Osaka area and all had parking and 400-tsubo lots.

Ownership

The work among the three partners was divided agreeably: Mr. Ito served as President and Treasurer, Mr. Sasaki as Vice President of Operations, and Mr. Hara as Vice President of Marketing/Sales and Corporate Development. Each of the three held 25 percent of the firm's stock; the remaining 25 percent had been offered to and was held by their investing parents and in-laws with a corporate buy-back agreement.

Staffing

Stores were staffed in a customary Japanese way, that is, full-time employees managed and part-time employees served as waiters, cooks, dishwashers, and janitors. Students and housewives comprised the part-time staff, which averaged about 20 hours of work weekly. Managers were trained within the firm by a combination of sessions with the personnel director and senior store managers, plus training on the job. Although the company usually created its own store managers, some of the managers came from among the trainees of Skylark, Royal, and Denny's companies, where they had grown impatient waiting for assignments as store managers.

Headquarters staffing was lean and offices were crowded with desks abutting. Many of the functions of advertising, store design and layout, and research were done by outside contractors as needed.

June 5

Promptly at 10 a.m., Osamu Ito, the president-treasurer, arrived at the bank to keep his appointment with Hoshino-san, the bank official with whom his firm had dealt for the past 11 years. Hoshino-san knew Frederica's management and

---

[1]A tsubo, a Japanese measure of land, is equal to 35.58 square feet.

history very well, and after courteous greetings and pleasantries, initiated a polite description of the bank's position regarding Frederica's recent request for a loan. He said,

> This bank and I personally have very high regard for the three of you at Frederica's. We admire the way you have used this bank's money to develop 15 fine stores. I congratulate you on your accomplishments; we are honored to have been permitted to assist you these past 11 years.

Mr. Ito bowed in acknowledgement.
Mr. Hoshino continued:

> We have particularly noticed the strength of your competition, the general slowing down of the growth-rate of some chain-restaurant companies, and the proliferation of their ideas to stimulate and accelerate new growth. In reviewing the material accompanying your request for a loan, I doubtless have missed that portion dealing with your strategies and plans for the renewal of such growth. All that I saw accompanying your application was a description of the remodelling and the new units you wish to add. I'm sure you already have what we need, so I suggest that you return in a week with the written proposal of your strategies and plans; I can then go to the loan committee with a more complete application. As it is now, your material is inadequate. But, of course, you are free to seek funds from other bankers . . .

The meeting moved then to a courteous conclusion. Ito raced back to the office. His partners were busily engaged in business discussions with outsiders, so he merely stepped through each office doorway for a moment and said as calmly as he could, "We should have lunch at Number 7, back table, 12:30. Agreed?"

He returned to his office then, but he was too tense to concentrate on his work.

At 12:30 the three partners met and began talking at once. Mr. Hara and Mr. Sasaki asked almost in unison, "What happened?"

"He turned us down — after 11 years of doing business . . ."

"Refused our request! Why? What did he say?"

"Well, he was polite, of course, and he didn't actually say *no* but the meaning was clear. He is very conscious of the industry slowdown and I think he is afraid that our business will be damaged when the big firms begin to compete more actively against each other. My understanding of his remarks is that either we elect to go elsewhere for money, or we make a much better case for the loans we want from him. Even with a strategy and the plans he now wants, we don't have any guarantee of getting the loan, but if we are going to hve any chance at all, we must present a valid proposal by next week."

Leaving their lunches virtually untouched, the three men talked intensely for 2½ hours. They explored their ideas about the firm and where it was going in the chain-restaurant industry — and where it should be going. As their meeting came to an end under the pressure of the schedule for other meetings that afternoon, Hara leaned back in his chair. He said,

> Let me tell you what is on my mind at this moment. It is very unfortunate that we have had to be placed in this crisis with the bank, but Hoshino-san has jolted us into confronting a situation we have not even considered. We have spent a few years just running this company as if no changes would ever occur. We have only found better, cheaper, or more streamlined ways of doing the same old thing. We've been solving problems as they have arisen, but not anticipating future problems. We've been fighting fires, but not preventing fires. But with *this*

problem that now faces us, we have begun to talk and examine alternatives and to plan the way we first did when we started the business. By working together like this, we are already beginning to act effectively.

Mr. Ito and Mr. Sasaki nodded. Mr. Hara continued,

All right, let's summarize what we plan to do between now and our next meeting—which has to be soon. I suggest that we meet for further discussion tomorrow. Meanwhile, I will write an observation paper on the following points: (1) the apparent causes of industry slowdown in growth; (2) what the impact of the slowdown could be on some firms in the industry; and (3) what the possible industry responses could be. I'll have the paper with me when we meet here tomorrow at 12:30.

June 6

Mr. Hara arrived early for lunch and reviewed the material he had prepared for Mr. Ito and Mr. Sasaki. Exactly at 12:30 the meeting began and Mr. Hara distributed copies of his observation paper to his partners.

Confidential Memorandum
Frederica's

TO: Osamu Ito, President-Treasurer
           Seiji Sasaki, Vice President Operations

FROM: Toshio Hara, Vice President Marketing/Sales, Corporate Development

RE: Observations regarding Japanese chain-restaurant industry slowdown in growth-rate (See Exhibits 42.1–42.4 for some statistical data on the market.)

1. Some of the major causes of the slowdown in growth of some of the chain-restaurant companies in Japan can be described as follows:

    a. Some firms have so many outlets that they are taking trade from each other.

    b. New firms continue to enter the market, thus limiting growth of some others.

    c. Consumer tastes appear to be changing; in some cases, consumers seem to be more sophisticated or more discriminating.

    d. There may be a general leveling-off of consumer interest in chain-restaurant foods.

    e. New forms of restaurant competition such as 7–11 and MY-STORE convenience groceries have entered the restaurant market.

2. Possible impact of chain-restaurant firm slowdown in growth can be described as follows:

    a. Company cash flow may be reduced, causing difficulty in meeting current obligations.

Exhibit 42.1   Growth of Japanese Restaurant Industry Annual Sales

Calendar Year	Yen (Billions)	U.S.$(Y240) (Billions)	Year-to-Year Growth
1982 Actual	Y 16,355	U.S.$ 68.15	8.7%
1983 Actual	Y 17,100	U.S.$ 71.25	4.6
1984 Estimate	Y 18,500	U.S.$ 77.33	8.5
	Y 18,010	U.S.$ 75.04	5.3

Note: In 1981 there were approximately 2 million retail establishments in Japan, of which 31 percent, or 620,000, were eating and drinking establishments. Of this number 167,000 were in greater Tokyo.
Source: The East Magazine, 1983.
Source: Sanyo Securities, 1984

Exhibit 42.2   Spending on Food and Eating Out in Japan, 1963–1983

Year	Income Spent for Food (Percent)	Income Spent for Eating Out (Percent)	Food Expenditures for Eating Out (Percent)
1963	38.7	2.5	6.5
1968	35.5	2.8	7.9
1973	31.9	3.2	10.1
1978	30.2	3.6	11.8
1983	27.8	3.9	13.9

Source: Sanyo Securities, 1984

    b.   Company executives may feel strong pressures to resume company growth pattern so as to show overall sales increases.

    c.   Some firms may make erratic and/or ill-considered decisions in order to cope with the slowdown, possibly inflicting damage on both their own firms and on competitors' firms.

    d.   As the firm's progress slows, less opportunity may occur for employee-advancement, causing a decline in employee-morale and an increase in employee resignations.

    e.   Company profits may decline, causing the price of stock to drop, thus reducing the ability of the company to float new issues and to obtain direct loans.

    f.   From a positive standpoint, good managers may be motivated to take positive, sensible, well-developed actions that will take advantage of the slowdown.

3.   Responses of some firms in the chain-restaurant industry can be described as follows:

    a.   The firms have become more interested in market-research studies to determine customers' current and projected interests in menu-offerings, store themes, decor, and locations.

    b.   The firms focus more attention on employee-performance, including service, training, conduct, and attire.

    c.   Some firms may increase systemization of operations, including such aspects as purchasing, food preparation, product distribution, in-store food preparation, and work flow.

Exhibit 42.3   Comparative Sales Figures for Selected Japanese Family Restaurant Chains, 1983

Firm	Number of Stores	Industry Rank	Sales (Y Millions)	Year-to-year Change	Per Store Sales (Y Millions)	Projected New Restaurants in 1984[a]
Skylark	417	3	67,660	20.3%	162.20	55
Royal[b]	275	6	56,900	11.9	197.34	39
Denny's	195	16	36,386	10.6	166.08	30
Frederica's	15	—	2,100	2.0	140.00	3

[a]Estimated cost each: Y80 million
[b]Consolidated figures including ice cream, bakery, and franchise stores
Source: Sanyo Securities, 1984; Frederica's Restaurant Co., Ltd. is fictitious.

Exhibit 42.4   Selected Family-Type Restaurant Chains in Japan — Comparative Financial Analysis, 1983

Restaurant Chain	Gross Profit Margin (Percent)	Net Profit Margin (Percent)	Quick Ratio (Percent)	Current Ratio (Percent)
Skylark	64.7	5.4	54.2	85.7
Royal	59.5	4.3	54.4	24.3
Denny's	63.3	3.4	67.0	87.6
Frederica's	57.0	2.0	40.0	60.0

Per store average sales growth for five years: Skylark, Royal, Denny's + 4.0 percent; Frederica's 2 percent.
Source: Sanyo Securities, 1984; Frederica's Restaurant Co., Ltd. is fictitious

d.   Some firms take a longer-run view of profits by shifting their focus from increasing present sales and profits to increasing market share.

e.   The firms pay increasing attention to market segments and what would be attractive to those segments.

f.   Designated old stores are being remodelled and recycled and new stores opened, all in accordance with perceived new market trends.

When they finished reading Hara's position paper, Mr. Sasaki, vice president of operations, began to talk.

Hara-san is right. If I were to add anything I would say that we failed to stay abreast of changes in the market. The truth is that we've been lucky to have come so far without any significant changes in our operations: Our menu has remained virtually unchanged in almost a decade; it still consists of the same hamburger sets, chicken sets, spaghetti, curry, little steaks, desserts, and salads — no specials for brunches, holidays and no food promotions like our bigger competitors are offering. We are "attracting" our customers only with lower prices.

Our stores are alike. If you see one, you've seen them all, which could be boring. Although we are getting family dinner business, the customers have below-average income and their visits to restaurants are infrequent; they seem to be up to only about 35 years old. The luncheon customers — the OLs[2] and middle and lower-level managers — seem to come to our restaurants mainly because of proximity to their offices. Evening business tends to be young people on dates and some over-50 night owls in the neighborhood. We get no business at other occasions such as morning coffee, or afternoon coffee or tea. I think we've been lacking imagination and creativity in our operations. We hve to act — and now.

Mr. Ito said,

Yes, I agree, but the dimensions of the problem are enormous. First, we have 15 stores, all of the same pattern and all with stale theme and design and static operations. Second, we have designs completed and contracts ready for three stores, all for the next 12 months, assuming approval of our loan. And third, we are suddenly confronted with a need to rethink our whole operation: new concepts, new products, and maybe new market and different locations — and still go back to the bank by next week with a strategy and some preliminary plans strong enough to satisfy the loan officers. I am overwhelmed at the task and the risks.

Mr. Ito thought for a minute, and took a deep breath and said quietly and with authority, "Let's get a consultant and tell him we need his recommendations in 60–90 days. I can go back to the bank and tell him we will have a strategy and plan for him in about three months. Agreed?"

"Agreed."

"Agreed."

September 10

OK Associates, a Tokyo restaurant-consulting firm, finished the initial report — and overview — and presented it to Frederica's Restaurants for review. Ito, Hara, and Sasaki gathered to discuss and to decide what steps to take.

The report stated that the company needed to take action to move Frederica's into a pattern more in keeping with industry changes. The report stated further that the principals of the firm had a choice of strategies, but current practical limitations foreclosed adopting all strategies at the same time. They had therefore to decide which strategy to follow.

Below are summarized three major strategies proposed by OK Associates:

Strategy I: *Franchising*

Concept.   Frederica's can maintain the present systems, decor, menus, and patterns of operations, but expand the number of units by selling franchises to qualified applicants.

---

[2]OL is a Japanese term standing for the English words "office lady," and is described generally as age 18–24, single, living with her parents, working, having high disposable personal income which she spends heavily on designer-label clothes and accessories, restaurants, and travel.

Rationale for Franchising

- Franchising permits the company to expand the number of outlets rapidly, limited only by the time required to locate and prepare qualified applicants to open units under the Frederica's name.
- Franchising requires little if any expenditure by Frederica's in that the franchisee bears the entire investment.
- The franchising fees paid to Frederica's can be a substantial source of new funds annually to the company.
- The entry into and the conduct of franchising operations can be relatively simple in that the operating systems, restaurant concept, recipes, and training programs are already in existence, tested, and documented with company manuals.
- Franchising permits an accelerated rate of growth in the number of Frederica's restaurants, thus serving to heighten consumer awareness and probably resulting in an increase in market share.

Strategy II: Opening in New Geographic Areas

Concept.   Frederica's can open new stores in towns and cities other than its present Tokyo and Osaka markets.

Rationale for Opening in New Geographic Areas

- Major Japanese family restaurant chains are now so heavily represented in Frederica's main trading area that competition is very difficult, highly segmented, and sophisticated.
- Frederica's current decor and menu may be not sufficiently up-to-date for present markets, but could be viable for some years yet in second-and third level cities before significant change is necessary.
- Frederica's can continue to grow while perfecting newer decor, menus, and systems.
- Second- and third-level cities have lower rents and lower wages, which will permit a lower break-even point.
- Second- and third-level cities have easier traffic and parking so that customers can be drawn from a wider geographic area.
- There are fewer up-scale restaurants now in second- and third-level cities, so Frederica's can be perceived as being at a higher level than in present Tokyo and Osaka markets; in many places, Frederica's might be the best place to eat.
- Prime locations are easier to obtain in small cities.

Strategy III: Target New Market Segments

Concept.   Frederica's can target new market segments, namely (a) persons over 35–40 years of age, and (b) women.

Rational for the over 35–40 Market

□ Japan's is the fastest-aging population in the world and already has a life expectancy exceeding all nations except Iceland; thus, the older market will grow significantly in Japan.
□ Frederica's competitors appear to be ignoring this aging population as a market for fear that older customers might drive out the younger ones already present. Older customers might prefer more traditional Japanese cuisine, which will require additional costly special full-time chefs. Persons over 35–40 in Japan are too careful in their food spending as a result of their poverty and hunger during the war and postwar years, and thus too difficult to gain as a viable market.
□ The validity of Frederica's competitor's beliefs (above) are unproven, but do form the basis for their current targeting of various market segments under age 35, thereby creating a window of marketing opportunities for Frederica's in the over 35–40 market.

Rationale for the Women's Market

□ Frederica's competitors have concentrated their marketing efforts or women principally on the OLs, but not on other segments of the Japanese female population, thus providing a market opening for Frederica's.
□ The restaurant market for women is not near full development, as evidenced by the fact that female lunch-time business is mainly from women workers eating together, and the evening meal business is predominantly male only.
□ Although the restaurant companies have mainly ignored the female business, the major hotels in Japan have very successfully targeted women over 40 to purchase luncheons—and even exhibits, lectures, concerts, and sponsored group tours.
□ Disposable personal income of Japanese women is encouraging for marketers, inasmuch as 50 percent of working women over 40 have taken employment in order to spend money socially, for pocket money, and for leisure.
□ Women's participation in the Japanese labor force (see table below) is long-lived and substantial, with some decline only in the child-bearing years.

Women's Labor-Force Participation Rate in Japan Age Category

	15–19	20–24[a]	25–34	35–44	45–54	55–64	65+
Millions of women	0.67	2.63	4.66	5.43	4.91	2.65	1.05
Labor force participation	17.2%	71.1%	50.2%	62.7%	62.8%	45.1%	16.0%

Note: More than 90 percent of working women are employed full time.
[a]About one-third of this group are considered OLs.
Source: Japan Statistical Yearbook, 1983

Time for Decision

Ito, Hara, and Sasaki completed reading the summary report then looked at each other in thoughtful silence. Ito spoke,

> I think that the consultants have given us a lot to consider here. Certainly there are other possibilities such as new restaurant products, or new concepts such as cafeterias, but I think that our answer must lie somewhere in what we've just read. Our job now is to decide on the direction we want to go and the strategy and plan for getting there. What do you men think?

Volkswagen of America: Automobile Introduction — The Quantum

Case 43

In 1981 Volkswagen introduced what was hoped to be the company's flagship for the 1980s — the Quantum. Called Passat in Europe, the Quantum replaced the Dasher, which was originally brought to the United States in 1974.

Background

The Volkswagen concept was developed in the 1920s by a young automobile designer, Ferdinand Porsche. Porsche intended the car to be a completely practical vehicle. At first his plans for an unconventional, small, inexpensive automobile were rejected by European automobile manufacturers. The rise of Hitler and his pledge to the German people that every man would own his own car, "The Volkswagen," made Porsche's dream a reality, and manufacture of the Volkswagen got underway. The car's production, however, was disrupted by World War II.

After the war, British Occupational Forces controlled the Volkswagen factory until 1949. The factory was then turned over to Heinz Nordoff, who faced the major task of rebuilding the Volkswagen organization. The basic design of the car, however, was not altered, and engineering emphasis was directed toward internal improvements of the automobile.

Gradually a global sales and service oganization developed. At present, Volkswagen A.G., located in Wolfsburg, is West Germany's largest industrial enterprise with factories located throughout the world.

In its early years, the "Beetle," which had become the car's nickname, had problems gaining acceptance in the American market. To gain initial sales, a foreign-car dealer who had been appointed exclusive importer and agent east of the Mississippi for Volkswagen advocated that dealers who wanted the more popular foreign cars should also purchase a few of the unconventional Beetles. His suggestion was accepted. From this rather humble beginning in the early 1950s, interest in and sales of Volkswagens soon began to increase rapidly.

Volkswagen sales peaked in 1970 at 582,500 cars, accounting for almost 7 percent of total sales in the United States. While imports expanded their share of the market as the 1970s continued, Volkswagen began to decline in market share and absolute sales. This decline came about because of the obvious increase in foreign-car competition and the step up of smaller car production by major U. S. manufacturers.

Source: From Roger D. Blackwell, James F. Engel and W. Wayne Talarzyk, *Contemporary Cases in Consumer Behavior.* Hinsdale, Ill.: Dryden Press, 1985.

The Quantum

The following information is from the media information used to introduce the Quantum to the United States.

Englewood Cliffs, N.J. — Volkswagen today announced the introduction of the all-new Quantum — the most technologically advanced and elegantly executed line of cars ever to wear a VW logo.

Conceived as Volkswagen's flagship line for the '80s, the Quantum comes in three body styles — a sporty Coupe, 4-door Wagon and 4-door Sedan. (The latter does not go on sale until Spring '82.) All three models are completely equipped, full five-passenger vehicles possessing the sophisticated road manners, functional-yet-handsome European styling and interior spaciousness and appointments of cars costing half again as much.

The technological superiority of the Quantum is most evident in two areas: aerodynamics and chassis design. The sleek, almost fluid silhouettes of the three cars are a result of extensive development work in VW's climatic wind tunnel in Wolfsburg, West Germany. The two-door hatchback Coupe, which features an integrated front air dam and rear deck lid spoiler, has a drag coefficient (c_d) of only 0.39, the lowest of the three and one of the best to be found on a vehicle of this size.

For improved ride comfort and stability, the frontwheel drive chassis of the new Quantum features a longer 100-inch wheelbase and wider track than the Dasher it replaces. In addition a completely new "twist-beam" with trailing arms and coil spring struts is being used for the first time on a vehicle as large as a Quantum.

This new "track-correcting" axle, as VW engineers call it, utilizes unique asymmetrical rubber-metal bushings at the pivot points to reduce the natural tendency for the rear wheels to "steer" under high lateral loads.

Not only is this new rear suspension fully independent, it is extremely light, and so compact that a 15.8 gallon fuel tank is located between the rear wheels underneath a low trunk floor.

To provide the best possible combination of space and comfort, the external dimensions of the top-of-the-line car are slightly larger than those of the Dasher. However, through exhaustive computer-aided analysis of the Quantum's components and material makeup by Research & Development at Wolfsburg, it has been kept lean and trim. In fact, the Quantum weighs only about 120 pounds more than the smaller Dasher.

Fuel Mileage Improved

Low curb weight, a clean, wind-cheating shape, and an efficient powertrain are responsible for the Quantum's impressive fuel mileage. The Federal Environmental Protection Agency rates the manual transmission Quantum at 28 miles per gallon in the city and 41 miles per gallon on the highway — a four-percent improvement over the gas Dasher.

Power for the Quantums comes from a 1.7-liter overhead cam fuel-injected gasoline engine mounted longitudinally under the hood and mated to a Formula E 5-speed gearbox. This new wide-ratio transmission features long-legged fourth and fifth gear ratios for economical, relaxed highway cruising, and shorter first through third gears for brisk acceleration and passing.

Power assisted rack and pinion steering is standard on all Quantums, as is a Formula E Upshift Indicator Light that tells the driver how to increase fuel economy at no expense in performance by shifting up the next higher gear.

Luxury Interior

The well-planned cockpit of the Quantum features fully reclining front seats with a height-adjustment lever on the driver's side, cut pile carpeting, padded four-spoke steering wheel, a passenger reading lamp and an electric rear window defroster. Both the sporty Coupe and Wagon come with fold-down 1/2–2/3 split rear seat backs for increased luggage capacity. The Wagon also has a rear wiper/washer system and bins in the cargo area so that small items such as a camera can be hidden from view. Befitting its sporting nature, the Coupe comes with a tachometer, LCD quartz digital clock and black exterior window trim and black front and rear spoilers.

Streamline remote-control outside mirrors, 5½ × 13-inch alloy wheels and 185/70-13 steel radials are standard on all models. Black accented 6 × 14-inch light alloy wheels fitted with low-profile 195/60-14 high-performance radials are optional.

Quantums can be specified with a GL package consisting of cruise control, power windows, central door locking, electrically operated outside mirrors, illuminated vanity mirror, adjustable rear seat headrests and "GL" identification on the rear deck lid.

Other options include a new push-button air conditioning and heating system, automatic transmission, sliding steel sunroof with tilt feature, AM/FM stereo with electronic tuning, auto-reverse cassette, automatic antenna, and four-speaker sound system.

Efficient aerodynamic design, an advanced suspension system together with the intelligent size of the Quantum reaffirm Volkswagen's technological leadership in automotive development. The Quantum is backed by a 12-month, 20,000 mile limited warranty that is honored by over 1,000 authorized VW dealers nationwide.

Product Description

Exhibit 43.1 provides a description of the rationale behind using the name "Quantum" in the United States. As originally introduced, the Quantum was available in three versions: coupe, four-door, and station wagon. The following information provides a description of the Quantum as "top-of-the-line Volkswagen":

Exhibit 43.1 Rationale for the Name "Quantum"

The 1981 Quantum will be Volkswagen's new top-of-the-line model, replacing the phased-out Dasher.

As a basic positioning statement (final statement forthcoming) it would be safe and fitting to describe it as a family car, available in notchback sedan, hatchback wagon and two-door coupe body styles. With a Turbo-diesel engine, the new model joins a select group of higher-priced imports in the luxury category.

Name criteria for this new model must convey characteristics and attributes that are consistent with the car's marketing image, i.e. top-of-line, sophisticated technology, superior engineering.

The name *quantum* directly relates to mathematics and physics. In scientific usage, it means an abrupt transition. The new model is a *quantum* leap above the Dasher on several styling, engineering and marketing levels. It is VW's entry into a higher class of automobile. The world has strong scientific connotations all of which are positive, important, and, to the layman, high-sounding.

Also important, the name must make a strong visual impression (look good on the printed page or nameplate on car) as well as sound good to the ear. It must also work well for all three body styles, *i.e.* fit the character of the various configurations.

Further, like all Volkswagens past and present, it must stand out from the pack, be unique but also very much to the point. Not different just to be different, but different because it portrays all of the special meaning inherent in the car. Lastly, the name should at once combine dignity with personality, the latter especially important for advertising/merchandising consideration.

In the name Quantum, we believe there is the embodiment of all the name criteria that are important. Moreover, since the new model will be priced higher than previous top line Volkswagens, the proposed name supports the price/value relationship in a very effective manner.

Among the scores of names that were considered, Quantum best measured up to the high standards that were set for Volkswagen's new top line automobile.

Styling Characteristics

- All steel unit body construction
- Dual rectangular halogen headlights
- Turn signals integrated in headlights and taillights
- Wrap-around side markers, front and rear
- Radiator grille, black with bright edge

Price

$10,400 Coupe, $10,700 Four-Door, and $11,000 Station Wagon

Model Versions

□ Body styles: 2-door Coupe, 4-door notchback, and 4-door station wagon
□ Engine: 1715 cc with CIS injection system (5 cylinder is proposed with automatic transmissions, on all models; turbo diesel will be an option on automatic or 5-speed models)
□ Transmission: 5-speed manual (standard)
□ Trim level: Deluxe

Interior Design

The interior design objective was:

□ to provide harmony with the overall character of the vehicle
□ to establish continuity between exterior and interior appearance
□ to promote the VW top-of-the-line image.

Engineering

Progressive: A large number of components are used from other VW models in line with the modular unit principle. The new models are larger and may give better fuel economy than the previous model. There has been no change in the transmission and engine, it is identical to the 1980 model.

Automobile Market Segmentation

The United States automotive market is often divided into three broad categories: family cars, luxury cars, and sports or sporty cars. Volkswagen positioned the Quantum to compete in two of these categories: (1) a coupe in the sporty car group and (2) a four-door sedan and station wagon in the family group. Exhibit 43.2 shows how Volkswagen perceived the competition and consumer characters in the various segments of the family group. Exhibit 43.3 indicates how Volkswagen perceived the competition and consumer characteristics in the segments of the sporty car market.

Quantum's Position

The basic positioning statement for Quantum was stated as: "Volkswagen's flagship cars for the 80's. Built with advanced German technology, European styling and sophisticated aerodynamic design and collectively offering superior performance, handling, and fuel economy without sacrificing spaciousness and comfort."

The following characteristics were used as aids in executing the positioning function:

Exhibit 43.2   Family Car Market Segments

Segment 1: High priced

    Audi 5000
    BMW
    Cadillac
    Lincoln
    Mercedes-Benz

Segment 2: Medium priced

  2a. Four-Door Sedans:
    VW Quantum
    Audi 4000
    Datsun 810/Maxima
    Renault 18i
    Toyota Cressida
    Volvo DL

  2b. Station Wagons:
    VW Quantum
    Datsun 810/Maxima
    Renault 18i
    Toyota Cressida
    Volvo DL

Segment 3: Low priced

    Volkswagen Jetta
    Chrysler K Car
    Fiat Brava
    Ford Fairmont
    GM X Body
    Honda Accord
    Mazda 626

Segment 1: Married, males

    30–55 years old
    Income—
      $35,000 +
    College Educated

Segment 2a: Married, males

    25–50 years old
    Income—
      $20,000 +
    Attended College
    Family size: 2.7
    Occupation—
      sales work,
      engineers, and
      proprietors

Segment 2b: Married, some females

    30–60 years old
    Income—
      $25,000 +
    College Educated
    Family size: 3.1
    Occupation—
      retired, sales
      work, proprie-
      tor, farmers,
      skilled trade

Segment 3: Married, males

    25–44 years old
    Income—
      $20,000 +
    College Educated

☐ *Quantum's high price:* Appeal to emotion and self-image.

☐ *Quantum's high resale value:* A way to counteract the original high price reaction . . . an intelligent investment.

☐ *Quantum's gas economy:* The key selling advantage . . . still a leader in this segment.

☐ *Quantum's Corporate Umbrella:* Utilize the VW image strengths that are high on these consumers' desired list, namely:
  ☐ well-built car
  ☐ reliable/trouble free operation

☐ *Advertising:* A new sophisticated approach; elegance rather than humor—a possibility "Quantum—by Volkswagen." Some introductory advertisements for the Quantum are shown in Exhibits 43.4 through 43.7.

Exhibit 43.3   Sporty Car Market Segments

Segment 1:   *Very high priced, super luxurious, ultra high performance, sports cars:*
Porsche 928
Porsche 911
Audi Quattro
Ferrari
Lamborghini
Lotus
Maserati
Mercedes-Benz 380SL

Segment 2:   *High priced, sleek, high performance, sports cars:*
Porsche 924
Porsche 924T
Alfa GTV6
Corvette
Datsun 280ZX/T
DeLorean
Mazda RX-7[a]
Triumph TR7/8[a]

Segment 3:   *Moderately priced, sporty cars, with some performance characteristics:*
VW Scirocco
Audi Coupe
VW Quantum Coupe
Chrysler TC3/024
Datsun 200SX
Ford Mustang
Honda Accord/Prelude
Plymouth Sapporo
Toyotal Celica/Supra

Segment 4:   *Lower priced, sporty type cars, with some performance:*
VW Rabbit
Datsun GX
Ford Escort
GM *J* Body Coupe
Honda Civic
Mazda GLC
Toyota Corolla—SR5

Segment 1:   *Strongly male, married*
30–54 years old
Income—
   $50,000 +
Education—Post
   Graduate

Segment 2:   *Mainly male, married*
25–49 years old
Income—
   $35,000 +
Education—
   College Degree

Segment 3:   *Some male, married*
25–40 years old
Income—
   $20,000 +
Education—
   Some College

Segment 4:   *Some male, married*
20–40 years old
Income—
   $17,000 +
Education—
   Some College

[a]Lower price, but sleek; definite competition.

Exhibit 43.4   Introductory Television Storyboard

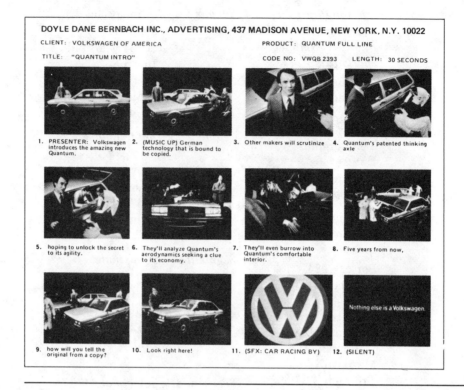

Exhibit 43.5   Introductory Television Storyboard

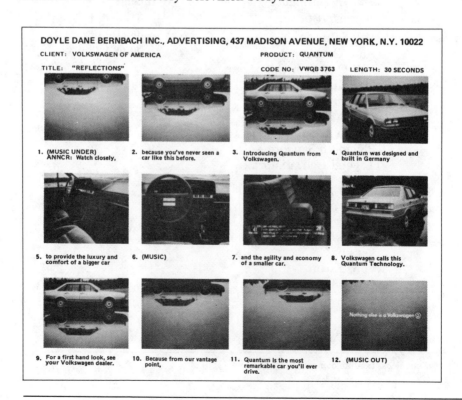

Exhibit 43.6   Introductory Newspaper Advertisement for Quantum

Source: Doyle Dane Bernbach, Inc.

Consumer Research

Rogers National Research of Toledo, Ohio conducts an annual survey among second quarter (January, February, and March) new car buyers. The Quantum portion of the 1982 study can be summarized as follows:

Exhibit 43.7   Introductory Magazine Advertisement for Quantum

Source: Doyle Dane Bernbach, Inc.

☐   Quantum owners' overall satisfaction with their new car is on par with Subaru, but below Cressida, Audi, and Maxima. "Excellent/very good" ratings are:

Vehicle	Percent Rating
Toyota Cressida	94
Audi 4000	93
Datsun Maxima	93
VW Quantum	86
Subaru	86

□ Dasher was behind these three vehicles in 1981; no upward movement by Quantum.

□ Basically, the same order applies for delivery condition ratings, with Subaru third and Datsun and VW dropping down one place.

□ While the overall opinion rating is comparable to Dasher's 1979/1980 level, the Quantum's delivery condition rating has slightly surpassed any of the Dasher's previous ratings. Quantum shows significantly higher owner satisfaction ratings than Dasher for: overall quietness, overall front seat comfort, overall interior roominess, overall exterior styling, riding comfort, overall ease of handling, overall power and pickup, smoothness of engine idle, ease of starting, absence of wind noise, and absence of water leaks.

□ Quantum, Maxima, and Cressida buyers list quality of workmanship, durability/reliability and ease of handling as their primary purchase motivators. The remainder, i.e., Audi 4000, Renault 18i, Subaru, Dodge Aries, Plymouth Reliant, and Oldsmobile Ciera supplant handling with fuel economy.

□ Before purchasing their car, more Quantum and competitive owners considered a GM product than any other vehicle. Subaru buyers are the exception, staying within the Japanese family of products. Few buyers seriously considered a Quantum.

□ Honda and Toyota are capturing a large number of previous Dasher owners. Quantum/Dasher owner loyalty is a very low 4 percent.

□ Many Quantum buyers disposed of a Volkswagen, with GM disposals a poor second. Some VW owners have apparently upgraded to the Audi 4000. Renault, Datsun, and Toyota are making heavy inroads in the domestic market. Dasher was capturing more of the domestic market than the Quantum is.

□ The Quantum buyer is a married male, about 44 years of age. He is a college graduate, earning approximately $41,000 per annum. This profile closely resembles that of the Dasher buyer.

Exhibit 43.8 shows the trends in how Quantum (Dasher) purchasers rate the automobile on various attributes. The importance of certain aspects of the automobiles and the purchase decision are shown in Exhibit 43.9. Exhibit 43.10 presents trend information about automobiles replaced as a result of the purchase of a Quantum (Dasher) from 1979 through 1982. Trends in consumer characteristics are presented in Exhibit 43.11

Exhibit 43.8   Owner Satisfaction Trend (Excellent/Very Good Ratings)

Overall, How Do You Rate Your Car on These Features?	New Quantum/Dasher Purchased in			
	1982	1981	1980	1979
Average MPG city	26%	37%	36%	31%
Average MPG highway	32	42	42	38
Overall average MPG	28	40	39	35
Overall opinion	86	74	85	87
Delivery condition	84	74	81	79
Value for the money	56	47	54	66
Overall quietness	65	26	42	*
Overall quality of workmanship	84	60	81	83
Overall front seat comfort	88	81	74	*
Overall interior roominess	84	45	48	58
Overall interior styling	83	76	74	79
Overall exterior styling	86	80	78	78
Mileage (Fuel economy)	75	93	91	94
Riding comfort	84	67	70	79
Overall ease of handling	97	77	83	89
Overall power and pickup	58	10	25	*
Smoothness of engine idle	74	48	51	63
Ease of starting	90	83	81	82
Absence of engine stalling	96	97	92	88
Proper fit of doors	92	82	93	89
Fit of other body panels	94	87	90	*
Absence of wind noise	84	70	73	74
Absence of water leaks	91	65	83	80
Fit of exterior chrome and molding	84	79	88	84
Lack of squeaks and rattles	71	59	75	59
Appearance of paint job	91	81	89	81

Exhibit 43.9   Important Reasons for Purchase Decision Trend

How Important Was Each of the Following in Your Purchase Decision?	New Quantum/Dasher Purchased in			
	1982	1981	1980	1979
Mileage/fuel economy	87%	100%	100%	98%
Fun to drive	56	31	—	—
Power and pickup	48	10	16	34
Ease of handling	92	72	—	—
Durability/reliability	95	97	—	—
Quality of workmanship	98	92	93	93
Technical innovations	57	56	—	—
Exterior styling	48	30	31	36
Interior styling	52	31	32	41
Riding comfort	82	66	56	63
Passenger seating capacity	57	43	—	—
Quietness	59	31	—	—
Safety features	76	63	—	—
Luggage capacity	77	60	50	51
Value for the money	75	83	70	83
Prestige	19	9	11	7
Resale or trade-in value	64	64	68	60
Cost of maintenance	54	49	53	81
Price or deal offered	58	57	39	57
Quality of dealer service	72	62	65	62
Warranty coverage	57	59	—	—
Dealer's finance plan	12	8	—	—

Exhibit 43.10   Source of Sales Trend

If You Disposed of a Vehicle at the Time of Purchase, What Was the Make?	New Quantum/Dasher Purchased in			
	1982	1981	1980	1979
Did not own a vehicle	2	—	—	3
Did not dispose of a vehicle	15	17	22	18
Vehicle disposed of:				
General Motors	17	25	26	21
Ford Motor Company	7	13	14	14
Chrysler Corporation	5	5	7	6
American Motors	2	1	1	1
Domestic trucks/vans	5	11	—	—
Total domestic disposals	36	55	48	50
Volkswagen	32	13	14	14
Audi	2	—	1	1
Honda	1	4	1	1
Toyota	1	2	2	2
Datsun/Nissan	2	2	2	2
Other imports	9	8	10	9
Total import disposals	47	29	30	29

Exhibit 43.11   Demographic Trends

About Yourself	Owners of a Quantum/Dasher that Was Purchased in							
	1982	1981	1980	1979	1978	1977	1976	1975
Sex: Male	68	73	77	73	62	73	69	77
Married	86	95	86	85	73	82	80	87
Age: Under 20	—	—	—	1	1	1	—	1
20–24	1	—	1	4	7	10	8	4
25–29	10	6	9	13	23	21	19	25
30–34	14	18	13	14	17	18	20	16
35–39	15	23	17	12	5	9	11	14
40–44	11	18	10	10	8	8	10	10
45–49	10	9	8	9	10	10	8	12
50–54	10	6	10	10	8	11	9	8
55–59	7	7	10	13	9	10	7	4
60–64	12	5	11	6	5	8	6	4
65 and over	9	8	11	9	6	6	4	2
Median age (years)	44	41	45	43	37	42	36	36
Education:								
High school or less	17	21	20	33	24	20	25	19
Some college	16	22	21	23	19	22	20	23
College graduate	23	18	20	19	18	20	19	20
Grad. study/degree	44	38	37	35	39	35	37	38
Total family income:								
Under $10,000	—	1	2	2	5	7	10	6
$10,000–$14,999	5	1	3	6	16	14	17	21
$15,000–$19,999	5	7	8	11	19	19	22	26
$20,000–$24,999	5	7	10	18	13	15	13	14
$25,000–$29,999	7	13	9	12	10	12	14	9
$30,000–$39,999	22	27	21	22	21	17	12	11
$40,000 Plus	46	36	35	29	17	13	11	13
Median income	41,000	36,700	35,600	29,400	24,000	22,900	20,400	19,300
Occupation:								
Professional/technical	25	22	30	30	32	31	44	41
Manager/proprietor	18	16	15	13	12	7	10	10

Case Index